AVIATION
LEARNERS, INSTRUCTI

Aviation Training: Learners, Instruction and Organization

Edited by
ROSS A TELFER AND PHILLIP J MOORE
The University of Newcastle, Australia

Routledge
Taylor & Francis Group

LONDON AND NEW YORK

First published 1997 by Ashgate Publishing

2 Park Square, Milton Park, Abingdon, Oxon OX14 4RN
711 Third Avenue, New York, NY 10017, USA

*Routledge is an imprint of the Taylor & Francis Group,
an informa business*

First issued in paperback 2016

British Library Cataloguing in Publication Data

Aviation training : learners, instruction and organization
   1. Airplanes - Piloting - Study and teaching
   I. Telfer, Ross, 1937- II. Moore, Phillip J.
   629.1'3252'07

Library of Congress Catalog Card Number: 96-79116

ISBN 13: 978-0-291-39837-6 (hbk)
ISBN 13: 978-1-138-25480-0 (pbk)

Contents

Part 2 Instruction

Part 3 Organization

List of tables

List of figures

x

List of contributors

Joey M Anca Jr.

Joey M Anca Jr. is Manager for Human Factors at Philippine Airlines. He pioneered the development of PAL's first CRM program in 1988 (called the Line of Position Workshop). His current interests are Line Operational Evaluation, redesign of the Flight Instructor's Manual, Pilot Judgement Training, and CRM/LOFT Training at PAL. He is a graduate of the Ateneo de Manila University and has written articles and conference papers on CRM, with a focus on Advanced Technology training, Culture, and optimising CRM training.

Graham Beaumont

A senior Check Airman with Qantas Airways, Graham Beaumont joined the airline in 1966 as a Cadet pilot following a brief career in education. He has put this experience to good use in Qantas where he has held several managerial positions in the Flight Operations Training Department. Currently he is CRM Coordinator with responsibilities for the development and implementation of CRM programs for both Cabin and Flight Crews.

John Bent

Captain John Bent was, until recently, the Flying Training Manager (Airbus) [A330 and A340] for Cathay Pacific Airways in Hong Kong, designing the launch training for this introductory program. His previous position was Flying Training Manager (Policy), engaged in the development of future training programs; a task to which he has now returned. The last half of his nineteen years in Cathay Pacific Airways have been spent in the Check and Training Section. Captain Bent has been flying for over 30 years, both with the Royal Air Force and in three airlines in civil aviation. His training experience has included military flying instruction, management of a flying school in Germany, and development and launch of a new multi-cultural pre-school and Primary School in Hong Kong (the latter in his free time over a period of five years). Between 1989 and 1992 he was co-designer and manager of a new Workshop Program for Aircrew Trainers, using broad research in the industry as the basis for design, with a strong human factors bias.

Jorg Bertram
Captain Jorg Bertram commenced flying for the regional airline, Nordair, flying mostly DC-3 and then B-737 aircraft. In 1973 he joined Air Canada as a Second Officer on the DC-8 before becoming F/O on the B-727. He flew various types, DC-9, DC-8 and B-747 until 1989. He was promoted to Captain and very shortly thereafter became involved in human factors as a CRM facilitator and member of the Air Canada LOFT development team.

Timothy Bilton
Timothy Bilton is a postgraduate student in the Department of Applied Psychology at Cranfield University in Bedforshire, England. He received his BSc (Hons) in Psychology from Manchester Metropolitan University in 1993, followed by an MSc in Applied Psychology from Cranfield University in 1995. He is currently working towards a private pilot licence and his research interests focus on CRM training and aircrew performance. He has worked with Virgin Atlantic Airways and Brittania Airways in the UK.

C T Chan
Captain C T Chan joined SIA in August 1968. He obtained his Commercial Pilot Licence with Instrument Rating from Airwork Services Training, Perth, Scotland in 1969. After obtaining command in 1977 on the B737, he has been in training positions on all aircraft types that he has been on since 1978. He has flown the F27, B737, B707, B727, B757, B747 and A340. He was appointed Deputy Chief Pilot (Training) B743 in July 1992 and Deputy Chief Pilot (Training) A340 in January 1996. He is also an Instructor and check pilot on the A340.

Norm Dowd
Captain Norm Dowd began his commercial flying career in Twin Otters over the Canadian Arctic. In his 22 years with Air Canada he has flown aircraft as diverse as the A320 and B747-200. Norm facilitated CRM from 1989, leading the team that developed Air Canada's LOFT. He also led the team which wrote the handbooks for Transport Canada fulfilling the ICAO requirement for human factors training for flightcrew. He represents Air Canada on the IATA Human Factors Steering Committee, where his focus is the training of CRM/LOFT facilitators.

Terry L Farquharson

Prior to joining an airline in 1979, Terry Farquharson served 13 years in the military where he qualified both as a flying instructor and an engineering test pilot, graduating from the Empire Test Pilots School in 1972. Having held management positions in both executive aircraft operating companies and airlines, he is currently employed by Cathay Pacific Airways where he is a line captain. In addition he is responsible for the acceptance and periodic flight testing of aircraft, acceptance and approval of flight simulators, and dealing with the authorities on regulatory issues. Terry holds a degree in Business from Curtin University and an MBA from Brunel. He has acted as a consultant to aviation companies on training and organisational issues.

Rick Fry

Captain Rick Fry is the Fleet Manager (Airbus) [A340 and A330] for Cathay Pacific Airways in Hong Kong. He has been in Cathay Pacific a little over 16 years and has been a management pilot since 1988, during which he has held various positions of Chief Check and Fleet Manager for the L1011. Rick started his career with initial training through the Qantas Cadet Pilot Scheme in 1969 and worked for several airlines including Air Nauru operating around the Pacific and South East Asia. He has flown in his civil career the F28, B737, 727, 707, 747 and L1011 aircraft before his first Airbus experience, the A320, on Dragonair network for 5 months.

Brett Gebers

Captain Brett Gebers is currently a training captain on the B737 with South African Airways based in Johannesburg. He is also an Instrument Rating examiner and has been involved in aviation training for the past 15 years. He was a member of the IFALPA Aircraft Design and Operation Committee for 6 years and is currently the President of the Airline Pilots' Association of South Africa.

Richard D Gilson

Dr Gilson is a Professor of Psychology, founder and former director of the Center for Applied Human Factors in Aviation. He received his PhD degree in Psychology from Princeton University. He is the co-ordinator of the PhD program in Human Factors at the University of Central Florida. Dr Gilson holds numerous pilot certificates as well as seven U.S.A. patents in the field of Aviation.

Brent Hayward

Brent Hayward is Managing Director of Asia Pacific Resource Management, an Australian company providing clients with a comprehensive range of consultancy services in aviation psychology and human factors. Brent is a registered psychologist, with 18 years experience within the aviation industry. Previous full-time employers include the RAAF Psychology Service, Australian Airlines, and Qantas Airways. Brent is founding President of the Australian Aviation Psychology Association, and holds full membership of the Australian Psychological Society, the European Association for Aviation Psychology, and the International Society of Air Safety Investigators.

Harry Holling

Captain Harry Holling started his aviation career in 1971, and has flown in Papua New Guinea, USA, and Australia. He is currently a Training Captain on the BAe146 with Ansett Australia, a company he joined in 1980. CRM is a major interest, having been a facilitator for three years, helped to develop three Ansett courses, and is now group leader of the CRM Development Program. His biggest project to date was writing, producing and filming a feature video on a BAe146 Loss of All Engines incident. This film is the central focus for a popular and successful CRM session.

David R Hunter

Dr David Hunter is a program scientist with the Office of Aviation Medicine of the Federal Aviation Administration in the USA where he is responsible for research dealing with pilot decision making. During his 20-year research career he has worked on helicopter system design for the US Army, on the selection of personnel for Air Force pilot training, and the selection of air traffic controllers for both the US Air Force and the Royal Air Force. He holds a BSc in Psychology (University of Texas, Arlington) and his PhD is from the University of Texas at Austin. He is aformer Army aviator and has instructed in both airplanes and helicopters. His current research interests include analyses of pilot decision making processes, the development and marketing of new safety programs, and investigations of pilot selection, training, and management procedures across the aviation industry.

Marvin Karlins

Marvin Karlins is professor of management at the University of South Florida, Tampa. He has a BA (*Summa Cum Laude*) from the University of Minnesota and MA, PhD in psychology from Princeton University. He has served as a consultant to Singapore Airlines for 14 years, and has authored 18 books and numerous popular and professional articles.

Freddie Koh

Captain Freddie Koh Sing Chong, currently the Assistant Director of Flight Operations (Line Operations), Singapore Airlines also has the responsibilities of Chief Pilot B777 fleet.

Captain Koh joined the Airline in 1964 as a cadet pilot. After basic training in Scotland, he became a second officer on the DC3/F27 fleet. He became a First Officer a year later, and was promoted to the Comet 4 fleet in 1966. He also flew as First Officer on B707, before becoming a F27 commander in 1972 and later a B737, B707 and B747 commander. After two years as a training captain on B747, he was promoted to Chief Pilot A300 in 1982. He became Chief Pilot B747 in 1986 and Chief Pilot B747-400 in 1988.

Captain Koh was appointed Assistant Director of Flight Operations (Line Operations) in January 1993. He has the main responsibility of overseeing all the fleet operations and crew management in Singapore Airlines

Jefferson Koonce

Professor Koonce joined the University of Central Florida in 1992 as Director and Chief Scientist of the Center for Applied Human Factors in Aviation (CAHFA). He earned his PhD in Engineering Psychology from the University of Illinois in 1974. He is a multi-engine commercial instrument rated pilot and flight instructor, a licenced psychologist, fellow of APA and APS, as well as a senior member of the Institute of Industrial Engineers.

Henry (Hank) R Lehrer

Professor of Aeronautical Science at Embry Riddle Aeronautical University at Daytona Beach, Dr Lehrer teaches both undergraduate and graduate courses. He has an ATPL, is a Certified Flight Instructor (Instrument and Multi-Engine) with over three decades of teaching experience. He is the founding editor of the Journal of Aviation/Aerospace Education and Research, and has an extensive background in research, publication and conference presentation.

Anne Marit Lie

Anne Marit Lie received her Master of Science from the Norwegian Institute of Technology in 1994, writing her graduating thesis in the field of organisational culture and aviation safety. After graduation she worked as a consultant in the Socio-Technical Systems Safety Sector at the Joint Research Centre in Ispra, Italy, developing human factors training courses. She is now at the Norwegian University of Science and Technology. Her main interests are the study of culture and the organisation, and how it may influence human factors training.

Dan Maurino

Secretary of the ICAO Flight Safety and Human Factors Group, Captain Maurino joined Aerolineas Argentina after acquiring a degree in education. He held several management positions, including that of Training manager, before commencing research in flight simulator training in Montreal, He joined ICAO in May, 1989, with the responsibility of developing and implementing its Human Factors program.

Len McCully
Captain McCully joined SIA in January 1963. He obtained his commercial pilot licence with Instrument Rating from Airwork Services Training, Perth, Scotland in 1963. After obtaining command in 1970, Captain McCully was appointed Chief Pilot (Standards) in June 1977. This position was retitled Chief Pilot (Training) in December 1981. He was appointed Assistant Director of Flight Operations (Training) in December 1989. He has flown the F27, Comet IV, B727, B737, B707, B747-300/400, Learjet 31 and the Airbus A300 and has been instructor and check pilot on all these aircraft except the Comet IV. He is currently an instructor and check pilot on the A340.

Norman MacLeod
A consultant specialising in the design of aviation ground instruction and the use of technology in training, Norman MacLeod was a training specialist in the RAF for 21 years. A graduate of Staff College, he has extensive experience of operational training, including CBT and simulation for transport, AEW and maritime strike/attack aircraft. He commanded a training school and had Staff Officer responsibility for ground training.

Paul McNabb
At the time of writing, Paul was completing an assignment for the United Nations in the Middle East. Previously, he was Manpower Planning Specialist for Air Niugini. He directed his own international consultancy in human resources strategic planning and management training between 1987 and 1993, following experience in training within the New Zealand Fishing Industry, contract training in Indonesia and New Zealand, directing a Tourism Human Resource Development unit. Following an initial science degree from Wellington (NZ), Paul gained a post-graduate diploma in Teaching English as a Second Language. Additionally, he maintains an active interest in human resource and training development.

Roger Miller
Captain Roger Miller is Manager, Standards and Compliance, at Ansett Australia. Having flown in airlines for over three decades, he has experience on aircraft from the DC3 to the 767, and has been involved in training, checking and standards at Ansett for twenty years. His background in CRM goes back to its inception at Ansett. He is also the proud owner of a DH-C1 Chipmonk.

Phillip J Moore

Dr Phil Moore is an associate professor in Education at The University of Newcastle, Australia where he teaches educational psychology in the Faculty of Education and instructional courses in the Department of Aviation and Technology. He holds a PhD from The University of Newcastle and is a member of the American Psychological Association. His research interests are in human learning, particularly motivation, strategies, and text processing. He is the recipient of a number of Australian Research Council Grants and has published his works in international journals. He is co-author, with Biggs, of the book *The Process of Learning*. With Telfer, he has been conducting joint research with a number of national and international airlines on pilot, instructor and organisational perspectives on learning.

Mustapha Mouloua

Mustapha Mouloua is a Senior Research Scientist at the Center for Applied Human Factors in Aviation and Assistant Professor of Human Factors at the University of Central Florida, Orlando. He received his M.A. and PhD degrees from the Catholic University of America, Washington, D.C. His research interests include attention and human performance, cognitive aging, and aviation psychology. He is editor of *Human-Automation Interaction: Research and Practice* (in press) and co-editor of *Human Performance in Automated Systems: Current Research and Trends* (1994), and *Automation and Human Performance: Theory and Applications*. (1996).

Werner Naef

With over 25 years experience in Swissair, Captain Naef has flown DC8, DC9, MD80 (instructor and check pilot) A310 (Captain). He has been a training officer with the Swiss Civil Aviation School at Oxford (UK) and Vera Beach (USA). Flying experience has also been gained with the Swiss Air Force since 1968, in which Werner has flown fighters (DH Venom, Hunter, F8E) and transport (PC6). He has been a squadron leader for 11 years, and Deputy Head of Mission Control. His engineering degree is combined with post-graduate study in psychoanalysis. Captain Naef is a member of the Board of the European Association for Aviation Psychology.

Stanley N Roscoe

Stanley N Roscoe was a transport pilot in the Troop Carrier Command during World War 11. He earned his PhD in aviation engineering psychology at the University of Illinois in 1950 and pioneered the application of human engineering principles and man-in-the-loop simulation in aircraft system design during the 1950-60s. He is retired from Hughes Aircraft Company (1977), where he was Manager Display Systems Department and Senior Scientist; from the University of Illinois at Urbana-Champaign (1979), where he was associate director for research of the Institute of Aviation and head of the Aviation Research Laboratory; and from Mexico State University (1986), where he was head of the Behavioral Engineering Laboratory. He is still occasionally active as professor emeritus of psychology at the University of Illinois at Urbana-Champaign and New Mexico University; as president of ILLIANA Aviation Sciences Limited, and as vice president of Aero Innovation Inc. He is the primary author of the WOMBAT Situational Awareness and Stress Tolerance Tests.

Anthony C Sasso

Anthony Sasso is the Senior Crew Resource Management Specialist for Northwest Airlines Incorporated. Before joining Northwest in 1994, he spent 9 years in the United States Air Force as an Advanced Combat Evaluator/Instructor Navigator on the Lockheed C-130 Hercules. He continues his active flying career with the Minnesota Air National Guard and to date has over 3000 hours in the C-130. At Northwest he is responsible for the CRM/LOFT training for all the pilot instructors. He also oversees the development and manages the facilitation of all the LOFT scenarios used by Northwest. Anthony is a member of the Airline Transport/AQP Instructor Evaluation Focus Group. He holds a Bachelors degree in Mathematics and Economics from Boston College, Chestnut Hill, Massachusetts and a masters degree in Operations Management from the University of Arkansas, Fayetteville, Arkansas.

Jill J Scevak

Dr Jill J Scevak is a lecturer in the Faculty of Education at the University of Newcastle in Australia where she teaches educational psychology. She holds B.A., Dip Ed, MEd Stud and PhD degrees from the University of Newcastle. Her research interests include the effects of text design on learning, especially in conditions where there are accompanying diagrams, charts, graphs, maps and the like. Her research has been presented at numerous international conferences and has been published in the world's leading scholarly journals. Dr Scevak is the recipient of a number of Australian Research Council Grants and is a member of the American Psychological Association.

Albrecht Schiewe

Since 1995, Albrecht Schiewe has been the Head of the Department of Human Factors of Deutsche Lufthansa/German Airlines. He received his M.S. in Psychology from the University of Hamburg, Germany, in 1987. From 1988-95 he worked as a psychologist at the DLR Department of Aviation and Space Psychology where he was responsible for developing and establishing a human factors training program for the group of German astronauts. He was involved in the psychological selection of pilots, air traffic controllers, and astronauts. His current research interests are in human factors in the development of crew resource management programs for airlines.

Ken Sellars
Since arriving in Papua New Guinea with 278 hours in his log book, Captain Sellars has gained considerable flying experience in the region in a wide variety of aircraft: 206, 402, Islander, Twin Otter, Bandeirante and Citation. He joined Air Niugini in 1984, flying the Dash 7 and F28. After filling the positions of Check Captain and Dash 7 Fleet Captain, he is now Manager Line Operations, Air Niugini. Captain Sellars plays a key role in developing company selection methods and the Head-Start Program to prepare National Cadet Pilots for overseas training. A keen off-road motorbike rider, he has ridden to the North-Western-most accessible point of PNG, and has crossed Australia directly from west to east.

Ross A Telfer
Formerly Foundation Professor and Head of the Department of Aviation at the University of Newcastle, Australia, Dr Telfer now heads his own international consultancy (Instructional Research and Development) which has been active with a number of airlines developing and evaluating training programs. Now an Emeritus Professor, he has authored, co-authored or edited several books (including *Psychology and Flight Training*, and *Aviation Instruction and Training*), articles and conference papers. His current research interest is in pilot learning and training.

Pamela S Tsang
Pamela S Tsang is an associate professor at Wright State University. She was an engineering psychologist at the Volpe National Transportation Systems Center, Cambridge, Massachusetts during 1995-96. Previously, she was a postdoctoral research associate at NASA-Ames Research Center, Moffett Field, California. She received her Ph.D. from the University of Illinois at Urbana-Champaign in Experimental/Engineering Psychology and her A.B. in Psychology from Mount Holyoke College. Her current research interests are cognitive aging and pilot performance, time-sharing performance, display/control integrality, and mental workload issues.

Mark W Wiggins
Mark Wiggins is a Lecturer in the Department of Aviation and Technology at the University of Newcastle, Australia. Having studied in both Australia and New Zealand, he has been teaching and researching the fields of aviation human factors and training for several years. He has a Masters Degree in Psychology

from the University of Otago, is a qualified pilot, and is currently undertaking a PhD in computer-based training and aeronautical decision-making.

Acknowledgements

The University of Newcastle's support of this book is acknowledged. The University not only provided infrastructure support but also study leave to one of us, Moore, for sustained research and writing time.

Prime thanks are due to the thirty one contributors who gave their time, energy and expertise in the production of the chapters. In demanding times, these people were able to meet deadlines and so make our job a little easier. Our intentions were to have an international perspective (Europe, North America, Africa, South East Asia, Australia and the Pacific region) combining both industry and research expertise. An examination of the chapters should show we have achieved that objective. Thanks.

We also wish to acknowledge the photographic contributions spread throughout the book. Valuable assistance in this area was provided by: Ansett Australia, Cathay Pacific Airways, Embry-Riddle Aeronautical University (Florida), Northwest Airlines, Philippine Airlines, Qantas, Singapore Airlines, South African Airlines, and Swissair.

Chris Byrne undertook the task of compiling the final manuscript. Her devotion and perseverance, her expertise in word processing and graphics, and her sense of humour are all very much appreciated. Ken Scott's valuable assistance on the photographic side is also acknowledged.

Finally, John Hindley is thanked for his support of this project.

Ross Telfer and Phil Moore
Newcastle
Australia
August, 1996.

Foreword

Captain Dan Maurino

Training and safety are integral components of the fabric of contemporary aviation. Furthermore, they are closely intertwined. The fact that training, safety and their indissoluble bond are part of a greater scheme of things has not always however been acknowledged by conventional wisdom. Traditional discussion has been biased towards considering training and safety as ends in themselves, rather than as services to achieve higher goals. Furthermore, training and safety have more often than not been taken out of context, ignoring that it is rather anecdotal and lacking foundation to discuss training and safety as abstract entities, without anchoring the discussion within real-life, socio-operational contexts. It is harmless - if meaningless - to consider training and safety in the abstract when engaged in philosophical meandering. In practice, training and safety do not take place in a vacuum, but within specific social contexts, exercised by groups with specific professional cultures, and they are perennial, specific victims - if not scapegoats - of recurring contextual constraints. It is therefore imperative that training development and safety practices spring from realistic assumptions. This in turn demands that applied training and safety research be context-conscious.

On-going debate on aviation training and safety presents, as of lately, interesting overtones. Under the auspices of organizational and cognitive science, traditional views on training and safety are under crossfire. For decades, it has been dogma in aviation that safety is an objective process supported by quantifiable data and based upon defined structures. This is partly true. However, when considering that although safety may well *rest* upon protocols and structures it essentially *evolves* from attitudes, a different picture emerges, one which presents safety as a state of mind. Safety is about hazards and risks, about the allocation of resources to cancel hazards and risks to life and damage to property and, ultimately, about the value of human life. Neither hazards nor the risks that they may generate are inherent to artifacts or procedures; they are an evaluation constructed in different manners by different social groups based on experience and learning. The different perceptions in different contexts - because of societal beliefs - about what constitutes hazard and acceptable risk inevitably lead to the fact that the value of human life will vary considerably across the global village. This does not imply amoral calculation, but rather that the allocation of resources to cancel hazards and risks will depend upon the prevailing attitudes within social groups. Safety is not the objective process heralded by dogma, but a subjective process of risk evaluation and acceptance. This suggests that the established practice of developing safety solutions for a particular context and then exporting them to other contexts hoping their effectiveness will remain unaltered is rather naive and needs revisiting.

The notion of safety as a social construct introduces interesting implications in its relationship with training. Like safety, training takes place within distinct social and organizational contexts and, in theory at least, one important need it fulfils is compensation for potential system deficiencies. A fundamental role of training is to cope with system deficiencies which were unforeseen - or ignored - at the time of system design. At the bottom line, training is a tool available to operational personnel to fulfil their role as last line of defence, as goalkeepers of safety in sociotechnical production systems when system deficiencies pop out unexpectedly. It is then inevitable that training is espoused - consciously or unconsciously - to the prevailing safety paradigm. Training in aviation has a successful track record, and if it is to remain a useful and applicable tool, it must be relevant to the needs of the end-users. In order to be relevant, aviation training must be based (a) upon an appropriate safety paradigm, (b) upon an understanding of systemic deficiencies, (i.e., what the *real* problems are) and therefore, (c) be context-specific. Here again, the established tendency of developing training solutions of universal value must be the object of serious re-consideration.

What has been the past, what is the present and, most important, what does the future hold for the relationship between training and safety in aviation?

In the past (roughly since World War II), the safety paradigm favoured by aviation - in line with prevailing worldwide beliefs in black and white, right and left, good and evil and other simplistic extremes without intermediate stops - was also simple: safety was considered a value of universal definition, and accidents were caused by individuals. Protracted abuse of the benefit of hindsight fostered the notion of human error as an aberrant form of behaviour and therefore a cause of accidents. Safety endeavours were mostly reactive, taking place only after safety breakdowns ("if it ain't broke, why fix it?"), and with focus in the outcome of the processes engaged by operational personnel regardless of the quality of the process. Within this state of affairs, prevention was aimed at the sharp end of the operational spectrum and training therefore aimed at individual performance. Generations of aviators have been trained while ticking boxes in training forms devised in North America and Europe, without much introspection as to the real, operational, end value of the assumptions defining the contents of such boxes, neither for the North American and European contexts nor for the rest of the worldwide aviation community. In terms of applied Human Factors knowledge, classical example of this approach are early Cockpit Resource Management training courses aimed at fixing the mythological "wrong stuff" and deemed to be of universal value and application with a few "cosmetic changes".

Today, in a world of shades of grey and trying to find a new socio-political balance amidst relentless change, it is hardly surprising that attempting to define the favoured safety paradigm arises mixed feelings and conflicting emotions. Those holding the majority, conventional view based on conservatism - and convenience - argue for the continuing relevance of the past safety paradigm. Others -and the ranks are slowly increasing - question the notion of safety as a value with unchallengeable universal definition and contend that distinct contexts present different safety and training problems which require distinct, culturally-calibrated solutions. Within this latter camp, the prevailing notion is that accidents are caused by work groups rather than by individuals - a notion with important underlying implications for training. Under the scrutiny of applied cognition, human error is considered a rather poorly-defined form of human behaviour and, most significant, as a normal component of human performance. Questions as to whether human error is a cause of accidents or merely a symptom of deficiencies in the deeper layers of the systems arise more frequently. Because of an increasing interest in the quality of the process incurred by operational personnel in addition to their outcome, reactive prevention - although still very much alive - shares the safety arena with proactive prevention which attempts to fix the system before it breaks. It is a fair statement that today's prevention aims at both the sharp and blunt end of the operational spectrum. In terms of training, even when large segments of aviation operational personnel training still aim at individuals, the focus is slowly changing towards a systemic approach to training, and a dawning interest in the organization and how it fosters or impedes learning is becoming increasingly conspicuous.

Normal evolution will hopefully lead to a state of affairs in which safety would be considered a distinct social value, and towards the notion that accidents are caused by system flaws rather than by individual misbehaviour. Human error would then be considered a symptom, a clue to indicate where the safety process should begin rather than end. Attention would be directed towards the processes incurred by the aviation system while pursuing its production goals - the safe and efficient transportation of people and goods -, regardless of the outcome of these processes. Prevention endeavours would concentrate in the blunt end of the system, truly the breeding grounds of system deficiencies, while keeping an eye in the front end, to ensure that goalkeepers continue to be proficient in discharging their tasks as progress dictates. Within such context, training would be considered a proactive, culturally-fostered organizational development rather than a fix for the "wrong stuff" or the dumping grounds of poor design, production pressures or managerial blunders. Training and human resource development will then change its present status as last great frontier of aviation safety, means of living for consultants, opportunity to generate research data, power tool from management or many of the others misperceptions flying around the international community, to that of a tool to improve safety and efficiency of the aviation system, with operational and social relevance.

Idle talk is abundant since offer usually exceeds demand. What has been sketched above has significant implications in terms of change, and change does not take place through idle talk or pontification. Commitment and decisive action by those in position to effect change is required. According to the universally accepted measuring stick of the aviation safety record - accident statistics - lapses and deficiencies in operational human performance continue to penetrate the system defences with periodicity. If this situation is to be contained, change *must* take place. The aviation industry cannot continue to resort to solutions employed in the past with the naive belief that they will work in the present or future contexts. The industry must look for solutions which anticipate and contain human error in operational contexts rather than continue to regret its consequences. Change is essential.

This book is an agent for change. It goes a long way into solidifying the relationship between context, safety and training; a relationship the understanding of which is essential to conduct business in aviation as we approach the year 2000. Its editors set the tone in the introduction, by advocating congruency among trainees, trainers and system as the foundation for training effectiveness. From there onwards, a team of numerous contributors - with a variety of backgrounds such that operational relevance and protection against academic monopoly is guaranteed - takes over and continues to build the bridge between applied research and training in context. On reflection, it may well be contended that this book stands as proof that there is hope for those willing to challenge the gloomy walls of dogma which, from time to time, imprison human intelligence.

Captain Dan Maurino,
Co-ordinator Flight Safety and Human Factors Program,
International Civil Aviation Organization,
Montreal, July 1996.

Introduction
The roles of learning, instruction and the organization in aviation training
Ross A Telfer and Phillip J Moore

There are significant potential differences in the perspectives on learning and instruction held by pilots, instructors and the range of organizations which administer aviation training and testing (Telfer and Moore, 1995). These organizations include flying schools, regulatory authorities and airline management. The degree to which congruence or alignment occurs across the three groups - trainees, trainers and system- determines the potency or dilution of training effectiveness.

At this stage, in the absence of substantiating data, this argument has to remain an assertion. It has, however, high face validity and our ongoing research offers encouraging results. It is hardly a wild or sweeping claim, as the literature suggests that optimal learning occurs when all participants' expectations align and they work collaboratively towards a common goal. The presence and extent of a lack of congruence - or conflicts in expectations - suggest the extent to which training effectiveness (the extent to which it attains its goals) and efficiency (the cost of doing so) are impaired. Our research has developed ways in which aviation training organizations can assess:

- pilots' perspectives on learning;
- the learning that instructors encourage; and,
- the learning that management and organizational culture shape.

These methods will be discussed later. At this stage, the three contributors to learning can be detailed.

Three levels of influence on aviation training

The outcome of training and instruction is largely determined by the motivation and strategies of the individual pilot or student, by the instructor's values, skills and knowledge, and by the nature of the organization (or system) in which the training occurs (Telfer, 1994). The last input is deceptive, for it is easily as complex as the other two. Organizational or contextual bias on aviation training consists of a hierarchy of interrelated variables: societal culture, government legislation, regulatory and licensing authority, policy, management, and organizational climate. This position is not over-stated. Consider how the schooling system or aspects of social and economic status affect the nature of the employment pool from which airlines recruit.

A summary of the three categories of variables and their practical manifestations is provided by Table 1.

Although the lists of variables are only indicative, in the absence of conclusive evidence at this stage of the research, they appear a reasonable basis on which to proceed. The individual learner alone can determine intrinsic motivation to become a professional pilot. The individual's attitudes and strategies decide the approach to an aviation syllabus, allocation of time to learning, and selection of methods of study. Yet the abilities and experiences of the learner, which will greatly affect the way the initial training is received, are predetermined as entry behaviours when training commences. They are determined by such socialising agencies as family, school, peer group and media.

In relative terms, instructors seem to have little autonomy. Perhaps this is why they tend to lack the parity of esteem, and salary, their experience and qualifications merit. To a large extent the syllabus, program and examination are prescribed. Some instructor variables are similar to those of the learner. Their experience and expertise would be reflected in their attitudes to instruction, learning and to the trainee; to the extent and types of instructional aids; and to their professional knowledge and skills of both aviation and instruction. There are many areas in which the instructor has a say, but in which the final determinant is probably in the form of constraints from higher authority. Such areas are the availability of funding for remedial or special instruction beyond the norm, participation in workshops or special instructor training, and in recognition of special professional qualifications or expertise. There may be no opportunity to implement skills or knowledge to improve the process of instruction, because the process is firmly established by authority or solid precedent.

The existence of professional groups, such as Associations of Flight Instructors, is the first step towards gaining greater control over the process, syllabus, and testing of training. There are several major hurdles, however, and these are typical of occupational groups seeking professionalisation. For example, there are several fronts upon which instructors need to keep advancing: adherence to a publicised Code of Ethics; a demonstrably professional period of preparation and qualification; and registration and licensing for practice by a body which is capable of disciplining its members for professional breaches, rather than an external regulatory or governmental organization.

There is incongruity in Table 1 in the extent to which the organization or system contributes to - even controls - the process. Compare the ticks. The government or its delegated authority; the employer; the board of directors; the chairman; the accountant: these are the gate-keepers who decide the vital inputs of aviation training. Just as the process of learning can be seen as several interdependent components linked in a system, so the process of training can be viewed in terms of the vital inputs, the way they are processed, the resultant output and how it feeds back to influence the nature of the inputs.This is shown in Figure 1.

Implications for training: influencing the gate-keepers

The irony, of course, is that we have been devoting the training budget to the instruction of pilots and instructors. Yet it is management and the organization (employing, regulating, licensing, governing, and so on) which is the largest determinant of the quality of learning. Table 1 presents the basis for an argument that we should be aiming a major effort at educating and persuading the gate-keepers who actually decide what sort of, and how much, training will occur. Figure 1 shows the critical position - and power - that the gatekeepers hold. They control not only the nature and extent of the inputs - but they actually filter the extent to which feedback can modify the inputs. They could, for example, choose to set up an evaluative review of a licensing system and then decide who will be on the committee, and whether or not to implement the results.

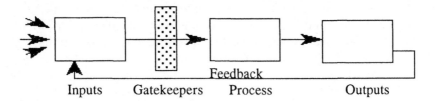

Inputs   Gatekeepers   Process   Outputs

Figure 1 The training system

It is not surprising that training and instruction in aviation are under pressure. What the individual pilot and instructor are seeking - even if collaboratively - may be in spite of rather than because of the system's demands. The all-important test may have little resemblance to what occurs in line flying. The optimal training aid may be outside the training department's budget.

The most obvious pressure is the organizational quest for efficiency. This quantitative interpretaion of training is usually viewed in terms of value for dollar and minimum time off-line. It may even be seen in terms of insurance savings, taxation deductions or gaining credit with the licensing authority. The instructor and pilot would probably favour a more qualititative framework seeking effectiveness in terms of the standard of training and learning. (Telfer, 1993).

The larger context of aviation operations is under examination, largely because of the focus of crew resource management. For example, the work of Hofstede (1991) in highlighting the extent to which culture and organizations can influence such key aspects as communication, individuality or attitude to authority. The implications of this work for aviation are being revealed by Johnston (1992) Merritt (1993) and Lambo and Lambo (1995). Increasingly, the insights of CRM has led to a widening focus. Initially, this was out of the cockpit to incorporate the crew. Then the crew concept extended beyond the aircraft to the total team involved in maintaining safe flight. Now the illumination extends to the company itself. Resource is the subject of management, regardless of its context.

An area yet to be explored in aviation, but one that is recognised in organizational and management theory and practice is that of *climate*: the set of internal characteristics that differentiates one airline or flying school from another and influences the behaviour of its members. Simply, it is the personality of the organization. A variety of measures and descriptions exist, and can be applied in aviation. For example, the organization can be seen as being:
- **open** (high degree of support, morale, leadership by example, and consideration) or,
- **closed** (low morale, high emphasis on rules, trivia and paperwork, close supervision and impersonality). It is not only justifiable, but wholly appropriate that organizational climate is described in terms of participants' perceptions as responses to a questionnaire or interview. Climate and morale result from what people think, not from objective fact. For example, one method of determining climate is based on the similarity or differences in responses by different groups in the organization to questions about who makes certain decisions; whether people associate outside work hours; whether there are emphases on people values as well as task attainment. As for the precise effects on training, the climate of the organization (like the culture of the society) merits further exploration. There can be little doubt, however, that this exploration will be as fruitful as it has been in other organizations undertaking instruction and training.

Table 1
Indicative determinants of training **efficiency**

	INDIVIDUAL	INSTRUCTION	ORGANIZATION
program		✓	✓
facilities			✓
materials		✓	✓
equipment			✓
funding			✓
scheduling		✓	✓
supervision		✓	✓
assessment		✓	✓
attitude/value	✓	✓	✓
skill	✓	✓	✓
knowledge	✓	✓	✓

The inertia of tradition

Another tension is the pendulum swing of innovation versus tradition. Those who head organizations have attained recognition and career success because of abilities, attitudes, knowledge and skills. These values and capabilities have been attained over years of practical experience. They know what works: especially because of its unique characteristic - *it worked for them personally, and has worked for the industry.* That cannot be said of any other, more recent, option. They know the right stuff when they see it.

It is difficult for people in this situation to not only accept but to encourage innovation which may pose both a threat to overt functionality and their own expertise. At extremes, this can be seen as a conservatism capable of inhibiting progress in both instructor and trainee learning. On the other hand, it can also be seen as prudent management. Apart from the personal risk, there are the high stakes of aviation safety that require caution in training methods as much as operating procedures.

Three levels of input to training in aviation

In summary, then, the learning that occurs as part of instruction and training in aviation is determined by major inputs at three levels:

- that of the individual trainee;
- that of the instructor; and,
- that of management, the organization and the system in which it is located.

It is reasonable to assume that the system would work best when all three inputs were congruent and a synergy developed. After all, that is what is now argued for flight crews, aircraft crews, and companies. Conflicts among or between levels would serve to weaken the system and reduce the output both qualitatively and quantitatively. How can we decide if they are working in harmony or conflicting? How can we promote the synergy in training?

The process of learning and these influences

One way of conceptualising learning is to see it not only as what occurs as a result of the actual process of instruction and training, but to extend the focus onto what occurs before and after that lesson, sortie or briefing. Biggs and Moore (1993) developed this so-called *3P model* stressing the interactivity of **Presage**, **Process**, and **Product** factors in learning. The 3P model is a system. Any change in one section of the model influences either directly or indirectly each other component.

Presage refers to the "baggage" that pilots, instructors, and the organization bring to any instructional setting. In aviation, the important presage factors typically are pilot experience, age, abilities, personality, and their preferred approach to learning (Deep, Surface, Achieving). Also within the presage factor are instructor characteristics, such as their experiences, their commitment and motivation, their abilities, their personalities and their views on how learning should be approached. Presage factors also include the organization and the variable discussed in Table 1: the emphasis it places on facilities, training procedure, supervision, scheduling, and the ways in which it adapts to the tensions between innovation, change, and traditional more conservative perspectives, particularly when safety is of such a major concern in the industry. By way of regulatory authority and government legislation, additional constraints and tensions are placed upon organizations through laws, regulations, licence requirements, obligatory tests and standards.

Process factors are concerned essentially with the ways in which pilots go about learning a particular task. Clearly the way in which this is done is influenced by their own motivations and strategic knowledge, their interpretations of the instructional context, and the instructor's expectations, advice or prescriptions. If it is explicit, another variable is their awareness of the organization's expectations as they relate to their training. The organization's expectations may be more implicit, however, manifesting themselves in the nature of the training materials, the norms of the peer

6

group, the quality of the training facilities and the ways in which the outcomes are assessed and evaluated. An important presage factor influencing the ways in which individuals learn is their preference for surface, deep, and achieving approaches to learning (Biggs & Moore, 1993), constructs that are central to this argument.

Approaches to learning

Surface learners are inclined to reproduce what they have learned and typically use rote learning as an end. Often minimalism and anxiety are associated with surface type learning. *Deep learners* are more inclined to see learning as gaining meaning and understanding. They thus use a range of elaborative and integrative strategies to achieve their goals. *Achieving learners* are keen to do well, competitive, and enjoy the boost to the ego that good learning may give (Biggs, 1987).

The *Product* component of the 3P model is concerned with the quantity as well as the quality of that learning and the more emotive outcomes such as self concept and feeling good about learning. Quantitative perspectives on learning seem to predominate in most systems in which aviation learning is located, being reflected in marks or percentages, Under such a system, the closer one is to 100%, presumably the more one has learned. Such a judgement, however, may say very little about the quality of what has been learned. A score approaching 100% could, for example, reflect knowledge of a whole host of unrelated facts. This leads to the nature of the assessment itself. Assessment has been shown to have "backwash", when the assessment tail wags the instructional dog (Biggs & Moore, 1993). If assessment is heavily biased towards low-level details, then it is likely that the subsequent backwash will not only influence learners but also their instructors and the environment in which they both work.

Who is responsible for learning in aviation, and avoiding such backwash effect? Given the nature of the 3P model, each participant is implicated: pilots, instructors, and organization (see Table 1). This might seem like stating the obvious, but there are important implications for quality learning which arise from this position.

Quality learning in aviation

There has been much discussion about the nature of quality learning (see, for example, Biggs & Moore, 1993; Cohen, 1987) and quality learning in aviation in particular (see, for example, Telfer, 1994; and Wiggins &

O'Hare, 1993). Quality learning results when meaning, understanding and interpretation occur. The learner becomes a problem-solver who is developing a well-structured knowledge base, using appropriate motivation, and interacting meaningfully with others while involved in substantial learning activities. The more social aspect (interacting with others) is a critical component of adult learning in which quality learning is more than mere acquisition of knowledge.

The learner becomes actively involved in developing an integrated, elaborated knowledge base. Indeed, Biggs and Moore view quality learning as "deep" learning where there is an interaction among what is known, motivation, interactions with others, and learner activity. They also suggest that learning is most effective when all components in their model are synchronised, congruent, and aligned (Cohen, 1987). This view of quality learning is consistent with the aviation context. For the most part, learning in aviation is concerned with meaning, understanding and considering the circumstances of line application or implication. Pilots need to be capable of problem solving, using their extensive knowledge and skills to handle either unpredictable situations or repetitive, routine operations.

Pilots and learning

How do pilots learn? Our research with *ab initio* pilots (Moore & Telfer, 1990) and experienced pilots (Telfer & Moore, 1993; Moore, Telfer & Smith, 1994) suggests that pilots do see learning in deep, surface, and achieving terms. Indeed, in the Moore (1994) and Moore, Telfer and Smith (1994) work, there is clear evidence that experienced pilots place significantly more emphasis on deep and achieving approaches than they do on surface approaches. This finding has weight in that it stands irrespective of airline affiliation, being drawn from five international carriers. In response to a structured questionnaire, experienced pilots agreed with deep-oriented items (as reflecting their approach to learning), tended to agree with achieving items, and disagreed or tended to disagree with surface items. There were, however, differences between airlines on each of the deep, surface and achieving scales, with the largest differences on the achieving scale. Given that the achieving scale is reflecting institutional effects (Biggs, 1987), these differences may come from the effect of organizational or system climate. This would include cultural, instructor and management perspectives on how effective learning might occur.

Instructors and learning

It has been argued that instructors are a major variable affecting the learning of their students (Telfer, 1988). Expectations, planning, methods, modelling, empathy, feedback, and collaboration have been shown to affect the rate of learning. It is probable that a deep and achieving learner would succeed in spite of a substandard and uncommitted instructor. It is also probable that a surface learner may fail. Like learners, instructors bring "baggage" with them to the job. How do they view instruction? As a profession with a parity of esteem with commercial or airline flying? Or as a means to that end? How do they see management's, or their flying colleagues' view of their position?

One can imagine situations in which professional and committed instructors could lose their incentive, and others in which ambivalents could become zealous. The optimal appears to be one in which the instructor, student, examiner and organization have a high regard for the task of instruction and the status of the instructor.

Instrument development

To investigate instructor approaches to learning we devised a 34 item (six point Likert scale) questionnaire based upon the deep, surface and achieving constructs. To provide an idea of the nature of the instrument, several items are shown below with their sub-scale intent identified.

"To pass, students only have to memorise what they are given." (Surface)

"Opportunities are provided to ensure that students really understand what they are being taught." (Deep)

"Competition brings out the best in students." (Achieving)

A parallel instrument, described below, was developed to analyse the organizational approach to aviation training.

Organization and Learning

The rationale for examining perceptions of the organization's relationships with learning came from three sources: pilots' approaches to learning; organizational climate; and the effects of culture. The argument was that the organization would be most positively related to learning when there was congruence with the pilots' and instructors' views about the importance of deep learning and the place of achievement and surface methods. The organization would help the process of learning most when it fostered high morale or esprit, providing an open climate, and when it recognised any potential for negative effects of culture and made allowances for them.

As with the *Instructor Questionnaire*, the instrument designed for managerial perceptions is in its initial phases of complete development. To date we have generated some 49 items, again using the deep, surface, and achieving constructs. In addition, we have included items designed to tap organizational climate, morale and potential effects of culture. Some representative items are shown below with their sub-scale identified in parentheses.

"A pilot's job is to operate the aircraft, not understand it." (Surface)

"The company's instructors aim at understanding and problem solving, not just training in procedures." (Deep)

"It is important to recognise those who do best on checks and tests." (Achieving)

"In this organization, management, instructors, check captains and pilots work together as colleagues." (Climate)

"There is an us-and-them pilot attitude towards management." (Morale)

" Individualism is seen to be more important than teams in the way we work." (Culture)

Congruence and Alignment

To repeat, it is argued that learning will be optimised if all participants in the outcome share common goals, values and expectations. If pilots are seeing deep learning as their preferred mode, as our data suggest, then having instructors and the organization see it similarly might be a fruitful way to proceed.

Does this congruence occur, though? Our initial evidence strongly suggests that it does not. Our concluding comments come from experienced pilots undergoing training to command glass-cockpit, wide-body aircraft.

"I would like the opportunity to 'play' with the simulator for several hours before C/L, etc."

"Make the groundschool phase longer with more human input. CBT is here to stay, but however good it is, it cannot substitute for a qualified instructor."

"During CBT, introduce tutorials to cover with discussion the work done on the screen."

There is a need for pilots, instructors, airlines, training departments or organizations, examiners and licensing authorities to work together with a common goal and clear understanding of relative roles. Expectations have to be shared, not segregated. That would prevent training and learning goals being different or displaced for reasons which have little to do with professional preparation for aviation.

**There is a need for learners, instructors and the organization
to have common goals**

References

Biggs, J.B (1987). *Student approaches to learning and studying*. Hawthorn:
Australian Council for Educational Research.

Biggs, J.B. & Moore, P.J. (1993). *The Process of learning*. Sydney: Prentice
Hall Australia

Cohen, S.A. Instructional alignment: Searching for a magic bullet.
Educational Researcher, 16, 8, 16-20.

Hofstede, G .(1991) *Culture and organizations: software of the mind*.
London: McGraw Hill.

Johnston, A. N. (1992) *CRM- Cross Cultural Perspectives*. Dublin: Aviation
Psychology Research Group, Trinity College.

Johnston, A. N., McDonald, N., & Fuller, R. (1994). *Aviation psychology in practice*. Aldershot: Ashgate

Lambo, R. & Lambo, R. (1995) Culture and the cockpit in context: A situational perspective on behaviour in the cockpit. In N. McDonald, N. Johnston and R. Fuller (eds.). *Applications of Psychology to the Aviation System*. Aldershot: Avebury Aviation

Merritt, A.C. (1993) "The influence of national and organizational culture on human performance." Sydney: *Proceedings of the Industry Seminar of the Australian Aviation Psychology Association*,

Moore, P.J. (1994). *Across airline differences in pilot learning*. Paper presented at the 21st Conference of the Western European Association for Aviation Psychology, Dublin, Ireland, March.

Moore, P.J. & Telfer, R.A. (1990). Approaches to learning: Relationships with pilot performance. *Journal of Aviation/Aerospace Education and Research*, 1, 44-58

Moore, P.J., Telfer, R.A. & Smith. M. (1994). Learning for automation: Generic versus specific approaches. In M.Mouloua & R. Parasuraman (Eds.) *Human performance in automated systems: Current research and trends*. (pp. 307-313). Hillsdale, NJ: Erlbaum and Associates.

Telfer, R.A. (1993). *Aviation instruction and training*. Aldershot: Ashgate.

Telfer, R.A. (1994). Improving aviation instruction. In N.Johnston, N.McDonald & R. Fuller (Eds.), *Aviation psychology in practice* (pp. 340-358). Aldershot: Ashgate.

Telfer, R.A. & Moore, P.J. (1993). *The role of rote learning for experienced pilots*. Paper presented at the Aviation Human Factors Symposium, New Zealand Psychological Society's Conference, Wellington, August.

Telfer, R.A. and Moore, P.J. (1995) *Learning, instruction and organization in aviation*. Paper presented to the 8th International Symposium on Aviation Psychology, Columbus: The Ohio State University, April.

Wiggins, M. & O'Hare, D. (1993). A skills based approach to training aeronautical decision-making. In R.A. Telfer (Ed.), *Aviation instruction and training* (pp. 430-475). Aldershot: Ashgate.

Acknowledgement

The theme of this chapter was first presented by the authors in a paper entitled Learning, instruction and organization in aviation (paper presented at the 8th International Symposium on Aviation Psychology, Columbus Ohio, April 1995).

Part 1
Learners

1 Introduction to Part 1 - Learners

Phillip J Moore

This section contains eight chapters designed to examine the learner in the instructional cycle. While it might be stating the obvious, learners do differ from each other in a number of ways including age, experience, levels of expertise, preferences in the ways in which they learn, and in the ways in which they learn for more automated contexts. While the underlying principles of flight instruction have been standardisation and adherence to traditional methods, there are compelling arguments from other learning and instructing contexts for instruction to take into account the differences that individuals bring to learning (e.g. Biggs & Moore, 1993). These issues are taken up in this chapter with the aim of alerting those involved in training to take into account such individual differences when designing, implementing and evaluating training programmes.

The first chapter, by Tsang, is timely for she comprehensively, and critically, reviews the literature on aging and pilot performance. She shows that the average age of pilots is increasing and the number of pilots in the USA over 60 years of age has increased five-fold over the last 20 or so years. Tsang focuses on perception and decision making and analyses accident data as a function of age. The picture to emerge from her analyses is complex, it is not a simple issue of older individuals being poorer performers. Indeed, the finding that individual differences within an age group tends to increase with age makes it increasingly difficult to predict anyone's performance on the basis of age alone. Tsang concludes by suggesting that, if age influences pilot performance, it is not easily detected in the literature she so comprehensively surveyed.

Hunter's chapter takes quite a different perspective by examining the characteristics of a particular group of pilots in the USA, pilots who are primarily private licence holders. Hunter argues that while there are well established training programmes for those in the military and large civil carrier organisations, continuing pilot education for the private licence holder requires a different approach, particularly when a large number of such pilots fly 2.5

hours or less per month. Specifically, Hunter reports on a U.S.A. Federal Aviation Authority (FAA) large scale survey of private licence holders that attempted to identify such things as skill and experience levels and when and how they fly. Hunter shows that the population of pilots has wide experience, as measured by hours, an average age of 50 years, and is relatively well educated. In looking at what should be trained, Hunter identifies fuel management incidents, flying visual flight rules (VFR) into instrument flight conditions (IMC), and personal minimums. Highlighted are the facts that some 20 percent of the private licence holders reported at least one instance in which they were so low on fuel they were uncertain if they would make it to an airport. Also one quarter of the pilots reported entering IMC while flying VFR. Such information, allied to analyses of seminars already conducted by the FAA, encourages Hunter to argue for training programs designed to meet the needs of this group of pilots through a variety of presentation modes including use of the Internet, computer software and video materials.

The third chapter, by Wiggins, looks at the nature of expertise. How is expertise characterised? How can the cognitive skills of expertise be identified? Wiggins then moves to examine ways in which transitions from novice to expertise can be enhanced through Cognitive Task Analysis (CAT), an analysis that focuses on decision-making, problem solving, the development and application of mental models as well as the integration and interpretation of relevant information. Armed with such information about the learners and the task, appropriate training objectives can then be developed. Wiggins argues that such an approach is likely to increase both training efficiency and pilot safety.

The issue of individual preferences about learning is raised in Schiewe and Moore's chapter on individual differences and Crew Resource Management (CRM) training. Do some people prefer to learn from lectures? Do some prefer to learn in groups through activities? Do some dislike anything they are presented with? They gathered information related to these questions as well as attitudinal and personal data (age, rank, previous CRM experience) from over 500 pilots undergoing CRM training with a large European carrier. From their analyses they report four groups of individuals: Enthusiasts, Dynamics, Cognitives, and Rejectors. Enthusiasts tend to like all methods of instruction. Dynamics tend to like group activity and team building while Cognitives tend to prefer lectures and presentations. Rejectors rate lowly all methods of instruction and content. Greatest changes in attitudes were seen in the Enthusiasts. Many of the results may surprise the reader as the groupings had very little to do with age, rank, previous experience in CRM, or pre training attitudes. The complex issue of how training organizations can take learning preferences into account is taken up in the concluding section of their chapter.

The two chapters by Mouloua, Gilson and Koonce (Chapter 5) and Moore and Telfer (Chapter 6) tackle the problem of increasing automation. While increasing automation may have reduced the burdens of excessive in-flight workload, increased fuel efficiency and enhanced all weather flying, it has resulted in other problems. These problems include loss of situational awareness, reduced monitoring efficiency, and increased mental workloads. Mouloua and his colleagues review very recent work on pilots' interactions with cockpit automation, human-automation monitoring, and automation and pilot training. They propose that understanding how pilots interact with automation in the cockpit is crucial for safety, pilot and system performance as well as for the design of systems themselves. Exemplifying the problems, they draw attention to the ever-increasing number of alert systems on modern aircraft. How do pilots react to such alarms? What are the implications for training?

Moore and Telfer further examine automation in the cockpit but also include discussion on movements to automate instruction through Computer Based Training (CBT). They trace the movement towards greater automation in both the cockpit and instruction whilst reviewing some of the recent investigations of pilots' attitudes to such developments. Taking a practical perspective, Moore and Telfer then report on the ways in which successful pilots go about learning when converting to more technologically sophisticated aircraft.

Almost like a companion chapter to Moore and Telfer's, Gebers brings his vast training experience with South African Airways to Chapter 7 where he proposes guidelines as to how crew members can achieve the best from the training courses they attend. Gebers stresses the importance of both mental and physical preparation for training and provides useful advice as to how trainees undergoing type training can gain the most from their ground school and the simulator. Reflections on route training and recurrent training enhance the chapter. He makes well the point that there are no easy methods for learning vast amounts of information in a short time.

The final chapter in this first section is by Sellars and McNabb from Air Niugini. In some senses the chapter is quite different from the others in this part of the book but its concerns for individuals and how they might better fit into an airline makes it compatible with previous chapters. The chapter is written in the context of two pressures: increased localisation in airlines in Asia and the Pacific; and the attrition rate in national cadet pilot training. Sellars and McNabb detail an innovative programme designed along the lines of the Head Start programs of the 1970s in Education. As the name suggests, the program is designed to give cadet pilots a "head start" before they actually undertake pilot training. The programme consists of four phases each with specific goals and objectives. The earliest phase focuses on quite detailed personal reports to the cadets which detail their strengths and weaknesses (as assessed during selection) and makes suggestions as to ways in which their weaknesses might be overcome. Sellars and McNabb provide examples of such reporting. This information provides a basis for the activities undertaken in Phase 1. Phase 2 sees the cadets posted to flight operations where they undertake a variety of tasks aimed at developing professional attitudes and standards. Mentoring is then introduced at Phase 3 while the last phase is the actual flight training out-of-country. For those interested in developing a Head Start type program, Sellars and McNabb provide a schedule of a typical program used by the airline.

In all, these chapters foreground learners as individuals who have wide ranging differences. Each person in a training program brings their own "baggage" with them, baggage that includes their abilities, past experiences, preferred ways of learning, motives and strategies for learning, levels of expertise, attitudes towards training and so on. Clearly some of these will be seen to be more important in some situations than others. The challenge for those designing, implementing and evaluating training programs is to identify which individual differences are important in the context of organizational constraints.

References

Biggs, J.B. & Moore, P.J. (1993). *The process of learning.* Sydney: Prentice-Hall Australia.

2 Age and pilot performance

Pamela S Tsang

The interests and concerns in age and pilot performance

One reason for the recent heightened concern and interest in aging issues is because the population is aging. Based on the Federal Aviation Administration (FAA) annual surveys and the National Transportation Safety Board (NTSB) annual reports from 1968 to 1987, Bruckart (1992) estimated that the mean pilot age increased from 35 to 40 years and the number of pilots over the age of 60 increased five-fold. However, an examination of the general aviation accidents showed a decrease in accident rate over the 20 years period for each age group of a 5-year interval from under age 20 to over age 60.

Measuring pilot performance is an enduring issue that has escaped simple solutions. There are three major approaches to assess pilot performance: subjective evaluation of actual flight performance by the instructor or check pilot, quantitative off-line performance measures (e.g., tracking error, degree deviation from a simulator flight course, reaction time), and accident rate. Subjective evaluations are difficult to compare and analyze quantitatively but they are highly accepted as the standard practice of the trade. Off-line simulator or laboratory task performance measures provide the most diagnostic information but may have limited generality and validity. Accidents may be the ultimate measure of safety but accidents are rare and accident rate can only reveal global trend information. Since each of these approaches has its strengths and weaknesses, information should be sought with as many different approaches as feasible (Birren and Fisher, 1995).

The present chapter reviews some of the known age effects on those cognitive functions such as perception and decision making that have been identified to be essential to piloting. Not discussed are natural aging effects on sensory and physiological functions. The relationship between pilot age, experience, performance, and accident rate will be examined.

Cognitive functions essential to piloting

Some of the cognitive functions judged to be essential for piloting are: perceptual processing (e.g., instrument monitoring), memory (e.g., maintaining information furnished by air traffic controllers--ATCs), problem solving (e.g., fault diagnosis), decision making (e.g., whether to carry out a missed approach procedure), psychomotor coordination (e.g., flight control), and time-sharing performance (e.g., instrument monitoring while communicating with ATC; maintaining aircraft stability while navigating). Each of these cognitive functions will be reviewed below.

Perceptual performance

There are two aspects of perception (Salthouse, 1982) that are crucial to flying: spatial and temporal perception. Spatial perception involves tasks such as perceptual organization, spatial manipulation, and selective attention. Temporal perception includes motion judgment, temporal integration, and visual masking. The psychological literature indicates substantial age-related impairments in both spatial and temporal perception. There is however little age-related deficits with simple judgments of lines and angles (Salthouse, 1982). In addition, Hunt and Hertzog (1981) pointed out that although older observers would be at a disadvantage with detecting rapidly moving targets at low levels of illumination, large age differences would not be expected for detecting a clearly distinct stimulus.

It seems unlikely that older pilots would be immune from perceptual deterioration that is prevalently observed in the general population. However, the extent to which these declines have any operational significance is not clear. For example, Crook, Devoe, Hageman, Hanson, Krulee, and Ronco (1957) found that older individuals needed more time to judge the possibility of collision among simulated airplanes. Although this might implicate a reduced safety margin for the older observers, it is noteworthy that none of the observers had any flying experience. Eyraud and Borowsky (1985) categorized the 1977-1982 flight records of all naval pilots according to age, mishap rates, and causal factors. Nine mishap causal factors were found to be age-related. Among the six factors that had the highest mishap rates for fighter and attack pilots 26-year-old or younger, only one was highly related to perceptual processing--overrun and undershoot during landing. In contrast, the other three factors whose mishap rates were highest among pilots at least 38 years of age were not perceptually related (violations of regulations, improper instrument procedure, and inadequate flight preparation). Granted, the "old" pilots in this investigation would not be considered old by most standards, it is nevertheless important to note that it was the younger pilots (and most likely less experienced pilots) who were more prone to perceptual error. In another investigation, Szafran (1963) compared a group of younger pilots (mean age = 31) with a group of older pilots (mean age = 49). Rate of information gain was not reduced with increasing age, except under the information overload condition. Even then the difference was small. Another study by Szafran (1968) found a decrease in the efficiency of older commercial pilots in extracting relevant information (signal) from a background of noise. However, the older pilots tended to select more optimal strategies for signal detection that overcame the reduced efficiency of their sensory mechanisms.

The findings reviewed here suggest that flight experience may hone skills that can compensate for natural age-related perceptual declines. Szafran also noticed that the individual differences *within* an age group were larger than those *between* age groups. Other research has shown that large individual differences in age-related decrements is a common finding.

Memory performance

Increased age has generally been associated with poorer memory performance. In fact, age selectively affects different facets of memory. Although there are minimal age effects in short-term memory span (STM capacity, Botwinick and Storandt, 1974), efficiency of the processing therein (also refered to as the working memory, Baddeley, 1986) tends to decrease with increased age (Hultsch and Dixon, 1990; Salthouse, 1990). In addition, there are definite age-related difficulties with long-term memory retrieval (Craik, 1977). Coyne, Allen, and Wickens (1988) added that age differences are primarily associated with the ability to encode information and to transfer them from short-term to long-term memory .

Two investigations revealed that memory performance could be used to enhance the prediction of pilot performance. In one study, Braune and Wickens (1984b) administered five information processing tasks (tracking, Sternberg memory, maze tracking, hidden figures, and dichotic listening) to 30 instrument-rated pilots between the age of 20 and 60. These tasks had previously been shown to be age-sensitive with nonpilot subjects (Braune and Wickens, 1984a). In the study using pilots, performance on the five tasks was used to predict performance on a simulated communication task with ATC and a series of maneuvers on a GAT-2 twin engine simulator. Results showed that performance on the information processing tasks generally correlated with the simulator and communication performance, the memory task being the best predictor. In contrast to the nonpilot study which demonstrated age effects in all five tasks, age effects were detected in only two of the tasks (hidden figures and dichotic listening) in the study with pilots. Braune and Wickens suggested that the pilot group, as a whole, may belong to a more select group that excludes individuals of lower ability or individuals more susceptible to age effects.

In another study, Mertens and Boone (1988) compared a group of 30-39-year-olds with a group of 60-69-year-olds. Although most of these subjects were not pilots, all subjects were required to pass the equivalent of a Class III airman physical exam, exhibit normal pulmonary function, and have normal or above normal intelligence. Subjects' visual acuity, blood pressure, pulmonary function, intelligence scores, and the WAIS digit span (a measure of STM) were used as predictors of performance on the Civil Aeromedical Institute's Multiple Task Performance Battery (MTPB). The MTPB includes tasks such as monitoring, mental arithmetic, target identification, tracking, and problem solving that were designed to have high content validity for aviation. Subjects time-shared two or more of these tasks simultaneously. Results showed that the digit span memory score correlated significantly with the MTPB performance scores. In fact, the inclusion of the memory measure among the predictors provided better prediction of time-sharing performance than without it. Of note was the finding that even without the memory measure, the predictors were more highly correlated with the MTPB performance than was age. These results showed that there was a host of variables that played a greater role than age in determining the performance of a set of flight relevant tasks. Results such as those obtained by Braune and Wickens and Mertens and Boone suggest that while memory performance is flight relevant, age effects on memory performance may be attenuated considerably with a more select group of subjects such as pilots.

Problem solving and decision making

Jensen and Benel (1977) reported that decision errors were responsible for 52% of the fatalities in the general aviation accidents between 1970 and 1974. This alarming statistic has engendered much attention to the need of understanding pilot decision making behavior (e.g., Buch, 1984; Giffin and Rockwell, 1984).

A general model of human decision making is offered by Wickens and Flach (1988). Environmental cues such as weather, remaining fuel, and aircraft performance are first sampled. These cues are interpreted against a knowledge base in long-term memory. Based on this interpretation, pilots formulate alternative hypotheses about the state of the world. Alternative courses of action are then considered and the choice of action is determined by the estimated values and costs associated with each action. For example, given the current weather situation and the amount of remaining fuel, the pilot may consider to: proceed with the course as planned, return to the point of takeoff, or seek additional information. The model further recognizes that these decision making processes are subject to attention and memory limitations so under time stress and high workload conditions, pilots do not always have the luxury of deliberating their decisions as prescribed above. In these instances, decision makers may adopt "rules of thumbs" that often work but do not always lead to an optimal decision (Wickens, 1992).

In two simulation research, Wickens and colleagues examined pilot decision about whether to assume tasks depending on the current workload. Raby and Wickens' (1994) subjects flew simulated landing approaches while performing additional tasks. Segal and Wickens' (1991) subjects flew a helicopter simulation while performing secondary and tertiary tasks. In general, subjects maintained performance of the high-priority tasks when workload demands increased, but performance of lower priority tasks suffered. In both studies, subjects failed to maximize the lower priority tasks by rescheduling tasks or by initiating some of the tasks earlier even though they had ample opportunity to do so (see also Laudeman and Palmer, 1993).

Pilot experience, however, may play a role in the quality of the decision made. Wickens, Stokes, Barnett, and Davis (1988) used the Micro-Computer Decision Simulator (MIDIS) to examine the relationship between information processing capabilities and decision making performance. Spatial abilities, working memory, mathematical ability, and factual knowledge was found to predict novice pilots' decision-making but not of experienced pilots'. Moreover, the experienced pilots were more confident about their decisions. Using a laboratory task, Wiggins and O'Hare (1995) observed both qualitative and quantitative differences in weather-related decision making between experienced (more than 1000 hours of cross-country flying) and inexperienced (less than 100 hours) general aviation pilots. They differed in terms of their information search and problem solving strategies. The inexperienced pilots also required more time to evaluate the situation and to come to a decision. Importantly, even experienced pilots can succumb to time pressure and other stress (McKinney, 1993).

Adams and Ericcson (1992) provided an in-depth treatment of the transition from a novice to an expert pilot decision-maker. Examining a series of accidents that occurred between 1983 to 1989, Adams and Ericcson observed that "experienced pilots quickly responded to emergencies for which there were no handbook procedures or previous training. They assessed the situation and *integrated* airmanship skills, trained procedures and aeronautical knowledge into a quick, effective decision making process" (p. 5). They further concluded that this pattern of behavior is in contradiction to what is taught in the Aeronautical Decision Making (ADM) training materials published by the FAA in 1987. The ADM approach adopts a linear, sequential, deductive approach such as relying on the acronym "DECIDE" (Detect-Estimate-Choose-Identify-Do-Evaluate, Clarke, 1986). Adams and Ericcson (1992) believed that although the ADM training program has been credited for reduced number of accidents and incidents in the inexperienced pilot group (less than five years), it has been less successful with the experienced group. Adams and Ericcson proposed that a better understanding of the characteristics of expert decision making is necessary for training more effective decision making and for accelerating the transition from novice to expert.

Drawing upon the vast psychological literature on expertise (e.g., Chi, Glaser, and Farr, 1988; Glaser, 1987; Lesgold, 1984), Adams and Ericcson concluded that expertise is mostly learned. The fundamental difference between a novice and an expert is the amount of acquired knowledge and problem solving skills. In addition to having acquired the basic factual, declarative knowledge, experts have a large body of procedural knowledge about causes and effects. Further, expert's knowledge is well structured and organized so that retrieving information is much easier. Within their area of expertise, experts can readily see meaningful patterns and continuously update their perception of the current situation. An accurate account of the current situation allows the experienced pilot to rapidly retrieve the appropriate course of action directly from memory and to anticipate future conditions. This is in contrast to novice pilots who have to deliberately search for specific information and whose behavior is primarily sequential and rule-based (if A then B).

Glanzer and Glaser (1959) conducted an early investigation and tested 454 aircrew officers of the Air National Guard and 90 commercial airline pilots between the ages of 20 and 50. The tests used were selected to be age-sensitive and job-relevant. Little relationship between age and performance on decision making and problem solving tasks was found. Similarly, Szafran (1968) found no significant difference in decision making between younger and older pilots. Mohler (1981) noted that there are numerous airline examples that attest to the fact that older healthy pilots have the experience, judgment, and capability to avert catastrophe. In particular, Mohler cited the example in which a B-747 captain made a safe landing despite that three engines failed at 22,000 feet due to ice. (The captain had to retire at age 60 a few weeks later.) Another example involves a seasoned crew (53 years experience, plus 21 years for check airman) of United Flight 232 who landed a nearly uncontrollable DC-10 despite a catastrophic in-flight engine failure. The flight crew was selected by Aviation Week for the 1989 Laurels award for their "notable feats of airmanship ... which demonstrates the value of having experienced crews in the cockpits of large jet transports" ("Aerospace Laureate," 1990, p. 17).

The laboratory findings and anecdotes reviewed above bring to the forefront an important relationship that is the subject of a recent FAA sponsored investigation (DOT/FAA/AM-94/20-23). Examined was the interactive effect of age and experience on pilot performance and accident rate. Whereas increased age is generally thought to have adverse effect on performance, the expertise literature indicates that extensive experience acquired through years of training is one of the principal ingredients for developing expertise and superior performance. It is only natural that in the aviation context, as in other contexts, the older one is, the more experience one has usually gained.

Psychomotor performance

Welford (1959) found that although some age-related psychomotor performance decrements clearly involve peripheral limitations (e.g., reduced grip strength), older people are primarily limited by central mechanisms (e.g., reduced efficiency of attentional resources). In general, slowing of simple reaction time (response time to a single stimulus) with increased age is slight, but slowing of choice reaction time can be substantial. Stelmach, Amrhein, and Goggin (1988) found the *reaction time* of older subjects (67- to 75-year-olds) to increase linearly with increased task complexity, as do younger subjects (21- to 25-year-olds). However, on the average, the older subjects were 94 ms slower than the younger subjects across tasks that involve one or two hands to perform. For *movement time*, the older subjects exhibited a proportional increase over the younger subjects as task complexity increased. Older subjects were also less synchronized when initiating and terminating bimanual movements, suggesting an age-related difficulty in bimanual coordination.

For continuous performance, Welford (1958) found that tracking performance changed a great deal with age at high speed of target movement but changed little at low speed. Jagacinski, Greenberg, Liao, and Wang (1993) found that a supplementary auditory display to a visual manual control task can be helpful to the older adults (60-69 years old). In Braune and Wickens' (1984b) study with the instrument-rated pilots, a strong relationship was found between tracking error and flight experience but not age. Given that continuous tracking tasks are closely related to aircraft control, proficient pilots would be expected to track well. Costello-Branco (1985, cited in Mertens & Boone, 1988) also observed that the psychomotor performance of medically fit airline pilots over age 60 was comparable to the 35-year-old nonpilots.

Time-sharing performance

For the young and the old, a major limitation of performance is an inherent limit of attentional capacity (e.g., Kahneman, 1973) or processing resources (e.g., Wickens, 1992). As task demand increases, more resources would have to be devoted to the task in order to maintain a constant level of performance. Task demands can be increased either by increasing the single task difficulty or by increasing the number of tasks to be performed simultaneously. Two or more tasks can be time-shared (performed simultaneously) without affecting performance, if the total demand of the tasks and their management do not exceed the total capacity available (e.g., Kahneman, 1973). Although capacity is limited, processing efficiency may be improved by training or by the use of more appropriate strategies (e.g., Kramer, Larish, and Strayer, 1995; Tsang and Wickens, 1988).

Time-sharing performance is an important component of many daily activities such as driving, it has also been identified as a critical element of pilot performance (e.g., Gopher, 1993; Griffin and McBride, 1986; Jorna, 1989; Tham and Kramer, 1994; Tsang and Vidulich, 1989; Wickens, 1987). Experienced pilots can therefore be considered to have expertise in time-sharing. It has been suggested that experience brings with it a level of automaticity and increased processing efficiency. This in effect increases the amount of processing resources available for performing other activities. Additional benefits of experience include smoother task coordination or increased effectiveness in the management of multiple tasks.

In contrast to the beneficial effects of experience, increased age has been proposed to be associated with reduced processing efficiency. However, the existing literature does not unequivocally show an age-related decrease in time-sharing performance beyond the differences observed at the single task performance level (see Guttentag, 1989; Hartley, 1992). As pointed out earlier, the effects of age and expertise on performance are intriguing since pilot experience, and thereby pilot expertise, tends to increase with increased age.

The relationship between age, expertise, and pilot time-sharing performance has been examined in two recent investigations. In an attempt to resolve some of the inconsistencies observed in the literature, flight relevant tasks and expertise developed in the natural environment were examined in these investigations. In the Braune and Wickens' (1984b) study described above, 30 instrument-rated pilots between the age of 20 and 60 were tested on information processing tasks and in a simulator where they had to do a secondary communication task. Their performance on the information processing tasks was used to predict the simulator and communication performance. In this study, time-sharing performance was found to have little to do with age.

In a second study by Tsang and colleagues (Tsang and Shaner, 1995; Tsang, Shaner, and Schnopp-Wyatt, 1995), the time-sharing performance of 90 subjects across a broader age range (from 20 to 80 years old) was examined. To examine the effects of expertise, a group of active pilots was contrasted with a group of nonpilots. Demanding and flight relevant laboratory tasks were used. Subjects time-shared a continuous acceleration-controlled tracking task with either a memory task or a spatial orientation processing task. Two aspects of time-sharing performance were studied: time-sharing efficiency (dual task performance level) and attention allocation control (task management according to task priorities).

The results strongly suggested an age-related deficit in time-sharing efficiency that was above and beyond that occurring at the single task level. Younger subjects also had better task management than older subjects. However, the age effect on management was not large until age 60 or beyond. Pilots time-shared more efficiently and had better task management than nonpilots. Pilots were better able than nonpilots to sacrifice a low priority performance in order to achieve a higher level of performance for a high priority task. When faced with increased task demand in the low priority task, pilots allowed its performance to degrade while protecting the high priority task. The premise that pilots should have some expertise in time-sharing thus received at least some support. Most interesting, pilot expertise was able to reduce some of the age-related decreases in time-sharing efficiency and task management. However, although the beneficial effects of long-term extended training was evident, even pilots with a mean total flight hours of 5547 were not immune to the age effects. On the other hand, it is important to note that although the experimental tasks were selected to capture the cognitive demands of flying, they bore little physical resemblance to actual flying. Nevertheless, flight experience appeared to protect the old pilots from some of the age effects observed in the general population. Again, the interaction between age and expertise was not prominent until age 60 or beyond. Because each age group spanned two decades (20-39, 40-59, 60-79), it was not clear at what age beyond 60 that time-sharing became problematic.

The two studies reviewed here seem contradictory. A possible account for the inconsistency is that Tsang and Shaner covered an older age range. If the age effect does not become evident until after age 60, it would not be evident in the Braune and Wickens' study as none of their subjects was over age 60. Another important difference between the two studies is that Braune and Wickens examined simulator performance whereas Tsang and Shaner examined laboratory task performance. Because expertise is domain specific (Adams and Ericcson, 1992; Wiggins and O'Hare, 1995), it is possible that the older pilots' performance would be even more protected in a simulator or actual flying. Future research will need to examine these possibilities more closely.

Accident rate as a function of age

Given that age and experience can greatly influence performance in different ways, only those investigations that have examined both factors are reviewed here.

In an early United States Air Force military flying study, Zeller, Lentz, and Burke (1963) observed, amongst other results, that accident rate (accidents per 100,000 hours of flying) for high performance jet flying increased with age from the middle thirties on. In contrast, for lower performance non-jet flying, the older pilots had a lower accident rate and were less dependent upon recent flying (number of flight hours in the last six months) for maintaining this rate.

In another study, Golaszewski (1983) examined the data from the NTSB accident database and the FAA Comprehensive Airman Information System (CAIS) medical database for the years 1976-1980. Pilots were categorized by their Class of Medical. The lower the Class number, the more medically "fit" the individual. For example, commercial airline pilots are required to have a current Class I medical certification whereas general aviation pilots are only required to have a Class III medical. Both recent flying time (number of hours flown in the previous year) and total flying time were inversely related to accident rate (number of accidents per total annual flight hours). For Class I and II pilots with less than 5000 total hours, the older pilots had more accidents than younger pilots. For Class III pilots with low total hours and fewer than 50 recent flight hours, accident rate increased with age, the converse was true for those with more than 50 recent flight hours. For pilots with less than 1,000 total flight hours, accident rate decreased with age for those with more than 50 recent flight hours but increased for those with less than 50 recent flight hours.

The Office of Technology Assessment (OTA, 1990) examined Golaszewski's (1983) data in conjunction with the NTSB 1990 data. This report was only concerned with Class I and II pilots. Accident rate for pilots with more than 1,000 total flight hours and more than 50 recent flight hours improved with age until age 50, beyond which an increase in accident rate was observed. For pilots who flew more than 100 hours/year, age and increased recent flying time were associated with lower accident rate. However, after age 60, accident rate increased even if pilots continued to fly over 400 hours/year. Lastly, the higher the total flight time the pilot had, the later in age was the onset of increased accident rate. For pilots with 501-1000 hours, accident rate increased after age 39; for pilots with 1001-5000 hours, accident rate increased after age 49; for pilots with over 5000 hours, accident rate increased after age 59.

Guide and Gibson (1991) examined the data from 1982 to 1988 obtained from the NTSB accident database, the Aircraft Owners and Pilots Association Air Safety database, the FAA Statistical Handbook on Aviation, and the COMSIS Research Corporation database. Pilots were categorized as air transport pilots, commercial pilots, or private pilots. Minimal age effect was observed across age groups (of 5-year interval) from age 20 to age 59. Again, recent flight time appeared to be an especially important factor in accident rates. Pilots with more than 400 recent flight hours had about one third the accident rate of those with less than 400 hours.

Kay, Hillman, Hyland, Voros, Harris, and Deimler (1994) offer perhaps the most analytical analysis to date. Records obtained between 1976 and 1988 were examined. Their major conclusions are summarized here. For Class I pilots with more than 2,000 total flight time, the more recent flight time a pilot had, the less likely the pilot would be in an accident, but no effect of total flight time was found. Because, in the USA, the Age 60 Rule prohibits commercial airlines from assigning a pilot who has reached age 60 as either the pilot-in-command or the co-pilot, no airline accident data exist for pilots older than 60 years old. When the accident rate of Class II pilots were examined, the accident rate for the 60-65 group did not differ statistically from that of the 55-59 group, but was lower than that of the 65-69 group. When Class III pilots with more than 500 total flight hours and more than 50 recent flight hours were examined, there was an increase in accident rate for the years 63 through 69. There was, however, no indication of increased accident rate for airline pilots at age 60. For Class III pilots with considerably fewer recent flight hours (50 hours) than a typical airline pilot (700 hours), the accident rate started to increase at age 63.

Does age affect pilot performance?

One consistent finding among the investigations reviewed here is a definite relationship between recent flying time and accident rate. The only investigation that attempted some quantitative analysis (Kay et al., 1994) showed that accident rates tend to increase after age 63 for Class III pilots with 50 recent flying time. However, it should be pointed out that 50 hours in the previous year amounts to about 4 hours per month and is certainly not comparable to the more typical 700 hours of recent flying time that airline pilots have. While not totally consistent, there certainly is no overwhelming evidence from the accident data that increased age is a significant contributor to increased accident rate. However, as noted by Kay et al. (1994), precise analysis of the accident data could be procedurally complicated and the necessary information is often not readily available. Improved mechanisms for collecting and recording the necessary information for informative and accurate accident analysis are thus needed.

Summary: Does age affect pilot performance?

Recent research efforts certainly have heightened the understanding of some of the pertinent factors and issues involved. The psychological literature shows definite age-related changes with certain cognitive functioning that have been identified to be essential for flight performance (e.g., perceptual processing, certain aspects of memory performance, and certain psychomotor control). The cognitive functions that do not yet exhibit clear effects of age tend to be the more complex ones that involve several stages of information processing such as problem solving, decision making, and time-sharing. On the one hand, there are ample data to suggest that the more complex the performance, the larger the age effect tends to be. On the other hand, complex performance developed through extensive training is found to be more resistant to negative age effects. Since expertise in many complex job performances, including flying, tend to develop with experience and age, the interactive effects of age and expertise and their relative contributions to performance need to be carefully studied.

What is clear is that, as Rabbitt (1993) has argued, it does not all go together when it goes (see also Schaie, 1993). There is certainly no indication that all goes at age 60. Not only does age affect the different cognitive functions to different degrees, the time of onset of significant age effects also differ across cognitive functions (e.g., Tsang et al., 1995). In addition, as noted by Rabbitt (1993), Szafran (1968), and many others, individual differences *within* an age group tend to increase with age. One implication of this increased individual differences is an increased difficulty of predicting one's performance based solely on one's chronological age. For example, Tsang (in press) examined the response distributions from the different age groups in the Tsang et al. (1995) study. The probability that a randomly selected individual from one age group would outperform a randomly selected individual from another age group was estimated. The estimates showed that 2 to 3 individuals out of 10 people over 60 years old are likely to time-share better than a randomly selected person between the ages of 40 and 59, despite reliable differences between the group means. That is, if age were used as the sole elimination criterion, 20-30% of the individuals in the old group would have been eliminated unnecessarily. If future research demonstrates similar findings with other cognitive performances, the efficacy of any policy that is based strictly on one's chronological age should be seriously questioned.

In conclusion, if age affects pilot performance, its effect has not been easy to detect. For example, Hyland, Kay, and Deimler (1994) found that although the instructor and check pilot evaluation of the pilot's simulator performance correlated with the pilot's age, the simulator performance did not. Accident rate also fails to reveal clear and significant adverse age effects (see also Stuck, van Gorp, Josephson, Morgenstern, and Beck, 1992). Among a host of factors that have been found to play a part in the relationship between age and performance, individual differences and recent flying experience are probably the two most consistent and critical factors. Certainly more research will be needed for a better understanding of this relationship. Besides establishing the validity of the laboratory tasks to flying, operational significance of the performance differences observed with these laboratory tasks will need to be established (Institute of Medicine, 1981; Tsang, 1992). Having a centralized system designed for recording all the necessary information in one place for accident analysis would make possible more rigorous and systematic examination of the accident data. Lastly, although subjective evaluation is the standard of the trade, having more objective and quantitative measurement techniques for assessing actual flight performance would certainly be helpful.

References

Adams, R. J., and Ericsson, K. A. (1992), *Introduction to Cognitive Processes of Expert Pilots* (DOT/FAA/RD-92/12), US. Department of Transportation, Federal Aviation Administration, Washington, DC.

Aerospace Laureate. (1990), *Aviation Week & Space Technology*, January 1, pp. 16-17.

Baddeley, A. (1986), *Working Memory*, Oxford University, New York.

Birren, J. E., and Fisher, L. M. (1995), 'Rules and reasons in the forced retirement of commercial airline pilots at age 60', *Ergonomics*, vol. 38, pp. 518-525.

Botwinick, J., and Storandt, M. (1974), *Memory, Related Function, and Age,*

Charles C. Thomas, Springfield, IL.

Braune, R., and Wickens, C. D. (1984a), *Individual Differences and Age-Related Performance Assessment in Aviators. Part 1: Battery Development and Assessment* (Final Tech. Rep. EPL-83-4/NAMRL-83-1), University of Illinois, Engineering-Psychology Laboratory, Urbana-Champaign.

Braune, R., and Wickens, C. D. (1984b), *Individual Differences and Age-Related Performance Assessment in Aviators. Part 2: Initial Battery Validation* (Final Tech. Rep. EPL-83-7/NAMRL-83-2), University of Illinois, Engineering Psychology Laboratory, Urbana-Champaign.

Bruckart, J. D. (1992), 'Analysis of changes in the pilot population and general aviation accidents,' *Aviation, Space, and Environmental Medicine*, vol. 63, pp. 75-79.

Buch, G. (1984), 'An investigation of the effectiveness of pilot judgment training,' *Human Factors*, vol. 26, pp. 557-564.

Chi, M., Glaser, R., and Farr, M. (eds.) (1988), *On the Nature of Expertise*, Erlbaum, Hillsdale, NJ.

Clarke, R. (1986), *A New Approach to Training Pilots in Aeronautical Decision Making*, AOPA Air Safety Foundation, Frederick, MD.

Coyne, A. C., Allen, P. A., and Wickens, D. D. (1986), 'Influence of adult age on primary and secondary memory search,' *Psychology and Aging*, vol. 1, pp. 187-194.

Craik, F. I. M. (1977), 'Age differences in human memory', in J. E. Birren, and K. W. Schaie (eds.), *Handbook of the Psychology of Aging*, Van Nostrand Reinhold, New York, pp. 382-420.

Crook, M. N., Devoe, D. B., Hageman, K. C., Hanson, J. A., Krulee, G. K., and Ronco, P. G. (1957), *Age and the Judgment of Collision Courses*, USAF School of Aviation Medicine, Randolph A.F.B., TX.

Eyraud, M. Y., and Borowsky, M. S. (1985), 'Age and pilot performance', *Aviation, Space, and Environmental Medicine*, vol. 56, pp. 535-538.

Giffin, W. C., and Rockwell, T. H. (1984), 'Computer-aided testing of pilot response to critical events', *Human Factors*, vol. 26, pp. 573-581.

Glanzer, M., and Glaser, R. (1959), 'Cross-sectional and longitudinal results in a study of age-related changes', *Educational and Psychological Measurement*, vol. 19, pp. 89-101.

Glaser, R. (1987), 'Thoughts on expertise', in C. Schooler and W. Schaie (eds.), *Cognitive Functioning and Social Structure Over the Life Course*, Ablex Publishing Corp, Norwoord, NJ, pp. 81-94.

Golaszewski, R. (1983), *The Influence of Total Flight Time, Recent Flight Time and Age on Pilot Accident Rates* (Final Report DTRS57-83-P-80750), Acumenics Research and Technology, Inc., Bethesda, MD.

Gopher, D. (1993), 'The skill of attention control: Acquisition and execution of attention strategies', in D. Meyer and S. Kornblum (eds.), *Attention and performance XIV*, Erlbaum, Hillsdale, NJ, pp. 299-322.

Griffin, G. R., and McBride, D. K. (1986), *Multitask Performance: Predicting Success in Naval Aviation Primary Flight Training* (NAMRL 1316), Naval Air Station, Naval Aerospace medical Research Laboratory, Pensacola, FL.

Guttentag, R. E. (1989), 'Age differences in dual-task performance: Procedures, assumptions, and results', *Developmental Review*, vol. 9, pp. 146-170.

Guide, P. C., and Gibson, R. S. (1991), 'An analytical study of the effects of age and experience on flight safety', in *Proceedings of the Human Factors Society 35th Annual Meeting*, Human Factors Society, Santa Monica, CA, pp. 180-184.

Hartley, A. A. (1992), 'Attention', in F. I. M. Craik and T. A. Salthouse (eds.), *The handbook of aging and cognition*, Lawrence, Hillsdale, NJ, pp. 3-49.

Hilton, Systems, Inc. (1994), *Age 60 Rule Research, Part I: Bibliographic Database* (DOT/FAA/AM-94-20), Federal Aviation Administration, Office of Aviation Medicine, Washington, DC.

Hultsch, D. F., and Dixon, R. A. (1990), 'Learning and memory in aging', in J. E. Birren and K. W. Schaie (eds.), *Handbook of the Psychology of Aging*, Academic, San Diego, CA, pp. 259-269.

Hunt, E., and Hertzog, C. (1981), *Age Related Changes in Cognition During the*

Working Years (Final Report), University of Washington, Department of Psychology, Seattle.

Hyland, D. T., Kay, E. J., and Deimler, J. D. (1994), *Age 60 Rule Research, Part IV: Experimental Evaluation of Pilot Performance* (DOT/FAA/AM-94-23), Federal Aviation Administration, Office of Aviation Medicine, Washington, DC.

Hyland, D. T., Kay, E. J., Deimler, J. D., and Gurman, E. B. (1994), *Age 60 Rule Research, Part II: Airline Pilot Age and Performance--A Review of the Scientific Literature* (DOT/FAA/AM-94-21), Federal Aviation Administration, Office of Aviation Medicine, Washington, DC.

Institute of Medicine, National Academy of Sciences. (1981), *Airline Pilot Age, Health and Performance*, National Academy, Washington, DC.

Jagacinski, R. J., Greenberg, N., Liao, M-J., and Wang, J. (1993), 'Manual performance of a repeated pattern by older and younger adults with supplementary auditory cues', *Psychology and Aging*, vol. 8, pp. 429-439.

Jensen, R. S., and Benel, R. A. (1977), *Judgment Evaluation and Instruction in Civil Pilot Training* (Final Report FAA-RD-78-24), National Technical Information, Springfield, VA.

Jorna, P. G. A. M. (1989), 'Prediction of success in flight training by single- and dual-task performance', in *AGARD Conference Proceedings, AGARD-CP -458* (21-1-21-10), Advisory Group for Aerospace Research and Development, Neuilly-Sur-Seine, France.

Kahneman, D. (1973), *Attention and Effort*, Prentice-Hall, Englewood Cliffs, NJ.

Kay, E. J., Hillman, D. J., Hyland, D. T., Voros, R. S., Harris, R. M., and Deimler, J. D. (1994), *Age 60 Rule Study, Part III: Consolidated Database Experiments Final Report* (DOT/FAA/AM-94-22), Federal Aviation Administration, Office of Aviation Medicine, Washington, DC.

Kramer, A. F., Larish, J. F., and Strayer, D. L. (1995), 'Training for attentional control in dual task settings: A comparison of young and old adults', *Journal of Experimental Psychology: Applied*, vol., 1, pp. 50-76.

Laudeman, I. V., and Palmer, E. A. (1993), 'Measurement of taskload in the analysis of aircrew performance', In *Proceedings of the Seventh International*

Symposium on Aviation Psychology, Ohio State University, Department of Aviation, Columbus, OH, pp. 854-858.

Lesgold, A. M. (1984), 'Acquiring expertise', in J. R. Anderson and S. M. Kosslyn (eds.), *Tutorials in Learning and Memory*, W. H. Freeman, San Francisco.

McKinney, E. H. (1993), 'Flight leads and crisis decision-making', *Aviation, Space, and Environmental Medicine*, vol. 64, vol. 359-362.

Mertens, H. W., and Boone, J. O. (1988), 'Functional aging: Further examination of Gerathewohl's model in prediction of complex performance from physiological and psychological measures', Paper presented at the 59th Annual Scientific Meeting of the Aerospace Medical Association, New Orleans, LA.

Mohler, S. R. (1981), 'Reasons for eliminating the "Age 60" regulation for airline pilots', *Aviation, Space, and Environmental Medicine*, vol. 52, pp. 445-454.

Office of Technology Assessment (1990), *Medical Risk Assessment and the Age 60 Rule for Airline Pilots*, Subcommittee on Investigations and Oversight, Committee on Public Works and Transportation, U.S. House of Representatives, Washington, DC.

Raby, M., and Wickens, C. D. (1994), 'Strategic workload management and decision biases in aviation', *The International Journal of Aviation Psychology*, vol. 4, pp. 211-240.

Rabbitt, P. (1993), 'Does it all go together when it goes? The Nineteenth Bartlett Memorial Lecture', *The Quarterly Journal of Experimental Psychology*, vol. 46A, pp. 385-434.

Salthouse, T. A. (1982), *Adult Cognition: An Experimental Psychology of Human Aging*, Springer-Verlag, New York.

Salthouse, T. A. (1990), 'Working memory as a processing resource in cognitive aging', *Developmental Review*, vol. 10, pp. 101-124.

Segal, L., and Wickens, C. D. (1991), *TASKILLAN II: A Study of Pilot Strategies for Workload Management* (Tech. Rep. ARL-91-1/NASA-91-1), University of Illinois, Aviation Research Laboratory, Savoy, IL.

Schaie, K. W. (1993), 'The course of adult intellectual development', *American Psychologist*, vol. 49, pp. 304-313.

Stelmach, G. E., Amrhein, P. C., and Goggin, N. L. (1988), 'Age differences in bimanual coordination', *Journal of Gerontology*, vol. 43, pp. 18-23.

Stuck, A. E., van Gorp, W. G., Josephson, K. R., Morgenstern, H., & Beck, J. C. (1992), 'Multidimensional risk assessment versus age and criterion for retirement of airline pilots', *Journal of the American Geriatrics Society*, vol. 40, pp. 526-532.

Szafran, J. (1963), 'Age differences in choice reaction time and cardio-vascular status among pilots', *Nature*, vol. 200, pp. 904-906.

Szafran, J. (1968), 'Psychophysiological studies of aging in pilots', in G.A. Talland, (ed.), *Human Aging and Behavior*, Academic, New York, pp. 37-74.

Tham, M., and Kramer, A. (1994), 'Attentional control and piloting experience', in *Proceedings of the Human Factors and Ergonomics Society 38th Annual Meeting*, Human Factors and Ergonomics Society, Santa Monica, CA, pp. 31-35.

Tsang, P. S. (1992), 'A reappraisal of aging and pilot performance', *International Journal of Aviation Psychology*, vol. 2, pp. 193-212.

Tsang, P. S. (in press), 'Boundaries of cognitive performance as a function of age and piloting experience' *International Journal of Aviation Psychology.*

Tsang, P. S., and Shaner, T. L. (1995), 'Age, expertise, structural similarity, and time-sharing efficiency', in *Proceedings of the Human Factors and Ergonomics Society 39th Annual Meeting*, Human Factors and Ergonomics Society, Santa Monica, CA, pp. 124-128.

Tsang, P. S., Shaner, T. L., and Schnopp-Wyatt, E. N. (1995), *Age, Attention, Expertise, and Time-Sharing Performance* (Tech. Rep. EPL-95-1), Wright State University: Engineering Psychology Laboratory, Dayton, OH.

Tsang, P. S., and Vidulich, M. A. (1989), 'Cognitive demands of automation in aviation', in R. S. Jensen (ed.), *Aviation Psychology*, Gower Technical, Brookfield, VT, pp. 66-95.

Tsang, P. S., and Wickens, C. D. (1988), 'The structural constraints and the strategic control of resource allocation', *Human Performance*, vol. 1, pp. 45-72.

Welford, A. T. (1958), *Aging and Human Skill*, Oxford University, London.

Welford, A. T. (1959), 'Performance, biological mechanisms and limiting performance in a serial reaction task', *Quarterly Journal of Experimental Psychology*, vol. 11, pp. 193-210.

Wickens, C. D. (1987), 'Attention', in P. A. Hancock (ed.), *Human Factors Psychology*, North-Holland, New York, pp. 29-80.

Wickens, C. D. (1992), *Engineering Psychology and Human Performance* (2nd ed.), Harper Collins, New York

Wickens, C. D., and Flach, J. M. (1988), 'Information processing', in E. L. Wiener and D. C. Nagel (eds.), *Human Factors in Aviation*, Academic, New York, pp. 111-156.

Wickens, C. D., Stokes, A., Barnett, A. F., and Davis, T. (1988), *A Componential Analysis of Pilot Decision Making* (Tech. Rep. AAMRL-TR-88-017), Armstrong Laboratory, Wright Patterson AFB, OH.

Wiggins, M., and O'Hare, D. (1995), 'Expertise in aeronautical weather-related decision making: A cross-sectional analysis of general aviation pilots', *Journal of Experimental Psychology: Applied*, vol. 1, pp. 305-320.

Zeller, A. F., Lentz, E. C., and Burke, J. M. (1963), 'Current flying, age, experience and non-jet accidents', *Aerospace Medicine*, vol. 34, pp. 222-225.

Acknowledgement

The writing of this chapter was supported by National Institute of Aging Grant AG08589 and the Operator Performance and Safety Analysis Division at the Volpe National Transportation Systems Center in Cambridge, Massachusetts where the author spent her sabbatical in 1995-1996.

3 Pilot characteristics

David R Hunter

Introduction

The training of pilots is a life-long process that continues long after they have finished the training required for their certificates. Pilots in the military and those working for large civil carriers have access to extensive in-house recurrent training programs designed to ensure that they retain their proficiency and remain abreast of new technological and procedural developments. Pilots in corporate aviation and many of those with smaller civil carriers utilize contracted training (such as that provided by Flight Safety International) to achieve much the same effect. However, there are hundreds of thousands of pilots (primarily private certificate holders) who do not have access to these training resources. The high cost of the training and limitations on time preclude these pilots from receiving this type of recurrent training.

Paradoxically, these are the pilots who are most in need of training, since they often fly infrequently and, generally, start with a lower skill level and knowledge base. Accident statistics for this group also reflect the differences between these groups and the need for effective training programs.

For the over 300,000 pilots in the United States who fall into this category, the Federal Aviation Administration (FAA) conducts an extensive program of continuing pilot education called the Aviation Safety Program (ASP). Training is largely delivered through Aviation Safety Seminars held throughout the country. Each year over 14,000 of these seminars are conducted with over 700,000 participants. Many of them are conducted by Safety Program Managers from the almost 80 FAA district offices, while many others are conducted by the 4,000 volunteer Aviation Safety Counselors. Safety information is also disseminated through the FAA Aviation News, a magazine published eight times a year that focuses on safety issues.

To achieve its desired effect, the ASP must reach as many pilots as possible with an effective and relevant training message. Knowledge of the characteristics of the targeted pilot population can help to maximize the impact of the program. This information could be used in two ways. First, knowledge of the relevant characteristics of the pilot population could be used to shape the content and format of training programs. Secondly, knowledge of the demographic characteristics of the pilot population could be used to improve the marketing of the training programs. Since not every pilot attends the FAA's Safety Seminars, two segments of the population that would be of particular interest are those who do and do not regularly attend.

Gathering data on the pilot population

Unfortunately, data on the general population of pilots are very limited. For the most part, investigators have examined only the characteristics of pilots involved in accidents (c.f., NTSB, 1989); although, some studies have been conducted to investigate specific aspects of the pilot population. For example, Platenius and Wilde (1986) surveyed 70,000 Canadian pilots in a study of pilot attributes and accident risk. In addition, a study of similar scope is underway to develop exposure data for pilots in New Zealand (D. O'Hare, personal communication, November 29, 1995). For the most part, however, only rudimentary data gained from the forms completed during the periodic medical examination are available for the vast majority of pilots who have never been involved in an accident.

FAA Survey

To address this shortcoming, the Federal Aviation Administration recently conducted a large-scale, nationwide survey of pilots. The overall purpose of this study was to obtain data to be used in support of research on aeronautical decision making (ADM). At the same time the survey provided an opportunity to collect collateral information which could be of significant use when planning a marketing strategy for new ADM interventions.

As noted earlier, at present the primary vehicle for disseminating safety information used by the FAA is the safety seminar. Yet, little is known about which pilots attend the seminars, why they attend, what formats of instruction and topics are favored, and how often they attend. Therefore, the survey included questions relating to training in general, and safety seminars specifically. In addition to questions on training issues, additional sections were developed to assess other factors which might be related to safety and accident involvement.

In its final version the questionnaire contained 143 items: 16 dealing with general aviation qualifications, 19 dealing with the number of hours logged during the last 6 months, last 12 months, and during the entire career of the respondent, 8 questions dealing with the type of aircraft flown most frequently over the past year, 3 dealing with the careers of professional airmen, 15 dealing with training experiences, 13 questions regarding critical aviation incidents, 34 dealing with personal minimums and practices, 27 dealing with attitudes about flying, 5 dealing with participation in future research studies, and 3 dealing with general demographic information.

The questionnaire was printed as an optically-scannable booklet and was mailed to a random sample of 19,657 pilots drawn from the population (approximately 561,486) of active airmen. Of that sample, 6,735 usable questionnaires were returned. Complete details of the development and evaluation of this survey are provided by Hunter (1995).

Designing training that meets pilots' needs

The contents of a training program are influenced both by the internal characteristics of the participants (for example, their skill and experience levels) and by their external characteristics (for example, when and how they fly). The external characteristics determine how often and under what circumstances they are exposed to potentially hazardous conditions. The internal characteristics determine how capable they are of dealing with those conditions. Deciding upon the content of a new training program thus requires that both sets of characteristics be considered. An ideal candidate for a new training program would be one that addresses a frequently encountered hazardous condition (for example, adverse weather), for which a large number of pilots lack the skills or knowledge required to deal safely with the situation.

Table 3.1
Recent and total flight experience

	Private	Commercial	ATP
Hours Logged - Last 12 Months			
Mean	50	108	340
Median	30	53	272
Standard Deviation	68	230	303
Hours Logged - Total			
Mean	819	2857	10412

Median	445	1574	9066
Standard Deviation	1293	3771	6809

Although the present study did not assess skill and knowledge levels directly, they may be inferred (as is the usual case in aviation) through the reported flight experience (hours logged). As shown in Table 3.1 there is a wide variation in both the total and recent flight experience of pilots as a function of their certificate level. Not unexpectedly, private and commercial pilots have far fewer total and recent flight hours than pilots who possess an airline transport rating and who, for the most part, are earning their living as pilots. As noted earlier, pilots employed by air carriers typically have access to a well structured system of continuing training and, except in a very few instances, the safety training programs that are conducted by the FAA are not directed toward that group. Hence, that group will be dropped from further consideration and all the subsequent tables will report data only for the private and commercial certificate holders. Commercial pilots are included because, although some of them may have access to formal training programs sponsored or conducted by their employers, many holders of the commercial certificate (approximately half, according to the survey results) have never flown in a commercial setting. These pilots, who may obtain a commercial certificate for the additional level of training and prestige which it imparts, are very similar to the private certificate holders in terms of recent and total experience, continuing training they receive, and the types of flights they undertake.

Even when targeted just at private and commercial pilots, new training programs must accommodate a wide range of total experience and must be suitable both for pilots who fly frequently and those who do so infrequently. For example, half of the private pilots fly only 2.5 hours per month *or less*. It seems reasonable to presume that the skill levels of these pilots and hence their training needs are substantially different from those who are able to engage in more frequent flights.

Other personal characteristics of the pilots that may influence the content and format of new training include both age and educational level. As was the case with experience levels, there is also a wide variation in these characteristics. In general, the pilot population is mature with an average age of approximately 50 years, and is relatively well educated as shown in Table 3.2. The large proportion of pilots with advanced degrees (particularly those who have completed doctorate level training) suggests that the level of new training (for example, the reading grade level of training materials) could be considerably higher level than that used for typical mass-media publications. Further, it cautions us against using overly simplified explanations in an effort to ensure complete understanding, since highly-educated individuals may resent what might be perceived as an affront to their capabilities. Nevertheless, there may also be a place for a primer-level instruction in some topics, to accommodate those pilots (approximately 36%) who did not complete a college-level education. The critical point is to realize that, as shown by the data, there is a large variation in these characteristics and effective training must be designed to allow for that variation.

Table 3.2
Educational attainment by pilots

Education Level	Private	Commercial
Grade School	1%	
High School	17%	15%
Associate Degree	19%	19%
College Degree	32%	33%
Master's	17%	19%
Doctorate	14%	13%

In addition to the internal characteristics, there are also the external characteristics to be considered in designing new training. The internal characteristics determine to some degree how training should be constructed and delivered, while the external characteristics help us to identify what should be trained. One way to identify training needs is to look at the situations in which pilots find themselves that present hazards and that could, under some circumstances, lead to accidents. One common cause of accidents is fuel mismanagement. This is reflected in Table 3.3 in which 20% of the private pilots and 33% of the commercial pilots report having experienced at least one instance in which they were so low on fuel that they were seriously concerned about making it to an airport.

The survey findings suggest that this is a situation that occurs fairly commonly. For the most part, of course, these situations are resolved and do not become accidents. However, had some other factor (such as deteriorating weather) also been present then the outcome might not have been benign. Thus, the survey results agree with findings from analyses of accident causes and strongly suggest the need for training in this area. However, whether the needed training should deal with improving the computational skills of pilots so that they are better able to estimate fuel consumption or whether it should stress better preflight inspections so as to ensure that the fuel tanks are completely filled before beginning a flight, remains unclear.

Another potentially hazardous event involves continued flight under visual flight rules (VFR) into an area of instrument meteorological conditions (IMC).

This sequence of VFR into IMC flight is the single largest cause of fatal accidents, accounting for about one fourth of the total. The data in Table 3.3 seem to reflect that tendency as about one fourth of the pilots report having entered IMC while flying under VFR at least once during their flying experiences. As with the low fuel experience, the results alert us to a need for more effective training on this subject, but they do not specify the nature of that training. However, additional data from that portion of the survey that dealt with personal minimums, the usual practices pilots follow when flying, and their attitudes toward flying can help clarify the training requirements.

In the FAA Survey many pilots had advanced degreees

Table 3.3
Involvement in hazardous events

| | Low fuel incidents | | Flown VFR into IMC | |
Instances	Private	Commercial	Private	Commercial
0	80%	66%	77%	78%
1	16%	24%	15%	14%
2	3%	7%	6%	5%
3	1%	2%	1%	2%
4		1%	1%	1%
5				
6+		1%	1%	1%

To help further specify content of new training, we might look at how pilots typically fly. In the example of fuel mismanagement given earlier, the practices of pilots with regard to checking their fuel tanks before they depart or in computing expected fuel consumption might well identify shortcomings that could be addressed by training. When asked how often they topped off or checked their fuel tanks before taking off, virtually every pilot said that it was done before every cross-country flight. However, when asked how often the expected fuel consumption was computed before a cross-country flight, about 20% of both the private and commercial pilots said that it was not always done. Of course, some allowance might be made for pilots who fly the same cross-country route frequently and, once having computed the fuel requirements, only recompute the fuel consumption when some major factor (such as greatly increased headwinds) changes. Still, the number who do not always compute fuel requirements seems suspiciously high, and one might wonder whether some pilots fail to compute this essential bit of information because they are not aware of its importance or because they do not know how to make the computation. Clearly, different training would be required to remediate the problem, depending upon which cause was predominant.

Pilots also report flying low beneath the clouds (commonly called "scud-running") with a frequency that gives cause for some alarm. About 25% of the pilots reported that they sometimes flew at 1,000 feet above ground level (AGL) to remain clear of the clouds, while about 7% reported having flown at 500 feet AGL to remain clear of the clouds. This is potentially a very hazardous condition and is commonly cited in reports of fatal weather-related accidents. These behaviors may reflect a lack of complete commitment to safety and adherence to legal operation procedures. When asked how much they agree or disagree with the statement, "I would duck below minimums to get home" slightly more than 60% chose the Strongly Disagree response, while the remaining 40% indicated some lesser degree of commitment to the notion that you should never do this. One might argue that for the 40%, there are some circumstances under which they will take a chance and ignore safety and legality. (Interestingly, about 70% of the Airline Transport certificate holders Strongly Disagreed -- as one might hope, they are more strongly committed to safety.)

Personal minimums

Closely related to what pilots report as their usual practices are their personal standards -- commonly known as their personal minimums. The FAA and civil aviation authorities in other nations set minimum standards for almost all aspects of aviation operations. Perhaps the best known of these standards are those which define the conditions under which flight under visual flight rules (VFR) may be accomplished. In controlled airspace, which now includes most of the continental United States, the requirements for visual flight are 3 miles of visibility and at least 500 feet below any clouds. Since there is also a requirement to remain at least 500 feet above the surface (over sparsely populated areas), this amounts to a minimum ceiling of 1,000 feet.

Table 3.4
Personal minimums for a day, cross country VFR flight

	Private	Commercial
Visibility		
1 mile	1%	1%
2 miles	1%	1%
3 miles	18%	26%
4 miles	3%	4%
5 miles	37%	41%
6 miles	6%	5%
8 miles	7%	5%
10 miles	20%	14%
15 miles	8%	4%
Ceiling		
1,000 feet	3%	6%
1,500 feet	5%	10%
2,000 feet	14%	22%
3,000 feet	38%	38%
4,000 feet	16%	11%
5,000 feet	24%	14%

While these are the minimum legal standards for VFR operations, many pilots elect to adopt more stringent standards, to the effect that they will not initiate a flight unless the weather conditions considerably exceed the legal minima. These personal minimums have been widely discussed in the popular aviation literature (c.f., Clausing, 1990) and Kirkbride, Jensen, Chubb, and Hunter (in press) have developed a procedure to assist pilots in managing risk during preflight planning through the construction of a personal checklist embodying clearly stated and documented personal operating minimums.

One might reasonably argue that adoption of higher standards by a pilot of limited total and recent experience is a prudent risk control measure which compensates to some degree for a lower skill level. Failure to observe this strategy or finding that some pilots would initiate flights under conditions which apparently do not meet the minimum legal standards suggest the need for training to address this issue. As noted before, finding that some pilots say they will fly under less than legal VFR conditions (as shown in Table 3.4) does not necessarily allow us to specify exactly what the training should be, but it does lead us to examine the area in more detail.

Designing training that is accessible to the pilot

Basing training content and format on the characteristics of the pilot population will allow us to produce training that addresses more accurately the needs of that group. However, even training that is exactly what the pilots need to improve their skills in a vital area is of little use if it is not marketed effectively. Lectures given to empty halls, videos that no one sees, and pamphlets that no one reads do not promote safety.

As noted in the introduction, the safety seminars are the major mechanism used by the FAA for the dissemination of safety information and the continued training of certificated pilots. However, as shown in Table 3.5, that program is not successful in reaching every pilot. Of the private pilots, for example, about a third reported not having attended a seminar in the last two years. If we define regular participation as having attended two or more seminars over the last two year period, then only about half of the pilot population would qualify as regular participants. Even so, the effect of the safety seminars on those who do attend may be substantial. Comparing those who attend with those who do not attend on the critical events described earlier shows that those who attend are better than those who do not on almost every comparison.

Neither are pilots who attend the safety seminars dissatisfied with the training they receive. Initial results from an ongoing evaluation of the safety seminars shows that participants are almost universally satisfied with the programs. Those who attend like it; but, how do we attract those pilots who do not attend regularly? When asked why they do not attend regularly, pilots most often reported that they were too busy. As shown in Table 3.6, location was another consideration. Although it may be possible to adjust the location of the seminars so as to make them more accessible, the personal schedule of the pilots is clearly not open in influence by the seminar organizers. Attendance might also be enhanced by offering training on the most appealing subjects (listed in Table 3.7), however, to a large degree these are the subjects already covered in the safety seminar programs.

Table 3.5
Attendance at FAA safety seminars

	Private	Commercial
None	35%	33%
One	20%	21%
Two to Five	38%	38%
More than five	7%	8%

Table 3.6
Primary reason for not attending safety seminars

	Private	Commercial
Location	17%	16%
Time	12%	10%
Irrelevant material	2%	4%
Too busy	20%	19%
Poor quality	2%	2%
Other	9%	9%
Not Applicable*	38%	40%

* Not Applicable was chosen by those who regularly attended seminars

Table 3.7
Most appealing seminar subject

	Private	Commercial
Federal Aviation Regulations	15%	19%
Airspace	14%	12%
Weather	22%	19%
Fight Planning	3%	3%
Pilot Techniques	23%	23%
Stall/Spin	3%	2%
Pilot Certification & Training	1%	3%
Local Flying Environment	16%	15%
Other	4%	5%

It seems likely that there are factors which are beyond the control of those designing, scheduling, and conducting the safety seminars. Because of the travel and time demands inherent in seminar-type training sessions, there may well be a considerable segment of the pilot population who will never attend, regardless of how interesting and relevant the seminar is. For these pilots, alternative forms of training delivery must be devised. Some possibilities include distribution of printed and videotape material directly to pilots (particularly if those most at-risk for accident involvement can be identified), distribution of material such as computer software over commercial networks or via the internet, and placing training materials at facilities such as pilots' lounges, libraries, or even commercial videotape rental establishments so as to make them more accessible to pilots. The extent to which these possible alternative training delivery mechanisms, along with several others, are feasible and acceptable to pilots is being explored in another large scale survey of pilots being conducted for the FAA by The Ohio State University. Data from that expressly marketing-oriented study should be available by the time this book reaches print.

Some conclusions

Training programs for certificated pilots must meet the criteria alluded to earlier. That is, they must address the training needs of the pilots and pilots must actually partake of the training. (I assume, perhaps hopefully, that the training actually has a positive effect.) In deciding upon a topic for training, in determining the format, and in marketing the resulting product, knowledge of the characteristics of the pilot population is essential. The eternal dictums of business are clearly applicable here:

- Know your product
- Know your customer

When the characteristics of the pilot population are examined it becomes clear that a broad array of training programs are required to meet the needs of the diverse pilot population. Likewise a broad spectrum of delivery mechanisms are needed in order to successfully impart the training message and achieve the desired effect -- safer pilots.

References

Clausing, D.J. (1990). *Improving your flying skills: Tips from a pro.* Blue Ridge Summit, PA: TAB.

Fowler, F. J. (1993). *Survey research methods.* Second Edition. Newbury Park: Sage Publications.

Henry, G. T. (1990). *Practical sampling.* Newbury Park: Sage Publications.

Hunter, D. R. (1995). *Airman research questionnaire: Methodology and overall results.* DOT/FAA/AAM-95/27. Washington, DC: Federal Aviation Administration, Office of Aviation Medicine.

Kirkbride, L. A., Jensen, R. S., Chubb, G. P., & Hunter, D. R. (in press). *Developing the personal minimums tool for managing risk during preflight go/no-go decisions.* DOT/FAA/AM-96/pending. Washington, DC: Federal Aviation Administration, Office of Aviation Medicine.

NTSB (1989). *Annual review of aircraft accident data: U.S. general aviation calendar year 1987.* NTSB/ARG-89/01. Washington, DC: National Transportation Safety Board.

Platenius, P. H., & Wilde, G. J. S. (1986). *A psychometric study of Canadian pilot license holders and their aviation accident risk.* Kingston, Ontario: Department of Psychology, Queen's University.

Rea, L. M., & Parker, R. A. (1992). *Designing and conducting survey research: A comprehensive guide.* San Francisco: Jossey-Bass.

Appendix

Some notes on generalizability

To better understand the results of the study from which these data were obtained, some issues dealing with the interpretation and generalizability of survey data must be addressed. In general, there are two sources of error for self-administered mail survey data such as those cited here: sampling error and nonsampling error. Sampling error is that error which is attributable to the sample drawn from the population of interest.

The samples obtained for private, commercial, and airline transport ratings were 2,548, 2,845, and 1,218, respectively. The associated 95% confidence intervals are 2.0%, 1.9%, and 2.9%. When examining the results for the private and commercial pilots, then, we may be sure (with 95% confidence) that if only sampling error is considered, the results are accurate within about 2%, while the results for the airline transport pilots are accurate within about 3%.

Nonsampling error is that error which is attributable to factors which include: nonresponse, erroneous entries or deliberate falsehoods by the respondent, and data scanning or entry errors. By far the largest potential source of nonsampling error in a mail survey is associated with nonresponse. In any survey of this type some number of persons who receive the questionnaire will fail to complete and return it.

Since this effort is largely concerned with safety issues, one might reasonably ask whether the respondent and non-respondent groups differed with respect to their involvement in aircraft accidents. To address this question, accident data were obtained by matching the sample against the database maintained by the National Transportation Safety Board. The accident rates of the respondent and nonrespondent groups are very similar (3.0% and 3.3%, respectively) and a nonsignificant chi square was obtained leading us to believe that past accident involvement did not influence the decision to respond to the survey. Although not reported in detail here, it was also found that, overall, gender (except for the airline pilots) was unrelated to participation, as was total flight time. However, respondents for all the certificate levels tended to be somewhat older that the nonrespondents and, except for the private pilots, to have slightly less recent flight experience. The results of these analyses suggest the results are not badly biased; however, caution is always required when interpreting self-report survey data and the interested reader is referred to the original report (Hunter, 1995) for a more complete description of the data analyses and to any of the several excellent texts on survey methodology (c.f., Henry, 1990; Fowler, 1993; Rea & Parker, 1992) which can provide more complete information on these issues.

4 Expertise and cognitive skills development for Ab-initio pilots

Mark W Wiggins

Introduction

As a result of numerous systematic and costly failures, a large number of technology-based industries have recognised the significance of effective training systems in terms of the prevention of human error in the operational environment. In particular, there is a growing recognition that personnel must be immersed within a learning-based environment from initial entry into the industry, and that the training process should continue on a regular basis. The emphasis of this type of ab-initio training is typically to encourage innovation and the promulgation of principles of safety through a training system which is firmly based within contemporary educational practises.

Contrasting the trend in other technology-based industries however, the systems currently in place for ab-initio training in the aviation industry, continue to be based upon education and training principles developed in the late 1940's (Henley, 1991). The primary emphasis during such training appears to involve the development of behavioural skills and procedural skills, such that the pilot has the capability to operate the aircraft within a reasonable level of tolerance. There is thus little explicit consideration at this level of the development of cognitive skills such as risk analysis, decision-making, situation awareness, or problem-solving. Rather, these skills are presumed to occur spontaneously as the pilot accumulates expertise within the operational environment.

Clearly, there are a number of disadvantages with this type of approach, not least of which involve training efficiency and pilot safety. Training efficiency is likely to degrade when there is a dissociation between the behavioural skills and the cognitive skills involved in the performance of a task. A pilot for example, may possess the behavioural skills necessary to land an aircraft, but lack the cognitive skills necessary to manage unexpected demands in the operational environment.

Cognitive skills such as problem-solving and decision-making derive from both a functional understanding of the components involved in the problem environment, coupled with a knowledge of the specific procedures which may be employed (Kieras & Bovair, 1984). These facilitate the transfer of skills and thus, it might be argued that ab-initio pilot training may be considerably more efficient and more effective if due consideration were given to the integration of behavioural and cognitive skills during the ab-initio training process.

Due to the restrictive nature of the typical ab-initio training environment, novice pilots often lack the cognitive skills necessary to operate safely within an uncertain and dynamic aeronautical environment. This has led to a number of aircraft accidents in which pilots appear to lack the skills necessary to either:
- recognise the requirement for problem-solving/ decision-making; and/or
- implement an appropriate problem-solving/ decision-making process (See Air Accidents Branch, 1988).

In addition to the fundamental lack of cognitive skills however, skill acquisition theory would suggest that the performance of a task will only improve through consistent, repetitive exposure to situations in which the skills are required, and from which task-related feedback will emerge (Anderson, 1987; Shiffrin & Dumais, 1981). This necessitates the exposure of relatively inexperienced pilots to situations which may be beyond their capability, and thereby increases the probability of erroneous behaviour.

Why the neglect of cognitive skills development?

The apparent neglect of cognitive skills development in ab-initio flight training has occurred for a number reasons including the perpetuation of historical training systems, the difficulty in developing suitable training systems, and the difficulty in characterising the development of cognitive expertise.

Historically, ab-initio flight instructors have been relatively inexperienced, progressing towards flight instruction as a means to acquire the hours necessary to obtain employment with an airline. The lack of practical and/or life experience amongst flight instructors is such that by necessity, they revert to the practises which were applied when they were learning to fly (Henley, 1991). This creates a situation in which little innovation occurs and there is a perpetuation of what might be regarded as very limited educational practises and training systems.

Coupled with flight instructor inexperience is the relative difficulty in developing suitable training systems for the acquisition and maintenance of cognitive skills. Since the aviation environment is both uncertain and dynamic, it is particularly difficult to locate the cognitive cues necessary for instructional purposes. Successful in-flight weather-related decision-making for example, is dependent upon the recognition and subsequent integration of a number cues, each of which may change from situation to situation. The aim, therefore, is to acquire a series of generalised principles, coupled with an accurate mental model of the situation, and to use this information to direct pilot performance within a range of task-related situations. This, in essence, is the nature of expertise.

Characterising expertise

Until recently, expertise, or mastery within a particular domain was defined primarily on the basis of the *outcomes* associated with task-related performance. During both World War II and the Korean War for example, expertise, in terms of aeronautical performance, was generally identified with the number of enemy aircraft destroyed, or the number of missions which had been flown successfully (Yeager & Janos, 1986). This was assumed to be indicative of a superior level of performance. Similar principles define mastery in such diverse domains as chess (Charness, 1991), billiards (Abernethy, Neal, Engstrom & Koning, 1993) and squash (Abernethy and Wollstein, 1989), in which expertise was, and in many cases continues to be characterised by the accumulation of successful, observable outcomes.

Superior overt performance is not however, always associated with expertise. Superior performance in terms of the rate of text production is a characteristic of literary novices rather than experts (Paris, 1986). Similarly, novices are generally better able than experts to construct the initial sentence in a paragraph (Zbrodoff, 1984). Therefore, in order to acquire a comprehensive understanding of the nature of expertise and thereby facilitate the development of instructional systems, it becomes necessary to consider both task-related performance itself, and the underlying intellectual processes upon which the particular outcome is based.

Schvaneveldt and others (1985) consider a tripartite approach to the characterisation of expertise. This involves a combination of: superior task-related performance; superior psycho-motor skills, such as tracking tasks or complex manual manipulations; and/or superior cognitive skills including pattern recognition, problem-solving and decision-making. This suggests that expertise is the product of a complex interaction between a number of related dimensions and that no single, underlying feature exists which determines precisely, the performance of an expert within a particular domain.

In addition to these three elements of expertise, it is possible to consider a fourth, affective component which may occur to a greater or lesser extent within particular domains. Stressful experiences in particular, have the potential to disrupt performance during both psycho-motor and cognitive activities (Holsti, 1971; Keinan, Friedland & Ben-Porath, 1987; Wright, 1974). In chess, for example, evidence suggests that experts are often more skilled than their peers in terms of managing and directing emotional experiences to facilitate performance (Tikhomirov & Vinogradov, 1970).

Relatively superior performance appears to be related (at least in part) to the ability to limit the impact of affective demands on cognitive tasks such as planning and decision-making (Isen, Means, Patrick & Nowicki, 1982; Svensson, Angelborg-Thanderz, & Sjoberg, 1993). On the basis of this evidence, expertise within a particular domain is dependent upon a combination of superior psycho-motor skills, cognitive skills, and/or affective skills, thereby leading to superior task-related performance.

From a training development perspective, the complexity of skilled performance is therefore such that each phase requires the development of psycho-motor (behavioural) objectives, cognitive objectives and affective objectives. In defining cognitive objectives it becomes necessary to specify generalised factors which contribute to the development and nature of cognitive expertise.

Characteristics of cognitive expertise

The characteristics of cognitive expertise have, for many years, been the subject of considerable debate within the domains of cognitive science and instructional design. From the cognitive science perspective, the notion of cognitive expertise has been of some interest for the development of expert systems and artificial intelligence. It has been assumed that by characterising the development and the nature of human expertise, guidelines might be developed to capture this knowledge in a series of rules, and use this as the basis for the development of computer-based applications (Tolcott, Marvin & Lehner, 1989).

Allied to this approach is the instructional design perspective, for which the motivation to characterise the nature of cognitive expertise stems from the expectation that it can facilitate the development of more effective and efficient instructional systems (Lesgold, 1988; Ryder and Redding, 1993). The aim is to use this information to augment instructional systems by either reducing the amount of extraneous information provided in the training environment, and/or providing the information within a framework which encourages the development of appropriate cognitive and psycho-motor skills.

Consistent with this perspective, isolating the precise nature of cognitive expertise is probably best achieved through a longitudinal analysis in which the learner is examined at frequent intervals during the transition from novice to expert. Unfortunately, this type approach requires a vast investment of both time and resources to reach a satisfactory conclusion. Moreover, this process is often conducted in an uncontrolled research environment so spurious variations may result.

Cognitive and skill development are linked

On the basis of this argument, researchers have typically avoided the longitudinal approach in favour of a cross-sectional methodology in which comparisons are made *between* individuals at different stages during the transition towards expertise. In recent years, there has been a plethora of such expert-novice comparisons in a number of fields as diverse as squash (Abernethy, 1990), map reading (Gilhooly, Wood, Kinnear & Green, 1988), medical science (Patel & Groen, 1991), fire fighting (Klein, 1989; Klein & Klinger, 1991), weather-related decision-making (Wiggins & O'Hare, 1995), and sonar operation (Kirschenbaum, 1992). These comparisons also help to differentiate between expert and novice performance.

As a prelude to the characterisation of expertise, it is important to note the level of inconsistency which appears to exist between research outcomes, particularly in terms of expert performance. There is inconsistency between the performance of experts in various domains. Whilst some expertise is reported as exceedingly accurate (Kirschenbaum, 1992), the performance of experts in other areas is relatively inaccurate (Goldberg, 1968). Thus, it might be argued that the differences evident between expert levels of performance may simply reflect differences which exist between various types of experts in various types of domains. Shanteau (1988) in particular, argues that there are three general classes of cognitive expertise, each of which involves a continuum, based upon the primary cognitive demands associated with a particular task. Since experts may be skilled in only one or two of these dimensions, changing the demands of a task to reflect other cognitive dimensions is likely to result in poor performance, irrespective of the overall level of expertise of the individual.

Classes of cognitive expertise

- The first of these continua characterises the distinction between perceptual expertise; such as that required for aerobatic flight; and cognitive expertise; such as that required for in-flight decision-making. Shanteau (1988) argues that the latter is relatively more dependent upon problem-solving skills, whilst the former is more dependent upon perceptual-motor skills. There thus exists a difference in terms of both the level of conscious control of performance and the reliance upon higher-order cognitive structures: a distinction which is consistent with Rasmussen's (1983) skill-based and knowledge-based classifications of human performance.
- The second continuum involves a distinction between knowledge expertise; such as that required by an historian; and diagnostic expertise; such as that required by a maintenance engineer (Shanteau, 1988). The former involves the capacity to integrate a vast amount of task-related information, whereas the latter involves the facility to develop accurate hypotheses based upon a limited amount of task-related information, often with level of uncertainty. Whilst the underlying cognitive structure emphasises the integration of information in both cases, the distinction identified by Shanteau (1988) is likely to reflect differences in terms of the operational environment. Time constraints in particular, tend to limit the extent to which large amounts of information can be examined and this, thereby encourages the development of task-specific strategies which rely upon a limited amount of task-related information (Hammond, Hamm, Grassia & Pearson, 1987; Klein, 1989; 1990).
- The final continuum distinguishes between experts who provide data acquisition and advice; such as financial consultants; and those who are skilled in the selection and implementation of decisions; such as managers or supervisors. In this case, expertise may involve the former acquiring sufficient task-related information to provide the latter with the information necessary to formulate an appropriate and timely decision. By implication, however, both must have an understanding of the relationship between the information available and the various outcomes: albeit at a different cognitive level.

In training, the cognitive dimensions outlined by Shanteau (1988) reflect the demands which exist during the performance of any cognitive task. The success with which a task is managed is dependent upon the skills necessary to recognise and respond appropriately to the particular cognitive demands associated with a task (See Figure 4.1).

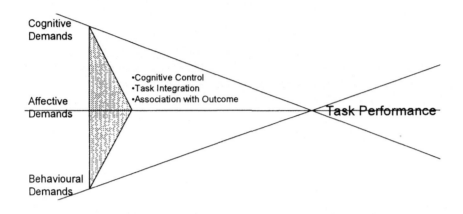

Figure 4.1 A representation of the cognitive, affective and behavioural dimensions which contribute to task performance and the interaction which must occur

A strategic decision-making task involving a board of directors, for example, may require significant levels of cognitive control and task integration, but little association with the implementation of the outcome. In contrast, a time-limited, weather-related decision involving an IFR operation may require significant levels of cognitive control, limited task integration, and a significant association with the implementation of the outcome. On the basis of this discussion, cognitive expertise can therefore be characterised as involving:

- The skills necessary to recognise the level of cognitive control/ intervention required in response to the cognitive demands of a task;
- The skills necessary to recognise and respond to the level of task integration involved in the performance of a cognitive task; and
- The skills necessary to select and implement the outcomes associated with the performance of a cognitive task.

Whilst these characteristics represent general dimensions of cognitive expertise, an effective training system requires the identification of the extent to which each of the dimensions is reflected in particular tasks. This will facilitate the development of cognitive objectives necessary for the purposes of Instructional Systems Design (ISD).

The identification and classification of cognitive skills

On the basis of Shanteau's (1988) discussion of the nature of cognitive expertise, successful cognitive performance within the aviation domain can be assumed to require the skills necessary to recognise and respond to:
(i)   the level of cognitive control involved in the performance of the task;
(ii)   the extent and amount of information which needs to be integrated; and
(iii)   the degree of active participation involved in the selection and the implementation of the task.

Each of these dimensions can be considered as a relatively independent skill, with expertise on one dimension not necessarily equating with similar performance on another. From a learning perspective however, the nature of each dimension with respect to a particular task must be determined explicitly, and one process through which this can be achieved is through Cognitive Task Analysis (CTA).

Cognitive task analysis

According to Edwards and Ryder (1991), cognitive task analysis (CTA) is one procedure through which cognitive performance may be devolved and thereby examined. It is assumed that the identification of task-related cognitive and procedural knowledge, coupled with the development of an understanding of their inter-relationship, will facilitate the construction of effective training strategies for the neophyte decision-maker.

In the learning domain, CTA is fundamentally a process designed to facilitate the identification of differences between experts and novices in terms of their perception and performance of a task, and to postulate subsequently, a process through which the transition from novice to expert may be enhanced. *More specifically, CTA focuses upon the characteristics of decision-making and problem-solving, the development and application of conceptual representations/ mental models, and the interpretation and integration of task-related information.* Consequently, CTA is regarded as particularly applicable within the aviation domain since many aviation-related tasks involve cognitive skills such as situational awareness, problem-solving, decision-making and the integration of a large amounts of information (Redding and Seamster, 1994).

The utility of CTA in the aviation domain has been demonstrated effectively by a number of researchers in detailed examinations of the performance of air traffic controllers (Schlager, Means and Roth, 1990; Harwood, Roske-Hofstrand, and Murphy, 1991; Redding, Ryder, Seamster, Purcell and Cannon, 1991). Some analogies can be made between the tasks performed by air traffic controllers and those performed by pilots since both operate in dynamic and complex situations for which the information available is often uncertain and the process of problem-solving is time-constrained.

Since cognitive expertise is presumed to involve performance across three dimensions, the CTA should be designed such that it involves a detailed analysis of: the level of cognitive control; the level of task integration; and the association with the selection and implementation of outcomes involved in the performance of a task.

CTA Methodologies

Whilst other approaches to task analysis devolve the process into task-related and psychologically-related components, CTA represents a more wholistic approach based on the assumption that the behavioural, cognitive and affective aspects of task performance are intrinsically related. As Redding and Seamster (1994) suggest however, there are a number of methodological strategies applied in CTA including protocol analysis, psychological scaling, performance modelling, cognitive modeling, neural network modelling, error analysis and cognitive interviewing. The main elements common to the various strategies associated with these approaches include an identification of the task components, a recognition of those elements of the task which require similar knowledge and/or skills, an understanding of the differences between expert and novice performance and the identification of those conditions which augment the process of learning.

The goal

Clearly, the overall goal associated with cognitive skill acquisition involves the development of expertise within a particular domain. This requires the combined skills necessary to recognise, process and respond to a variety of situations. Whilst empirical research indicates that the transfer of expert performance across domains is relatively poor, performance within domains remains relatively consistent (Glaser & Chi, 1988). The relative acquisition of cognitive skill can therefore be evaluated against the Z-effect.

Based on the three-stage skill acquisition theories of both Fitts and Posner (1967), and Anderson (1987), the Z-effect refers to the differences which exist between expert, intermediate and novice performance during familiar and unfamiliar situations within a given domain. In the case of novices for example, the lack of task-specific skills is such that performance is relatively limited, irrespective of the relative familiarity or unfamiliarity of the particular task. The performance of intermediate pilots however, will improve beyond novice performance during familiar tasks, but will remain consistent with novice performance during unfamiliar tasks. This results from the development of localised expertise which has yet to progress to the stage in which the skills become domain-general. Finally, experts can be expected to perform relatively consistently above both intermediate and novice pilots during both familiar and unfamiliar tasks. The effect is depicted diagrammatically in Figure 4.2.

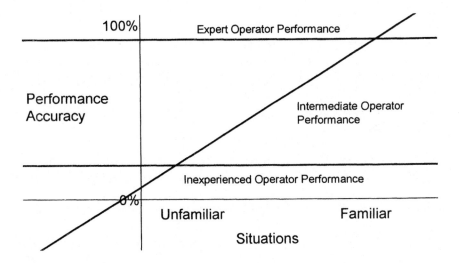

Figure 4.2 **A diagrammatic representation between the performance accuracy of expert, intermediate and inexperienced operators during familiar and unfamiliar situations**

Evaluating cognitive performance involves an assessment of performance in both familiar and unfamiliar situations. In general, expertise equates to the extent to which performance during an unfamiliar situation is consistent with that evident amongst experts. The development of expertise requires the successful integration of cognitive training within both the behavioural and affective dimensions of skill development. Lintern (1995) argues that the development of cognitive skills should be situated within the operational environment within which, these skills are expected to be performed. This is designed to contextualise the skills and provide the foundation for the subsequent development of expertise.

Summary

The aim of this discussion was to provide a framework within which the development of cognitive training systems could occur. The general characteristics of expertise were defined in terms of behavioural, cognitive and affective elements, and this provided the basis for the subsequent examination of the general characteristics associated with cognitive expertise. According to Shanteau (1988), the cognitive demands associated with a task can be divided along three dimensions and cognitive performance must therefore involve an accurate assessment and response to the particular cognitive demands. From a training perspective, the extent and nature of these demands can be determined through the application of information acquisition strategies including cognitive task analysis. This serves to clarify the training objectives necessary to develop and implement cognitive training strategies in the ab-initio training environment and therefore, is likely to increase both training efficiency and pilot safety.

References

Abernethy, B. (1990). Anticipation in squash: Differences in advance cue utilisation between expert and novice players. *Journal of Sports Sciences, 8,* 17-34.

Abernethy, B., & Wollstein, J. (1989). Improving anticipation in racquet sports. *Sports Coach, 13,* 3-7.

Abernethy, B., Neal, R., Engstrom, C., & Koning, P. (1993). What makes the expert sports performer better than the novice? *Sports Coach, 16,* 31-37.

Air Accidents Investigation Branch. (1988*). Report on the Accident to Cessna F 172M OO-JEL in the Sea, 3 Nautical Miles East-North-East of Ryde, Isle of Wight on 30 April, 1987.* London, UK: Her Majesty's Stationary Office.

Anderson, J.R. (1987). Skill acquisition: Compilation of weak-method problem-solutions. *Psychological Review, 94,* 19-210.

Charness, N. (1991). Expertise in chess: The balance between knowledge and chess. In K.A. Ericsson & J. Smith (Eds.), *Toward a general theory of expertise.* Cambridge, UK: Cambridge University Press.

Edwards, B.J., & Ryder, J.M. (1991). Training analysis and design for complex aircrew tasks. In R.F. Dillon & J.W. Pellegrino (Eds.), *Instruction: Theoretical and applied perspectives.* New York: Praeger.

Fitts, P.M., & Posner, M.I. (1967). *Human performance.* Westport, CN: Greenwood.

Gilhooly, K.J., Wood, M., Kinnear, P.R., Green, C. (1988). Skill in map reading and memory for maps. *Quarterly Journal of Experimental Psychology, 40A,* 87-107.

Glaser, R. & Chi, M.T.H. (1988). Overview. In R. Glaser, M.T.H. Chi, & M.J. Farr (Eds.), *The nature of expertise.* New Jersey: Lawrence Erlbaum.

Goldberg, L.R. (1968). Simple models or simple processes? Some research on clinical judgements. *American Psychologist, 23,* 483-496.

Hammond, K.R., Hamm, R.M., Grassia, J., & Pearson, T. (1987). Direct comparison of the efficacy of intuitive and analytical cognition in expert judgement. *IEEE transactions on Systems, Man, and Cybernetics, 17,* 753-770.

Harwood, K., Roske-Hofstrand, & Murphy, E. (1991). Exploring conceptual structures in air traffic control. *Proceedings of the Sixth International Symposium of Aviation Psychology,* Columbus, OH, Ohio State University, pp.466-473.

Henley, I. (1991). The development and evaluation of flight instructors: A descriptive survey. *The International Journal of Aviation Psychology, 1,* 319-333.

Hoffman, P.J., Slovic, P., & Rorer, L.G. (1968). An analysis of variance model for the assessment of configural cue utilisation in clinical judgement. *Psychological Bulletin, 69,* 338-349.

Holsti, O.R. (1971). Crisis, stress decision-making. *International Social Science Journal, 23,* 53-67.

Isen, A.M., Means, B., Patrick, R., & Nowicki, G. (1982). Some factors influencing decision-making and risk-taking. In M.S. Clark & S.T. Fiske (Eds.), *Affect and cognition.* Hillsdale, NJ: Erlbaum.

Keinan, G., Friedland, N., & Ben-Porath, Y. (1987). Decision-making under stress: Scanning of alternatives under physical threat. *Acta Psychologia, 64,* 229-243.

Kieras, D.E., & Bovair, S. (1984). The role of a mental model in learning to operate a device. *Cognitive Science, 8,* 255-273.

Kirschenbaum, S.S. (1992). Influence of experience on information-search strategies. *Journal of Applied Psychology, 77,* 343-352.

Klein, G., & Klinger, D. (1991). Naturalistic decision making. Crew System *Ergonomics Information Analysis Centre Newsletter, 2,* 1-4.

Klein, G.A. (1989). Recognition-primed decisions (RPD*). Advances in Man-Machine Systems, 5,* 47-92.

Lesgold, A. (1988). Problem solving. In R.S. Sternberg & E.E. Smith (Eds.), *The psychology of human thought.* New York: Cambridge University Press.

Lintern, G. (1995). Flight instruction: The challenge from situated cognition. *The International Journal of Aviation Psychology, 5,* 327-350.

Paris, P.L. (1986). *Goals and problem solving in written composition.* Unpublished doctoral dissertation, York University, Toronto.

Patel, V.L., & Groen, G.J. (1991). The general and specific nature of medical expertise: A critical look. In K.A. Ericsson and J. Smith (Eds.), *Toward a general theory of expertise.* Cambridge, UK: Cambridge University Press.

Redding, R.E., & Seamster, T.L. (1994). Cognitive task analysis in air traffic controller and aviation crew training. In N Johnston, N McDonald, & R Fuller (Eds.), *Aviation Psychology in Practice:* Aldershot, UK: Avebury.

Redding, R.E., Ryder, J.M., Seamster, T.L., Purcell, J.A., and Cannon, J.R. (1991). *Cognitive Task Analysis of En-route Air Traffic Control: Model extension and validation,* Report to the Federal Aviation Administration, McLean, VA, Human Technology Inc. (ERIC Document Reproduction Service. No.ED 340 848).

Ryder, J.M., & Redding, R.E. (1993). Integrating cognitive task analysis into instructional systems development. *Educational Technology Research and Development, 41,* 75-96.

Schlager, M.S., Means, B., & Roth, C. (1990). Cognitive task analysis for the real (-time) world. *Proceedings of the Human Factors Society, 34th Annual Meeting,* Santa Monica, CA, Human Factors Society, pp. 1309-1313.

Schvaneveldt, R.W., Durso, F.T., Goldsmith, T.E., Breen, T.J., Cooke, N.M., Tucker, R.G., & De Maio, J.C. (1985). Measuring the structure of expertise. *International Journal of Man-Machine Studies, 23,* 699-728.

Shanteau, J. (1988). Psychological characteristics and strategies of expert decision-makers. *Acta Psychologia, 68,* 203-215.

Shiffrin, R.M., & Dumais, S.T. (1981). The development of automatisation. In J.R. Anderson (Ed.), *Cognitive Skills and their Acquisition.* Hillsdale, NJ: Erlbaum.

Svensson, E., Angelborg-Thanderz, & Sjoberg, L. (1993). Mission challenge, mental workload and performance in military aviation. *Aviation, Space and Environmental Medicine, 64,* 985-991.

Tikhomirov, O.K., & Vinogradov, Y.E. (1970). Emotions in the heuristic function. *Soviet Psychology, 8,* 198-203.

Tolcott, M.A., Marvin, F.F., & Lehner, P.E. (1989). Expert decision making in evolving situations. *IEEE Transaction on Systems, Man, and Cybernetics, 19,* 606-615.

Voss, J.F. & Post, T.A. (1988). On the solving of ill-structured problems. In R. Glaser & M.T.H. Chi (Eds.)., *The Nature of Expertise.* New Jersey: Lawrence Erlbaum Associates.

Wiggins, M.W., & O'Hare, D. (1995). Expertise in aeronautical weather-related decision-making: A cross-sectional analysis of general aviation pilots. *Journal of Experimental Psychology: Applied, 1,* 304-319.

Wright, P. (1974). The harassed decision-maker: Time pressures, distractions and the use of evidence. *Journal of Applied Psychology, 59,* 555-561.

Yeager, C., & Janos, L. (1986). *Yeager.* London, UK: Arrow.

Zbrodoff, N.J. (1984). *Writing sorties under time and length constraints.* Unpublished doctoral dissertation, University of Toronto.

5 Individual differences and CRM training

Albrecht Schiewe and Phillip J Moore

Introduction and background

There is little doubt that one of the major changes in aviation training over the last decade has been the introduction of CRM (Crew Resource Management) programs as part of recurrent training (Helmreich, 1993; Weiner, Kanki & Helmreich, 1993.). Such programs aim to modify attitudes and behaviours in three major areas: communication, judgement and decision making, and teamwork with the ultimate objective of producing more effective crew co-ordination and cockpit resource utilisation for safer flight.

As Schiewe (1995) notes, however, the general focus of CRM research has been on the outcomes of CRM training, the question of whether or not CRM training makes any difference. Certainly there is evidence for positive changes in attitudes and behaviour (Helmreich & Foushee, 1993) but there is counter evidence also suggesting that, for some, CRM training effects are negative (Helmreich & Wilhelm, 1989; 1991). The pursuit of such outcomes or product based questions is undoubtedly important but we would argue that a more process based question is of equal importance, the question of how participants in CRM programs actually feel about the content and the methods of instruction they are experiencing. There is a strong literature showing the vital role of feelings about the instructional context (e.g. the curriculum, instructional methods, evaluation etc) in determining quality learning (e.g. Biggs & Moore, 1993).

While some attempts have been made to answer this latter question, much of the focus has been on an overall rating of the CRM program (e.g. How useful was the program?). Answers to such questions are useful as a general metric of "success" for those designing programs but in the long run the data do not allow for any determination about which parts or units of the training program are perceived to be more useful than others. Armed with such information, designers can modify the program by reworking the units seen to be least useful and relevant.

Perceptions of the relevance of the material and the usefulness of the training methods, however, might be mediated by individual differences. Individual differences such as interpersonal skills and the need to achieve have been shown to influence attitudes to CRM (Helmreich & Wilhelm, 1991) and it is likely that individual differences also play a part in perceptions of particular units or parts of any CRM training program. The recent research by Schiewe (1995) amply demonstrates such differences and because of its importance to the work reported in this chapter we will spend a little time detailing his study.

Schiewe's study used over 700 pilots undergoing a three-day CRM training program which contained 17 training units dealing with teamwork, communication, and judgement/decision making (Maschke, Goeters, Hormann & Schiewe, 1995). The program contained a mix of methods of instruction with some units being presented as lectures, others as lectures and videos, and others as group activities and role plays. The participants were asked to evaluate the whole course as well as the individual units for relevance of the specific content and usefulness of the methods of instruction.

In analysing the results, Schiewe used a statistical procedure called cluster analysis which groups or clusters together people who have similar response patterns. Schiewe found four clusters of people. One cluster was classified as "enthusiasts" for they consistently rated both content and method highly. Accounting for about 50% of the participants, these individuals seemed keen on any form of CRM training. By way of contrast, a second cluster (about 7%) was labelled "decliners" for they consistently rated content and method lowly. Schiewe called his third cluster "cognitives" (about 17%) as they appeared to favour instructional methods that focussed on transmission of information (e.g. "How to provide helpful feedback") while his last group, the "dynamics" (being about 26% of the participants) seemed to favour methods of instruction that employed group activities, they liked experiential learning rather than discussion and more direct instructional methods.

The importance of Schiewe's (1995) findings lies in identifying the ways in which different people perceive the individual CRM units in terms of content and method. However, a logical extension of that work would be to examine more substantively the role that differences within individuals might play in the perceived differences in any one CRM units' worth. For example, are Captains, who are obviously more experienced, more likely to be enthusiastic than their less experienced F/Os? Or is it that the younger crew, commencing their careers, are more enthusiastic?

Also what of attitudinal effects? Do participants entering CRM training with negative attitudes towards CRM and psychologically oriented training change their attitudes? Can clusters be defined by such attitudes? Is it that the "decliners" in Schiewe's (1995) research were those who were "anti-CRM" before the training was undertaken?

Answers to questions such as those posed above are important for they have the potential to provide a greater understanding of the ways in which individuals are effected by their recurrent human factors oriented training. If it can be identified that certain biographical or attitudinal characteristics play a role, then CRM trainers may be able to modify programs to accommodate such differences, with the ultimate aim of ensuring positive outcomes.

In quick summary then, this chapter follows from Schiewe's (1995) work by further investigating another group of pilots undergoing CRM training. Specifically, the chapter examines whether or not meaningful groupings of participants can be established from this sample and also what roles factors such as age, position, fleet affiliation and pre-training attitudes to training may have in defining those groupings. Also of interest are the effects of the program on attitudes towards CRM training as well as attitudes towards psychological training modifying behaviour. The next section of the chapter outlines the training program.

The training program

The three-day CRM training course conducted by the airline included 14 units from which pilot data were gathered. The units covered specific areas such as Communications, Judgement and Decision Making, Teamwork and seminar related units (see Schiewe, 1995). The particular content and method of presentation of the rated units are shown in Table 5.1. It can be seen for example, that Unit 2 focuses on human error in aviation and the mode of presentation is lecture and associated videos. By way of contrast, Unit 7's content relates to Teamwork with the method of instruction being group activities and practical exercises.

Participants

Over a period from April 1995 to May 1996, 544 participants were asked to evaluate the whole course as well as the specific units. In particular they were asked to rate both the relevance of the particular content of each unit and its instructional method using five point Likert scales. For content, the range was from 1 ("absolutely unimportant, a waste of time") to 5 ("extremely important/useful for daily work routines") while for method the range was from 1 ("uninteresting, boring ...") to 5 ("excellent, very helpful in transmitting the content"). Hence a higher score implies more positive feelings towards the dimension under consideration. Due to incomplete data from some pilots, the final data set consisted of 501 pilots.

Table 5.1
Sequence of training units from which data were gathered

Unit	Domain	Content	Methods
2*	J & D	Human Error	Lecture/video
3*	SRU	Seminar overview	Lecture/group discussion
4*	Team	Stereotypes (The first impression)	Group activity and discussion
5*	J & D	Decision Making Strategies	Case study, group discussion
6*	Com	Inquiry and Listening	Group activity/discussion video
7*	Team	To become a team player	Group activity/practical exercise
8*	Team	Authority and Assertiveness	Video, pair activity
9*	Com	Advocacy	Video, group discussion, lecture
10*	J & D	Situational awareness	Group discussion, case study
11*	Com	Barriers of communication and	Group discussion, roleplay with
12*	Com	Feedback	group activity/discussion
13*	J & D	Attitudes and risk assessment	Video, self and group activity
15*	SRU	Seminar transfer	Self-assessment
16*'	Team	Problem solving groups	Roleplay, scenario, peer feedback

In addition, data were gathered regarding position (Captain, F/O, FE), age, and attitudes towards CRM and training that incorporates psychology/human factors content. Specifically, six questions were asked, the first four (1,2,3,4) related to attitudes before training, the last two (5,6) to attitudes after training: Question 1 was related to previous experience with CRM training; Question 2 was concerned with previous participation in seminars with psychology/human factors content; Question 3 centred on attitudes to CRM; Question 4 centred on attitudes towards psychologically oriented training modifying behaviour; Question 5 focussed on attitudes to CRM after training; and Question 6 asked for attitudes towards psychologically oriented training modifying behaviour after the training program. Each question was answered on a 5-point scale, with higher scores representing more positive attitudes.

The findings

Cluster analyses

Following Schiewe's (1995) earlier research, we conducted cluster analyses using the ratings of the units to see if there were meaningful clusters of individuals (see Ward, 1963). Inspection of Ward's co-efficients for the last ten steps indicated three and four cluster solutions. Use of discriminant function analyses (SPSS "Discriminant" SPSS Inc, 1993) confirmed that the four cluster solution was more appropriate with 94.6% correct classification cases (compared to 84.4% for the three cluster solution). Cluster 1 consists of 117 participants, Cluster 2, 140, Cluster 3, 11, and Cluster 4, 233. The means for the clusters for both content and method are shown in Table 4.2. An inspection of the table suggests labels similar to Schiewe's earlier work: Cluster 1, the "Dynamics"; Cluster 2, the "Cognitives"; Cluster 3, the "Rejectors"; and Cluster 4, the "Enthusiasts". In general terms, for Method, "Enthusiasts" rate all units highly whereas "Rejectors" rate them lowly. It is pleasing to see, however, such a low number of those who reject such training content and methods. The "Cognitives" rate lecture oriented units (e.g. Unit 10) highly but group activity units (e.g. Unit 7) lowly while "Dynamics" appear to be the opposite to the "Cognitives"in their ratings. For Content, there are fewer differences between "Cognitives" and "Dynamics" as might reasonably be expected.

Table 5.2
Means for methods and content by cluster

	Enthusiasts		Dynamics		Cognitives		Rejectors	
Unit	Method	Content	Method	Content	Method	Content	Method	Content
2	4.30	4.35	3 69	3.93	3.98	3.92	2.63	3.81
3	3.92	3 95	3.19	3.44	3.20	3.47	1.91	2.09
4	4.45	4.35	4.27	4.04	4.03	3.90	1.91	3.00
5	4.61	4.77	3.94	4.61	4.11	4.50	2.91	4.09
6	4.42	4.33	3.67	3.99	3.77	3.98	2.81	3.63
7	4.12	4.16	4.44	3.82	2.29	3.36	2.09	2.72
8	4.15	4 40	3 29	3.76	3.48	3.97	2.00	3.27
9	4.04	4.19	3.26	3.78	3.38	3.87	2.63	3.82
10	4.43	4.57	3 75	4.27	4.25	4.40	2.36	3.54
11	4.56	4.38	3 97	3.96	3.74	3.84	1.91	3.00
12	4.19	4.34	3.21	3.96	3.26	3.86	2.18	3.63
13	4.39	4.42	3.53	3.98	3.60	3.98	2.18	3.72
15	4.07	4.17	3.34	3.67	3.30	3.62	2.00	2.27
16	4.77	4.64	4.64	4.55	4.08	4.30	3.09	3.45
Overall	4.42	4.42	3.85	4.00	3.37	4.09	2.09	3.00

Age, position and fleet

When an overall rating of the seminars was examined considering age, position (e.g. captain, F/O), and fleet (long, medium and short hauls), the results showed no differences. In other words, older participants did not rate the CRM program differently from younger ones, nor did Captains differ from F/Os and FEs.

Whether the participants flew long, short, or medium haul also made no difference to the overall rating of the program. While the results for the individual units themselves showed some differences, this occurred in less than 10 percent of the comparisons and no trends were apparent.

When we considered age, position and fleet using the clusters (Enthusiasts, Rejectors, Cognitives, Dynamics) a similar pattern of no differences emerged. For example, there were proportionally no more Captains than F/Os in the "Enthusiasts", and there were proportionally no more older pilots in the "Dynamics". In terms of "Rejectors", no specific age, position nor fleet dimension described them differently from other clusters.

So to summarise to this point: age, position, and fleet affiliation seem to play little, if any, role in the ways in which participants rated the whole program or rated the individual units comprising that program. Furthermore membership of the clusters was not related to any of these variables. Next we look at whether or not the clusters were different from each other in terms of the previous experience in human factors type training.

Previous experience with CRM and psychological training

Questions 1 and 2 asked the participants to rate their previous experience in both CRM and seminars with a psychological/human factors content. When we compared the four clusters we found no significant differences between the groups on either question. That is, they reported similarly their experiences in these areas. Cluster membership thus had very little to do with one's previous experiences for those who had more experience were not found predominantly in any one of the clusters. Neither were those with less training experience. Next we consider attitudes towards CRM and psychologically oriented training.

Attitudes towards CRM and psychological training

Attitudes towards CRM and psychological training modifying behaviour were assessed, as indicated above, by two questions related to pre-training attitudes (Questions 3 and 4) and two related to post-training attitudes (Questions 5 and 6). We examined whether or not cluster membership could be defined by attitudes towards CRM training and psychological training influencing behaviour. Firstly, we looked at attitudes pre-training. No significant differences were found between the clusters in terms of initial attitude to CRM. This pattern was repeated for the pre-training attitudes towards the likelihood of training influencing behaviour. So, in terms of their attitudes to begin with, the four clusters (Enthusiasts, Rejectors, Cognitives, Dynamics) were quite similar.

However, analyses of their attitudes after the training program showed a number of interesting differences. After training, 98 percent of the Enthusiasts were positive or very positive in their attitudes towards CRM compared to near 90 percent of the Dynamics and Cognitives. The Rejectors, while only being a relatively small group, showed only 45.5 percent in the positive direction. For the Enthusiasts, 33.3 percent had an ambivalent attitude before training, but only 1.9 percent after. In addition, a low 13.4 percent of the Enthusiasts reported "very positive" before training but 50 percent responded this way after the course. For the Enthusiasts it appears that an appreciation of content and methods of the program also showed a change in attitudes towards CRM.

For the Rejectors, none had a negative attitude to CRM beforehand, but, after training some 36 percent had moved to the negative end. For both Dynamics and Cognitives the patterns at pre and post training were somewhat similar.

In terms of post-training attitudes to psychological training modifying behaviour, there was also a significant difference between the clusters. Here we found that almost 90 percent of the Enthusiasts were positive or very positive in their views on psychological training modifying behaviour compared to 77.5 percent for the Dynamics, 73 percent of the Cognitives but only 36 percent of the Rejectors.

Perhaps one of the most interesting findings emerges from the comparison of before and after attitudes towards training modifying behaviour. Prior to training, across all clusters, less than 50 percent of each cluster reported positively on the matter. After training all clusters, except the Rejectors, moved to a more positive position, the Dynamics increasing by 30 percentage points, the Cognitives by 31 percentage points and the Enthusiasts by a substantial 43 percentage points.

People's enthusiasm towards team activities varies

Discussion

We have attempted in this chapter to both replicate previous research by Schiewe (1995) and tease out more fully the role that individual differences such as age, position, fleet, and attitudes might play in CRM training. We have presented a fair amount of information in the chapter in order to demonstrate, in one sense, the complexity of the issue. Nevertheless, we see a number of major findings that might prove of benefit to those involved in training. We present them in point form below.

* There are identifiable differences in the ways in which pilots perceive the relevance of the content and the usefulness of the methods used in the CRM training program.
* Individuals form into four quite clear groupings or clusters: Enthusiasts, Rejectors, Dynamics, and Cognitives. These groupings are very similar to those identified by Schiewe (1995) using another group of pilots.
* Enthusiasts (46.5 percent of participants) consistently perceive content to be highly relevant and methods of instruction useful. Rejectors (2 percent) report quite the opposite. Cognitives (28 percent) appreciate more the lecture and video presentation methods, suggesting perhaps a passive, individualistic preference to learning, while Dynamics (23.5 percent) seem to like methods which incorporate group work, team building, suggesting interpersonal, interactive preferences in learning. The distribution of participants to groups differs slightly from Schiewe (1995) where Enthusiasts accounted for 50 percent, Cognitives 17 percent, Dynamics 26 percent and "Decliners" 7 percent.
* Age, position, and fleet seem to play little part in whether or not a pilot is an Enthusiast, Rejector, Dynamic or Cognitive.
* Prior experience with CRM type programs also seems to play little role in whether or not a pilot is an Enthusiast, Rejector, Dynamic or Cognitive.
* After training, attitudes to CRM training *and* recognizing that such training could modify behaviour were more positive for the Enthusiasts, the Dynamics and the Cognitives (especially for the Enthusiasts).
* After training, the Rejector attitudes to CRM and psychological training were more negative.

What individual differences should trainers look for then? Our results would suggest that it may not be necessary to look at the age of the participants, nor whether or not they are a Captain or F/O, nor which type of aircraft they operate. Also our findings would suggest that attitudes to CRM and psychological training on entry to the program may not be the starting point. Further, previous experience with human factors type training had very little influence. It appears that what happens to the pilots in the program makes a difference, the more the pilot appreciates the method and content of the units (as best exemplified in the Enthusiasts), the greater the changes in attitudes to CRM and psychologically oriented training influencing actual behaviour.

How can an airline take into account such differences as seen, for example, between the Dynamics and the Cognitives? It is probably not feasible, nor financially viable, to devise entirely different units for the CRM training program, one extensively using lecture/video presentations, the other focussing on group interactivity. While such may satisfy these two groups, the application of one mode may have an adverse effect upon the Enthusiasts as it may be that the mix of methods across the units contributes to their general level of enthusiasm. An alternative way of attacking the problem could be to ensure that there is a mix of instructional methods in each unit (e.g. some lecture/video, some group activity), as long as the particular aim of the unit could be achieved through such mixed methods. A modification of this could be to have a common introduction to a unit with participants then following their preferred way of learning, through lectures and the like or group, team activities. (It would be informative to discuss with the Dynamics and Cognitives how the program methods might be modified to better suit their learning preferences.) A social psychological perspective would suggest having Enthusiasts in all groups undergoing training, their enthusiasm might "rub-off" on the others. However, all of these suggestions are tempered by the reality of training budgets within an organization and training sections must optimise learning within a variety of constraints. What may be educationally the best solution may not be possible and compromises will undoubtedly need to be made.

What of the Rejectors? Give them up as lost cases? We think not. If it is possible, we would argue that there may be some merit in following up such individuals with interviews and discussions in an attempt to locate the source of their discontent. Our data indicate that it is not in their initial attitudes, suggesting that the program itself contributed to their increasingly negative attitudes and general lack of enthusiasm to the program. What is it that turns them negatively? Can the program be changed to accommodate their concerns?

Before concluding we acknowledge the limitations of the work reported in this chapter. We used a sample of pilots from one airline and the results are clearly influenced by national culture as well as the organizational and training culture of that airline (see Telfer & Moore, 1995). Attitudes were measured with single questions leaving open the question of the reliability of the responses and we were not able to ascertain the relationships between cluster membership and actual operational performance. Nevertheless, we are confident that the findings will prove beneficial to those involved in designing, implementing and evaluating CRM type programs.

75

In conclusion, it is pleasing to find such a low number of rejectors of both methods and content of training in CRM/psychological training. The finding of groups similar to those identified by Schiewe (1995) suggests that CRM training methods and content do play a part in the ways that participants' perceive the relevance and utility of such training. Our findings, however, extend that work by showing that attitudinal change is greatest in the Enthusiasts, followed by the Dynamics and Cognitives to a lesser extent. Age, position, and fleet affiliation were not important in explaining cluster group membership, nor were initial attitudes, nor were previous experiences. What actually happened in the training program seems to have been the most significant force in producing change. Of course, there still remains the question of how such clusters perform in the simulator and aircraft. Do the Enthusiasts, for example, utilise CRM principles more effectively in the cockpit than others? Such questions are clearly worthy of pursuing as the answers to them will bring greater understanding of the relationships between training and ultimate operational performance.

Note: Full details of the analyses can be obtained from Schiewe. Dr Melissa Monfries is thanked for her comments on an earlier version of this chapter.

References

Biggs, J.B. & Moore, P.J. (1993). *The process of learning*. Sydney: Prentice Hall Australia.

Helmreich, R.L. (1993). Whither CRM? Directions in crew resource management training in the cockpit and elsewhere. In R.Jensen (Ed.). *Proceedings of the seventh international symposium on aviation psychology*. Pp 676-681. Columbus: Ohio University Press.

Helmreich, R.L. & Foushee, H.C. (1993). Why crew resource management? Empirical and theoretical bases of human factors training in aviation. In E.L.Weiner, B.G. Kanki & R.L. Helmreich (Eds.) *Cockpit resource management*. Pp 3-42. San Diego: Academic Press.

Helmreich, R.L. & Wilhelm, J.A. (1989) When training boomerangs: negative outcomes associated with cockpit resource management programs. In R.S. Jensen & D.Neumeister (Eds.). *Proceedings of the fifth symposium on aviation psychology* pp 692-697. Columbus: Ohio University Press.

Helmreich, R.L. & Wilhelm, J.A. (1991). Outcomes of crew resource management. *International Journal of Aviation Psychology*, 1, 287-300.

Maschke, P., Goeters, K.M., Hormann, H.J., & Schiewe, A. (1995). The development of the DLR/Lufthansa crew resource management training. In N.Johnston, R.Fuller & N.McDonald (Eds.). *Aviation psychology: Training and selection* pp 23-31. Aldershot: Ashgate.

Schiewe, A. (1995). On the acceptance of CRM methods by pilots: Results of a cluster analysis. In R.S.Jensen & L.A. Rakovan (Eds.). *Proceedings of the eighth international symposium on aviation psychology.* Pp 540-545. Columbus: Ohio University Press.

SPSS Inc. (1993). *SPSS for Windows, Professional statistics,* Release 6.0. Chicago Illinois.

Telfer, R.A. & Moore, P.J. (1995). Learning, instruction and organization in aviation. In R.S.Jensen & L.A. Rakovan (Eds.). *Proceedings of the eighth international symposium on aviation psychology* pp 1183-1188, Columbus: Ohio University Press.

Ward, J.H. (1993). Hierarchical groupings to optimize and objective function. *Journal of the American Statistical Association,* 58, 236-244.

Weiner, E.L., Kanki, B., & Helmreich, R.L. (1993). *Cockpit resource management.* New York: Academic Press.

6 Automation, flight management and pilot training: issues and considerations

Mustapha Mouloua, Richard D Gilson & Jefferson Koonce

The aviation industry has experienced a considerable level of automation control in the past twenty years. For almost any task, pilots, crew members, maintenance operators, air traffic controllers, as well as, other specialized personnel can now benefit from the use of automation. For pilots, automation has reduced the burden of excessive in-flight workload and resulted in fuel efficiency and enhanced all weather flying. However, such use of automation has also resulted in a number of behavioral problems related to flight management and systems safety. These problems include a loss of situational awareness (SA), monitoring inefficiency, increased mental workload, and sometimes, pilot's inability to effectively revert to manual control in cases of system breakdowns or malfunctions (Mouloua, Parasuraman, 1994; Parasuraman & Mouloua, 1996; Wiener, 1988; Wickens, 1994). Clearly, These pitfalls can be attributed to technology-centered "conventional" automation, in which the function between the pilot and automation remains fixed at all times. Understanding how pilots interact with automation in the cockpit is crucial for safety, pilot and system performances, as well as for system design. The present chapter describes some of the human factors issues associated with automation design and presents some considerations for future pilot training and system design.

Pilots' interaction with cockpit automation

Research on pilots' interaction with advanced automation has increased in recent years because of the need to ensure that new technology would not have a detrimental impact on pilot performance and safety. Even test pilots have had problems with automation, as exemplified by the recent Airbus

A330 crashed on June 30, 1994 while the crew were testing the effectiveness of the autopilot with an engine out. Such automation centered incidents have resulted in the loss of many crew members and others on board. Consequently, researchers as well as aircraft designers are now concerned with the outcome of such increased automation in the aviation industry. Although much has been written about the advanced flight deck (Norman, 1990; Billings, 1991; Wiener, 1993), little research has been devoted to pilot's understanding of and knowledge of such advanced "automated" flight deck, as well as the various mechanisms involved in pilot-automation interaction. Recently, pilots' attitudes towards automation have begun to be heard; however, they still remain far from being applied into training programs. McClumpha and James (1994) surveyed pilots' attitudes toward flying advanced technology aircraft. A total of 1372 UK registered pilots were compared to 982 International Air Transport Association (IATA) pilots on several specific advanced automation-related issues. Nine areas invloving design, reliability, flight management system (FMS), outputs/feedback, skills, training, crew interaction, workload, and overall impressions were surveyed. The results indicated that the factors that underlie the attitudes that pilots have towards automation appears to be stable and consistent across the two populations of pilots (UK and IATA). Pilots of advanced technology aircraft reported an inappropriate level of feedback from the automation. They also indicated that their understanding of the system is not necessarily improved with advanced technology flight decks. For perceived understanding of a system, these attitudes appear to be regulated by situational factors (i.e., pilot's hours on type and the aircraft level of automation). However, for crew coordination and trust, the pilots' responses were determined by experiential factors (i.e., pilot's total flying hours).

A subsequent large-scale study by Rudisill (1994) surveyed pilots operating thirteen types of commercial airplanes across five manufacturers (Airbus, Boeing, British aerospace, Lockheed, and McDonnell Douglas), and 57 air carriers/organizations were also surveyed. A total of 1,914 questionnaires were completed for analysis. The analyses involved factors related to: general observation with regard to flight deck automation, comments concerning the design of automated systems, crew understanding of automation and the crew interface, crew operations with automation, and personal factors affecting crew/automation interaction. The results indicated most pilots were positive about the technology; however, they also reported some critical concerns about the design of advanced flight decks. Many displays were noted as being not easy to use and adequate display symbology should incorporate some human factors aspects in order to ease the pilot-automation interaction. Several concerns with use of the FMS were also reported by the pilots. For example, too much head-down time may force the pilot out-of the loop because of preoccupation with the FMS or for reprogramming. Pilots were also concerned with the need of constantly monitoring what the automation is doing and felt distanced from the aircraft. Other concerns included higher levels of workload during abnormal situations as well as the negative effect of automation on cockpit management and crew communication sometimes. Pilots wished that a new approach to training should be developed in order to resolve some of the adverse effects of advanced automation.

A recent study by Gonos, Shilling, Deaton, Gilson, and Mouloua (1996) examined pilots' attitudes towards current alarm/alert display system technology, training methods employed for alarm/alert systems, and recommendations for future diagnostic systems. The results overwhelmingly indicated that the flight crews would prefer to be kept in the decision loop for responding to alarm/alerts especially in life threatening situations.

The results of these different studies clearly contribute to the definition of guidelines which may be used during design of training programs as well as design of future aircraft flight decks. Increased levels of automation may not be always the best viable option to help pilots cope with increased workload during different flight phases.

Human-automation monitoring

The human monitoring of advanced automated systems is generally poor (Parasuraman, 1987; Wiener, 1988). Several recent investigations also empirically demonstrated that human performance is not immune to "complacency" or what it is sometimes referred to also as "automation-induced monitoring inefficiency" (Parasuraman, Molloy, & Singh, 1993).

Following these serious human factors concerns associated with poor design encountered in "technology-centered" automation, another form of automation known as human-centered "adaptive" automation was proposed in the 1970s. Adaptive automation or adaptive aiding is a form of automation that is implemented dynamically in response to changing task demands on the pilot (Morrison & Gluckman, 1994; Rouse, 1988, 1994). Adaptive automation is known to be less susceptible to the behavioral problems associated with traditonal or "static" automation because it provides for maintenance of pilot situational awareness and other skills (for in depth discussion of these problems, see Rouse (1977); Mouloua & Parasuraman (1994); and Parasuraman & Mouloua (1996)).

Often, situation awareness is not acquired and may even be lost because of system malfunction or programming conflicts. The results are decisions without full information that may, at best, not address the difficulty, or worse may exacerbate the problem into life threatening situations. Several examples of the later are explored by Sarter and Woods (1994) in their study of automation-induced errors. The cry-wolf effect expectations also can interfere with rational analyses. For example, the anticipation of false alarms leads to non-compliance or to guessing outcomes (probability matching) without utilizing substantiating back up information (Bliss, Gilson, and Deaton, 1995). Likewise, anticipating automation sequences can lead to acceptance without verification based on incorrect assumptions.

Automation and pilots' training

It appears at this writing that the 1995 American Airlines B757 into a mountain in Cali, Columbia, occurred as a combined effect of loss of situation awareness and an unfamiliarity of reprogramming the flight management system which was coupled to the autopilot. An unanticipated Air Traffic Control request was followed without sufficient verification as to automation outcomes.

The new generation of aircraft will include an even increasing level of automation for routine in-flight operations. Air crews will be alerted to system [even situation] abnormalities through a growing number of alarms that may occur simultaneously or in hierarchies. Therefore, multiple alarms will add a higher workload and more confusion for untrained operators and may result in inappropriate responses and unnecessary aborted missions.

Current training procedures developed to respond to single alarms may be inadequate for the current generation of multiple system alarms found in sophisticated civilian and military aircraft. The proliferation of alarms has led to the increased likelihood of multiple alarm events and the consequent inability of the operator to determine the underlying cause of the alarms (Gilson, Deaton, and Mouloua, in press). Traditional procedure training alone cannot encompass all possible causes and combinations of such alarms. As a result, uncertainties detract from critical mission tasks, missions are unnecessarily aborted, or in the worst case, accidents resulting in the loss of life and equipment occur. In many cases, these "worst case" events would have been avoided with redesigned alarm systems and improved training.

Critical reviews of accidents, as well as post-incidents interviews have revealed that the current approach to the development of warning systems lacks direction. There appears to be inadequate indications and procedures to anticipate all contingencies and cope with problems before they lead to out-of-bounds conditions. In instances where many subsystems are co-dependent, critical events often lead into cascading or multiple alarms, such states could result in misdirected diagnosis which was unanticipated in the original design.

This state of affairs makes it even more difficult for the operator, at the worst possible time, to adequately identify and manage (respond) an emergency when faced with what may appear to be a plethora of unrelated alerts. In such situations it is crucial for the operator to diagnose the underlying cause(s) that produced the pattern of alarms, and not only the secondary or symptomatic indications.

Alerting systems notify operators, e.g., the pilot or flight crew, that a system abnormality has occurred (or is about to occur), prompting for corrective actions. Typically, sensors for alerts are placed at strategic locations for specific systems, such as engine, fuel, electrical, hydraulic, pressurization, etc., to allow monitoring of various parameters. When an upper (or lower) threshold boundary is exceeded an alert is displayed. New "intelligent" alerting systems now are triggered by trends or adaptively alter thresholds depending on historical data. Aircrews are highly trained to respond according to prescribed procedures set out in operating manuals available in paper or electronic form, but are less prepared for "soft/fuzzy" triggers.

Alerting systems are an issue in automation

System- versus procedural-based training

Traditional Manual training assumes that alerts are true and that procedures must be applied as published. Indeed, most pilot evaluation is largely dependent upon such an assumption. However, in the real world this can lead to false alarms remaining unverified and, if reactively responded to, can actually create problems not originally there. For example, according to The Aviation Consumer (1994), "... federally mandated emergency locators for aircraft have only 33% real alarm reliability [hit rate] and have an astounding 97% false alarm rate." This has caused the loss of between 23 and 58 lives each year for a 1990-1992 study period.

System-based versus knowledge-based training has certain merit but must be studied with caution before use. For example, the complexities of system analysis may overwhelm or delay aircrews during critical moments. On the other hand, novel or unexpected circumstances require a deeper analysis, and at times unusual procedures. Training selection criteria should depend on a balance among such issues as pilot experience, likelihood of occurrence, and time requirements to collect data for analysis, at the least.

Considerations for training

In the latest generation aircraft, the increased number of alerts and messages is not obvious to the viewer. Although the actual number of displays has declined with the application of multi-function CRTs in the "glass" cockpit, the amount of information has increased via software hierarchies, thereby resulting in multiple alerts and at times cause confusion. The following points should be considered in order to ensure optimal performance:
* Prioritize sufficient system knowledge like alerts
* Teach verification techniques for alerts
* Train with unusual "what if" scenarios to expand understanding
* Provide time available to consider alternate options before a response is required
* Develop risk analysis techniques based on overall situation factors and goals

Considerations for systems design

Records of aircraft accidents/incidents, as well as behavioral studies, have shown that even highly trained operators exhibit a variety of human errors in responding to alerts, e.g., delays, outright failure to respond, responding to false alarms, confusion with multiple alarms, etc. For example, Goldstein (1981) reported that "operators on the scene of Three Mile Island complained that the growth [in the number of alarms] prevented them from obtaining good information concerning initial, primal conditions that led to other, secondary failures." Appropriate design recommendations should be taken into account to facilitate a better interaction with the technology. The following design

recommendations should be considerations for pilot-automation interfaces:
* Consider suppression of alarms, when responses would be inappropriate
* Restrict normally displayed information based on needs
* Provide options to obtain processed or raw data
* Provide expert system recommendations for responses in life threatening situations
* Create designs that cluster or sequence information to naturally facilitate appropriate response(s)
* Consider the use of automation to take over when human response is unlikely

Conclusions

A new era of automated systems and alerts demands a re-evaluation of design and training techniques. Subtilities of interactions must be considered by the research, training, and operational communities to appreciably reduce the already low accident rates. A "clean slate" approval may be necessary, given the progressive shift from manual control emphasizing rapid and accurate responding to supervisory control emphasizing judgement and decision making. Tailored training to new designs should reduce the high percentage of human error prevalent in aircraft accidents.

Acknowledgments

This research was supported in part by Contracts Nos. 11-72-318 and 11-72-318 from Navy, ONR, NAWC/TSD. The views presented in this in this article are those of the authors and do not necessarily represent the views of the Navy. We thank Tonya Lewis for her technical assistance.

References

Billings, C.E. (1991). Toward a human-centered aircraft automation philosophy. The *International Journal of Aviation Psychology, 1*, 261-270.

Bliss, J.P., Gilson, R.D., & Deaton, J.E. (1995). human probability matching behavior in response to alarms of varying reliability. *Ergonomics, 38*,(11), 2300-2312.

Gilson, R.D., Deaton, J.E., & Mouloua, M. (in press). Development of training strategies for alarm diagnosis in the cockpit. *Ergonomics in Design.*

Goldstein, L.P. (1981). Discriminative display support for process operators. In J. Rasmussen & W.B. Rouse (Eds.), *Human detection and diagnosis of system failures.* New York: Plenum Press.

Gonos, G.H., Shilling, R.D., Deaton, J.E., Gilson, R.D., & Mouloua, M. (1996). Cockpit alarm diagnostics and management systems: current status and future needs. *Special Report 96-001. Naval Air Warfare Center Training Systems Division,* Orlando, Florida.

McClumpha, A., & James, M. (1994). Understanding Automated Aircraft. In M. Mouloua & R. Parasuraman (Eds.). *Human performance in automated systems: Current research and trends.* Hillsdale, NJ: Earlbaum.

Mouloua, M., & Parasuraman, R. (1994). *Human performance in automated systems: Current research and trends.* Hillsdale, NJ: Earlbaum.

Norman, D. (1990). Commentary: Human error and the design of computer systems *Communications of the ACM,* 33(1), 4-7.

Parasuraman, R., Molloy, R., & Singh, I.L. (1993). Performance consequences of automation-induced "complacency". *The International Journal of Aviation Psychology,* 3, 1-23.

Parasuraman, R., & Mouloua, M. (1996). *Automation and Human Performance: Theory and Applications.* Hillsdale, NJ: Erlbaum Associates.

Parasuraman, R. (1987). Human-Computer monitoring. *Human Factors, 29,* 695-706.

Rouse, W.B. (1977). Human-computer interaction in multi-task situation *IEEE Transactions on Systems, Man, and Cybernetics.* SMC-7(5), 384-392.

Rudisill, M. (1994). Flight Crew Experience with Automation Technologies on Commercial Transport Flight Decks. In M. Mouloua & R. Parasuraman (Eds.). *Human performance in automated systems: Current research and trends.* Hillsdale, NJ: Earlbaum.

Sarter, N.B., & Woods, D.D. (1994). Pilot interaction with cockpit automation II: An experimental study of pilots' model and awareness of the flight management system. The *International Journal of Aviation Psychology,* 4(1), 1-28.

Wickens, C.D. (1994). *Designing for situation awareness and trust in automation.* Paper presented at the IFAC conference on Intergrated Systems Engineering. Baden-Baden, Germany. September 27-29, 1994.

Wiener, E.L. (1988). Cockpit automation. In E.L. Wiener & D.C Nagel (Eds.) *Human factors in aviation.* San Diego: Academic Press.

Wiener, E.L. (1993). Life in the second decade of the glass cockpit. In R.S. Jenson & D. Neumeister (Eds.), *Proceedings of the Seventh International Symposium on Aviation Psychology* (pp.1-11). Columbus, OH: Department of Aviation, The Ohio State University.

7 Learning for new technologies

Phillip J Moore and Ross A Telfer

Introduction

One of the inevitabilities for pilots in commercial aviation in the 1990's and beyond is that they will need to become competent in the efficient and effective use of a range of ever increasingly complex technologies. In the case of automation of systems, the machinery is allocated functions that would otherwise be assigned to humans. New technologies have emerged, for example, in training with computer based training and full motion simulators, on the flight deck (the glass cockpit) and in the very way in which flights are managed, as with the use of datalink. Indeed, it could be argued that for the majority of pilots undergoing conversion training, grappling with "new" technologies plays a substantial role in both line operations and training. The level of difficulty is commensurate with the novelty of the technology.

In this chapter we address the complexities of these issues and provide a glimpse of how experienced pilots tackle the problems of learning about and using new technologies.

Glass cockpit

Much has been written about the introduction, benefits and problems of glass cockpits "The what's it doing now" phenomenon (e.g. Rudisill, 1994). Indeed, work by Billings (1991) and more recently Jorna (1996) highlights the ways in which pilots have become increasingly distant from the operation of the aircraft. Figure 7.1 below, adapted from Billings (1991) by Jorna (1996), shows how 60 or so years ago the aircraft was controlled by the pilot through controls. However, by the mid 1990s between pilot and aircraft there are data link, flight management systems, flight mode, autopilot then control.

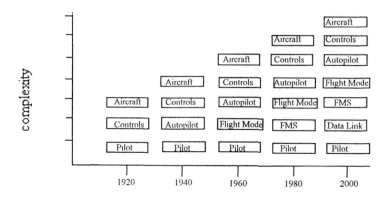

Figure 7.1   Trends in distancing pilot from aircraft operations (Jorna, 1996)

Recent work by Funk, Lyall and Riley (1995) systematically, and comprehensively synthesises much of the available literature regarding human factors problems of flightdeck automation. A few details will demonstrate the thoroughness of their approach. They identified over 400 documents (e.g. journals, technical reports, newspaper articles) related to flightdeck automation problems and reviewed 13 accident reports in which automation was a likely contributing factor. In addition, some 590 reports of incidents (from Aviation Safety Reporting System-ASRS) were analysed as were 128 questionnaires completed by "experts" (e.g. pilots, ATCs, aviation psychologists). From these data Funk et al developed a taxonomy of perceived problems and concerns related to flightdeck automation. In brief, concerns about automation issues such as capabilities, failure, authority, complexity, and standardisation accounted for nearly 40 percent of the concerns, with 50 percent of the citations showing concerns for the pilot (e.g. role changing, understanding, attention, workload, situational awareness). The remaining concerns were for crew co-ordination and training.

McClumpha and James (1994) also examined pilots' attitudes towards automation and flying advanced technology aircraft. Using questionnaire data from both UK and IATA pilots, McClumpha and James were able to identify seven factors:
* Workload and task efficiency;
* Form and content of the displays;
* Handling skills and airmanship;
* Reactions to problems;
* Feedback;

* Trust/co-ordination; and
* Understanding.

Interestingly, the researchers highlighted the pivotal role that the last four factors (those related to aspects of pilots' understanding) play in pilots' concerns about automation. In other words, flying advanced technology aircraft affects the form and content of a pilot's understanding of the system. Age also was shown to be an important variable with younger pilots reporting better understanding of error messages than older pilots. At the level of actual cockpit operation, Mosier, Skitka, Heers and Burdik (1996), showed that the patterns of use of automation may not be as designers may have anticipated, pilots may become over reliant on the system and not use the facility to aid decision making. Quite clearly then the introduction of new technologies impacts upon a wide variety of factors, many of them implicating learning and of course, training.

Training

In contrast to the pyramidal progression in the development of technology as shown above, instructional methods and media have maintained a core of tradition approaches, supplemented by options made available from hardware. This view is conveyed in Figure 7.2.

The distractor in current training for new technologies is that it could be claimed, on the basis of pass rates, that the system works. In input/output terms this is apparent. Our point is that the system works primarily because of the efforts, experience, application, strategies and organization of the trainees. An extreme view is that they may succeed in spite of the training system. With an appropriate instructional design, learning for new technologies can be enhanced to the extent that there are new benefits for aviation organizations. These benefits would be mainly in the affective domain of learning, one that is costly for airlines to induce. Consider, for example, attitudes such as pride in their company's professionalism, increased morale, attitudes towards their employer and the new technology; the messages they will be conveying to their peers, and so on.

Why has not aviation instruction kept pace with commensurate changes in technology? The reasons are so many and so interrelated that it is a wonder that any change has occurred. First, this is a highly specialised industry in which increasing degrees of sophistication depend upon a traditional set of skills and knowledge: provided by ab initio for pilots, for example. Then there is almost a guild system of development through aircraft types with increasing technical demands and degrees of professional responsibility. This works. There is an attrition rate, it is not all that efficient, but what comes out in the end meets the industry's needs.

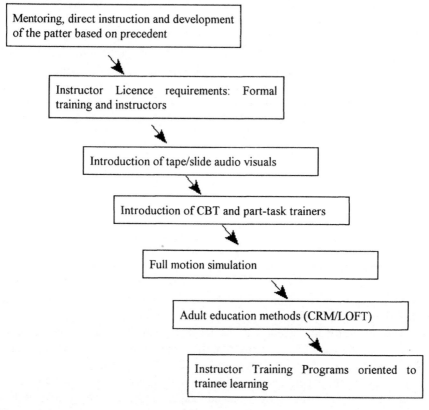

Figure 7.2 Instructional developments

In order to adopt any other approach to pilot training means that you need to stop doing this. There are two costs here. One is involved in taking people off the usual production line (which will continue working if you just leave it alone); the other is the risk that something new may not work as well even though it will inevitably be costing more. Finally, the introduction of new methods means that existing expertise is redundant. This is not pleasing for either management or experienced instructors.

The spread of CRM extended the range of methods in the industry, especially those appropriate to adult education. Discussion groups and role plays supplemented lecture presentations and tended to replace chalk and talk; the range and extent of instructional videotapes were boosted. Participants were recognised as motivated, experienced individuals who had something to offer. They were active: no longer passive recipients of facts, figures and skills.

Attitudes and values became important, too.

In a subtle twist, the teaching and testing of attitudes became important, for the changes being sought by CRM were primarily in the affective domain of learning. The traditional instructional patter incorporated airmanship and judgement: but integrated in the skills and knowledge of practical flight. How could such matters be taught as topics in themselves? As it had been forced in the initial development of CRM, the industry searched for answers in both education and industry. New norms were established for instructors as facilitators and presenters.

Computer-based training (CBT) and computer-based flight training devices, such as Koonce, Moore and Benton's (1995) Basic Flight Instruction Tutoring System (BFITS) have recently made an impact on training. For example, Lufthansa's Integrated Type-Rating for conversions to new generation aircraft (see Buehle, 1995) comprehensively uses CBT in an interactive way for understanding of flight management systems. Their five phase training program uses CBT in the early stages but for Phases 4 and 5 (LOFT oriented), CBT is no longer used. Indeed, pilots seem to appreciate CBT but not to the exclusion of human input (Moore, Farquharson & Telfer, in press; Walley, 1995). Perhaps the instructional message is not to get carried away with instructional technology.

The Basic Flight Instruction Tutoring System (BFITS) is a computer-based approach to teaching ab initio pilots to fly (Koonce, Moore & Benton, 1995). BFITS teaches manoeuvres by questioning, demonstrating, and then having the student actually perform the manoeuvre on the computer. Throughout, feedback is given and if operational tolerances are exceeded during performance, BFITS provides hints to the student on how to rectify the problem. Upon completion of any manoeuvre, the system then informs the student of their competence. A play-back facility allows the student to review their performance and BFITS points out where the tolerances were exceeded. An initial examination of BFITS by Koonce et al indicated reduced time to solo for those undertaking BFITS when compared to more traditional training methods.

However, the perception pilots have of their training, particularly conversion training, is not all rosy. There are many quality things going on, but there is room for improvement. Walley's (1995) thorough analysis of UK pilots demonstrates a real concern for the depth of knowledge that pilots feel they have about systems and how they interact. She suggests that the treatment of abnormal systems operation in isolation ignores the fact that on occasion there may be a complex interaction among a number of malfunctioning systems. In a similar way, the UK pilots saw insufficient time being allocated to training which exacerbated their problems of depth of knowledge. Hands-on-practice also emerged as a major concern with many pilots arguing for greater time to practice, even if not in actual flight conditions.

Recent work by Moore, Farquharson and Telfer (in press) and Telfer, Moore and Farquharson (in press) reinforces Walley's findings. Their pilots were undertaking conversion training for state-of-the-art glass cockpit aircraft. Positive aspects of the training included the integration of simulator and ground school, the opportunity for self-pacing on the video and computer based instruction system, the relatively large amount of time allocated to simulator training, comprehensive documentation and the positive role of the instructors. However, overall time allocation ("unnecessarily time-compressed"), level of knowledge ("computer-based training and audio-visual approach" taught "how to pass the test rather than anything of substance"), and the need for more human interaction through chalk and talk, seminars, tutorials and end-of-day question and answer sessions were seen as issues requiring attention. Consistent with Walley was the perceived need for more time to practice on flight management computers ("A stand alone FMC be provided for individual practice").

There are complexities in learning for new technologies in aviation

Pilots and their learning

How do pilots go about their learning when confronted with new technologies? Of course there are many individual differences in the ways in which pilots go about their learning but over the years we have been able to identify a number of motivational and strategic ways in which pilots ensure success (e.g. Moore, Farquharson & Telfer, in press; Moore, 1995; Telfer, Moore & Farquharson, in press; Telfer & Moore, 1993). At a general level, it appears that there is a strong need to understand whilst also realising that rote type learning can be useful on some occasions. A combination of will and skill is required prior to learning, during learning, and after learning. Self-regulation, especially understanding that learning may not be proceeding as expected, seems to be critical.

Prior to learning

Having a positive attitude to begin with is very important to set the scene for quality learning: "Setting a high standard" for oneself and being willing to "work hard". Setting goals, organising how time will be allocated to the different components of the training program and establishing a dedicated study space are seen as important for success. Prioritizing and allocating attention to key elements help reduce demands. Indeed, some pilots examine the whole conversion course to identify where the most difficult sections are, then organize their studying to stay ahead, " ...my colleague and I re-organised the course structure to fit ourselves. We looked at the time that would be needed to learn each of the topics and figured that the last section on the 'glass cockpit' would be hectic, so we stayed ahead of the class presentations".
Others like to "...allocate time to look at and follow-up tangents". For each exercise undertaken, it is vital to know the aim of the exercise so all effort can be targeted in that direction. Seeking advice from colleagues who have been through the course before can be helpful as it sets up expectations about learning and may alert the learner to possible areas of difficulty and the ways in which the colleague handled such difficulties. One pilot commented, " ...pick the brains of previous courses to see what are the goals of the course and then put in priority the aspects to be studied versus the time available...".

During learning

As would be expected, there are many strategies that successful pilots employ in actual learning. Taking notes is common, often transferring important information onto cards or small notebooks that they then use for self-checking. These notes include diagrams, charts and other visuals to help them understand the information. Others link the new information with their prior knowledge to see how the new system is different from the ones they have been used to, " I compare the old with the new and work on the changes". Reading and rereading are dominant strategies with key information being focussed upon and noted. The powers of mental imagery and rehearsal are recognized, with visualising how things work and mentally rehearsing scenarios. Some pilots like to sit in the simulator, when it is not in operation, to check their levels of understanding in the "real" context rather than in a study room. They realize that learning is very much contextually bound. Mixing ground school and simulator training seems to be appreciated, the links between theory and practice can be amply demonstrated.

Pilots also recognize the usefulness of overlearning in areas such as checklists and memory items so that recall occurs almost instantaneously and automatically, particularly in times of stress. Recognition of overloading is also prevalent, " I break the day into half-hour lots, sometimes taking a novel for an hour to give me a rest - stops overloading". Related to this is self-pacing and self questioning ensuring that learning is progressing as planned and that the appropriate level of understanding is being achieved. If it is not then "fix-up" strategies are used such as discussing with fellow crew (even over a beer!) and questioning instructors. Indeed, it is quite common for pilots to talk of co-operative and collaborative learning in conversion training. The opportunity to "play" with flight management systems and other complex technologies found in cockpits is very much appreciated. Having the chance to see "what happens if..." in a simulated situation not only provides motivation but also has the potential to enhance understanding of how the system operates.

After learning

The end of a training course is not the end of learning. Self-evaluation of how one has gone on a course is important, particularly when matched up against the course goals and individual goals and plans. Useful questions include, Have I achieved what I set out to achieve? Could I have used better strategies in parts of the course? What would I do differently if I were to do this course again? What did I do to ensure that I succeeded? Could I have used the resources more effectively? Discussion with fellow course participants on their learning motives and strategies might give an expanded view on ways in which changes could be made.

Finally, if there is a course evaluation conducted by the training personnel, make comments constructive so that the designers and implementers of the program can see the strengths and weaknesses of their endeavours.

Concluding comments

In this chapter we have attempted to show the complexities of learning for new technologies in aviation. In the initial section of the chapter we illustrated how there was an ever-increasing distance between the pilot and the actual aircraft and that changes in training had not necessarily kept pace with the relatively rapid changes to automated systems. A brief look at the literature on training for automated systems showed many positive points but also highlighted several areas of concern, especially the need for human input to be combined with the more technologically instructive systems such as CBT. The chapter concluded by looking at ways in which successful pilots approach training for technologically more advanced aircraft.

References

Billings, C. (1991). Towards a human-centred aircraft automation philosophy. *International Journal of Aviation Psychology*, 1, 261-270.

Buehle, E.H. (1995). The integrated type-rating. In Johnston, N., Fuller, R. & & McDonald, N. (Eds.). *Aviation psychology: Training and selection.*pp298-301. Aldershot: Avebury Aviation.

Funk, K., Lyall, B., & Riley, V. (1995). *Perceived human factors problems of flightdeck automation. Corvallis.* Oregan State University.

Jorna, P.G.A.M. (1996). Cockpit automation: The challenge for enhanced human performance. Paper presented at the Second Automation and Human Performance Conference, Cocoa Beach Florida, March.

Koonce, J.M., Moore, S.L., & Benton, C. J. (1995). Initial validation of a basic flight instruction tutoring system (BFITS). In Jensen, R., & Rakovan, L. (Eds.). *Proceedings of the Eighth International Symposium on Aviation Psychology*, pp 1037-1040.

McClumpha, A., & James, M. (1994). Understanding automated aircraft. In Mouloua, M & Parasuraman, R. (Eds.). *Human performance in automated systems: Current research and trends.* Hillsdale: Erlbaum.

Moore, P.J. (1995). Across airline differences in pilot learning: The roles of experience and qualifications. In Johnston, N., Fuller, R., & McDonald, N. (Eds.). *Aviation psychology: Training and selection* pp 302-307. Aldershot: Avebury Aviation.

Moore, P.J., Farquharson, T., & Telfer, R.A. (In press). Automation and human performance in airline pilot training. In Mouloua, M. (ed). *Human-*

automation interaction: *Research and practice.* Hillsdale: Erlbaum.

Mosier, K. L., Skitka, L.J., Heers, S., & Burdick, M. (1996). Patterns in the use of cockpit automation. Paper presented at the Second Automation and Human Performance Conference, Cocoa Beach, Florida, March.

Rudisill, M. (1994). Flight crew experience with automated technologies on commercial   transport flight decks. In Mouloua, M. and Parasuraman, R. (Eds.).*Human performance in automated systems: Current research and trends.*pp203-211. Hillsdale: Erlbaum.

Telfer, R.A., Moore, P.J. & Farquharson, T. (In press). Pilot learning and conversion training. In Hayward, B. & Lowe, A. (Eds.).*Applied aviation psychology:Achievement, change and challenge.* Aldershot: Avebury Aviation.

Telfer, R.A. & Moore, P.J. (1993). The role of rote learning for experienced pilots. Paper presented at the Aviation Human Factors Symposium, New Zealand Psychological Society's Conference, Wellington, April.

Walley, S. (1995). Conversion training for commercial pilots. In Johnston, N., Fuller, R., & McDonald, N. (Eds.). *Aviation psychology: Training and selection* pp 324-329. Aldershot: Avebury Aviation.

8 The flight crew member's responsibility and role in aviation training

Brett Gebers

"The social consequences of operational failure in Aviation, for whatever reason, are sufficiently grave to demand the level and type of professionalism that can be afforded by higher education" (Pippin 1993).

Introduction

The airline industry has become a very competitive business with cost control and increased productivity becoming more and more important. It is logical therefore that airline training should be scrutinised to see if it can be done more cost effectively whilst retaining standards that satisfy the regulatory authorities and the insurers. Airlines spend a fortune on initial type qualification and recurrent training annually. Yet very few, if any, airlines really explain what is required of their trainees during their training.

Vast amounts of money have been spent by the airlines, manufactures and regulatory authorities on Crew Resource Management (CRM), aircraft design, improved engines and ergonomics. Surprisingly little has been spent on researching and teaching aircrew members how to learn this material effectively. Flight crew have usually been left to their own devices in terms of how to study and learn whilst attending ground school and simulator courses. With airlines becoming more cost conscious, flight crew and airline training departments will have to ensure that the desired learning is achieved in what is almost inevitably going to result in less and less time in the simulator and classroom. This places a heavy burden on the flight crew member to make the best use of the facilities and time available.

This chapter is not intended to be a highly technical or academic discussion of airline training problems but rather to offer some practical guidelines as to how crew members falling primarily into the following categories can achieve

the best from the training courses they attend.
  * Initial type qualification (conversion) onto first airliner.
  * Initial command.
  * Type rating qualification (conversion) for Captain, First Officer and Flight Engineer.
  * Recurrent training at pre-determined intervals.
  * Requalification training following illness or layoffs.

First, however, let us consider the learning process, memory, and psycho-motor skills.

The learning process

The learning process may be described as "the acquisition of skills or information through interaction with the environment" (Biggs & Moore, 1993, p. 527). There are a number of facets to the process of learning:
  * Meaningful learning is much easier if it takes place in context.
  * Voluntary learning requires that the trainee is motivated.
  * There are different approaches to learning.
  * All the senses are used in the gaining of knowledge with visual and auditory senses playing major roles.
  * Actual learning is achieved through experience which requires that the trainee expend energy.

Learning in context

Learning something within the context of its use is much easier than learning something out of context. For example, learning the meaning of the word 'aileron' makes far more sense to a trainee when he or she is shown a picture of it, than reading the definition from a glossary of terms. If the trainee is taken to an aircraft and shown the aileron it makes even more sense. When the trainee is later taken for a flight and shown the effect of aileron application it is highly likely that meaningful learning will have taken place. An experienced crew member transitioning to a new type will have much less trouble putting things into context, because of his or her greater knowledge and experience, than a new crew member converting onto his or her first airliner.

Motivation

The old story of 'you can take a horse to water, but you can't make it drink' is just as true with learning. An unmotivated trainee is less likely to learn what is required or will not remember what was learned for any length of time. A trainee about to embark upon an initial type qualification course is likely to be highly motivated as in most instances the training is a step forward in a crew member's career. The same crew member is more likely to be less motivated when doing recurrent training as he or she will have 'seen it all before' and may well regard it as a drag. During any course there are bound to be times when enthusiasm flags a little and it is essential that whoever notices this takes positive steps to regenerate or revitalise the motivation. Maintaining a positive outlook is vital to the success of any training course.

The different approaches to learning

There are three basic approaches to learning as described by Biggs (1987) during extensive research at high schools and universities. These approaches are classified as Surface, Deep and Achieving. Surface learners are generally motivated to achieve the minimum course requirements. They achieve their aims through rote learning and only learn the bare minimum. Deep learners make a real effort to understand what they are learning. The learners who follow an Achieving type approach are highly motivated people who work really hard to achieve high grades and who enjoy the thrill of being top student or at least being better than average. Moore and Telfer (1990) carried out a study which showed that ab initio pilots who were inclined towards Deep learning flew solo earlier than those who were less inclined towards Deep learning.

Knowledge and the senses

Of all the knowledge that we are likely to acquire in life, sight and hearing play the most important roles. This explains why audio visual aids are so popular in the teaching environment. The more of our five senses that we can use during the learning process the easier and the more meaningful our learning will be.

Quality learning requires the expenditure of energy

On-the-job learning or trial-and-error practices are not an option for the aircrew member. Learning and education in the aviation industry is a serious business and for good learning to take place energy and mental effort must be expended

(Biggs & Moore, 1993). The more effort the learner puts into the learning process the better he or she is likely to learn what is required. It is important to remember that the learning is accomplished by the trainee and not the instructor. This makes it essential that the student is an active participant in the process of learning (Hawkins & Orlady, 1993).

Memory

Memory can be divided into 3 different sections: sensory registers, working or short term memory, and Long term memory.

The sensory registers

The sensory registers are the parts of the brain that take note of the inputs or physical stimuli from the senses. Such information is only held for very short periods (1 to 5 seconds) and if not moved into working memory, will be lost.

The working or short term memory

Inputs to the working memory from the sensory register are affected by factors such as expectation, and stress. These inputs are taken into the working memory where they are worked on or discarded. The capacity of the working memory is limited to between 5 and 7 items at any time. The quality of the items placed in the working memory is important because it can only hold 7 items of information. The working memory could hold 7 individual numbers or 7 chunks of information. Think of how you chunk telephone numbers to remember them. All this means that in any learning, simple facts or bits of information need to be combined to form chunks so that valuable working memory is not wasted.

A more practical example of this is learning to fly on instruments. When a pilot first starts learning to fly on instruments the first few lessons are rather hectic and he or she, like most student pilots, wonders how they are ever going to learn to keep the aircraft on an even keel, track to a beacon or listen to and respond to radio calls. After a few more lessons it becomes apparent that it will be possible to do all of this. Part of the reason is the development of the pilot's psychomotor skills and the other is that the chunking of information has occurred. During the first few lessons the inputs acquired through looking at the instruments had to be interpreted and combined according to established procedures on a one by one basis before the required action was taken. This saturated the working memory. As the pilot becomes more proficient he or she starts to combine or chunk the individual procedures and stores them in the long term memory where it is readily accessed. It is worth noting that in the late 1980s the Royal Airforce found that their trainees failed their flying training courses primarily because of insufficient spare mental capacity when subjected to a high workload, a lack of awareness, slow thinking and poor retention of instruction (Smallwood & Fraser, 1995).

The long term memory

This is the part of the memory where information is stored for later use. If something is to be remembered, effort must be expended to ensure that the desired information in the working memory is coded and stored in the long term memory for later recall. The process of coding attaches long term understanding and meaning to information, connections are thus made between old and new information. Of course, the better these connections, the more likely the information will be recalled when required latter.

Psychomotor skills

The psychomotor skills are those skills used when driving a car or playing sport. With enough practice it becomes possible to carry out these actions without thinking about them. This of course frees working memory which can be used for other purposes such as carrying out a conversation whilst driving a car.

Now let us turn to flying training, in particular traditional and contemporary training.

Traditional flying training

Traditional flying training focused on general aeronautical knowledge such as meteorology, flying skills, procedures and regulations. When the Wright brothers made their first flight the emphasis was very clearly on psychomotor skills and little in the way of management. Flying a modern airliner clearly still requires psychomotor skills but these skills form a much smaller proportion of the total knowledge and management skills required of today's pilot.

The training courses of the past required that the crew had to attend ground school for a few weeks where the instructor explained the intricacies of the innards of the aircraft to the trainees using a blackboard. The trainees then wrote examinations on the systems and limitations. This was followed by training in simulators or in some instances in the aircraft. The final checkout was sometimes carried out in the aircraft due to the poor simulator fidelity which prevailed at the time. No one really knew any better and cost was not a big issue. Training has changed vastly over the last 25 years.

One may argue that there are many old technology aircraft still in operation and that following traditional training courses on these aircraft is still acceptable. The counter argument is that these old aircraft now operate in a far more sophisticated environment and that new training methods are required to ensure that the crew are able to cope in this environment. Another point is that in order to remain competitive, training costs and training times have to be trimmed. This places a rather heavy burden on the crew member.

Contemporary flying training

In modern day training centres very little use is made of instructors and the chalk and talk method of teaching the aircraft systems. Audio visual systems and interactive computer based training systems (CBT) are used extensively. This phase is usually integrated with fixed base trainers or part task trainers ultimately leading up to a number of sessions in full flight simulators. The final proficiency check is done in the simulator and in many instances the trainee's first flight in the aircraft is a revenue flight under the watchful eye of a training captain.

The new way of training is not without its problems. A number of surveys conducted amongst pilots indicate that however great the CBT systems are they cannot ever replace the instructor. Some crew members still want some interaction with the instructor and as a result some learning centres favour a mix of instructor leading the lesson and CBT being used to reinforce what has been learned. A survey done amongst BALPA pilots in 1992 indicated that too much emphasis was being placed on teaching pilots only what they needed to know (Walley, 1994). This was felt by the majority to leave them with insufficient system knowledge and was perceived to be the biggest threat to them doing their job well.

The use of part task trainers and computer based instruction can be a big advantage to a pilot learning how to use Auto Flight and Flight Management Systems (FMS) as it provides an opportunity for hands on practice. Another advantage of the new system is that it is usually 'self pacing'. This allows slow learners to learn the correct techniques on devices such as a FMS and then practice until they are comfortable with their ability to use the system. This may be particularly valuable to older crew members converting onto the new 'glass cockpit' aeroplanes.

Preparation for the training home environment

With a type rating qualification or other training course drawing near it is essential for the crew member to try and tidy up any loose ends in his or her private life so as to be able to concentrate on the training course. It is advisable that during all training courses the crew member should try to ensure that he or she has as few distractions as possible. The support of family members is important.

Mental preparation

Trainees must prepare themselves mentally for the course ahead. This preparation should include:
* ensuring a positive outlook on life
* understanding what he or she wants from this course
* setting realistic goals in terms of standards to aim for
* knowing what his or her weaknesses are and where possible how to compensate for them
* putting all prejudices aside
* adopting a mentor

If a negative attitude is allowed to prevail during the course, the crew member is likely to become highly stressed and this will rub off onto those around him or her. This inevitably impacts negatively on the learning process. Think back to the more pleasurable moments in life. It is doubtful if they happened in the presence of negative people. These training courses require a lot of work and ought to be made as pleasant as possible. Create a positive environment by talking positively.

Part of the process of motivation is the setting of realistic achievable goals. It is important for the crew member to know what he or she expects from the course ahead as it helps in setting realistic goals. The crew member should know the minimum standard required and whether it is acceptable to achieve this standard or should he or she aim higher? Aiming too low is a risky business because nervousness in a test inevitably impacts negatively upon performance. If goals have been set it is possible to evaluate one's performance in respect of those goals during the course and to modify one's strategy to ensure that the goals are going to be achieved.

We all have weaknesses of some kind or another and it is essential that we face up to them and learn how to compensate for them as far as possible. An example of a shortcoming is that one may be easily distracted, making it difficult to study. Facing up to this and admitting that one is easily distracted may make it easier to resist the temptation to go and do something else. It sometimes helps to set oneself a task to study for say two hours and then allow a reward of 30 minutes of watching television (a big distraction) for example.

Prejudices can affect the learning environment and one has to be very careful not to allow them to get in the way. For example one may dislike the way that someone in the class dresses or the fact that he or she may be of a different culture. One may also be prejudiced by statements such as "He is an appalling lecturer" and so make one less receptive to what may be good information. Dislikes or prejudices in cases like this can very easily detract from the learning that should be taking place.

A trainee, particularly a beginner, who forms a mentor relationship with an older, more experienced crew member can find a useful source of information on how to handle the various aspects of undergoing aviation training.

Physical preparation

It is essential that the trainee has sufficient rest during and prior to commencing the course. Fatigue influences many aspects of learning such as concentration, attention span, motivation and patience. Being physically fit is also a great way of minimizing the effects of stress. The trainee must make time for leisure activities during the course. A study amongst some volunteers proved that depriving people of leisure activities resulted in them feeling tired, unreasonable and showed them to be less creative (Edwards, 1990). Every effort should be made to follow a balanced diet whilst attending the ground school and simulator course.

Next, the focus is on ground school.

Ground school

The ground school phase of any type rating course is often seen as a drag and as a necessary evil. There are many reasons for this which include:
* uninteresting material
* poor presentation
* too much time or insufficient time allowed
* lack of relevance or integration with the succeeding phases on the fixed base trainer or simulator

This phase of the training is essential and it can be made interesting. Unfortunately the technical manuals provided for the course are often not written in an easy to understand style. CBT and good ground instructors can make this material come alive. Failing that, the trainees themselves can form small groups and work on trying to make the material more interesting by asking each other questions, by redrawing the diagrams and playing 'what if type games.' For example what would happen if one was dispatched with a fuel pump unserviceable and another one were to fail during the flight? Asking this type of question can take what initially appears to be a dry piece of text and make it really interesting whilst achieving depth of understanding. Learning is far more effective and easier if it can be done by doing something rather than watching or listening to someone. The trainee should not hesitate to make his or her own notes. Photo-copying someone else's notes is not conducive to effective long term learning because little or no effort will have been expended on making these notes. To be really effective your notes should combine the information from all the reference material and the instructor into your own structure and format. Some people find that using mind maps is a very effective way of learning new and revising old material (e.g. Bunzan & Bunzan, 1990).

If a ground school course is allowed to drag out for too long the trainees are likely to start becoming demotivated particularly if they are not kept mentally stimulated. It is more usual to allow barely sufficient time for the ground school course. This unfortunately puts the trainees under pressure to keep up with the material and does not encourage deep or achiever type learning. As a trainee it is important to recognise this and to ensure that the material is adequately revised later on when more time is available.

The problem of apparent lack of relevance or integration of material with the preceding and succeeding phases of training is a difficult one for the trainee to solve. Once again playing 'what if type games may be useful in trying to tie seemingly irrelevant detail into the systems or procedures which are being studied. Forming discussion groups or talking to other crew members currently operating the same equipment may also be useful. The use of fixed base training devices can provide the required stimulus in trying to integrate what has been learned with the more practical training to come. Taking a jumpseat ride if allowed by the airline or operator can be a great help in coping with these problems as it may be possible to ask experienced crew members to explain the relevance of learning certain material. In order for a jump seat ride to be productive it is essential that the trainee compiles a list of questions to be answered prior to travelling.

The simulator

The realism achieved in full flight simulators has developed over the last 30 years to a point where zero flight time training is possible. Very little airline training will be done on the actual aircraft in future because of the cost and the dangers associated with trying to simulate emergencies. Simulators are excellent training tools but there are a number of problems that a trainee may encounter during his or her simulator training. These include:

* inter personal conflict with the other trainee or trainees in the simulator;
* conflict with the simulator instructor;
* learning plateau;
* over controlling or pilot induced oscillation.

There are several potential barriers to learning in a simulator

Not all people get along well together and occasionally inter personal conflict develops. It sometimes happens that as the course progresses and the trainee's stress levels rise, so people become impatient and start to snap at each other. This is normal and not something about which one should unduly worry. One way of sorting out the conflict whilst in the simulator is to keep the conversation on an 'Adult to Adult' level and to focus on what is right and not who is right or wrong. The focus should be on the task, not the person. Once the simulator session is over, if considered necessary, the trainees should talk about their problems and what made them upset over a beer or two.

If a personality conflict with the simulator instructor occurs it is usually sensible to ask for a change in instructor. Such problems, whilst being rare, are not unheard of and are best dealt with before they start to influence learning. If a change of instructor is not possible, it is probably best to discuss the situation and once again focus on the task, not the person.

There comes a time in most people's studies when one just cannot seem to make any progress. This is known as a learning plateau and the experienced instructor will spot this problem and help the trainee through it. If the instructor has not noticed the problem or is not helping, then the other crew member should provide moral support until the problem is overcome and normal progress is assumed.

Ideally procedures should be overlearned in the simulator so as to ensure that recall will be possible when working under stress. Few airlines can afford to allow the crew members enough simulator time for overlearning. To compensate for this the crew member should make use of time between sessions to sit on a chair and visualise the procedures required to be learned. Going through the procedures in his or her mind until they are overlearned is an important step towards ensuring that procedures are 'chunked' and that working memory is freed. The use of cockpit mock-ups for familiarisation purposes cannot be over-emphasised. If the crew members practice procedures together before and after simulator sessions using the cockpit mock-ups progress in the simulator is likely to be much quicker.

Most simulators can be difficult devices to 'fly' accurately unless one is prepared to 'fly by the numbers' as they lack aerodynamic stability. It often happens that a crew member seems to be fighting the simulator whilst trying to make it do what he or she wants. This leaves the crew member with limited free working memory to deal with the other problems or for learning. The main reason this happens is the crew member's lack of appreciation or knowledge of attitude flying. Knowledge of the correct attitudes and approximate thrust settings for the various phases of flight cannot be over emphasised. These attitudes and thrust settings should be available from the simulator instructor or from the Flight Crew Training Manuals. As a general rule level flight in most transport aircraft will be achieved with a pitch attitude varying between approximately 2° at high speeds to about 10° at low speeds. Other than for emergency descents a pitch attitude of less than 0° is seldom required. This means that most flying other than take-off is done with a pitch attitude varying between 0° and about 10°.

Once the desired performance has been achieved through the correct pitch attitude and thrust setting, the simulator must be correctly trimmed. An out of trimmed condition is often accepted, as although the control forces on the elevator are often well balanced throughout the speed range, they are often relatively light (Van Rooyen & Lithgow, 1991). It is therefore often not easy for an inexperienced pilot to recognise that the aircraft is not actually in trim. Regular releasing of the control column and observing the divergence from the required flight path will indicate whether or not the simulator or aircraft has been trimmed correctly. These problems are greatly reduced in fly-by-wire type aircraft such as the new Airbus series and the B-777.

Route training

The crew member about to embark on the route training phase would do well to try and familiarise him or herself with the planned routing and airports to be visited prior to the flight. This can be done by taking a jumpseat ride if allowed, by talking to other line crews and by borrowing approach charts and maps. When taking a jumpseat ride it is important that you establish what you want to learn during the flight. This requires writing out a list of questions that you want answered either by observation or asking one of the crew members for an answer.

A call to the training captain prior to the route flight asking what he or she would suggest you prepare can make the flight a far more rewarding learning experience. Approaching the route training in this manner will show the training captain that you are really keen and enthusiastic. Enthusiasm is usually infectious and you are like to get far more from the training than if you were somewhat indifferent and waited to be taught everything. First impressions are lasting impressions. A keen student will often motivate an instructor or training captain to give more of him or herself enabling the trainee to get more from the training session.

It sometimes happens that trainees are warned of a training captain, or line captain for that matter, being difficult to work with. Probably the best way of approaching this situation is to assume everyone is not guilty until you have personally had a chance to assess the situation. Should you be so unfortunate as to end up with a really difficult training captain try to establish common ground at an appropriate point by finding out what interests him or her or perhaps where they learned to fly. This usually works and can make the environment far more tolerable.

Recurrent training

Recurrent training at periodic intervals can be a pleasant experience or something that has to be done. With the right attitude it is likely that recurrent training can be a useful learning experience. One of the reasons it is likely to be hard work is that the crew member has not remained on top of the technical material learned during the initial training onto type.

If the crew member sets him or herself a task of revising one or two systems a month after the initial qualification it is relatively easy to stay on top. If the revision is left to a day or two prior to the recurrent simulator session anxiety is probable with the inevitable deterioration in performance. Recurrent training does not have to be stressful if planned in advance and goals set.

Conclusion

There are no easy methods of learning what is usually a vast amount of information in a short period of time. To make matters worse, what you learn during an aviation course has to be learned almost perfectly, as it must be applied perfectly from the first flight. This is unlike some other professions where a lower level of proficiency can be tolerated as there is room for on the job learning. In order to learn something, energy has to be expended and the more a subject is analysed and the more notes made, the more meaningful the learning will be. As an aircrew member one has a large amount of responsibility and it is essential that every effort is made to get the most you can from the training course that you are about to follow.

References

Biggs, J.B. and Moore, P.J. (1993) *The Process of Learning*, Prentice Hall, Australia.

Bunzan, T. and Bunzan,B. (1993) *The Mindmap Book*, BBC, London.

Edwards, D.C. (1990) *Pilot - Mental and Physical Performance*, Iowa State University press, Ames.

Hawkins, F.H. and Orlady, H.W. (Ed), (1993) *Human Factors in Flight*, Ashgate, Aldershot.

Jensen, R.S. (Ed) (1989) *Aviation psychology*, Gower, Aldershot.

Moore, P.J. (1994) Across Airline Differences In Pilot Learning: The Roles Of Experience And Qualifications, Paper presented at the 21 st Conference of the European Association for Aviation Psychology (EAAP) Dublin, April.

Moore, P.J. and Telfer, R.A. (1990). Approaches to learning: Relationships with pilot performance. *Journal of Aviation/Aerospace Education and Research, 1,* 44-58.

Pippin, W.E. (1993) Educating the Aviation Professional. In R. A. Telfer (ed) *Aviation instruction and training.* (Pp309-322). Aldershot: Ashgate.

Smallwood, T. and Fraser, M. (1995) *The Airline Training Pilot*, Ashgate, Aldershot.

Telfer, R.A. and Biggs, J.B. (1988) *The Psychology of Flight Training*, Iowa State University Press, Ames.

Trollip, S.R. and Jensen, R.S. (1991) *Human Factors For General Aviation*, Jeppesen Sanderson, Englewood.

Van Rooyen, E. and Lithgow, S. (1991) *B737 Pilot Instructors Guide*, South African Airways, Johannesburg.

Walley, S. (1994) Conversion training for commercial pilots, Paper presented at the 21 st Conference of the European Association for Aviation Psychology (EAAP) Dublin, April.

Acknowledgements

My wife Claire and Mrs. C.E. Du Plessis for proof reading. Capt. Johan Du Plessis of SAA for his enthusiasm and constructive criticism. First Officer Colin Gibson of SAA for his suggestions. Janet Clarke of SAA for photographs.

9 Reducing attrition rates of cadet pilots

Paul McNabb and Ken Sellars

A common problem for the airlines of Asia and the Pacific is the combination of pressure for localisation and the attrition rate encountered in national cadet pilot training. Several reasons have been provided: apparent lack of motivation and commitment; lack of prior experience as a guide; lack of knowledge of the basics; uninformed decision-making; lack of resources; homesickness. The list is familiar.

Having considered its options, *Air Niugini* has introduced an innovatory program which appears to be solving the problem. The twelve-month program was developed from a design suggested by two consultants: Professors Phil Moore and Ross Telfer of the University of Newcastle. They used a knowledge of the Head Start educational programs of the 60's, and their current research into pilots' learning (see Chapter 1) as the bases for systematic personal development of the cadet pilots.

Head Start, which began in the USA in the mid 1960's, was designed to prepare pre-school children to attend school. As the name suggests, the young children were given opportunities to develop socially and intellectually, through specially designed programs, so that when they entered school they had a "Head Start", they were prepared for their future. Translated to the airline, this meant the preparation of newly selected cadet pilots so that on their entry into actual ab initio training, they would have had a period of "working" in the airline in various departments and also would have had the opportunity to work at rectifying any weaknesses identified through the selection process. Importantly, the Head Start candidates would have been in direct contact with the organizational culture of the airline.

Stage 1 of the Air Niugini's Head Start Program

The starting point for the year of Head Start is the feedback provided each successful cadet applicant immediately after the selection interviews and testing (see Self Development Objectives).

AIR NIUGINI NATIONAL CADET TRAINING

Self Development Objectives

Introduction

Congratulations on your progress to date in the Headstart Program.

Shortly you will depart on the next phase of your Headstart Program, being the secondment to a department of the Flight Operations Division. You will recall that we have emphasised that the headstart program lasts throughout this year, and thus provides you the opportunity to continue developing your overall potential so as to successfully pass your future flight training.

In recent days you have been introduced to a range of techniques that will assist you be successful in your chosen career. These include Communication skills and Team-building skills. As well, it is usual to learn a lot about ourselves while we are interacting with other Cadets.

Consequently both you and the MRDU itself have now amassed a large amount of data on your strengths, and your developmental areas. This data is drawn from both your performance during this first week of Headstart, as well as the Assessment Centre results and research conducted by the University of Newcastle into such aspects as your learning style.

Rather than retain this data in our files we felt it would be of most use as Feedback to yourself, for if you know as much as the airline about our personality and approach to tasks, this gives you the maximum opportunity to work on improving your overall ability as a Pilot.

The enclosed information is therefore offered in a helpful manner. It is now up to you to ensure you employ this knowledge to your own advantage.

Figure 9.1 Self development objectives

Typical of the feedback content (which is personal and confidential) would be details of strengths (perhaps mentioning mathematics, spatial relations, ability to interpret aircraft instruments, and generalised aspects of personality); some Developmental Targets (perhaps completing a specified number and type of mathematical problems derived from aviation operations; developing vocabulary and spelling systematically by working through and adding to a list of aviation terms), and some Personal Advice from the Headstart Co-ordinator (based on insights gained from observation and results of the selection procedures. These could include suggestions on interpersonal skills, study methods, achievement, decision-making, or leadership): as shown in the following example.

A Sample of the Individual Reports

PERSONAL AND CONFIDENTIAL

Strengths

Maths/Spatial Relations:	Quite good results in the 60% of these tests that covered maths knowledge and spatial relations of 2 to 3 dimensional figures. (Refer* below).
Aviation:	Average or slightly above average in the skill of interpreting a set of aircraft instruments.
Personality Tests:	Good adjustment, and good social maturity and motivation to do well in learning

Development Targets

Maths Application:	* While acceptable in general maths knowledge, below average results for *the application* of mathematics to aviation problems. You should set yourself the objective of completing at least five maths problems per week, that ask you to solve aviation-related calculations typically faced by flight crews.
Language:	Near average or slightly below in all tests (Grammar, spelling vocabulary). Using the technical aviation textbooks available from Flight Operations, circle no less than 20 words per week that you are unsure of, and clarify the meaning of these words with senior Flight Crew, and/or the Training Department. Then consciously make use of these words in your own daily speech.

> You are fortunate - being surrounded by others speaking 'aviation English' all day you will show rapid progress in your language skills!
>
> General
>
> a.   You could benefit from improved ability in the area of interpersonal skills; being those you encountered during the first week of the Headstart program. Ask your colleagues to monitor and provide feedback to you in this area - it requires you to practice at least weekly in the next three months (You will find that the 'Language' area above and this area of 'Interpersonal Skills' will benefit each other).
>
> b.   At times you 'tune out' of group discussions, and consequently miss some of the learning benefits. You must concentrate from now on, if necessary by making summarising notes or diagrams to ensure you have to maintain you attention to the learning experience. While you have easily reached the standard in your previous academic studies, from now on your professional development is going to demand that you perform at ever-higher levels. Developing superior methods of learning **now** will be the key to your ongoing success.

Figure 9.2 A sample of the individual reports

Counselling given to the cadets with their personal reports advises them to be honest with themselves in recognising their current strengths and weaknesses, and to be proactive in doing something about them. Suggestions include regular self-testing, practice and exercises, using the analogy of preparation for competitive sport.

Study and learning methods are discussed in detail, with reference to the results of the Moore and Telfer international study and the implication for ab initio training success. Here Biggs' (1987) notions of Deep, Surface, and Achieving approaches to learning are presented, encouraging the cadets to be well organised and keen to do well (Achieving) and understanding what they learn (Deep). The importance of motivation for achievement is emphasised as are strategies for effective studying.

Several days are allocated to induction to the company. Integrated with this introduction is an intensive period of skills development. Indoor and outdoor projects develop confidence, planning skills, personal management, participation, leadership, decision-making, and positive attitudes.

Another emphasis at this early stage is the development of key knowledge and skills to support the new values and attitudes. A special focus is the range of interpersonal skills such as active listening, effective communication, resolving conflict, and team building. Cadets are expected to demonstrate these skills at every opportunity. There was evidence quite early of the group dynamics: especially the team climate, supportiveness and cohesion. If one of the group has problems with a project or assignment, others are ready to help. Individuals are expected to learn to ask for assistance, and to recognise their weaknesses and strengths. This is a performance-based program in which the cadets have to demonstrate competency at each stage before moving on.

For example, before leaving the first stage, the cadet has to communicate effectively; plan projects (both individually and as part of a team); act as a leader (or follower); and show an ability to identify his own developmental needs and a way of working on them. Many of the communication skills (and situational leadership) introduced at this early stage of their careers will flow easily into CRM and LOFT later. For example, they discuss attentive silence, paraphrasing, attentive body language, open and closed questions, and open and closed body language.

The project planning sequence requires an objective to be confirmed; resources to be identified; options listed and a best option selected; tasks to be allocated, and the results evaluated. Again, this will have pay-offs down the track in terms of cockpit problem solving.

The 1994 group of pilot cadets developed a pocket sized check list of a decision-making/problem/solving model which was laminated and distributed.

Stage 2

In the second phase of *Air Niugini's* Head Start schedule, cadets are posted within flight operations. Here they undertake a variety of tasks: taking supernumary flights requiring written reports; or relay radio messages to catering and engineering. While being exposed to the professional standards of aviation, they are being required to demonstrate reliability, commitment, and an ability to remediate deficiencies.

Stage 3

Personal mentors enter Head Start at this phase. These are experienced Air Niugini pilots who have volunteered to participate as individual advisers. A matching technique is used to try to optimise the relationship, which includes not tutoring for the BAK subjects, but the notion of modelling professional values. Pilot Cadets provide personal details (such as their developmental objectives for Head Start, and their ideas on the nature of the mentor experience or mentor personality which they think would be most helpful).

The match-up is done by the Manager, Line Operations (Captain Ken Sellars). Mentors and cadets make regular joint progress reports.

Typical of the intention and operation of Head Start was that the cadet group developed its own study plan and timetable for the Basic Aeronautical Knowledge (BAK) and Navigation examinations.

Stage 4

Having successfully completed each of the preceding stages, cadets depart for Commercial Pilot flight training, which is out-of-country. Here their progress is monitored by the training organization and also, on a regular basis by senior aircrew from the airline itself. The developmental program allows for more informed decisions about any problem that may arise during this stage. A typical annual program developed in consultation with Professors Telfer and Moore follows (see next page).

So?

The Head Start at *Air Niugini* trades-off the loss of a year's flight training against a grounding in aviation knowledge and a demonstrated commitment to a flying career with the company. The view of both personnel and flight operations departments is that the balance is very favourable for both the individual and the company. Each cadet pilot acquires knowledge, skills and attitudes which make success in pilot training more probable (and failure or withdrawal less probable). *Air Niugini* receives trainees who are compatible with the company's operating values and procedures. Most importantly, the pilots have a commitment to a career in the company. They see command promotion as their goal, and they are working on it from day one.

\[Month\]	Location	Requirements*

AIR NIUGINI CADET PILOT HEAD START PROGRAM
1996

Month	Location	Requirements*
1	Flight Despatch	Computer Course Study Schedule Monthly Meeting with Captain L. Sabumei
2	" "	Start theory studies Monthly meeting
3	" "	Start Supernumary flights Monthly meeting
4	" "	Load Control Dangerous Goods Monthly meeting
5	" "	Theory studies cont'd Flights cont'd Monthly meeting
6	Tech. Crew Scheduling	Control Tower Visit Monthly meeting
7	" "	Supernumary Flights cont'd Studies cont'd Monthly meeting
8	Operations Control	Human Factors/CRM Monthly meeting
9	" "	Final meeting

*NOTE:

117

Head Start is the final stage of selection. It is in your interest to complete it at as high a standard as possible, and to use it as an opportunity to demonstrate the qualities which Air Niugini is seeking. At the end of each month an evaluation is conducted, and at the end of each appointment the Section Head will report on the cadets involved.

The requirements on this sheet are only descriptive. The specific assignments are as scheduled by the individual or prescribed by Captain Sabumei (or other Air Niugini staff).

The responsibility for completing the Head Start program satisfactorily is the individual cadet's. **If in doubt, find out.**

Only the personal study schedule and the study of theory subjects has to be undertaken individually. All of the other exercises are intended to be undertaken collaboratively. Presentations will be either joint or in rotation. In any collaborative work, **all members of the team will receive the same mark or grade, so it is important that the best possible report or assignment be provided.** Cadets will need to use their initiative to find information, contact people, and gather resources in order to complete some assignments. This is part of the task.

REQUIREMENTS FOR EACH LOCATION

FLIGHT DESPATCH (Reports to the Flight Despatch Manager)

At this location cadets are expected to undertake:
- updating approach plates;
- preparation of flight plans;
- updating operations manuals;
- gaining knowledge of the operations of flight despatch;
- other assigned duties.

Assignment:
Describe how to get weather information and NOTAMs, and how to file a flight plan.

OPERATIONS CONTROL (Report to the Senior Ops Controller)

At this location cadets are expected to:
- make a list of daily aircraft movements.
- note the decision process in allocating aircraft types
- trace the progress of adjustments to the schedule throughout the day.
- note the ways in which Operations interacts with other parts of the organization on a day to day flight operational basis;
- other assigned duties.

Assignment

Provide a 10-15 minute talk on the functions of Operations Control in Air Niugini.

TECHNICAL CREW SCHEDULING (Report to Supervisor, Crew Scheduling)

At this location, cadets are expected to:
- note the daily roster of technical crew;
- be aware of the legal limitations of crew scheduling;
- observe monthly and daily rosters and any differences in them.

Assignment:

How can crew scheduling be improved? Present your views in the form of an essay which justifies the points you make.

SPECIFIC REQUIREMENTS

1. **Computers**: Become computer literate and, if possible, complete all assignments by using a word processor.

2. **Aviation Theory Subjects:** devise a study schedule which will enable completion of the assigned reading by month 8, and submit this schedule for approval to Captain L. Sabumei by the end of Month 1. For each subject, present a ONE PAGE summary of the important points, and be prepared for questioning on it.

This is the ONLY independent study.

3. **Supernumary Flights**: between Month 3 and Month 8 complete 50

supernumary flights. Complete and submit reports on each flight.

4. **Load Control and Dangerous Goods:** complete as prescribed by Captain Sabumei.

5. **Human Factors and CRM:** complete as prescribed by Captain J. McDonald.

6. **Control Tower:** organised and scheduled by cadets. Be prepared to discuss.

7. **Monthly Reports:** at each monthly meeting each cadet will provide a report indicating progress over the past month, and personal goals for the next month (in addition to those prescribed in the Head Start Program).

Figure 9.3 Air Niugini cadet pilot head start program

References

Biggs, J.B. (1987). *Student approaches to learning and studying.* Australian Council for Educational Research: Hawthorn.

Part 2
Instruction

10 Introduction to Part 2 - Instruction

Ross A Telfer and Phillip J Moore

This section contains nine chapters with a focus on the second major variable in training effectiveness: the instructor. Motivated and capable trainees may succeed in spite of their instructors, but instruction remains a key variable in the quality of airline training.

The recognition of the need for aviation instructional methods to keep pace with the rapid technological change in the industry is not new. See, for example, Telfer and Biggs (1988), Telfer (1993) and Moore, Farquharson and Telfer (in press). What is new is the planned remediation which is exemplified in the contributions to this section. The innovations include strategies for combining the training of flight crew with other members of the production team which enable airlines to fly safely and commercially; a means of surveying an airline to identify training and instructional weaknesses; a proven method for training instructors to provide Human Factors training; a means of evaluating CRM programs; some practical means of improving instructional curricula and methods in aviation; an insight into the design and development of computer-based selection and training methods; practical techniques derived from experience of the in-house development of support materials for a CRM program; an innovative approach to an organization's training of airline captains; and an insight into how training manuals can be produced so that learning is facilitated.

A second feature of the contributions to this section is the blending of theory and practice. It is gratifying (perhaps even indulgent when one's own research is involved) to see a mutual recognition of the interdependence of academic research and industry practice. On close examination, many of the traditional methods of industry can be seen to have an implicit rationale in theoretical principles. These can only be identified by systematic observation and scientific methods to ensure reliability, validity and significance. The aviation industry provides rich source of data about instruction and learning, and a reservoir of

123

many years of expertise and experience which can provide valuable insights. All these resources need to be used, and the contributions to this section provide excellent guides for those who wish to do so.

Finally, the contributions to this section demonstrate a willingness to tackle the perplexing questions of how non-technical or Human Factors training can be integrated with technical training for not only aircrew, but all those involved in the mission of a safe flight.

There are some innovative solutions which are now reaching beyond instructional design towards assessment. Until validity and reliability can be established for Human Factors testing, potential litigation makes jeopardy-checking in the simulator or on the line potentially litigious. We may not have reached this solution, but we are probing the envelope.

In the first chapter, Naef starts with a quantitative interpretation of the dynamics of skills and behaviour in team performance. What he calls "The Real Stuff" is identified in terms of interaction. The concept of a team in the aviation industry is defined broadly, then appropriate training for such teams is described. Training for the full team - "joint training"- is what he advocates. Helpfully, he provides both the formal guidelines and the actual experiences of Swissair. We follow the actual development of the courses and seminars, and see how they were refined by evaluative feedback.

Naef indicates the basis for future development of CRM and Instructor Training in the company. He sees the significant variables as increasing specialization, cost pressures and the organizational dynamics. Cabin and cockpit crew have to form a cohesive entity in both training and line operations despite these variables.

In Philippine Airlines, Anca has conducted a major survey of instruction and training. He describes the methodology, the results and what he sees as the implications for the company and for instruction in the industry. His analysis of the data in terms of the congruence or conflict between categories of respondents provides a few surprises: especially the responses and approaches to learning of groups differing according to status, age or experience; and the extent of the difference between the perceptions of the company's instructors and other groups such as management and pilot groups. These differed in their views of training effectiveness. This difference was evident not only in the views of instruction, but of training notes and manuals, too.

For any who wish to replicate the exercise, the survey instrument and relevant references are provided in full detail. According to Anca, there is a need for systematic evaluation of ground instruction and for more attention to be given to the selection of instructors. His argument is persuasive.

Next, Bertram and Dowd discuss Air Canada's innovative LOFT Facilitator Training, designed by their development team. How the course and manual evolved makes interesting reading: especially for others wishing to achieve a similar program of equivalent high quality. They provide a day by day analysis of the course content and how it is presented. As an example, course notes are provided for the instructional skill of questioning. Further examples include the ways in which an evaluation form rates Human Factors aspects of training, and how the workshop is evaluated.

Air Canada's LOFT Facilitator Training provides a model for assessment and training in Human Factors. For example, the identification of five blocks for self-critique and feedback will be valuable not only in the context of specialised LOFT Facilitator development, but in the more general training in Human Factors.

Bilton then reports on his evaluation of Virgin Atlantic's CRM training program. Commencing with an examination of the factors which influence pilots' behaviour he goes on to trace the development of an evaluative questionnaire and structured interview. His examination of the ethical issues in such a study is quite timely and informative. Few would argue with his view that the place to really test CRM is in terms of the pilot behaviours demonstrated when flying the line. This chapter will prove helpful for those wrestling with the methodological issues of rigorously evaluating a company's CRM program.

Although we are experiencing rapid technological change in the aviation industry, Lehrer is able to point to an approach to training which has not kept pace with changes in the work place. By taking us through the three domains of learning (knowledge, skills and values) he is able to demonstrate the assistance that learning objectives can provide. Performance objectives can be constructed by using what he terms "action verbs".

His description of "approach tendencies" provides a very useful strategy for Check and Training Captains or Instructors who seek indicators of the degree of acceptance and use of new attitudes. They will also find the ways in which American Airlines made use of "Ten Commandments of Good Crew Co-Ordination" a useful approach.

Lehrer sees the final stage of the development of an aviation curriculum - the evaluation of learning - a problem area. This is especially so when we seek to evaluate the effectiveness of teaching attitudes, values or beliefs about aviation such as judgement or airmanship, which are in the affective domain of learning. To find a solution, Lehrer describes the options we have by using a questionnaire, rating scale, interview or role play to collect data. For those who wish to make use of existing instruments, he lists further alternatives and their origins and applications.

Almost two decades previously, Roscoe had referred to "Situational Awareness" as a way of describing the seminal pilot behaviour for predicting and enhancing flightdeck performance. In this chapter he traces the changes in terminology and the development of the WOMBAT and DuoWOMBAT to increase situational awareness, attention-management abilities, and management of the collective resources of flight crews. He points out that despite expenditures on R & D, the military has been unable to produce selection batteries capable of accounting for more than around 25% of the variance in training success.

There would have to be widespread support for Roscoe's assertion that there is a need for a valid test of whether pilots can "stay ahead of the airplane"; show "good judgement", "airmanship" or "situational awareness". He described how the WOMBAT approaches this problem by obtaining measures of situational awareness and stress tolerance. The analysis of the problems of validating tests is salutary for all those involved in pilot selection. The two descriptions of studies using the WOMBAT give a greater understanding of how such validation can be obtained, and where the difficulties are. Can we predict for nearer-term success as well we can predict the probability of distant future success?

The description of the DuoWOMBAT relates to earlier chapters on CRM or Human Factors training design and evaluation. DuoWOMBAT is designed to contribute to the development and testing of team attitudes and strategies.

Airlines face the choice of either importing an off-the-shelf CRM program, or producing one in-house. For those in the latter group, Hollings' chapter offers some home-grown guidance.

As leader of a group of pilots who produce Ansett Australia's annual component to their cycle of CRM programs, together with the accompanying pre-reading, manual and audio-visual aids, he provides a concise how-to-do-it. The ten step guide to producing an in-house videotape is a clear guide which owes at least some of its clarity to a video Holling's produced on the teamwork and resource management evidenced in a BAE146 engine roll-back incident over the West Australian desert. The simple steps will undoubtedly encourage others to follow the advice in his concluding sentence: "Let's try it".

In the next-to-final chapter, Beaumont brings his years of experience at Qantas to bear on the problem of producing airline captains in quantities to meet the company's requirements and timing, with a consistent quality. The industry appears to have difficulties in preparing captains in an effective and efficient manner. Commercial imperatives may dominate.

After giving an overview of the traditions, he provides table of overt and covert demands on the airline captain. This can be related to the typical career path he traces, demonstrating that there is really little time, relative to years of experience, on actual preparation for the role. The integrated model he designs as a response takes into account the training culture and established precedents. The response takes into account potential barriers and likely modifiers. The major need, which his model is designed to provide, is the calibration of check and training airmen to provide consistency in both approach and expectations.

The last chapter takes quite a different perspective from the others by looking at the ways in which training manuals can be improved. With an ever-increasing use of in-house training manuals, this chapter has a fair amount to offer. Here Jill Scevak, an expert in text processing, joins us to produce a checklist that can be used by organizations to "test" the quality of their training manuals. By examining content, format, readability, structure, graphics and illustrations, and reader involvement, those involved in training will be able to identify the strengths and weaknesses of the manuals used in training. The chapter provides guidelines on how weaknesses in manuals can be remediated.

It is no wonder that instruction has such a pivotal role in aviation. It has major inputs from ab initio through to endorsement, recurrent, emergency, base, ground and promotional training. Through instruction people are prepared for entry to aviation; for an ongoing role in the industry, and for ultimate management of it. It determines safety, profit, comfort, and achievement. It is worth taking seriously.

References

Moore, P.J., Farquharson, T., & Telfer, R.A. (In press). Automation and human performance in airline pilot training. In M.Mouloua (Ed.). *Human-automation interaction: Research and practice*. Hillsdale: Erlbaum.

Telfer, R.A. (Ed.) (1993) *Aviation Instruction and Training*. Aldershot: Ashgate.

Telfer, R. & Biggs, J. (1988) *The Psychology of Flight Training*. Ames: Iowa State University Press.

11 Joint training and "The real stuff"

Werner Naef

Background: Experience from "the real stuff"

This article on joint training primarily discusses the cooperation and synergy construction that result when a team of people with great potential are brought together. Adequate methodological and didactic skills and the acquisition of technical skills on the part of the individual staff member or trainee are taken for granted and are not treated here.

Simply put, it can be said that each team performance (P_T) is a product of its participants' individual skills (S) and the behaviour (B) expressed in interhuman modalities:

$$P_T = S * B$$

This formula shows, albeit in a simplified manner, that a 100% effort of skills and behavior results in a product that is equally complete, i.e., a 100% team performance:

$$P_T = 1 * 1 = 1$$

But if both these contributing factors are reduced to a level of 50%, then the team effectiveness is much lower, namely only 25%:

$$P_T = 0.5 * 0.5 = 0.25$$

Even with the learned skills at 100%, a collapse results when behavior is so damaged that team members can no longer implement their own capabilities. This effect can be found in many subpar performances or production by committee in industrial and service-related operations, in partnerships or, last but not least, in the case of aircraft incidents:

$$P_T = 1 * 0 = 0!$$

I call this dramatic dependency of team performance on interhuman processes *"the real stuff"*. This can be found in daily operations as well as in all borderline cases. This is what our investigations have revealed as the central causal factor in incidents, accidents or even simple mistakes (Hamman, Seamster & Edens, 1995; Eissfeldt, 1995).

When analytically investigating aircraft incidents, the connection between skills and behavior can been traced quite distinctly with the aid of voice and data recording equipment. Because data protection laws prohibit the use of such equipment in other service sectors or industries, it is difficult to make similar claims in these corresponding sectors. Those people in positions to know, however, have verified the fact that certain industries are greatly interested in our research efforts. Using training programs similar to those we have developed (HPL, CRM or other designations), they hope to implement qualitative growth steps based on the relevance of interhuman processes. Ongoing development into the issue of "Human Factors in Operating Rooms", currently under study by Helmreich (NASA UT) among others, is a good example of this. Air traffic control has adapted the Crew Resource Management (CRM) concept under the name "Controller Resource Management" (Wiener, Kanki & Helmreich, 1993).

The equations listed above, interesting although relatively unscientific, illustrate the significance of interhuman processes.

The goal of process-oriented basic and supplementary training is, more than anything, to highlight the interplay between potential and the process of forming synergies via individual skills or, in short, the genesis of a team performance. We took this step in the cockpit a few years ago. In doing so we moved away from cultivating exclusively individual pilot capabilities, the idea of a one man show, toward a training aimed at team performance, the crew concept, as the central focus. Our main maxim here was "uncovering mistakes equates to a positive team performance". It is my belief that we must now concentrate on consistently implementing the guidelines of association training, team development and interdisciplinary synergy development. Goeters (1995) also spoke in favor of including interfaces in joint CRM training. This places substantial requirements on how one forms a program because one must consider the psychological variances of the different professional groups (Harris, 1994; Chute and Wiener, 1995; Amundsen, 1995).

In our industry there have been, and still are to a large extent, separate training procedures for various personnel groups, such as cockpit crews, cabin crews, maintenance staff or dispatchers, even though these groups must work closely together in order to ensure daily aircraft operations. This is partly due to the fact that these diverse personnel groups are generally placed in diverse organizational units of an airline. The line management, training and administration of these units are structurally separated. But when performing their primary duties, they are required to function as a team.

These types of structurally-oriented organizational forms harbor the seeds for conflict and discord relating to daily flight operations. Value systems, superordinate priorities, territoriality, group thinking or behavior in any borderline form is not often unified or transparent and fails to form any part of a joint discussion. Clichés abound and preconceived notions tend to color any type of awareness. An example of such problem areas in the cockpit-cabin is offered by "Cockpit-Cabin Communication; I. A Tale of Two Cultures" (Chute/Wiener) "The International Journal of Aviation Psychology" (volume 5, number 3, 1995). The interesting realization reads: "Yes, many of the joint sessions turned into gripe sessions, but that is instructive in itself, in that it revealed that just below the surface of cordial (if not very friendly) relationships lurked a considerable hostility. Flight safety demands that this be brought above the surface and dealt with in a professional manner" (pp. 275).

Swissair CRM discussion group

The requirements of team behavior on a crew become downright dramatic in hijacking cases. It is very necessary to create a bridge function in basic and supplementary training of these personnel groups.

Studies on passenger fatalities in aircraft evacuation involving a fire on board have shown that an effective team performance by the crew would have significantly improved the chances of limiting fatalities. It is unfortunate that emergency training still largely takes place on a crew-internal basis.

In their model of the "Four Ps" Degani and Wiener (1994) show that after Philosophy, Policies and Procedures, Practices is a necessary and integral part of airliner operation. We do not believe that this can be realized on an isolated basis where crew categories are viewed separately.

All of these reasons bring us to the conclusion that joint training is an improvement that is indispensable to airline personnel training. If we were to ignore these facts, we would open ourselves up to charges of management deficiencies, as defined in the "model of accident causation" by Reason (1994). The next two sections of this article will be devoted to illustrating representative experiences and current Swissair projects on the topic of joint training.

An ample supply of formal guidelines may be found. Here are a few examples:

ICAO:

Annex 6, Chapter 9, "Aeroplane Flight Crew" para 9.3.:

"....The training of each flight crew member, particularly that relating to abnormal or emergency procedures, shall ensure that all flight crew members know the functions for which they are responsible and the relation of these functions to the functions of other crew members".

Annex 6, Chapter 12, "Cabin Attendants", para. 12.4.d) "Training":

"...These training programs shall ensure that each person is :

....d) aware of other crew members' assignments and functions in the event of an emergency so far as is necessary for the fulfillment of the cabin attendant's own duties..."

JAR OPS:

The European regulatory network, to be implemented in 1998 is calling for such joint training in a wide range, including simulator observer sessions by senior flight attendants during their purser training.

National Regulations:

These differ widely, however some states have fully included joint training into their national regulations.

Figure 11.1 Example of guidelines for joint training

Experiences with joint training

Swissair has practised joint training in past years. There has been a systematic increase in these methods, however, since 1987:

GSR/EPR

Annual Ground School Refreshers (GSR) for cockpit personnel, and the Emergency Performance Refreshers (EPR) for cabin staff have had a joint training sequence since 1991. Depending on the program, these sessions last between 60 and 90 minutes and include videos, slide shows and a short discussion period. The fact that approximately 12 cockpit crew members and up to 18 cabin crew members took this class resulted in the majority of participants experiencing it in a passive manner. Time parameters also prohibited the ability to enter into deeper discussions or group work. Emergency instructors were purely technical, having no field experience as a moderator as we prescribe for CRM trainers. Thus, the effectiveness of this sequence was far from optimal and was limited to the fact that the responsible line and training units felt compelled to do some type of joint training.

Valuable flight safety videos were shown only to cockpit crew members in a cycle of GSR courses. The videos were produced in-house and have become a valuable part of airline training worldwide. Topics such as stress, automation, the human loop, airmanship and perception were scientifically designed and transmitted in "edutainment", user-friendly videos for pilots. This cycle showed quite clearly that the topic was very valuable and was also greatly appreciated but that the relatively short discussion period among cockpit crews, of approximately 30 minutes, was frustrating because central relevant questions were handled in a manner that only scratched the surface of the topic.

The fact that we had outstanding methodological, didactic and thematic material was countered by the reality that we structured the supplementary training program in such as way that our people were unable to take proper advantage of the material presented. This look into the process highlighted the view that we needed to create a joint training program. One that would offer a certain degree of substance. I will return to the issue of joint training in the next section.

Basic Instructor Course

Future cockpit instructors, irrespective of aircraft type, were traditionally trained in so-called Basic Instructor Courses. Over the course of five days, topics such as awareness, behavior, communication, dealing with faults, and assessment were handled with an emphasis on training in the cockpit. We trained both captains and first officers in these courses. We also made a point of inviting participants from business aviation, from ATC or from the aviation authorities to sit in on these classes as they were officially acknowledged as instructor courses by the national authorities. This mixture of captains, first officers and visitors from the other groups mentioned above resulted in a quite positive joint training effect. The clarification of individual roles among future check airmen (captains) and instructors / first officers proved greatly beneficial during subsequent joint instruction of second officers during practical training sessions.

The fact that various independent "train the trainer" courses exist in the sector of "flight crew training", namely for cockpit personnel, cabin personnel, for instructors of basic pilot training as well as for emergency and systems instructors, prompted us to create a joint basic training course for future instructors in order to eliminate duplication and repetition. I will speak on this topic at greater length in the next section.

Security seminar 1987

Under the acute danger of hijackings, prevalent at that time, Swissair organized security seminars in 1987. Participation was limited to cockpit crew members, pursers and Maitres de Cabine and was voluntary. We planned to carry out five-to-eight afternoon joint training seminars. In addition to the security-relevant lecture, a video was shown and there was enough time for a thorough discussion. Although the seminars were voluntary, because of the shortage in crew members at that time in the company, and because the relevant units expected about 50% participation, the cycle was extended from May through October 1987 and the number of seminars was expanded from an original maximum of eight to a total of 19. This example of joint training was a great success. But there were also latent points of conflict that developed between the participating personnel groups. In hindsight the one missing ingredient was a proper forum and the instruments with which to process and resolve these conflicts.

Joint leadership course

Until 1994 our leadership training for future captains was traditionally focused on the flying aspects of the job. The focal points were being able to maintain control of the aircraft in every possible situation and being able to land it safely.

Leadership training consisted of what amounted to a single conversion training course in the simulator and in the aircraft where, as opposed to co-pilot training, abnormal and extreme situations were practiced. The next step was generally a monitored, three-month flight training course which ended in promotion to captain. During the initial year after this command course, after the regular captain duties had been assumed, all junior captains who had been promoted were offered a four-to-five-day course that was conducted by the corresponding aircraft's chief pilot. Topics in these internal courses included various experiences that had been gathered, cooperation with the chief pilot, the training of younger co-pilots, communication and professional perspectives. This completed the actual management training.

Beginning in 1995 a new concept was developed. In addition to a stronger emphasis on joint training, the most significant developments over the previous course are listed below:
– An initial, comprehensive five-day management seminar, completed before the actual command course. Topics are wide-ranging and fleet superordinate.

- Among other sections, this five-day course contains a two-day joint training section that includes pursers. One pilot and one flight attendant are assigned to a learn crew for the duration of the training period.
- The course is based on an intensive, individual phase of preparation that has been structured by Swissair.
- During this individual preparation phase, future captains and pursers concern themselves with the requirements, professional profiles and guideline booklets of other staff groups.
- In accordance with future JAA regulations, the purser observes one of the training captain's flight simulator sessions.
- The new captain and purser are then paired for one rotation (approximately five days) on the same short-haul flights during route training, allowing them to check and modify in practice what they have learned in theory.

This ensures joint training in both cockpit and cabin staff training programs. We are convinced that this type of consistent training, completed together and including key situational aspects, is most effective in promoting team performance.

Line-oriented leadership training (LOLT)

Feedback that we have received from the initial joint training exercises confirm the currentness and importance of joint training: Subsequent to the actual course, the acceptance of the individual subjects and methods was confirmed by means of a questionnaire.

Evaluation scale:
Low Rating: 1
High Rating: 5

The highest ratings were achieved by:

Table 11.1
Results of ratings

Subjects:	Score	Methods:	score
Process analysis	4.91	Practical leadership exercise	5.0
Learning partnership	4.83	Group of two	4.83
Exchange of roles	4.83	Process-oriented, personal presentation	4.66

The feedback we received has shown us that we are on the right path. The staff members from both professional categories were positively motivated in team integration which contributed substantially to flight safety-relevant advantages and also had a positive effect on customer service. The positive impression of the initial course participants was easily and quickly identifiable. This resulted in an increased demand for similar procedures.

In the framework of management instruction, the next and final step of joint training is sessions in moving evacuation trainers. These units are comparable to simulators and include a section of an MD-11 or A320 cabin plus the corresponding cockpit on a scale of 1:1. They move atop a hydraulic platform and can be used as a training device for evacuation drills in particular. They possess original doors, public address systems, interphones for cabin-cockpit communication and can be filled with synthetic smoke. We will conduct joint training with the future captains and pursers in these mock-ups and practice normal, abnormal and emergency operations based on a number of pre-programd scenarios. The task then is to apply two-way communication, decision making and all other components of joint training in the phase of joint operation. Concluding debriefing sessions include video feedback. This monitoring system ensures reinforcement of what has been learned. This also enables us, in our view, to guarantee effective joint training which will vastly improve the efficiency of the crew as well as their reliability when dealing with emergency situations.

Joint Training with Swiss Air Ambulance Company ("REGA")

Our long-standing and constructive association with the SWISS AIR AMBULANCE Company (REGA) has provided another opportunity for joint training. Based on Crew Resource Management, the exercise includes close to 60 staff members and deals with winged aircraft. A mixed work group, consisting of two CRM trainers (active line pilots) contributed by us, and one pilot, one doctor, a flying nurse and two dispatchers from REGA. This crew created a specific CRM seminar based on Swissair's existing "conflict" CRM model.

This seminar was also headed under the title "conflict" and deals with the following goals:
1. To make aware of the importance of certain interhuman processes.
2. To promote process-oriented, conflict-relevant knowledge.
3. To implement application of the knowledge gained and behavior suitable to avoid conflict.
4. To initiate the transfer of the skills acquired during everyday practice.

Similar to the Swissair CRM seminar, this particular seminar took place in a baroque convent which is run as seminar center. The first course day consisted of various modules that concerned the topics of communication, value systems, conflict rationale, elements of conflict, conflict dynamic and solution.

Role playing was at the center of the second, interactive day of the seminar. The role play concerned the typical situations from daily life of an emergency team operating in a fixed-wing aircraft en route from Zurich to Hong Kong. The four sequences focused on one of the participating groups: pilots, doctors, nurses and rescue team members. Since role playing is not one of the regular vocational aspects of the course participants, allow me to clearly define our intentions:
1. Systematic analysis of typical situations from "daily operation"
2. Practical structuring of the decision-making process.
3. To make aware of certain, typical conflict elements of daily life.
4. To give and receive feedback according to the set regulations.

The schedule for the second day of the course was formatted as follows:
08:15 : "Feedback" – significance and practice of giving and receiving feedback
09:15 : Introduce the role play into the group at large
09:45 : Coffee break
10:15 : Role play in small groups, scenarios 1–4 debriefing on decision-making and conflicts
12:30 : Lunch
13:15 : Guided tour of the convent, including a brief organ concert
14:15 : Feedback in small groups regarding personal behavior during the role

play including video feedback.

16:45 : Short exchange of experiences among the entire group.

17:15 : End

The role play was based on a simulated operation taking place on a flight from Zurich to Hong Kong, via Prague and Alma Ata. The actual topic dealt with the transport of a seriously injured person from Hong Kong back to Zurich. Unexpected occurrences were incorporated into this scenario that were totally within the framework of reality, i.e., they had happened before and could bound to happen again.

The active role play crew consisted of a small group of the following participants:

> 1 enlarged cockpit crew (2 captains and 1 co-pilot)
>
> 1 doctor
>
> 1 nurse
>
> 2 dispatchers

The aircraft crew (pilots, doctors and nurses) and the dispatchers were visually separated by means of a flexible wall and had to communicate via two-way communication device. Fax, telephone and radio contact were simulated.

During the role plays, which took place inside a specially outfitted room, the players were filmed with a video camera by the CRM facilitator but they were also watched live by a team of observers. The observer crew was basically a shadow group of the active role players, who had the same professions as those people represented in the role play crew.

The observer crew was charged with the following:

- Follow and judge the decision-making process in the four roles according to facts, opinions, risks and benefits, decision, execution and control (FORDEC by DLR, Hörmann, Dublin 1994).
- Which conflicts occur?

  - how are they dealt with?

  - are there suppressed conflicts that were not dealt with or "swept under the rug"?

During the substantial debriefing after the four role plays, the following points were discussed with the observer crew as well as the CRM facilitator:

- decision-making process
- roles within the crew, formal and informal roles, hidden roles
- personal feedback relating to behavior
- video feedback
- relevant, operational hot findings
- consequences, subsequent steps, action plan.

Results

It can generally be said that the seminars, regarding both the contents and methods used, were viewed very positively by the participants:
- emphasis on more opportunities for joint discussion and joint analysis of processes in the future,
- improved mutual understanding of motives and course of action,
- high esteem for feedback on perceived behavior, and
- a newborn feeling for the common mission.

The evaluation of the questionnaires completed by all course participants immediately after the course finished, confirmed our general impression:

Of the 21 questions on the questionnaire, regarding course implementation, methodology, contents, realism, presentation, etc., we find the ratings on the following six questions to have great significance:

1. Good performance	vs.	Poor performance
2. Course leader includes participants	vs.	Course leader ignores participants
3. Daily schedule too long	vs.	Daily schedule too short
4. Course was interesting	vs.	Course was uninteresting
5. Course was worth the effort	vs.	Course was not worth the effort
6. Course offers great practical benefits	vs.	Course of little practical use

Rating scale: (1 best - 7 worst)

Average rating per question:

Question 1 "performance"	1.5	
Question 2 "inclusion"	1.5	
Question 3 "schedule"	3.3	(4.0 would have been the ideal grade on this question)
Question 4 "interesting"	1.3	
Question 5 "worth effort"	1.3	
Question 6 "practical"	1.7	

The well above-average ratings form a clear statement that the REGA staff members were highly motivated to take the course and that they viewed the contents, goals and performance of the course to be very positive. Motivation and acceptance are the most elementary of factors that we could define in order to ensure that the training would be acknowledged effectively in actual practice.

Two developing projects in the field of joint training

Two important courses regarding joint training are being developed:

CRM

In conjunction with Swiss national civil aviation authorities (the FOCA, or Federal Office for Civil Aviation), all cockpit crew members have been required to complete a CRM course every two years since 1993. In January 1996, a work group began the task of putting together a two-day CRM seminar for the 97/98 CRM cycle entitled "Human Behavior in Emergency". As mentioned at the beginning of this chapter, studies have shown that joint training on the topic of "emergency" is a great necessity. Both current and planned regulations in Europe point to this fact.

Based on this, Swissair has decided to devote a day of the 97/98 CRM course to cockpit personnel and pursers together. Now the task is to lay the foundation for behavioral training. This, together with the joint GSR/EPRs (see part II "GSR/EPR), and with the product-oriented training of the overall crew, should promote the idea that the crew sees itself as an integral part of an equation and acts accordingly in routine aspects, service questions, in extraordinary situations and, last but certainly not least, in emergency situations.

Joint basic instructor course, comprehensive train the trainer course

In part II, Experiences with Joint Training, I have listed positive experiences that have been made by including external participants in the cockpit-related instruction courses. This finding, coupled with the more difficult operating framework and the importance we place on the "unité de doctrine" have moved us to initiate a comprehensive train the trainer course. We will train future instructors in the following basic courses beginning in summer 1996:
>   -cockpit training
>   -cabin training
>   -basic pilot training
>   -emergency instruction
>   -CBT and classroom instruction.

In future, the participants will be subject to a two-part course carried out over twin four-day sessions. These sessions will contain the topics of presentation technique, moderation, qualification, communication, learning and learning styles. In the second half of the course the participants will implement what they have learned and will also make a presentation that they have completed between the two sections of the course, (approximately 1-2 months). By means of discussion, feedback and video feedback, the participants will not only be able to assimilate elements of their future vocation, but also will be able to get some direct hands-on experience in behavioral instruction.

The diversification of the course and the participation of various future instructors from different areas within the company promotes mutual understanding and helps to reduce prejudices while supporting the joint platform for product design in the market.

Instructors will be taken from among key people in various sectors of the company. Their understanding and implementation of findings in areas such as human factors, human resource development, product design and strategic positioning will be of great interest. Instructors are important signal makers and sensors. It is therefore of central importance that the selection, training and supplementary instruction is comprehensively regulated within the company. This only reinforces our opinion of the importance of joint training.

Summary

We observe that:
- specialization in various areas of the company is increasing,
- polarizing, centrifugal and other powers result from the creation of profit centers or cooperation in general,
- cost pressures are increasingly gaining momentum

These are all factors that have a massive effect on training within a company. The danger is great that these factors, particularly the pressure to reduce costs across the board, are pressurizing strategic investment and comprehensive solutions over the long term. We must give the highest priority to the idea that a company's primary duties, in our case product design in flight operations, must be reflected in aspects of training. The passenger cannot have the feeling that the cabin and cockpit crew were hired by two separate companies.

This is why we take the opportunity whenever we can to train and educate our staff in a product- and duty-oriented manner. As is currently the trend in the USA, this applies to the most varied professional categories and may include, in addition to flight crews, maintenance and ATC staff members.

References

Amundson, J.M. (1995). Line Oriented Flight Training (LOFT) to improve cockpit-cabin communications. In N. Johnston, R. Fuller and N. McDonald (eds), *Aviation Psychology; Training and Selection* (pp. 81-86). Aldershot; Avebury Aviation.

Chute, R.D. & Wiener, E.L. (1995). Cockpit-Cabin Communication: A Tale of Two Cultures. *The International Journal of Aviation Psychology*, 5 (3), 257-276.

Eissfeldt, H. (1995). CRM-Training in Air Traffic Control. In H. Eissfeldt, K.M. Goeters, H.J. Hörmann, P. Maschke & A. Schiewe (eds.), *Effective Work in Teams: Crew Resource Management Training for Pilots and Air Traffic Controllers* (pp. 21-23). Cologne: DLR.

Hamman, W.R., Seamster, T.L., & Edens, E.S. (1995). LOFT/LOE in air carrier training. In N. Johnston, R. Fuller and N. McDonald (eds.) *Aviation Psychology: Training and Selection* (pp. 87-92). Aldershot; Avebury Aviation.

Harris, D.H.R. (1995). Perceived working relationship between flight deck and cabin crew. In N. Johnston, R. Fuller and N. McDonald (eds.) *Aviation Psychology: Training and Selection* (pp. 75-80). Aldershot; Avebury Aviation.

Wiener, E.L., Kanki, B.G. & Helmreich, R.L. (eds.) (1993). *Cockpit Resource Management*. San Diego: Academic Press.

12 Evaluation and the instructor

Joey M Anca Jr.

Learning foundation and theory

In the latter months of 1994, Philippine Airlines (PAL) commissioned a survey to assess the effectiveness of instruction and instructors within its Flight Training organization. What started off as an initial diagnosis of the training organization revealed data which appear sterile and straightforward from a statistical standpoint, but meaningful if viewed from the context of culture in an Asian flight training organization.

In a broad sense, learning is one's reaction to a previous experience. As Westrum (1991) would put it, 'a glance in the rear view mirror.' Learning is realized once an individual draws from the brain latent recorded experience, which when retrieved, is hopefully (and successfully) applied to a particular problem situation at hand. Therefore, one can posit that the level of learning is largely dependent upon the frequency with which relevant experiences are brought forth to difficulties and opportunities presented in life. Assuming that this position is sufficient, how then can an individual (a pilot for that matter) perform in situations where no recorded experiences can be cull from? Say, flying into an airport that the pilot has never been to or dealing with a new crewmember or instructor? In the former scenario, the problem could be well addressed through series of route training and qualification checks. But in the second scenario, the pilot may remain helpless in the exercise of trial and error by dealing with a new crewmember or instructor. One of the crucial issues in any learning environment therefore is: did the instructional institution or the learner himself prepare to anticipate future and unforeseen events?

To a large extent, the preparation for learning is determined by the context that the learner brings into the classroom or the aircraft. One of the most basic and, I believe ephemeral, literature on learning classifies the motivation and strategies of a learner into three approaches: Surface, Deep and Achieving (Biggs, 1987; Biggs & Moore, 1993).

Biggs defines the three approaches as: Learners with a 'surface approach' are motivated to meet minimal course requirements and achieve their goals by rote learning and strategies just to reproduce what they have learned. On the other hand, learners using a 'deep approach' are more intrinsically motivated, (they) seek to personalize their learning and undertake meaning-oriented learning activities. Finally, learners with an 'achieving approach' are more intrinsically motivated to seek high grades, to enhance their egos through competition, and to organize themselves for learning.

Putting learning into context

Whereas data from the three approaches incipiently came from university settings and, later, student pilot populations (Moore & Telfer, 1993), this chapter will be concerned with using the same model but from an organizationally longitudinal perspective, meaning differences between samples of position, age, flying hours and years in position. It is in this hope that the findings can provide data and suggestions which other researchers can build upon. The underlying caveat in this study is that the data represent the context and culture of an Asian airline and therefore, the findings do not necessarily represent other cultures and contexts.

Description of the study

The PAL Flight Training Survey Questionnaire (composed of 20 questions on learning, instruction and instructing, and three related to administration) was given at random to the total flightcrew population of Philippine Airlines of 650. A total of 82 responses were gathered. The questionnaire used a four-point scale of 1=Always; 2=Usually; 3=Rarely; and, 4=Never, lower scores being better endorsements of the questions. Statistical measurements were used (eg. Analyses of Variance and t-Tests for significance) to determine differences among groups. The responses were classified as below:

Using Biggs' (1987) approaches to learning, the twenty questions were then examined, on a relatively subjective basis, and categorized into the three approaches. Some questions pertained to more than one approach and thus were classified into either two or three combinations of approaches. The three additional questions were intrinsically administrative ones. They intended to get comments on additional training tools and resources and thus, did not impact directly into any of the three approaches.

143

Table 12.1
Survey samples

According to Position	According to Age	According to Years in Position	According to Flying Hours
Flight Engineer	less than 25 years old	1 year or less	500 hours or less
First Officer	26 to 36 years old	2 to 5 years	501 to 1000 hours
Ground Instructor	37 to 45 years old	6 to 9 years	1001 to 200 hours
Check/Instructor Pilot	45 and above years old	10 and above years	2001 and above hours

(From PAL Flight & Ground Training Survey Questionnaire, 1994)

Table 12.2
Classification of survey questions

Survey Question	Surface	Deep	Achieving
Are training objectives clear?		✓	
Are tests, checks or evaluations related to these objectives?		✓	✓
Do the tests, checks or evaluations indicate who is the best pilot?			✓
Does the training help to produce better flightcrew?		✓	
Are training methods appropriate?		✓	
Is training provided in the correct sequence?		✓	✓
Are training notes and manuals in sufficient detail?	✓	✓	✓
Are they easy to read?	✓	✓	✓
Can you easily understand them?	✓	✓	✓
Is enough time allocated to training and instruction?	✓	✓	✓
Is the scheduling of training suitable?	✓	✓	✓
Do checks and tests provide a valid indication of ability?			✓
Are training grades/remarks accurate reflections of attainment?			✓
Are you able to learn in a way that suits you best?		✓	✓
Are instructors able to cater for individual differences in trainees?		✓	
Are your flight instructors competent in teaching?	✓	✓	✓
Are your ground instructors competent in teaching?	✓	✓	✓
Are the things learned in training applicable to actual line operations?		✓	
Is there adequate preparation for advance technology, glass cockpit training?		✓	
Are the items taught in the classroom, checked in the simulator?		✓	✓

(Based from PAL Flight and Ground Training Survey, 1995)

After all questions were grouped into one of the learning approaches, the responses were clustered according to the four different sample populations: Position, Age, Flying Hours and Years in Position. This was done in an attempt to find out whether any sample population (s) drawn out from the total 82 submissions was significantly different from any of the other sample populations. A t-Test between groups was used to identify these differences.

Generally, the responses based on Age, Flying Hours, and Years in Position did not produce as many significant differences as the demographic item of Position. Significant differences are those values for probability (p) which are less than or equal to .05. For Position, the observation was that there were significant differences between scores of management instructors (flight and ground) as against line personnel (captains, first officers, pilot trainees etc.). On most items, ground instructors scores differed significantly with the scores of all other groups. This finding, when probed later on from the standpoint of the organization's culture, confirms various anecdotal experiences about the relationship of pilot and non-pilot instructors--the 'caste system' that operates within an airline and perhaps attendant discriminatory practices between these two groups. We shall now discuss the findings in particular.

'Deep' items

The items contained in this cluster are questions which directly impact on the learner's concern for being <u>internally</u> motivated to learn. Deep learners are described as those who reflect on the implications and potential problems which the subject matter may contain. Often Deep learners discuss matters with others, reading widely and relating the new learning with what they already know (Telfer, 1992). As such, the survey questions clustered in this approach revolve around the clarity of learning objectives, the efficacy of training in producing better flightdeck crew, the appropriateness of training methods, the ability of instructors to cater to differences of trainees, the applicability of learning to actual line operations and lastly, the level of preparation for advanced technology glass-cockpit training. All of the respondents scored the Deep items in between the range of 'Always' and 'Usually' (Mean Range of 1.634-2.39).

An examination of Figure 12.1 shows that the items on preparation for advanced technology training and the ability of instructors to cater to individual differences of trainees, in particular, revealed less favorable scores. To a lesser extent, the same could be said for applicability for actual line operations. Taking these findings into context, it may well be concluded that the respondents agree that the curriculum of studies (learning objectives, training methodology and the ability to produce better flightdeck crew) is not the area where training improvements could be done. In fact, the curriculum of studies is PAL's strength as seen from the positive endorsement of the Deep items. Historically, PAL's curriculum is patterned closely after KLM. It was only recently, with the introduction of the B747-400, F50 and B737-300 into PAL's fleet, that the curricula varied from that of KLM. In a ny case, the general sentiment of pilots (especially the more veteran pilots) is of belief and reliance for the KLM curriculum.

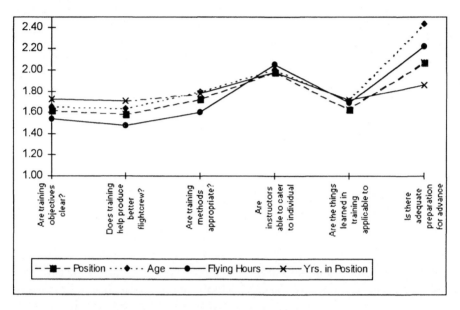

Figure 12.1 Average mean for Deep approach (lower scores indicate more preference for Deep approach)

We further examined the differences between each of the demographic groups with respect to the Deep items and found out that Age, Flying Hours and Years in Position responses were not significant. However, the grouping of Position showed greater discrimination. In most cases, ground instructors gave significantly more favorable scores than all other positions. Meaning, training objectives were clearer, training produces better flightcrew, methods are more appropriate, etc., from the standpoint of the ground instructors. Table 12.3 provides the data for significant differences between ground instructors and the demographic groupings.

Table 12.3
Significant differences between ground school instructors and other positions

Questionnaire Item (DEEP)	Ground Instructors and:				
	Management Pilot (N=10)	Line Captain (N=16)	First Officer (N=21)	Systems Engineer (N=7)	Pilot Trainee (N=18)
	Mean (SD)	Mean (SD)	Mean (SD)	Mean (SD)	Mean (SD)
Are training objectives clear?	1.6* (.516)	1.813* (.403)	1.619* (.498)	1.857*	1.722 * (.575)
Does training help to produce better flightcrew?	1.5 (.527)	1.688* (.479)	1.714* (.463)	1.714* (.756)	1.722* (.575)
Are training methods appropriate?	1.8* (.632)	1.875* (.342)	1.762* (.539)	1.571 (.535)	1.944* (.416)
Are instructors able to cater to individual differences?	1.9 (.994)	2.188* (.403)	2.095* (.436)	2.286* (.951)	2.00* (.594)
Are things learned applicable to line ops?	1.5 (.527)	2.063* (.443)	1.667* (.483)	1.857* (.378)	1.722* (.461)
Is there adequate preparation for advanced technology/glass cockpit operations?	2.4* (1.08)	2.438* (.629)	2.143 (.854)	2.571* (.787)	2.778* (.808)

(*= significant)

'Achieving' items

Learners who are motivated through an 'achieving' approach tend to seek out high grades in the process of the course. They are further motivated through competition and they put a high premium on being on the top of the student's list. In many ways, their gratification from the learning experience is largely due to the standards they place upon themselves and the impact of high grades upon their personal ego. The questionnaire items which were identified as exclusively impacting on the 'achieving' approach are: Do tests, checks or evaluations indicate who is the best pilot?; Do checks and tests provide a valid indication of ability?; and, Are training grades and post training remarks accurate reflections of attainment?

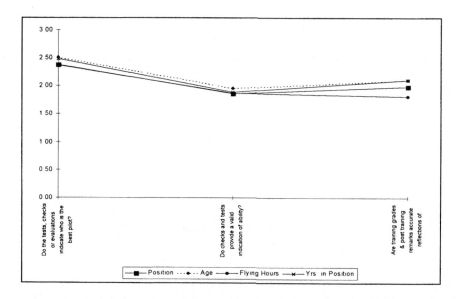

Figure 12.2 Average mean for Achieving approach (lower scores indicate more preference for Achieving approach)

The average mean scores from all demographic groupings in the Achieving items were higher than those found in the Deep items. (Compare Figures 12.1 and 12. 2.) This emphasis on the Achieving approach is consistent with an earlier study (Telfer, 1992) indicating higher mean scores of PAL pilots compared with six European and Asia Pacific airlines with respect to the Achieving approach. In that study, mean scores of PAL pilots were 4.35 compared with 3.93 for all other pilots.

On the items of 'Do checks and tests provide a valid indication of ability and Are training grades and post training remarks accurate reflections of attainment,' we found no differences between the scores of all demographic groups. The only differences we found were between line captains and first officers on the one hand, and ground instructors and check/instructor pilots on the other, in the item 'Do the tests, checks or evaluations indicate who is the best pilot.' We can only surmise that the difference may lie in the perspectives of the term 'best pilot' and that there may be sub-cultural issues in these perspectives.

In a hallmark research on cross-cultural dimensions (Hofstede, 1980), the

Philippines was ranked fourth highest (Malaysia, Panama and Guatemala were higher) in a survey among 53 nationalities, on the dimension of Power-Distance. A high power-distance index is indicative of highly paternalistic societies where leadership is viewed more as 'directing' than a 'sharing', the latter being where all members of the team participate in the decision-making and leading functions. Since the milieu of flight training is generally done in the classroom or the simulator, the directing style would seem more appropriate than would a shared or democratic leadership style. This is even bolstered by the finding that Philippine leaders (and instructors) are more predisposed to higher Power-Distance leadership or mentorship styles than would their other Asian or western counterparts. Therefore, we could expect that ground instructors and check/instructor pilots possess a tendency towards pinpointing the best pilot among his students. But in the case of line captains and first officers, who we may classify into the sub-culture of students, we see a more modest response towards the identification of being the best pilot.

The Filipinos live within a 'high context' culture (Gochenour, 1990). At a very early age, Filipinos learn the value of the groups or the contexts wherein they belong. They consider themselves as individuals, but within a group and feelings about personal accomplishments are only valid if shared with the group. Hence, Filipinos live in a context where they can only claim personal accomplishments if the group's effort is likewise acknowledged as instrumental to one's own success. An attitudinal fallout in this regard therefore is modesty when adjudged as the best pilot (positive attitude) or pulling down the successes of others through backbiting and gossip (negative attitude). The Filipino's vernacular coinage for this latter attitude is *crab-mentality* - to personify a basket of crabs who incessantly pull down others who are trying to get out of the basket.

As a postscript to this discussion, the value of indicating the 'best pilot' may be more understandable in a western, individualistic society and uncomfortable for the Filipino (perhaps, Asian) pilot.

'Deep-achieving' items

These items are those which can be classified in both the preceding two learning approaches. The items discuss: the linkage of tests and checks with the learning objectives, the sequencing of training subjects, the atmosphere of learning (i.e. are you able to learn in a way that suits you best), and the relationship between items taught in the classroom and items checked in the simulator. Figure 12.3 represents the average mean scores for the Deep-Achieving items.

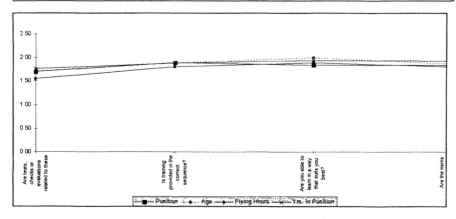

Figure 12.3 Average means for Deep-Achieving approach (lower scores indicate more preference for Deep-Achieving approach)

It would appear that there are similar scores among the average mean of all demographic groupings. However, when we looked into the differences between these groups, we found very significant differences especially in two items, namely, are tests, checks and evaluations related to training objectives and are items taught in class checked in the simulator.

Notably, both items directly pertain to whether students are evaluated on what they have actually taken up during the course. We found that Line Captains and First Officers scores significantly differed from Management Pilots and Ground Instructors. In the aspect of whether checks, tests and evaluations are related to training objectives, we found Line Captains indicated that training objectives are not as related to performance evaluation as would Management Pilots (p=.043) and Ground Instructors (p=.011). Related to this finding, Line Captains felt that there are differences between what was taught in class with what was checked in the simulator. Their scores in this item varied significantly with Management Pilots (p=.016) and Ground Instructors (p=.001).

By these differences alone, there is enough reason to evaluate the integrity of the curriculum and performance evaluation itself. There appears to be a differing view between the instructor group and the student group. While the instructors endorse that classroom topics are those checked in the simulator or in actual proficiency checks, this view does not hold true with respect to students.

Surface-deep-achieving items

Items in this cluster pertain to all learning approaches and are not singly or dually classified in any of two approaches. They were classified as such

150

primarily because of their importance in all three learning approaches. These items pertain to the comprehensiveness and readability of training notes and manuals, the allocation of time given for training and instruction, the suitability of training schedules and the competency of ground and flight instructors.

Training notes and manuals

Management Pilots significantly differed in their opinion about the overall comprehensiveness, readability, and understandability of training notes and manuals. For instance, Pilot Trainees (p=.033) felt that training notes and their Ab Initio manual were not sufficiently detailed; Line Captains (p=.003) and First Officers (p=.011) felt that the notes and manuals issued to them were not as easily readable and understandable. Such differences in scores would predictably vary because of the airline's practice to literally lift the manufacturer's training manual and adopt it in its own syllabi of studies. Though from a technical standpoint, aviation terms may have scant variability, what may indeed be not understandable is the applicability of the manufacturer's (or another airline's) philosophy into Philippine Airlines training and operational experience. Herein lies the mammoth task of training designers and developers in utilising what is intrinsically applicable to the airlines' operating condition.

Competency of flight and ground instructors

We compared the perceived competency levels between the two groups of instructors (flight and ground) and found out that as a whole, flight instructors were viewed as more competent than their ground counterparts. Expectedly, ground instructors rated themselves as more competent than flight instructors. However, we saw significant differences in this perception. Whereas ground instructors perceived themselves as competent 'always', Line Captains and First Officers (p=.002), Systems Engineers (p=.028) and Pilot trainees (p=.003) gave the opinion that ground instructors are actually less competent. What we found interesting is that even the Management Pilots (who are part of the administration and training function) had similar views (p=.007) about the competency of ground instructors.

We qualify this as a critical area for instructor development with regard to this finding. This is perhaps largely due to the amount of training and development given for ground instructors as compared with flight instructors. While flight instructors undergo standard recurrency programs, there is little evidence for continuing training given to ground instructors. Furthermore, the finding extends itself to uncovering differing treatment of flight and ground instructors. In fact, we may have unknowingly discovered subcultures within the training organization and confirmed their disparities based on the results of the data.

This could form the basis for investigation and research in the future.

**Ground instructors viewed the effectiveness of their instruction
differently from others in the airline**

Quo vadis?

If there is anything worth underscoring in this study of instructorship, evaluation and learning, it is the value of collaboration between academia and the training organization within the airline. In a country where indigenous expertise on aviation psychology is wanting, we have explored assistance through the use of western implements. Previous research (Telfer, 1993) revealed the tendency of the Filipino pilot towards a more Deep and Achieving learning approach. By further investigating approaches to learning across the organization, other findings unfolded:

- Demographic groupings of years in position, age and flying hours proved less 'sensitive' data: We did not get as many significant differences in scores when compared to grouping by position. This could perhaps be attributed to the Filipino as belonging to a 'high context' culture, where social position and affiliation define roles in the organization. Naturally, significant differences in scores are readily evident:
- The evaluation of instruction showed that there is a great opportunity to re-evaluating performance evaluation (proficiency checks, tests, simulator checks etc.) to reflect the curricula given in the classroom;

• Significant differences were observed between opinions of the instructor groups (flight and ground) and that of the students (line captains and first officers). Specifically, ground instructors were more positive in their opinion than would all the other respondents in the study. However, the airline may have to look at upgrading the competency of ground instructors who are mainly perceived as less competent than their flight instructor counterparts;

A conclusion which can be drawn from this Philippine Airlines study is that there is a need for systematic evaluation of ground instruction. This is part of the cycle of both learning and instruction. Indeed, systems theory implies a loop from results of instruction feeding back as an input to the system which can lead to improvement. Though leaders of airline organizations are usually selected because of the quality of their technical abilities, there is increasing evidence that we should be selecting instructors for their teaching competencies.

Acknowledgements

We acknowledge the spirit of co-operation by Professors Ross Telfer and Phil Moore in the conduct of this study.

References

Biggs, J.B. (1987). *Student approaches to learning and studying*, ACER, Melbourne.

Biggs, J.B. & Moore, P.J. (1993), *The Process of Learning* (3rd ed.), Prentice-Hall, Sydney.

Gochenour, T. (1990), *Considering Filipinos*, Intercultural Press, Yarmouth, ME.

Hofstede, G. (1980), *Culture's consequences: international differences in work-related values*, Sage, Beverly Hills, CA.

Moore, P.J. & Telfer, R.A. (1993), Pilot's approaches to learning, in Telfer, R.A. (ed.), *Aviation Instruction and Training*, Ashgate, Aldershot, pp.121-122.

Telfer, R.A. (1992), Pilot learning processes project: report to Philippine Airlines, The University of Newcastle, Newcastle.

Telfer, R.A. (1994). Instructional evaluation survey, Philippine Airlines. Bolton Point, Instructional Research and Development.

Westrum, R. (1991), *Technologies and society: the shaping of people and things*, Wadsworth Inc., Belmont, CA., pp. 354-358.

13 Loft facilitator training

Jorg Bertram and Norm Dowd

Background

In 1989, Air Canada began three-day workshops designed to increase its crew's awareness of the impact Crew Resource Management (CRM) has on flight safety. These three-day workshops, however, were clearly insufficient to implement lasting change. Air Canada's management recognized the need to reinforce the concepts explored in these workshops so Capt. W. MacLellan, Vice President of Flight Operations, tasked Captain Norm Dowd to research the programs that other airlines and the academic community were currently undertaking to reinforce this valuable training. After attending seventeen human factors conferences and seminars worldwide, and visiting several airlines, Dowd concluded that Line Orientated Flight Training (LOFT) in the simulator was the most effective method of continuing CRM training. This would provide a needed-opportunity for crews to practice and receive feedback in Crew Resource Management.

Captain Jorg Bertram and Captain Joe Leslie, both CRM Facilitators, then joined Captain Dowd to form Air Canada's LOFT Development Team. On behalf of the team, Leslie spent two very beneficial days with Delta Airline's Flight Operations Training in Atlanta, Georgia. (Delta had already begun human factors training in their simulators.) Upon his return, with the benefit of Delta's experience and the most current worldwide data that Dowd had collected, Leslie wrote the *LOFT Facilitator's Manual.* Betram produced Air Canada's first A320 LOFT scenario, which became Chapter 8 of the manual. This manual was designed to serve as a reference source for the facilitators. The last four chapters were assembled as stand-alone guides, each focusing on two of the eight human factors elements addressed by Air Canada. These guides were constructed to be used as prompts during the LOFT session proper and during the debriefing segment.

Once the manual was complete, the team turned to the design of a LOFT Facilitator's Workshop. This workshop would provide the forum needed to transfer the knowledge, skills and attitudes gleaned from our research, to the facilitators for their use as leaders in our LOFT program.

A consultant provided the course structure and methodology for this informational transfer. The *Spiral Curriculum* structure proved to be an effective training model in such applied practical skills (Telfer, 1991). In addition, the profile and background of the course participants - very motivated, skilled, professional pilots - were considered most important when choosing the instructional design. The following description provides the methodologies that were employed, as told by the team.

There were six basic aspect of the instructional design. These are presented in summary form, then described in more detail.

Summary of training design

- **Group Size:** Total number of participants between 8 and 16, in groups of 4, to satisfy all group activities.
- **Activity:** A hands-on, interactive workshop using video feedback parallelling a LOFT session.
- **Style:** Workshop using same number of participants as would take place in a LOFT (3 or 4).
- **Involvement:** Role-playing pilots participating in a LOFT as well as role playing pilots shown in the videos.
- **Adult learning:** Addressing participant concerns on flip charts before the course and at the end of the course to ensure the items were addressed.
- **Mirroring:** Videotaping group tasks to give feedback and hands-on training of VCR operation and use.

The structure of the course

LOFT is divided into three stages : briefing, conducting and debriefing. On days one and two of the workshop, each of the three stages was reduced to its elements and thoroughly examined. On day three, the stages are combined, giving each participant the opportunity to conduct a full briefing and debriefing. The design thus progressed from analysis to synthesis: from the whole, to the parts, and back to the whole.

The focus of the training is on the importance of briefing and debriefing. Briefing is important because it primes learning whereas debriefing reinforces learning. Ideally each should be no more than 45 minutes in length, with a summation at the end. We believe it is important that the facilitators leave with this concept clear in their minds:

> *It takes time to identify that communication, interpersonal skills, and management styles influence effective problem-solving and decision-making. This is the process that crews experience.*

Further, we believe that it is counterproductive to cloud the issue with too many concepts or ideas at the one time. Hence, there is an emphasis in each LOFT session on only two human factor elements although all elements will be present in every period.

Course description

The three day LOFT Facilitator Workshop covers a range of activities from discussion, seminar presentations, video analyses to additional tasks to be completed as "homework". Below, the day to day schedule is outlined. It should be noted that each of the major activities identified below may consist of a number of minor related activities.

Day 1

Introduction and welcome (Activity #1)

The purpose of this initial session is to introduce participants as well as providing a background to the program, establishing the research basis and comparison to other airlines LOFT programs and setting expectations of the course through presentation of the performance objectives. Ice-breaking clearly is important at this initial stage.

As part of *team building* we acknowledge the personal attributes that led to their selection as facilitators:
-great interpersonal skills,
-credibility among their peers,
-wide technical knowledge,
-positive professional attitudes (our workshops consisted of instructors, check pilots and CRM facilitators). The success of a LOFT program is

directly related to the selection and training of the LOFT facilitators (role modelling).

For *setting expectations* we map out to the participants where we have been and where we are going with the overall program. This is also a good time to provide them with a road-map of where and how they are going to operate in the next three days.

In this first session, we next review the *performance objectives* with the participants so that they will have a clear understanding of what they should be able to do at the end of the course. Each participant should be able to:

1) Explain why Human Factors training is critical to flight safety.
2) Identify the Human Factors *root cause* of technical deficiencies.
3) Focus the training on the crew output and recognition of how one team member's performance affects the crew's results.
4) Conduct the simulator portion of the LOFT, acting in multiple roles as ATC, FA, flight dispatch, etc.
5) Conduct an effective debriefing using questioning which draws out the participants through self-critique.
6) Operate the VCR marking system and to identify the events on the tape that focus on both effective and less-than-fully effective Human Factor elements and their technical implications.

One challenge is equipping facilitators with the skills necessary to enable them to recognize ineffective crew resource management that leads to a technical deficiency. Because the participants were nearly all check pilots and instructors, their strong technical background tends to lead them to focus on the technical deficiency itself rather than the human factors root-cause that *led* to the deficiency.

The debriefing (Activities #2 and #3)

The first element that we touch on after the introduction is the debriefing. We want to take advantage of primacy learning with what we consider the most important constituent of LOFT: the debriefing. We introduce the participants to the debriefing using two videos: one with an effective debrief and one that is totally ineffective. In the ineffective video, we make use of humour and exaggeration to emphasize the key elements of all debriefings:

- an open climate;
- stating goals;
- starting with effective behaviour;
- keeping all crew members involved; and,
- drawing out the feelings and views of the participants as opposed to personal views.

Next is group discussion (Activity #3) to involve the participants and have them identify the key elements rather than our simply stating them. These were recorded on a flip chart as they were catalogued and served to provide an immediate answer to the, yet unspoken, question many participants harboured: can I do this human factors thing?

After this short introduction on debriefing, we touch upon it again on day two and allow each participant to conduct a full debriefing on day three.

Root cause (Activity #4)

Before lunch on day one, we next touch on the root cause of accidents and incidents. We have found that it is a big challenge for instructors and check pilots to find the human factors root cause of a technical deficiency. We begin their awareness with the description of a pilot-proficiency check in which the F/O has difficulty programming a hold. The captain subsequently becomes involved in the programming and the aircraft passes the holding fix, violating their clearance. A short group discussion follows to identify the human factor root cause. This moves the focus to the crew coordination and workload management instead of the consequent airspace violation. (The crew had the necessary technical skills because the captain eventually programmed the hold but they lacked the human factors skills necessary to maintain a safe operation.)

This is introduced just before lunch to take advantage of lunch hour discussions among the participants. The next discussion on root cause involves the participants examining eight incidents as homework and then discussing them in class to hone these skills. We revisit the subject again in activity #4, on day 2. Here we watch vignettes on video depicting crew situations that demonstrate human factor deficiencies and have the participants specify the human factors components involved.

Briefing (Activities #5 and #6)

The briefing can be separated into the following components:
1. Overview
2. Creating the atmosphere
3. Conveying the instructional roles
4. Clarifying and reviewing two of the components of effective crew performance
5. Describing the scenario

Each LOFT participant receives a pre-work information package. We ask the facilitator at this point to use the art of questioning to probe the candidate's understanding of the training process they are entering. This provides an opportunity for the facilitator to clear up any misunderstandings before conducting the session and establishes an even base line for the group.

At this point we have the participants working in groups offering feedback for each of the pre-brief elements. The idea is to use the same technique you would like the participants to use: effective questioning and feedback. There is an exercise at the completion of day one to deal with effective questioning. It is introduced late in the day after the participants have had time to digest the significance of the concept.

Conducting the LOFT session (Activity #7)

In this session we discuss the conduct of the LOFT itself. Conducting the LOFT is broken down into the following parts.

Conductor

- Become intimately familiar with the operation of the simulator and video equipment.
- Refrain from interfering with the flight regardless of developments.
- Refrain from adding to the scenarios to improve the exercise for the more effective crews. We need accurate feedback of crew response to the LOFT exercise.
- Act as a "dumb and dutiful" simulator operator along for the ride.

Facilitator

- Provide voice communications for the push-back tractor, ATC, the company, maintenance and flight attendants in the most realistic fashion possible.
- Follow the ATC script outlined in the scenario verbatim. The pacing and timing are build into the scenario.
- Remember that as voice facilitator, if you are not told as ATC, company, or flight attendant, of the problem, you do not know it exists.
- Refrain from modifying the script, with one exception: if a crew is observed to be so overloaded that further learning is impossible, reasonable judgment should be exercised to prevent further compounding of the crew's situation.

Observer

- Monitor, record and assess crew performance in both the technical and CRM areas to assist in the debriefing.
- Be alert to any non-verbal communication that may be missed by the crew but potentially useful in debriefing.
- Note the time on the video display of crew interaction that you want brought out at the debriefing.

Active listener

- Much of the time we spend conducting the LOFT will be spent listening with the third ear.

Each of these elements is important in the conduct of the LOFT and requires a thorough understanding of the difference between a LOFT and the traditional forms of training.

Effective questioning (Activity # 8)

It is of vital importance for the facilitator to understand that this is the most effective method of drawing out the participants in both the briefing and debriefing stages. This skill is essential to draw out the participants views of what transpired during the LOFT rather than giving them the facilitators subjective opinion. This fosters crew interaction and allows them to explore the situation as they saw it individually. The video can then be used to clarify the events as seen by an impartial observer, that is the camera. The reverse process can also be used whereby the facilitator runs a portion of the video first and then uses effective questioning to stimulate discussion around a significant human factor event.

We show a video of Eastern Flight #401 and have the participants make up questions using the scenario as the basis for their questioning. We use the handout shown in the next box (see *Air Canada Questioning Handout*) at this time. For "homework" the facilitators examine eight incidents preparing them for discussion the next day.

Day 2

The Eight Human Factors Components (Activities #1 and #2)

The following eight human factors components provide the basis for the early activities on the second day:

1. Communication process(IMPART Model of Communication)
2. Team enhancement
3. Problem solving and decision making
4. Situational awareness
5. Communication styles(Influence model)
6. Feedback and conflict resolution
7. Judgement style
8. Workload management

Participants are asked to thoroughly read one of the components and to prepare a short lecture to feedback their understanding of each component, thereby, broadening the group knowledge of the components. They are also asked to prepare questions that a facilitator may use in highlighting this human factor component during a debriefing. We ask the facilitators to use a three step process when working on this activity:

1. Read the theory of what each component represents.
2. Explain the theory in layman's terms to their fellow participants.
3. Develop questions to draw out the LOFT participants' understanding of these components as they may relate to a real LOFT scenario.

Video vignettes of cockpit scenes are re-introduced at this stage as well. Here we revisit the *root causes* from the previous day, analysing the human factor deficiencies and specifying which of the above eight factors are involved.

Crew performance evaluation form (Activities #3, #4, and #5)

These activities centre on analysing the Crew Performance Evaluation Form, using it to evaluate an incident, then reaching consensus through discussion.

This evaluation is used to quantify the crew's performance in both technical and human factors in our continuing effort to validate the effectiveness of the LOFT program as well as the crew's performance during the session. This training segment is a five-step operation:

1. Review the performance form with a Likert rating and the key to the rating defining each scale value.
2. View a video of a 747 accident in Kuala Lumpur (stopping the video just before they crash).
3. Let each participant rate the crew as seen on the video.
4. Have the participants break into small groups and devise a common rating.
5. Compare ratings in the class and discuss variances to clarify diversities in the rating scale.

Again this is done before lunch to stimulate discussion during lunch regarding the material distributed. After lunch, *Activity 6* is conducted, which focuses on conducting a debriefing, technical versus human factors.

Air Canada Questioning Handout

The eight types of questions are provided below, with a brief explanation and example. Please write your question in the space provided.

B) List the question numbers so that they form a sequence from *surface* to *deep* learning.

1. **CLOSED** - only one answer possible. "You did not enjoy the video, did you?"

---

2. **OPEN** - a variety of answers are possible. "How valuable was the video?"

---

3 **STRUCTURED** - when crews have difficulty in responding to a question which is too demanding. The structured question provides necessary knowledge leading to the response
"You have seen the video of aircraft accidents and discussed the importance of communication as a human factors When could improved communication have prevented any of these accidents?"

---

4. **REQUIRING RECALL OF INFORMATION** - can be factual, such as, "How many gallons of fuel were lost?"

---

5. **REQUIRING COMPREHENSION OF MEANING OR SIGNIFICANCE** - testing understanding "Give us your definition of the term `team enhancement' "

---

6. **REQUIRING ANALYSIS OF RELATIONSHIPS OR COMPONENTS** - requires respondent to examine previously unrelated aspects and decide how they are linked "What is the relationship between communication and good decision making?"

---

7. **EVALUATION BY MAKING A JUDGEMENT** - requiring a decision which may be based on personal values "To what extent does recurrent LOFT training enhance safety?"

---

8. **BLENDING DIFFERENT SOLUTIONS OR IDEAS** - requiring respondents to balance arguments or conclusions and to compromise conflicts or extremes. "Given government policy, economic downturn and deregulation, what is the probability of Canadian / Air Canada merger?"

Figure 13.1 Questioning handout

VCR operational use in LOFT (Activity #7 and throughout)

The best training tool is to have a VCR available for the facilitators during the workshop and allow them to experiment with the various functions during the breaks. Discussion at this time should be centred on how to mark the tape and play it back. Ideally, one should play back to a point approximately 30 seconds before the event so that one can set the stage leading up to the event. At this time it would be valuable to discuss and caution against overuse of the video. It is not necessary to view every event that you feel is worthwhile. This can lead to tuning out (attention span is approximately 50 minutes).

Day 2 homework

Each participant receives a video with two other participants doing a LOFT leg. The objective is to review the LOFT and mark the tape where significant human factors events occurred. One may do this by writing down the time as one would in a real LOFT. The facilitator may also at this point prepare some questions to be used the following day during an actual debriefing.

The participants will appreciate mapping out the following day's events and the preparation time they are given for tomorrow's tasks.

Day 3

Principles of LOFT Design (Activities #1 and #2)

The group is again divided into teams of four and are given a LOFT design worksheet handout. The task is to design a LOFT using the guidelines found in chapter seven of the LOFT facilitators' manual. *Realism is the key in the use of the following guidelines:*

- Company route and flight number;
- Realistic departure time;
- Realistic weights and performance data;
- Load Sheet;
- Most time-consuming option is to land in one hour forty minutes;
- Normal distractions built in;
- Allow periods of time where nothing extraordinary happens.

The *specific objectives* in the design of CRM LOFT scenarios are that:
1. They are totally representative of Air Canada line operations;
2. The problems and situations developed emphasize crew cooperation,

crew management, leadership, and problem solving skills;
3. The scenarios provide the highest degree of realism possible;
4. They provide the crew with opportunities to confront complex decision making situations and to hone communication skills rather than the completion of a series of abnormal checklists.

After the LOFTs have been designed, the group can discuss each one to see if it fits within the design guidelines. *Do not overload crew in the scenarios.*

LOFT differs from traditional forms of training

Pre-brief exercise (Activity #3)

Here we allow each facilitator to conduct a briefing. It is helpful to prepare a flip chart as depicted below to provide a clear map as to everyone's roll during the ensuing exercise.

Depending on the number participants, we have groups of three or of four. In every group each person receives hands on practice along with a review of each human factor component. It is imperative that there is clear direction to the participants at this stage. Adults hate confusion.

Step I (15 Minutes)

Name	Role	Human factors Component
Jim	Conduct Pre-briefing:	Communication Styles and Team Enhancement
Jack	Captain of Crew	
George	F/O of Crew	

Nathan   Observer (will provide feedback on performance)

Each briefing should take ten to twelve minutes after which the observer is asked to give a two to three minute feedback to the Pre-briefer of what he or she, as an outside observer, noticed. Each of the briefings should be video recorded with the camera on a tripod to keep the coordinator free to observe and assist where required.

At this point we take a lunch break. The participants have been working hard and a break is an excellent opportunity to discuss the key elements of a briefing over lunch.

Debriefing exercise in teams and fostering self-critique (Activities #4, #5 and #6)

Again we split into teams of four with each participant having a chance to debrief a crew based on the video viewed the previous night. The crew being debriefed should be the crew seen the previous night. Again there will be an observer to provide some feedback for the debriefer.

Clarity is essential in this task and a flip chart to map out the roles is very helpful for the participants. Each debriefing should be recorded on the same tape as the briefing. This way the individual can take home and observe their own performance. A group discussion should ensue after everyone is finished to flesh out the important debriefing points.

We also at this time discuss some key concepts and issues in using feedback as positive reinforcement. In brief, this could be: Why the mission went well and how this knowledge can be used to make future flights safer.

We have found the following as blocks to self critique and feedback

1. Embarrassment
2. Power gradient Capt-F/O
3. Personality conflicts
4. Preoccupation with personal problems
5. Airline culture
6. Communication style

How do we train the facilitators to overcome these blocks?

- Embarrassment - commence with the positive aspects to encourage openness and focus on what happened not who did what;
- Power gradient - initiate discussion with the F/O focus on team output rather than individual performance;
- Personality conflicts - focus on this as a learning experience and complement team performance to promote cohesion:
  - the crew must have a shared mental model or an understanding of each other's situational awareness. For example, in decision making, the captain may be tending to focus on risk and F/O tends to focus on time;
  - train the facilitators to lead the crew into discussing the bases of their understanding.
- Preoccupation with personal problems - continually draw participants back into the team with questioning. The most effective captains are sensitive to other crew members' personal problems and their potential to affect the operation.
- Airline culture - focus on change in the airline's culture;
- Communication style - the facilitators reinforce a developmental communication style with their own method of communication, demonstrating a concern for their influence as well as the influence of others.

Course critique (Activity #7)

The course critique (shown in the Figure 13.2 - Loft Facilitator's Workshop Evaluation) enables us to review how well the facilitators feel they have been trained to conduct a LOFT. The questions in the critique are related to the performance objectives dscussed at the opening of the workshop.

LOFT FACILITATORS' WORKSHOP EVALUATION

THIS EVALUATION IS ANONYMOUS.

Please rate the extent to which each of these objectives was attained. If you circle 'NOT AT ALL' or 'POORLY' please comment over page to help us improve the program.

Return the completed sheet to the box at the front of the room before 15:30 on Day III as the evaluations will be discussed in the final session.

---

1) I am able to explain to the pilots how a recurrent LOFT Program enhances safety

--------------------------------------------------*-------------------------*-------------------------*

Not at All   Poorly   Adequately   Well

2) I am able to debrief the crew.

--------------------------------------------------*-------------------------*-------------------------*

Not at All   Poorly   Adequately   Well

3) I can operate the simulator and VCR marking system for the LOFT sessions.

--------------------------------------------------*-------------------------*-------------------------*

Not at All   Poorly   Adequately   Well

4) I am able to enact, in a realistic fashion the role of F/A, ATC, LEAD, etc

--------------------------------------------------*-------------------------*-------------------------*

Not at All   Poorly   Adequately   Well

5) I can identify behaviour that enhances flight safety and reinforce this conduct through comments or questions.

--------------------------------------------------*-------------------------*-------------------------*

Not at All   Poorly   Adequately   Well

6) I can assist the crew identify areas of potential improvement in both resource management and technical skills

--------------------------------------------------*-------------------------*-------------------------*

Not at All   Poorly   Adequately   Well

WORKSHOP EVALUATION

7) I can debrief the crew and foster the process of self-critique by participants.

----------------------------------------------------------------*--------------------------------*--------------------------------*

Not at All   Poorly   Adequately   Well

8) I can identify technical deficiencies and rectify them by reviewing the correct procedures.

----------------------------------------------------------------*--------------------------------*--------------------------------*

Not at All   Poorly   Adequately   Well

9) I can explain how human factors and technical skills relate and how their interdependence affects flight safety.

----------------------------------------------------------------*--------------------------------*--------------------------------*

Not at All   Poorly   Adequately   Well

10)   I can demonstrate the skills of:

a) **Questioning**

----------------------------------------------------------------*--------------------------------*--------------------------------*

Not at All   Poorly   Adequately   Well

b) **Explaining**

----------------------------------------------------------------*--------------------------------*--------------------------------*

Not at All   Poorly   Adequately   Well

c) **Empathy**

----------------------------------------------------------------*--------------------------------*--------------------------------*

Not at All   Poorly   Adequately   Well

Summation:

Figure 13.2 LOFT facilitators' workshop evaluation

Conclusion

Document key components of the LOFT on a flip chart and compare with the key components recorded in the introduction. The learning techniques used in the workshop and during summation, should model the techniques to be used in the LOFT such as effective questioning, and video debriefing to draw out participants.

There is emphasis on the human factors root cause of accidents. However, it is important to review the fact that a human factor failing usually precedes a technical deficiency. Technical expertise cannot guarantee a safe operation. It is only when we marry technical expertise with effective crew resource management that our odds of avoiding accidents increases.

The eventual path that LOFT may take once human factors training is accepted as quantifiable and measurable, is that competency in both technical and human factors performance will be accepted as a requirement for licensing, at all levels of aviation. As the LOFT program identifies training deficiencies, methods for training human factors skills will be more easily developed.

By encouraging awareness of and a positive attitude towards the benefits of effective crew resource management, Air Canada hopes to improve the level of safety on every flight.

Reference

Telfer, R.A. (1991) The design of airline HF training. *Report of the Flight Safety and Human Factors Regional Seminar*. Bangkok: ICAO. 36-39.

14 The evaluation of Virgin Atlantic Airways' Crew Resource Management training program

Timothy Bilton

The unacceptably high level of aviation incidents and accidents involving human error has caused the industry to look more closely at the human element of the system. One of the initiatives implemented in an attempt to reduce the number of human error related accidents and incidents is that of Crew Resource Management (CRM) training. CRM can be defined as: *"the most effective use of all available resources to achieve the optimal functioning of the aircraft"*(Bilton 1994). The training of CRM principles focuses on social skills as opposed to technical skills.

In the United Kingdom (UK), the Civil Aviation Authority (CAA) mandated CRM training in September 1993 (AIC 143/1993). This required that all pilots flying for the purpose of public transport attended a course on CRM by 1st January 1995. The CAA subsequently issued AIC 37/1995 'Crew Resource Management Training' in May of 1995. This required that company training manuals should state how recurrent CRM training would take place. It also made recommendations for Cabin Crew CRM training.

The need for evaluation

In both of the CAA circulars there is one area of CRM training that has been somewhat neglected, that of evaluation. This is surprising as there is a tangible need to demonstrate through evaluation the ways in which training improves safety. There are three main groups who will benefit from the evaluation of CRM training, namely, the individual, the airline and the industry.

- *Benefits for the individual.*

  By requesting that all the participants provide feedback on the training, each individual is able to contribute his/her feelings and opinions about the training.

Individuals will feel that their opinions are of value and that they are making a valid contribution. This is especially important for trainees who have had particularly poor or particularly beneficial experiences.

- *Benefits for the airline.*

By evaluating training, the airline will be able to identify the areas of the course that require revision, thereby verifying the training curriculum and identifying areas of possible improvement. From Virgin Atlantic Airways' perspective (the focus of this chapter), evaluation of CRM training can provide data to justify training costs, and more importantly through comprehensive evaluation, it is possible to measure the benefits throughout the airline.

- *Benefits for the industry.*

As stated above, the UK CAA has mandated CRM training. By evaluating the training across the UK industry, the nature of the effect that the training is having will become clear. For example, it may be that different sections of the industry learn from each other with regards to best and worst practices for CRM training.

Virgin Atlantic acknowledged the benefits of a formal evaluation of their CRM training program and this chapter details the initial evaluation conducted by Cranfield University in the UK.

Methodology for the development of the evaluative tool / evaluation

Typically, CRM training has been evaluated at the attitudinal level, with the assumption often being made that a successful course can be identified by a positive change in attitudes. The research justification for using attitudes as a measure of the success of a CRM training course was that firstly, there was no readily available culturally specific behavioural check list with which behaviours could be measured. Secondly, attitudes are subject to change from seminar instruction, making them accessible to the researcher. Thirdly, as this was intended as a longitudinal study, the logical starting point (for the evaluation) was the evaluation of attitudes, with the intention of subsequently looking at behaviours.

Figure 14.1 shows the CRM training, attitude change and behaviour change link, as well as listing several concomitant factors that also influence CRM behaviours.

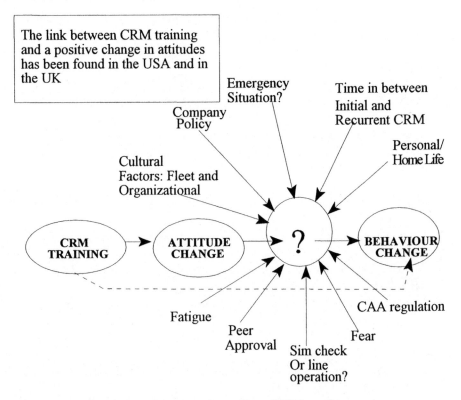

The link between CRM training and a positive change in attitudes has been found in the USA and in the UK

Figure 14.1 Examples of factors that affect CRM performance

The message of Figure 14.1 is that although it is essential to ultimately observe CRM behaviours in order to quantify them, in evaluative terms, behaviours are influenced by a variety of factors, making attitudes and attitude change the best place to start evaluation of the effectiveness of CRM training.

Virgin Atlantic was conducting CRM training in accordance with the CAA AIC 143/1993. Virgin Atlantic's Human Factors Department was responsible for the CRM training and subsequently commissioned Cranfield to design and conduct an evaluation. The Human Factors Department felt that by having an independent party evaluate the training, the results of the evaluation would be more meaningful. This is in accordance with Givens'(1993) assertion that '...*the evaluation process would best be conducted by a neutral, someone with no vested interest in other stages of the training program*'.

In association with the airline, Cranfield devised a methodology for the evaluation of the CRM training program. This involved an evaluation of attitudes towards CRM both pre-training and post-training. To do this an evaluative tool that was reliable, valid and sensitive was required. As no culturally specific tool was readily available, it provided Cranfield with the opportunity to develop one.

Questionnaire development

As a part of the questionnaire development, items were generated that related to CRM issues. This was done by asking four open ended questions to two groups of Virgin Atlantic aircrew. The groups were a mix of Captains, First Officers and Flight Engineers. The questions were based on factors identified by Helmreich and Wilhelm (1991). (Their factor names are given in bold type). The questions were:

- What do you think are the important issues surrounding *communication and co-ordination?*
- Do you think that the *responsibility of command* gives you the right to do as you wish?
- To what extent can the *recognition of stress* improve flight efficiency and safety?
- How important is it to avoid *interpersonal conflict* on the flight-deck?

With consent, the group answers to the four questions were tape recorded and transcribed. From the transcription, information was used to form items for the questionnaire. For example:

- *Interview question* "What do you think are the important issues surrounding communication and co-ordination"?
- *Answer* "I think communication's main function on today's aircraft is to overcome boredom, especially in the more technically advanced aircraft".
- *Questionnaire item* "Communication with other crew members is one of the best ways of alleviating boredom on a long sector".

These items developed for the questionnaire, were in the form of a five point Likert type scale. This process was repeated for both of the transcriptions until no more questions could be created, which resulted in a 28 item questionnaire. Any items that were derived from responses to question one, 'What do you think are the important issues surrounding communication and co-ordination?' were used to form the communication and co-ordination scale. Items derived from question two were formed into the responsibility of commands scale. Similarly, items from responses to question three formed the recognition of stress scale and items derived from question four formed the avoidance of interpersonal conflict scale. The questions were placed in a random order on the questionnaire. Two questionnaires were developed, one for completion prior to the CRM training, and one for completion after the CRM training, the only difference between them being that the post-training questionnaire also contained some demographic questions.

Questionnaire identification

The main aim of identifying the questionnaires was to match up the pre and the post questionnaires for each participant. This was a necessary requirement if attitude change was to be assessed over time. However, by matching up the pre-training and the post training questionnaires two ethical issues arose.

Firstly, there was the requirement to protect the identity of the individual participant. The evaluation required CRM participants to complete a pre-training and a post-training questionnaire. For these questionnaires to be compared the system of identification had to be confidential. It was also important to note the political sensitivity surrounding CRM and its subsequent evaluation. For example, there have been a limited number of occurrences whereby tutors and trainees have had major disagreements on CRM courses resulting in further action being taken. The political fallout of this should not be underestimated. If CRM training is marketed as non-jeopardy, that is what it should be. With regards to evaluation, it should always be stated clearly that the identification of participants during CRM training is for statistical purposes only. To avoid these problems the participants on the course were given a reference number that they had to write on both the pre-training and the post-training questionnaires.

Secondly, there was the need to discriminate between Virgin Atlantic employees and employees from other organizations who were on the training course in order to avoid cross-organizational contamination of the data. This was due to the Virgin Atlantic course being commercially available to other UK airlines. This situation complicated the longitudinal analysis as personnel from the airlines who bought in to the initial Virgin Atlantic Airways CRM training may not have been the same as those who were involved at a later date. A solution was found whereby Virgin Atlantic participants added the prefix 'V' to their identification number. This enabled the data to be coded in a manner that allowed all the Virgin Atlantic participants to be grouped together.

Questionnaire administration

The questionnaire was posted to the participants prior to the course along with the pre-course material distributed by the airline. Accompanying the questionnaire was a covering letter from the manager of the airline's Human Factors Department. The post-training questionnaire was administered at the end of the second day's training and collected immediately, thereby ensuring a high response rate.

Results of evaluation

The total number of CRM course participants who fully completed both questionnaires was 182 (46 Captains, 110 First Officers and 26 Flight Engineers).

The questionnaires were analysed to determine if any significant attitude change had taken place as a result of the training. A comparison of the pre-training and the post-training composite attitude scores revealed a significant difference in the desired direction, that of being increasingly favourable towards CRM (on three of the four scales). This is illustrated in Figure 14.2. Composite scores were constructed by summing the total responses of each participant across each relevant scale.

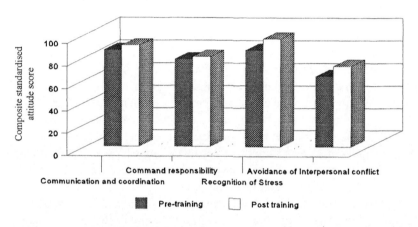

Figure 14.2 Composite standardized attitude scores of trainees pre and post CRM training

Figure 14.2 shows that after CRM training, participant's responses were more favourable towards CRM concepts across all four factors. The biggest relative increase was seen for factor three, recognition of stress, with the smallest increase occurring for factor four, avoidance of interpersonal conflict.

Further analysis revealed that flying in a two crew or three crew aircraft had no significant effect on attitude change experienced by the participants, and also that favourability towards CRM did not increase in all participants. A small number of the participants' attitude scores remained unchanged (two people), and some even decreased (eight people).

These results are consistent with the findings reported by Helmreich and Wilhelm (1991). They found little evidence to support the fourth factor and dropped it from their analysis. They also found that a significant number of trainees rejected CRM training and showed less favourable attitudes post CRM training than they did pre CRM training. This was labelled as the Boomerang Effect.

Implications for the airline

The positive attitude change experienced by participants on the CRM training course is the first step towards a better understanding of CRM, both for Virgin Atlantic and the UK aviation industry as a whole.

The results of the evaluation demonstrate that the Virgin Atlantic CRM training course does result in a significantly favourable change in attitudes towards CRM issues, thereby justifying the financial cost of the course development. Because the course is successful, it facilitates the transition to the next stage of CRM training, that of recurrent CRM.

A direct benefit to Virgin Atlantic is a reduction in the development time and costs of the recurrent training package. The successful initial CRM training for flight crew could also be used as a basis for broadening CRM-type training into other areas of airline operations for example, Ground Maintenance Resource Management.

Implications for the industry

The results from the survey strongly suggest that there was a high initial acceptance level of CRM training. This could possibly be attributed to the CAA legislation, in that less resistance is encountered by the CRM instructors due to the CAA mandating that the training must be conducted.

The biggest increase across the four scales was seen to occur in scale three, the recognition of stress. This has important implications, as the primary aim of CRM is to decrease the chances of a fatal human error occurring on the flight-deck of an aircraft. However, human errors often occur as a result of severe stress. In highly stressful situations people tend to revert to their dominant behaviour patterns, and when such regression occurs, any training that has not been overlearnt will be discarded in favour of the more familiar behaviours. CRM principles must therefore be integrated and evaluated at all levels of pilot training if they are to be successful when they are needed. By increasing participants awareness of the effects of stress and how to recognise it, the possibility of stress becoming severe and having a negative effect has been reduced. The other scales also increased, showing that the participants became more aware and more positive towards communication and co-ordination, and command responsibility. This is another benefit for flight safety as these areas, among others, were shown contribute to many of the accidents and incidents that originally led to the need for CRM training. This study shows that the awareness of CRM principles, and in particular, the recognition of stress, was successfully increased for the CRM participants.

The CRM training did not positively change the attitudes of every single participant. Some participants changed their attitudes negatively after the training. This underlines the issue of CRM 'failures', those people who are less in favour of CRM after being on a CRM course. In future CRM training, should participants who have decreased their favourability towards CRM be targeted for more training? If so, how can they be identified without contravening the confidential identification system under which the data was originally gathered? If they are identified, there may be a possibility that co-operation in future CRM seminars will not be forthcoming. As the aim of the CRM training is to decrease human errors occurring in the aviation system, individuals who are less favourable towards CRM concepts after their training could be perceived as more likely to be subject to human error themselves. It is therefore not unreasonable to suggest that these individuals are targeted for further training. However, it is also important to view the evaluation of CRM participants in the context of the airline culture. By referring back to Figure 1, it can be seen that some of the influences on behaviour apart from attitudes are things like company policy, for example, management attitude towards CRM or fleet culture (for example a highly automated fly by wire aircraft or a more traditional flight deck). These factors should be taken into account when evaluating CRM training, as they undoubtedly affect the level of ultimate CRM performance.

The first stage of CRM training has been aimed at increasing awareness of human factors related issues in the everyday operations of line pilots. This training has for the most part been evaluated at the attitudinal level. The next stage is recurrent and or combined CRM training. This should be aimed at giving the CRM trainees the opportunity to practice the skills deemed to constitute effective CRM performance and should be evaluated at the behavioural level.

Further study

As recurrent CRM training begins there is an ideal opportunity to study the effects of recurrent CRM on attitude change, as well as studying the relative permanency or decay of the attitude change resulting from the initial training.

In evaluative terms it is essential to observe CRM behaviours for change, as a change in attitude is more valuable in terms of aviation safety if it can be directly linked to a change in behaviour. It would therefore be necessary to observe CRM behaviours in context. Previous research into attitudes and behaviours has suggested that behaviour is influenced by a number of factors other than attitudes. (Fishbein and Ajzen 1980).

In terms of the research effort into CRM, the attribution of behaviour change through CRM courses solely by the measurement of participant's attitudes is only the first stage. In order to attribute behaviour change to CRM training it is necessary to observe the behaviour. This has been recognised by the UK CAA who have commissioned Cranfield University to develop a set of performance indicators for the evaluation of CRM at the behavioural level.

Conclusion

Ultimately, this study can be seen as the first step in the evaluation of CRM in the UK, in that it shows the training of CRM principles significantly effects participants attitudes in a favourable manner. The next stage is to evaluate behaviour change resulting from CRM training.

References

Bilton, T. (1994). *Development of a framework for the evaluation of a UK airlines' Crew Resource Management Training.* Unpublished MSc thesis, Cranfield University.

Fishbein, M., &, Ajzen, I. (1980). *Understanding Attitudes and Predicting Social Behaviour.* New York: Prentice Hall.

Givens, K, C. (1993). The Evaluation of Training in Telfer, R. (Ed) *Aviation Instruction and Training* (1993). Aldershot: Ashgate.

Helmreich, R, L. & Wilhelm, J, A. (1991). Outcomes of Crew Resource Management Training. *International Journal of Aviation Psychology* 1(4), 287-300.

United Kingdom AIC 143/1993 (Pink 90) 23rd September. *Crew Resource Management.* Aeronautical Information Service.

United Kingdom AIC 37/1995 (Pink 110) 4th May. *Crew Resource Management Training.* Aeronautical Information.

15 The evaluation of aviation curriculum in the affective domain: Some preliminary thoughts

Henry R Lehrer

Introduction

It is a marvelous time to be associated with the field of aviation. Airplanes have become quieter and more efficient and simulators have gotten cheaper as well as more realistic. In navigation, it is now possible to accurately cover long distances and to execute instrument approaches procedures in a more accurate and reliable way. The days of high-technology in aviation seem to be upon us.

In the training and education sector of the aviation industry, it is now possible to benefit from the use of computer-aided instruction or even take classes via distance learning and independent study. If taking a Federal Aviation Administration (FAA) exam, applicants can now know immediately whether they have passed or not. One might assume that the educational process is as advanced as it can be, however, such an assumption would be in error. What has not kept progress with the rest of the industry's rapid gains is that we still tend to evaluate the learning of air crew members, maintenance personnel, air traffic specialist, and the myriad of other aviation professionals in much the same way that we have done for decades.

The reference here is not to the maturation and use in aviation training and education of computer-based training, distance learning, or advanced simulation. Also not referred to is the implementation of one of the new instructional paradigms that have emerged in the arena of instructional technology. Where aviation has not made progress is in the evaluation of just how well we educate and/or train someone in such private and personal things as values, beliefs, convictions, morals, ethical behavior, observation of rules, or respect for other. This omission seems faulty since the evaluation of "These realities as perceived by an individual are just as important, if not more so, as the so-called . . . facts" (Combs, 1962, p. 200).

However, before we can determine how to better evaluate aviation education focused on the affective domain, we must first have a basic understanding of the three recognized domains of learning. Also exceedingly important is the manner in which performance objectives, the measurable achievement of learning, are developed.

The domains

Learning is usually categorized as belonging in three specific domains, cognitive (knowledge), psychomotor (skills), and affective (values and beliefs).

Cognitive domain

The Taxonomy of Educational Objectives: The cognitive domain of Bloom (1956) is perhaps the best know of the educational domains. In developing educational objectives in this domain, the focus is on education for the sake of knowledge and information. There is a hierarchical taxonomy for the domain which includes:
1. Knowledge: knowledge of facts and terminology; ways of utilizing trends and sequences, classifications and categories, as well as criteria and methodologies; and generalizations and theories.
2. Comprehension: comprehension that deal with the translation, interpretation, and extrapolation of information.
3. Application: abstractions of a particular situation.
4. Analysis: breaking a whole knowledge concept into parts and being able to distinguish elements, relationships, and organizational principles.
5. Synthesis: putting together the parts of a concept into a unique plan, operations, or abstract form.
6. Evaluation: making judgments in terms of both internal and external logic and consistency (Ornstein and Hunkins, 1993).
   In aviation, educational objectives in the cognitive domain refer to knowledge that might be gained as the result of attending a pilot ground school, reading an aircraft systems manual, listening to a pre-flight briefing, reviewing meteorological charts and reports, or taking part in a computer-based training module on avionics repair. The highest level educational objectives in this domain may also be illustrated by learning to correctly evaluate the execution of a flight maneuver, repairing an airplane engine, or reviewing the syllabus of an aviation program for breadth and completeness of training. All these activities require various uses and application on differing levels of knowledge. Learning activities in this domain are well formed and accepted in aeronautical settings

and the evaluation of achievement of specific performance objectives is quite straight-forward.

Psychomotor domain

Educational objectives in the psychomotor domain center on skills and the execution of various physical tasks. Included in this domain are:
1. Perception: awareness of a sensory stimulus through stimulation and cue selection followed by translation.
2. Set: the preparedness to take a particular action. Based on the mental, physical, and emotional readiness to act.
3. Guided Response: early learning of a complex task imitation of the instructor or trail and error. Usually judged by an instructor or against a suitable criteria.
4. Mechanism: the habitual performance of an act with some confidence and ability. An emphasis on gaining proficiency often at various levels.
5. Complex Overt Response: performance usually emphasized by quick, smooth, accurate performance requiring a minimum of energy. A lack of uncertainty and performance is automatic.
6. Adaptation: modification of skills to fit a special circumstance or problem situation.
7. Origination: creating new movements (Simpson, 1972).
   The development of skills is quite important in aviation and is exemplified by such activities as learning to perform specific flight maneuvers within a certain set of guidelines, being able to operate a piece of maintenance equipment, or the actual programming an aircraft's flight management system. However, as the psychomotor task becomes more complex and sophisticated, the need for integration of cognitive knowledge with specific psychomotor skills becomes more pronounced. In essence, we are combining performance from more than one domain.

Affective domain

Perhaps the least understood and in many ways, the most important domain of learning, is that which is centered in the affective domain. This domain deals with values, beliefs, and attitudes. The five major categories of the affective domain are outlined in Krathwohl (1964) and include:
1. Receiving: an awareness and a willingness to receive a stimulus.
2. Responding: a learner's active attention to stimuli with acquiescence (consent without protest) and a demonstrated willingness to receive in a satisfied way.
3. Valuing: a learner's beliefs and values addressed in the form of acceptance, preference, and commitment.

4. Organization: an internalization, with respect to conceptualization and organization, of an individual system of values and beliefs.
5. Characterization of a Value Complex: having a value system that is internalized and used as a philosophy for action. Behavior is now pervasive, consistent, and predictable.

Action verbs and objective development

The preparation of learning objectives (or performance objectives in certain schools of thought) is an accepted part of the instructional design process and for the development of virtually any educational event; aviation is no exception. A performance objective is something that indicates what is to be learned and in many cases includes a criteria against which the accomplishment of the objective will be known. "For an objective to be meaningful and therefore useful in guiding educators. . . it should be measurable" (Ornstein & Hunkins, 1993, p. 217).

The learning objective is typically framed in this manner: The learner (trainee or student) will be able to compute the great circle route from New York to London. The intent is clear; prior to the instructional period, lecture, training session, the leaner will expect to learn what is required so that after the learning takes place, he or she will be able to compute the great circle route as required. The objective contains two required parts, an action verb which is "compute" and a subject content reference "the great circle route from New York to London." Two other conditions can be included such as to "complete the task within 10 minutes" by "using an Avstar Flight Computer." Although the writing of learning objectives is not the subject of this chapter, it does help to understand the construction of such learning objectives. However, what is critical to understand is that we now have something to measure to determine either the effectiveness of the instruction or the completeness of the student's learning.

In the cognitive and psychomotor domains of learning, the action verbs usually give an evaluator and the student if the verb is explicit, a very clear indication of what is to be measured. In Table 15.1, several verbs are included that illustrate the hierarchical order; there are many more instances of appropriate verbs for a specific level of each domain that are not illustrated.

Action Verbs by Domain

Cognitive Domain Action Verbs

Knowledge	define, describe, identify, name, point to, or recognize
Comprehension	convert, explain, locate, report, restate, select, or sort
Application	compute, demonstrate, employ, operate, or solve
Analysis	compare, discriminate, distinguishes, or separates
Synthesis	compile, compose, design, reconstruct, or formulate
Evaluation	assess, evaluate, interpret, judge, rate, score, or write

Psychomotor Domain Action Verbs

Perception	choose, detect, identify, isolate, or select
Set	begin, move, react, respond, or start
Guided Response	assemble, build, calibrate, fix, grind, or mend
Mechanism	Same as above except with greater proficiency
Complex Overt Response	Same as above except more highly co-ordinated
Adaptation	adapt, alter, change, rearrange, reorganize, or revise
Origination	combine, compose, construct, design, or originate

Figure 15.1 Action verbs (Source: Gronlund & Linn, 1990; Kemp, 1985)

To develop a performance objective that can ultimately be measured, one must select the level of the domain in which the learning is anchored, choose an action verb that best describes what is to be learned and how, then extend the objective by adding the subject content reference, and finally - if required - add the condition(s) and criteria. As mentioned earlier, the evaluation of learning objectives in the cognitive and psychomotor domain is very straight forward. We measure, quantitatively, whether the objective has been met or not. Granted, as instruction becomes more complex, there are times when an objective is both cognitive and psychomotor and becomes quite complex. For example, if the learning objective was to for the student to be able to execute a Category II Instrument Approach Procedure to the lowest published minimums to airline transport pilot rating tolerances, the implication is that the cognitive domain objective (knowledge of all that is intellectually required for such an instrument approach) has been met and the psychomotor domain objective (skill to execute the approach in the prescribed manner) is possible. The candidate is either able to do it or not.

The same logic holds true with respect to combining domains and measuring the outcome for maintenance operations. That the maintenance examinee can correctly time the magnetos of a Cessna C-152 in 15 minutes must be evaluated with respect to determining if the knowledge and skill are both present. However, evaluation of learning objectives in the affective domain is not quite so easy.

The affective domain in aviation

The development of learning objectives in the affective domain follows the same logic as development of objectives in knowledge and skill areas. One selects the domain in which learning is to occur, determines the level within the hierarchy that exemplifies what is to be learned, selects the action verb (see Table 15.2), adds the subject content reference, and completes the objective with condition(s) and criteria as required. A learning objective in this domain might be constructed in the form; upon completion of this training, a chief pilot will be able take responsibility for the development and implementation of a Crew Resource Management (CRM) program within his or her company. While the action verb selection is quite routine, the addition of the subject content area to the learning objective presents a whole new set of problems for the curriculum developer and ultimately for the evaluator.

Action Verbs for the Affective Domain	
Domain Action Verbs	
Receiving	ask, choose, give, locate, select, rely, or use
Responding	conform, greet, help, perform, recite, or write
Valuing	appreciate, follow, join, justify, show concern, or share
Organization	accept responsibility, adhere, defend, and formulate
Value Complex	assess, delegate, practice, influence, revise, and maintain

Figure 15.2 Action verbs (Source: Gronlund & Linn, 1990; Kemp, 1985)

The problem centres on the fact that:

> *when we turn to the affective domain - attitudes, feelings, and appreciations - we find difficulty in specifying objectives in clearly observable and measurable terms. Most often we indicate these objectives only indirectly by inferring from what can be observed. . . . Some behaviors in this area are difficult to identify, let alone name and measure.* (Kemp, 1985, p. 85)

How then do you measure an attitude of appreciating the need for better crew co-ordination on the flight deck of an air carrier airplane or developing a better understanding of the relationships necessary between the maintenance and the flight operations units of a corporate flight department? The evaluation of these types of learning objectives, becoming more important in aviation every day, is the crux of the matter.

One way to determine if such an affective instructional goal had been attained may be to look for evidence of accomplishments that in part are indicative of a change in behavior. In the case of the maintenance/flight relationship above, evidence of a changing corporate culture with respect to how the two departments interact might be:

1. The development of a joint maintenance operations manual by the two departments that shortens maintenance down-time and consequently lowers operational costs.

186

2. A decrease in the number of down-time hours for maintenance (assuming of course that all correct procedures are followed).
3. More productive flight hours during a specific period (month, year).

Admittedly, attainment of a learning objective such as those above are only an indication of the possible successful fulfillment of an attainable objective and do not measure it directly. Mager (1968), however, calls these attitudinal objectives *approach tendencies* toward exhibiting a positive attitude to a subject or situation. The learner's attitude is considered as negative if he or she shows "avoidance tendencies." In general terms, to measure and thus begin to evaluate the achieving a positive attitude about an activity, post-instruction might be, the learner:

1. Says he or she likes the activity.
2. Selects the activity in place of other possible ones.
3. Participates in the activity enthusiastically.
4. Shares his or her interest in the activity by discussing it with others and/or by encouraging others to participate.

Additionally, Mager suggests that if company employees are to exhibit *safety consciousness*, they can be expected to exhibit the following behaviors such as reporting safety hazards, wearing appropriate safety equipment, following safety rules, keeping the work area free of loose tools, and encouraging good safety practices in others by reminding them to wear safety equipment. An extension of these ideas to CRM might be to use the 10 Commandments of Good Crew Co-ordination from American Airlines (American Airlines, 1978) to develop affective domain learning objectives. Affective domain learning objectives based on this work might include, after instruction, the captain will:

1. Appropriately delegate tasks and assignments to crewmembers.
2. Carefully assess problems and avoid preoccupation on minor ones.
3. Clearly communicate all plans and intentions to crew members.

The evaluation of whether someone has met these affective objectives while difficult to do quantitatively, is not impossible. However, using the traditional evaluation benchmarks of aviation, the written exam or the practical test, may not be appropriate and a new evaluation paradigm may need to be fostered.

Toward better affective evaluation in aviation

The evaluation of learning is an integral part of the educational scheme and its importance is critical to not only determining whether educational objectives have been met but also as an aid in future educational event development. In an aviation specific curriculum model, the *Aviation Curriculum design Matrix (ACDM)* by Lehrer (1993), the final step in the matrix was "how can the effectiveness of the curriculum be evaluated" (p. 274). Such evaluation should be included no matter the domain in which the learning has taken place.

Cognitive, affective or psychomotor learning?

Traditionally, tests of learning in aviation - particularly those that evaluate the accomplishment of learning outcomes in the cognitive and psychomotor domain, have tended to be limited to multiple choice, true and false, essay, short answers, practical demonstrations, and oral quizzing. However, such an evaluation scheme used with educational objectives that relate to ones values, emotions, and beliefs, falls short of the mark.

One of the inherent problems in measuring affective domain learning objectives is that quite often, one's feelings and beliefs are considered a very private and personal matter. Additionally, possession or presence of the "desired value complex" can be measured only by a response, verbal or written, from the person being evaluated. Although Mager's approach to evaluation of affective learning by observing whether *approach* or *avoidance tendencies* is a first step, more reliable and valid evaluation tools are needed. Compounding the difficulty even more is the fact that an individual may give the answer that is socially acceptable or one that is perceived as being the desired response; additionally, the effect of a learning experience many not be know until much later. Nonetheless, we must begin to attempt to more accurately assess the learning of values, beliefs, and feelings in aviation settings, particularly as they relate to issues of safety issues, crew resources management, leadership, and areas of human resources management. We should also include in our quest, ways to more accurately assess the corporate culture, an integral part of how a company's own value system can affect one's own behavior.

Kemp (1985) suggests several ways that the affective domain may be evaluated. Among these methods are the questionnaire, use of a rating scale, and interview. Additional methods included below are feedback situations, role playing, self-assessment, and group evaluation. Evaluation can also include combinations of these strategies.

Questionnaire

The construction of a questionnaire may take on either of two forms, open-ended and close-ended questions. While closed-ended questions may be easier to grade, tally, and quantify, use of such questions may limit the possible responses from the learner. However, if open-ended questions are used, a more varied range of responses should result. Although such a response may be more desirable and actually what we are really seeking, summarizing open-ended responses will probably take considerably more time since the categorizing of a specific response may not be quite difficult.

Examples of close-ended questions that might be used in a questionnaire focused at determining whether affective educational objectives have been met after a training unit of CRM might be:
1. After completing the CRM training unit:
   a. I feel the topic challenged me intellectually.
   b. I was generally attentive in class.
   c. I was not stimulated very often.
   d. I do not feel the topic was worthwhile.
2. When I evaluate the unit on CRM that I just completed,
   a. I could see how the concepts on this topic were interrelated.
   b. The instructor attempted to cover only the minimum amount of material.
   c. I did not know where the instructor was heading most of the time.

It is entirely possible that in the above questions, there can be more than one answer chosen or that there may be a specific answer that has higher value than another; the combinations can be varied. Possible open-ended questions for the same instructional unit might take the form of:
1. What was your general reaction to the CRM instructional unit in terms of content that was covered, how the subject was taught, and how free you felt to participate?

2. In your opinion, what was the single most important concept that you learned as a result of the CRM training module you just completed?

One important consideration in developing such a bank of questions is that "the evaluator should provide a framework for the respondents' understanding of the program. Not asking 'How satisfied are you with the program?' but asking 'What do you think of this program?' (McNeil, 1996, p. 281). Such a strategy allows the learner to be less restricted in their response or feel that there is one "right" answer.

Rating scale

The use of a rating scale is a modification of the questionnaire form of evaluation in which the learner replies to a question by selecting some point along a scale. Questions using a rating scale can take the form:

1. I now better understand the need for teamwork between the dispatch and the maintenance department.

___ Yes   ___ No   ___ Unsure

2. How do you rate the recent flight department team-building workshop. (Check the appropriate box)

No Use   Slightly   Useful   Satisfactory   Good   Excellent

_____   _____   _____   _____   _____   _____

3. Indicate your feeling about the overall value of the recent re-engineering project undertaken in the avionics shop.

Little or no Value   1   2   3   4   5   6   Great Value

In a rating scale, the respondent is forced to make a choice of an answer. Forcing such a choice can make statistical analysis of the responses from a rating scale more accurate. You may also wish to include a section with each question for respondents to add anecdotal responses as well.

Interview

An interview is a face-to-face meeting between the learner and the evaluator seeking to determine, by use of certain questions, the extent to which learning takes place. In such a scenario, McNeil (1996, p.281) cautions that "persons are more likely to 'fake' their attitudinal responses. Hence, mild deception is often used so that the learner will not know the [exact] purpose of the inquiry or that they are being observed." Situation might be contrived and thus learner reactions are interpreted to mean certain things; since situations in this area may have many psychological overtones, assistance of a professional in the field is desirable.

An interview situation might be structured around privately asking each of a flight deck crewmembers a single question: What is your opinion of the performance of your crew during the recent Line Oriented Flight Training (LOFT) exercise that you just participate in as part of your recurrent training? The evaluator, armed with an interview guide, would lead the learner through a series of questions that relate to the exercise, tabulating responses as the questioning progresses. The format is quite flexible and the face-to-face contact is desirable; good rapport between the learner and the evaluator is essential.

Role playing

The evaluation of values and beliefs may also be evaluated through the use of role playing scenarios. In role playing, a scenario is carefully outlined, various roles are assigned, and the action begins. A very structured format may be used that includes certain questions that need to be answered or the role playing can be quite free-form. One important characteristic of role playing is that it allows a learner to "try out" a certain set of emotions and feelings; such a technique has found acceptance in behavior modification work. The main difficulty in using this method is that the evaluator for role playing must be well trained in leading as well as evaluating such an exercise.

Action verbs facilitate effective instruction

Conclusions

The evaluation of aviation learning outcomes in the affective domain is sure to be a controversial as well as an extremely challenging undertaking. The process is also fraught with danger in that results may be inaccurate, inappropriate, and with little meaning. In addition, data on the evaluation of aviation-specific objectives in this domain are very limited. However, such obstacles should not keep aviation educators from striving to learn how to better measure the effectiveness of such value-laden aviation instructional programs like leadership training, motivational efforts, or any program that focus on measuring and ultimately improving the way that individual form their unique beliefs and convictions.

The findings of Kantowitz and Casper (1988) do begin to provide some insight as to a direction in which to proceed. Although the original reference was focused on the use of subjective ratings to assess workload in aviation, the same methodology can be used in assessing affective domain outcomes. Operators (or in our cases, the student or trainee) are simply asked:

> *how hard they feel they worked in a particular task either during or after the task has been completed. The method has the advantages of being nonintrusive and easy to implement. On the other side of the coin, however, its disadvantages include the lack of a theoretical framework, difficulties in comparing results between experimenters using different rating scales, and the problem of yielding relative rather than absolute results. Last but certainly not least is the problem of applying valid statistical tests to data obtained from subjective ratings.* (p. 176)

Two sources of aviation attitude assessment questionnaires show promise. The first source is the *Cockpit Management Attitudes Questionnaire* (CMAQ; Helmreich, 1984; Helmreich, Wilhelm, & Gregorich, 1988); the CMAQ is composed to three underlying dimensions: Communication & Coordination, Command Responsibility, and Recognition of Stressor Effects. Another source is a series of aviation evaluation instruments being pioneered by Telfer and Moore (1995). The instruments in this series include the *Pilot Instruction Process Questionnaire* (PIPQ), the *Organizational Training Culture Questionnaire* (OTCQ), and the *Pilot Learning Process Questionnaire* (PLPQ). Although data are still quite preliminary for the Telfer and Moore PIPQ and OTCQ instruments, early results are encouraging.

Aviation is becoming more technologically complex each day and there is a need to better prepare the human to interface with these advances. The issue is not more skill development or more knowledge acquisition; we do those things quite effectively now. The challenge is how to prepare the individuals to function as team members, as better followers, and ultimately as better leaders. Also at issue is how to prepare aviation professionals to be better problem-solvers and critical thinkers; such learning is heavily affective domain centered.

It is the hope that the discussion and thoughts outlined above can act as a catalyst. A catalyst in the process of looking more closely at just how the education of aviation professionals can become more meaningful and ultimately more effectively evaluated with respect to values and beliefs.

References

American Airlines Flight Academy (1978). The 10 commandments of good crew co-ordination. *Flight Deck*, p. 12.

Bloom, B. (1956). *Taxonomy of education objectives: Handbook I: Cognitive Domain*. New York: McKay.

Combs, A. W. (1962). *Perceiving, behavior, becoming: A new focus for education*. Washington, DC: Association of Supervision and Curriculum Development.

Gronlund, N. E., & Linn, R. L. (1990). *Measurement and evaluation in teaching*. New York: Macmillan.

Helmreich, R. L., Wilhelm, J. A., & Gregorich, S. (1988). Revised versions of the cockpit management attitudes questionnaire (CMAQ) and CRM seminar evaluation form. NASA/UT Technical Report 88-3. Austin, TX: University of Texas.

Helmreich, R. L. (1984). Cockpit management attitudes. 583-589.

Kantowitz, B. H., & Casper, P. A. (1988). Human workload in aviation. In E. L. Weiner, & D. C. Nagel (Eds.) *Human factors in aviation* (pp. 157-187). San Diego, CA: Academic Press.

Kemp, J. E. (1985). *The instructional design process*. New York: Harper & Row.

Krathwol, D. (1964). *Taxonomy of education objectives: Handbook II: Affective Domain*. New York: McKay.

Lehrer, H. (1993). Instructional design and curriculum development in aviation. In R. Telfer (Ed.), *Aviation instruction and training* (pp. 272- 290). Brookfield, VT: Ashgate.

Mager, R. F. (1968). *Developing attitude toward learning*. Belmont, CA: Pitman.

McNeil, J. D. (1996). *Curriculum* (5th.ed.). New York: HarperCollins.

Ornstein, A. C., & Hunkins, F. P. (1993). *Curriculum foundations, principles, and issues* (2nd. ed.). Boston: Allyn and Bacon.

Simpson, E. J. (1972). *The classification of education objectives in the psychomotor domain*, Vol 3. Washington House, Gryphon House.

Telfer, R., & Moore, P. (1995). Learning, instruction and organization in aviation. Paper presented at the Eighth International Symposium on Aviation Psychology. Columbus: April.

16 Predicting and enhancing flightdeck performance

Stanley N Roscoe

Beyond raw intelligence and motor skills, pilot performance depends largely on *situational awareness*, the overarching ability to attend concurrently to multiple sources of information, evaluate alternatives, establish priorities, and work on whatever has the highest momentary urgency. Crew duties add a social dimension to individual performance that is addressed by training in crew resource management. The PC-based WOMBAT™ test was designed to measure the situational awareness and attention-management ability of individual crew members under stress. The new DuoWOMBAT™ addresses the abilities of flight crews to manage their collective resources under similar conditions.

The problem

As I wrote in 1980 in a book titled *Aviation Psychology* (p. 127):

> *The world has many fine pilots. For those who fly regularly, performance is remarkably standardized. Indeed the variability in their control of any aircraft performance variable is slight, and they all handle routine cockpit housekeeping and communications procedures by the numbers. Yet these pilots are not all the same. Some will be far more successful than others despite their apparent uniformity of skill. Giant differences among pilots are revealed as tension and confusion mount under operational stress. The problem is to discover these differences early in the selection and training sequence.*

Psychologists have developed reliable tests of intelligence and useful instruments for describing and measuring personality. Unfortunately we have been less successful in identifying in advance the aptitude for controlling air and surface traffic or for deciding, as a copilot, what to do when the pilot in command rejects a final approach and turns outbound with the fuel almost exhausted (NTSB, 1979). The military have invested huge sums developing selection batteries that account for no more than about 25 percent of the variance in training success and have no measured correlation with operational performance.

The need for valid prediction

Historically the long-range prediction of who will rise to the occasion in an operational crisis has always been based on a foundation of psychological quicksand. As can happen with flight crews and air traffic controller teams, the individuals involved may gain all the skills and knowledge normally required but be unable to put them together in the confusion accompanying a major emergency. To cope with the problem, most of the world's airlines offer training courses in crew resource management. By subjective consensus, CRM has high face validity. Nevertheless, to select future pilots and assess the actual benefits of CRM training, objective measuring instruments are needed (Roscoe, 1994). Moreover, the need for valid tests of operational aptitude is increasing as information technology and automation make more complex operations possible and the cost of placing the wrong person in charge greater than ever. Increasing the information available gives the operator more to attend to, and automation makes it all the more important and difficult to keep track of everything that is going on and decide when some intervention is critical. Pilots used to refer to it as "staying ahead of the airplane", "good judgment", "airmanship", and even "residual attention" (Roscoe, 1980). In 1996, it is called "situational awareness".

Simple tests versus complex operations

The costs of mistakes in selecting and evaluating crew members are not limited to those resulting from mismanagement of critical operations. It is also costly to train individuals who fail to meet training standards or, worse yet, meet all requirements but then are unable to stand up under the stress of an operational crisis. Frequently even well trained and experienced pilots and copilots, cabin attendants, traffic controllers, and ground personnel, are suddenly unable to decide what to do first in the confusion of an accident scene or a major equipment failure. The situation may simply be too complex for them to sort out. Traditional pilot aptitude tests have been crippled by the notion that performance of complex operations depends on a collection of individually simple abilities. Based on this idea, batteries have been developed to test reaction time, manual dexterity, short- and long-term memory, spatial orientation, and the like. The fact that such batteries account for only about 25 percent of the variance in training success depends in part on the high correlations among the so-called constructs measured by the individual tests. Any one or two of the tests provides almost as much predictive power as the entire battery. Administering the rest of the battery is a waste.

Situational awareness

The concept

At a conference on "Situational Awareness in Complex Systems" held in Orlando, Florida in 1993, David Hopkin of the Royal Air Force Institute of Aviation Medicine advanced the notion that *situational awareness* is a unitary though complex human quality, above and beyond the sum of the component abilities currently measured by psychomotor test batteries. The idea was not new, but it had not previously been so well stated. The PC-based WOMBAT-CS (complex systems) test, which was demonstrated at that conference, had been developed by ILLIANA Aviation Sciences during the late 1980s to assess that same ability.

The WOMBAT, in turn, was the outgrowth of research done during the 1970s at the University of Illinois (Damos, 1972, 1977; Crooks, 1973); Gopher and North, 1974a, 1974b; Jacobs, 1976; Jacobs and Roscoe, 1980; Kraus, 1973; Kraus and Roscoe, 1972; North, 1977; North and Gopher, 1974; North, Gopher, and Roscoe, 1980; Roscoe, Jensen, and Gawron, 1980; Roscoe and Kraus, 1973; Roscoe and North, 1980). The research program at Illinois evolved from analyses of the functions performed by pilots and their airplanes in the performance of operational missions, as shown in Figure 16.1 (Carel, 1965; Roscoe, 1980; Williams, 1947, 1971, 1980; Williams and Hopkins, 1958).

The cerebrum-shaped portion of the diagram represents the functions performed by the pilot or crew, and those in the remainder of the diagram are performed by the airplane's various subsystems. The crew functions, somewhat arbitrarily, can be sorted into three activity categories: procedural, perceptual-motor, and decisional. Procedural and perceptual-motor activities include sensing, transforming, recollecting, recognizing, and manipulating. Decision making is basically cognitive, but with emotional overtones, and consists of choosing courses of action from the perceived alternatives. Situational awareness is the stuff that good decisions are made of.

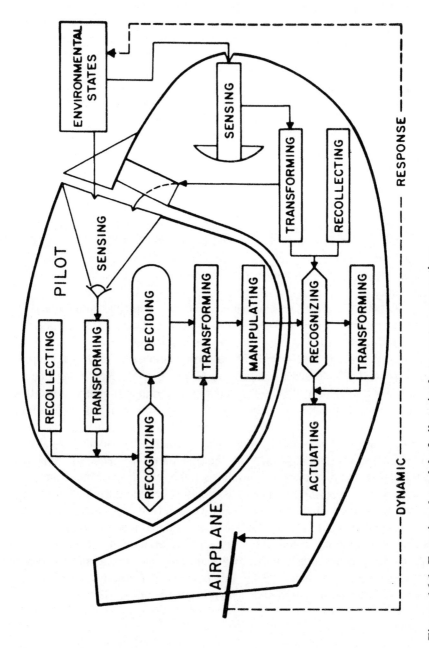

Figure 16.1 Functional model of pilot-airplane system operations

Measurement approach

The WOMBAT Situational Awareness and Stress Tolerance Test, produced and distributed by Aero Innovation, Inc., was designed to address the complexity of this overarching unitary quality by creating a situational scenario of similar complexity (Roscoe, 1993). The automatically adaptive scenario calls on a testee to scan multiple information sources, evaluate alternatives, establish priorities, and select and work on the task that has the highest priority at the moment. While there is growing recognition that situational complexity is necessary to measure situational awareness, complexity alone is not sufficient.

To avoid confounding basic aptitude with the effect of prior training in specific tasks such as flying airplanes, the elements that comprise the test must be unlike any real-world activities, unlike operating computers, unlike controlling any specific vehicle. Also, the individual tasks must be sufficiently simple to allow their mastery in a short practice period before combining them in the test situation. Situational complexity is achieved by the manner in which the individually simple subtasks are combined in an adaptive scenario involving multiple sources of information and multiple response alternatives.

The WOMBAT test was designed to embody all these requirements and constraints. The individual tasks involve pursuit tracking, pattern recognition, short-term memory, and spatial orientation, and on each a testee can reach an asymptotic performance level after a short practice period. The 3-D tracking task is unlike anything called for in controlling any vehicle. In a quadrant-location task, as each pattern of numbers is learned, it is replaced by a more difficult pattern of greater scoring worth. A two-back serial digit-canceling task, with no counterpart in everyday life, is both tedious and frustrating. The 3-D figure rotation and matching task (adapted from Shepard and Metzler, 1971) is a game that requires spatial orientation and calls for a self-assessment of confidence.

These four tasks comprise the menu of scoring alternatives available on request. Each task is relatively culture free in that it has no real-world counterpart, and each can be learned quickly by the apt testee. The attention demands of the WOMBAT scenario are expanded by situational information presented by peripheral indicators. To score well the testees must monitor the indicators vigilantly to follow the shifting priorities of the various tasks as indicated by their potential scoring worths and current scoring rates and to detect indications of failure modes that may require immediate termination of one activity in favor of another.

Typical group learning curves on the 90-minute WOMBAT-CS test initially show gradual improvement in the rate of scoring, with relatively uniform scoring after about the fourth or fifth 10-minute segment. On a retest of the same group of 17 students at George Mason University, Deborah Bruce (personal communication, 1995) found an increase of only six percent between the average scoring rate for the last 30 minutes of the original test and the first 30 minutes of the retest. Furthermore, the rank difference correlation of 0.88 that Bruce obtained between the two sets of scores gives an indication of the test-retest reliability of the WOMBAT-CS.

Test validation

The difficulty of developing tests of high predictive validity for operational aptitude involves several factors, the first of which is the usual clouding of operational performance criteria against which to validate any such test. If measures of operational performance are unreliable, as they typically are, there is no way that the true predictive validity of the test can be shown statistically. The pass-fail criterion is virtually useless when all operational personnel are given whatever amount of simulator refreshment is needed for periodic recertification, and rating scales are no better when almost everyone receives the same grade.

The objective evaluation of a test of situational awareness requires a valid criterion of operational success, one that is unlike any of our traditional validation criteria. Given the fact that instructors' ratings and pass-fail tests do not discriminate among pilots accurately, where can the investigator turn? Surely measures of performance during training, no matter how objective, are not ideal criteria, because the ultimate purpose of aptitude tests is not to predict immediate success but *future* success as a pilot in command.

In an *ideal* validation study, a large number of applicants for pilot training would be tested, all would be trained, and all who completed training, whether certificated or not, would be assigned to flight operations and their performances evaluated objectively over an extended period. In addition, all would be retested on the original selection test, and a demographically matched control group, who received no flight experience in the interim, would be tested and retested as a basis for assessing the possible effect of flight experience on test scores. In the *real* world of pilot training and flight operations, none of these conditions, save the first, is practical.

Because a longitudinal study of all the same people over several years is not a feasible approach, an alternative plan is requiredÑone that will still address the predictive validity question in a realistic manner. One such approach is a stratified experimental plan in which independent groups representing the various stages in the sequence of selection, training, and increasingly complex operations are tested. The mean scores for the successive groups are then compared to assess the reliability and magnitude of the anticipated successive increases in the group means.

A stratified pilot-group experiment

One study of this type has been performed with the WOMBAT-CS test at the University of Otago in Dunedin, New Zealand (O'Hare, 1995, draft report and personal communication). An unusual opportunity presented itself in January 1995 when pilots from around the world participated in the Omarama Cup soaring competition at Omarama, New Zealand, preceding the 24th World Gliding Championships. David O'Hare of the University of Otago recruited fourteen of the competing pilots to demonstrate their situational awareness on the WOMBAT-CS test.

Eight participants were classified as "elite pilots" on the basis of their consistently superior performances in gliding competitions at national and international levels. Six of these were national champions competing for the world championship. An additional two were highly successful soaring competitors with distinguished careers as professional pilots with both military and test flying experience. The other six pilots were also highly experienced but without notable competitive honors.

A group of twelve male nonpilots was closely matched with the pilots in age and occupational achievement to serve as experimental controls. The occupational status of the control and experimental subjects was based on the New Zealand *Standard Classification of Occupations*, which assigns every occupation to one of nine categories. The three groups (elite pilots, experienced pilots, and nonpilot controls) were shown not to differ significantly in either age or occupational achievement.

The elite pilots had higher WOMBAT scores than the other highly experienced but less successful pilots, and both pilot groups scored higher than the demographically matched nonpilot controls. A score of 200 is a frequently used selection threshold. None of the elite pilots scored below 200, and 62.5 percent of them scored above 250. Only one of the less successful pilots scored above 250, and two scored below 200. No control subject scored above 250, and 75 percent of them scored below 200. Despite the relatively small number of subjects involved, the mean scores for the three groups differed significantly beyond chance expectancy.

Situational awareness versus underlying abilities

Prior to testing the glider pilots, O'Hare had investigated the relationships between the WOMBAT scores of 24 nonpilot males, varying widely in age and occupational status, and their scores on four tests from the Walter Reed Performance Assessment Battery (Thorne, Genser, Sing, and Hegge, 1985). The tests were selected to measure the individual abilities hypothesized to underlie performance on the component tasks in WOMBAT, namely, pattern recognition, short-term (working) memory, visual search and recognition, and spatial imagery (Roscoe, 1993). The selected tests were Pattern Recognition 2, Digit Recall, Six-Letter Search, and Manikin.

The only ability measure to correlate significantly with WOMBAT scores was Pattern Recognition 2, indicating that the WOMBAT test does indeed measure something not measured by conventional test batteries. Figure 16.2 graphically illustrates O'Hare's model based on his experimental findings in this regard. The WOMBAT scores also initially showed a significant correlation with video game experience, but this diminished during the 60-minute test period. If the rate of decline were to continue to the end of a normal 90-minute administration, the correlation would not be significant.

WOMBAT performance is the measured criterion variable. Pattern recognition, working memory, visual search, and spatial imagery are the measured predictor variables. Situational awareness is the unmeasured theoretical construct that is hypothesized to account for most of the variance in WOMBAT performance. This model is consistent with the data from the O'Hare experiment in which only pattern recognition accounted for a significant proportion (10 percent) of the unique variance in the criterion. Other measured variables that failed to predict a significant amount of unique variance included age, occupation, computer experience, and video game experience.

In a general way, O'Hare's findings support the original premise that the individual cognitive tasks and the underlying abilities they are designed to measure are relatively unimportant in the context of situational awareness. Rather, what is important is how these relatively easy and largely culture free tasks are managed according to rules, both learned and inferred, to maximize overall performance. To be sure, the ability to perform the individual tasks does have an impact on the rate of scoring, but its contribution is secondary to the overriding demands of situational awareness and attention management under stress.

The O'Hare experiments provide the best evidence to date of the validity of the WOMBAT-CS in predicting *distant* future success as a pilot, but there is additional fragmentary evidence of its near-term predictive validity as well. Gavan Lintern (1994, personal communication) at the University of Illinois found a correlation of -0.80 between WOMBAT pursuit tracking scores and the number of practice landings required before flying solo; those with the higher WOMBAT scores required fewer practice landings. The fact that there was a slightly lower correlation with overall WOMBAT scores possibly reflects the weight landing places on perceptual-motor skills.

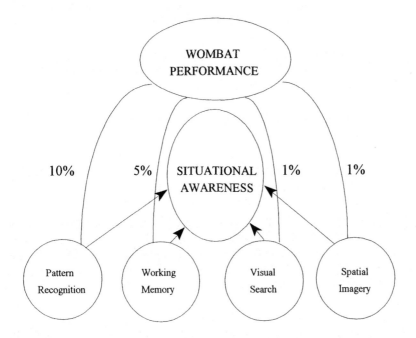

Figure 16.2 A model of performance on the WOMBAT test

Managing crew resources

The solo WOMBAT-CS Situational Awareness and Stress Tolerance Test was designed to assess the inherent aptitude of individuals to operate complex systems without regard to their interactions with other individuals in a team or crew relationship. The latter situation calls for additional personal attributes, primarily social in nature but with a cognitive component. The importance of social as well as cognitive factors in the cockpit has gained the attention of airline management and government regulators, leading to worldwide formal training in crew resource management. By consensus, CRM works.

Although certain so-called personality tests are believed by some to reflect traits conducive to effective and harmonious interactions with other team or crew members, until recently there was no test, other than flight simulator exercises, specifically designed to call for the application of those traits. As the WOMBAT test came into use by airlines and air and surface traffic control agencies, it soon became apparent that the higher-order cognitive demands it imposes on individuals could be extended to encompass the social aspects of team performance. To measure how well crew resources are managed, the solo WOMBAT-CS was expanded into the DuoWOMBAT Crew Resource Management Test, as illustrated in Figure 16.3.

DuoWOMBAT performance is the measured criterion variable. Pattern recognition, working memory, visual search, and spatial imagery are the measured predictor variables. Situational awareness, in the DuoWOMBAT model, includes awareness of the abilities, functional status, current activities of both participants and the resources that must be managed effectively for optimum team performance.

Sitting side-by-side at two linked WOMBATs, testees work out their strategies for trading off duties to maximize the team's combined score. The original test scenario was expanded by the addition of duet versions of the primary tracking task and of each of the three secondary bonus tasks, and other modifications were made to facilitate teamwork and adjust the scoring logic and weights appropriately. The 90-minute test consists of two 30-minute phases of dual performance sandwiched between three 10-minute solo phases (10-30-10-30-10). The three solo phases provide a learning curve for each individual to serve as a basis against which the team's CRM performance is evaluated.

Evaluating CRM

Objective evaluations of CRM training and testing are surely not beyond reach, but a new experimental approach may be called for (Roscoe, 1994). Evidently the airlines' CRM training programs have an observable effect in the desired direction on crew behavior in the cockpit. If that is indeed the case, the change in the individual crew member's behaviour should be reflected by improved performance on the DuoWOMBAT test (beyond that attributable solely to taking and retaking the test). Conversely, continued practice on the DuoWOMBAT would be expected to develop team behavioural attitudes and strategies that would readily transfer to the operational situation.

Few would deny that objective evaluation of pilots is vital to flight safety. Monitoring crew behavior via cockpit voice recording, in conjunction with flight data recording, has made major contributions to the high technical standards attained in commercial aviation. However, such contributions for the most part depend on the occurrence of accidents. Fortunately accidents are extremely rare, but as a consequence the lessons learned from them are also infrequent. The DuoWOMBAT provides a method for evaluating the routine, noncatastrophic interactions of flight crews, thereby completing the instructional cycle of Line-Oriented Flight Training and Crew Resource Management enhancement.

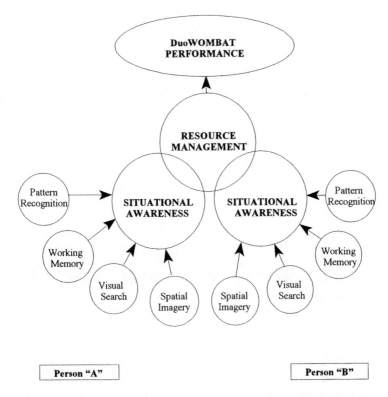

Figure 16.3 A model of performance on the DuoWOMBAT test

References

Bruce, D. (1995). "Test-retest reliability of the WOMBAT-CS", Personal communication. *Measurement of Residual Attention To Predict Pilot Performance* (TR ARL-77-11/AFOSR-77-10). Ph.D. dissertation, University of Illinois at Urbana-Champaign.

Carel, W.L. (1965). *Pictorial Displays for Flight* (Contract Nonr 4468(00), JANAIR TR-2732.01/40, AD 627669). Hughes Aircraft Company Research and Development Division, Culver City, CA.

Crooks, W.H. (1973). *Varied and Fixed Error Limits in Automated Adaptive Skill Training* (ARL-73-8/AFOSR-73-4). Ph.D. dissertation, University of Illinois at Urbana-Champaign.

Damos, D.L.(1972). *Cross-Adaptive Measurement of Residual Attention To Predict Pilot Performance* (TR ARL-72-25/AFOSR-72-12). University of Illinois, Aviation Research Laboratory, Savoy.

Gopher, D., and North, R.A. (1974a). *The Measurement of Operator Capacity by Manipulation of Dual-Task Demands* (TR ARL-74-21/AFOSR 94-15). University of Illinois, Aviation Research Laboratory, Savoy.

Gopher, D., and North, R.A. (1974b). "The Measurement of attention capacity through concurrent task performance with individual difficulty levels and shifting priorities". *Proceedings of the Human Factors Society, 18th Annual Meeting.* Human Factors Society, Santa Monica, CA.

Hopkin, V.D. (1993). "Situational awareness in air traffic control". Paper presented at a conference on Situational Awareness in Complex Systems, held in Orlando, FL, February 1-3 by the Center for Applied Human Factors in Aviation, a joint venture of the University of Central Florida and Embry-Riddle University.

Jacobs, R.S. (1976). *Simulator Cockpit Motion and the Transfer of Initial Flight Training* (TR ARL-76-8/AFOSR-76-4). Ph.D. dissertation, University of Illinois at Urbana-Champaign.

Jacobs, R.S., and Roscoe, S.N. (1980). "Simulator cockpit motion and the transfer of flight training", in S.N. Roscoe (Ed), *Aviation Psychology* (pp. 204-216), Iowa State University Press, Ames.

Kraus, E.F. (1973). *A Parametric Study of Pilot Performance with Modified Aircraft Control Dynamics, Varying Navigational Task Complexity, and Induced Stress* (TR ARL-73-10/AFOSR-73-3). Ph.D. dissertation, University of Illinois at Urbana-Champaign.

Kraus, E.F., and Roscoe, S.N. (1972). "Reorganization of airplane manual flight control dynamics". *Proceedings of the Human Factors Society, 17th Annual Meeting.* Human Factors Society, Santa Monica, CA.

Lintern, G. (1994). "Preliminary assessment of the predictive validity of the WOMBAT-CS Test in Private Pilot training", Personal communication.

National Transportation Safety Board (1979). *Accident report: United Airlines, Inc., Flight 173; Portland, Oregon; December 28, 1978.* Author,

Washington, DC.

North, R.A. (1977). *Task Components and Demands as Factors in Dual-Task Performance* (TR ARL-77-2/AFOSR-77-2). Ph.D. dissertation, University of Illinois at Urbana-Champaign.

North, R.A., and Gopher, D. (1974). "Basic attention measures as predictors of success in flight training". *Proceedings of the Human Factors Society, 18th Annual Meeting.* Human Factors Society, Santa Monica, CA.

North, R.A., Gopher, D., and Roscoe, S.N. (1980). "Manipulation and measurement of concurrent-task performances", in S.N. Roscoe (Ed), *Aviation Psychology* (pp. 134-144), Iowa State University Press, Ames.

O'Hare, D. (1995). "Cognitive ability determinants of elite pilot performance", Draft report and personal communication.

Roscoe, S.N. (1980). "Cockpit workload, residual attention, and pilot error", in S.N. Roscoe (Ed), *Aviation Psychology* (pp. 159-169), Iowa State University Press, Ames.

Roscoe, S.N. (1993). "An aid in the selection process-WOMBAT". *Civil Aviation Training,* vol. 4, no. 2, 48-51.

Roscoe, S.N. (1994). "Evaluating CRM". *CRM Advocate,* vol. 94, no. 1, pp. 20-21.

Roscoe, S.N., Jensen, R.S., and Gawron, V.J. (1980). "Introduction to training systems", in S.N. Roscoe (Ed), *Aviation Psychology* (pp. 173-181), Iowa State University Press, Ames.

Roscoe, S.N., and Kraus, E.F. (1973). "Pilotage error and residual attention: The evaluation of a performance control system in airborne area navigation". *Navigation,* vol. 20, pp. 267-279.

Roscoe, S.N., and North, R.A. (1980). "Prediction of pilot performance", in S.N. Roscoe (Ed), *Aviation Psychology* (pp. 127-133), Iowa State University Press, Ames.

Shepard, R.N., and Metzler, J. (1971). "Mental rotation of three-dimensional objects". *Science,* vol. 171, pp. 701-703.

Thorne, D.R., Genser, S.G., Sing, H.C., and Hegge, F.W. (1985). "The Walter Reed Assessment Battery". *Neurobehavioral Toxicology and Teratology*, vol. 7, pp. 415-418.

Williams, A.C., Jr. (1947). *Preliminary Analysis of Information Required by Pilots for Instrument Flight* (Contract N6ori-71, Task Order XVI, Interim Report 71-16-1). Office of Naval Research, Special Devices Center, Port Washington, NY. (Also incorporated in: Williams, A.C., Jr. (1971). "Discrimination and manipulation in goal-directed instrument flight". *Aviation Research Monographs*, vol. 1, no. 1, pp. 1-17; and in: S.N. Roscoe (Ed), *Aviation Psychology* (pp. 11-30), Iowa State University Press, Ames.

Williams, A.C., Jr., and Hopkins, C.O. (1958). *Aspects of Pilot Decision Making* (WADC TR 58-522; AD 209382). Wright Air Development Center, Aero Medical Laboratory, Wright-Patterson Air Force Base, OH.

17 Production of CRM programs

Harry Holling

This chapter looks at an important aspect of the delivery of airline CRM programs, the production of quality visual media which includes manuals, slides/overheads transparencies and video presentations. Because of the success of our video presentations, a major section of the chapter is devoted to that medium. The focus is on pointers for the production of effective CRM Programs. First, though, some background.

At Ansett Australia, the small number of CRM facilitators who present the program have the task of putting together a new program each year. Our aim is to produce the best quality, most interesting material possible. This means varying the content and presentation through our audio-visual means. Current communication technology offers a wide variety of media and impressive presentations can now be composed on a Personal Computer in a few hours. It is relatively easy to create documents and slide transparencies which are colourful, attractive, informative and readily comprehended. This technology is in the hands of many of our customers, the aircrew, so they use high standards to judge our CRM presentations.

Following are some of the lessons we've learned so far. The three presentation media we use are manuals, slides and videos. Each has its own place. Let's now look at how we go about producing manuals, slides, and videos.

Manuals

Once you've decided what to say, and how to say it, the manual will be starting to take form. Our early attempts were basically photocopied magazine articles attatched to a letter with some questions attached. It had a "disposable" feel about it and I suspect that is how it was received. The customer, the aircrew, would glance through the stack of paper to find anything of importance (such as set questions) and then discard the rest. The photocopied articles may have

209

interested many, but the quality of reproduction was so poor that they were almost unreadable.

What we do now is present the written material in a bound booklet. All material is prepared on a Personal Computer and a lot of attention is given to details such as spelling, page numbering, layout, typeface and binding. This immediately gives the impression of quality which reflects on the underlying CRM message. Microsoft Word was used to write the manuals and we have found it a very useful program because it is capable of importing text from most other word processors and has the ability to handle text and graphics. When the final script is to be bound, leave a margin to accommodate the binding. This margin is on the left of page one, but on the right of page two. This will be done automatically if you set up your document correctly. Adding a Header and Footer on the pages will help them look uniform throughout. Add page numbers and maybe a logo and your manual will look great.

As each of your developers completes his or her section, have them submit their script on disk and then add it to the master document using a uniform font and type size to ensure the manual is consistent throughout. Don't forget to save a copy of the document at each stage so that if a disaster occurs you can go back and rebuild it.

Pictures and graphics are very effective in making your manual more visually appealing. A lot of computer "clipart" is available. Maybe you can use some that suit your needs. Otherwise, draw your illustrations, diagrams or cartoons and have them scanned into computer images. "A picture speaks a thousand words" and a cartoon can convey a message that would take a full page of script. When people first open a book or magazine, they often glance at the picture or cartoon first, then the text. Never underestimate the power of communication of a simple picture or cartoon in an aviation manual but be sure that it is the right one or an inappropriate message may be conveyed.

Let's now turn to slides.

Slides

When your Facilitator presents your CRM material, the aim is to make a series of points that the customers will comprehend and remember. To organize them, headings or pointers can be written on a board. You can help by having those points written on overheads or slides. Make the slides on the computer. There are programs which produce files that allow photographers to print slides directly and the results are very good. Use colour, shape, shading, size and position to get your message across.

Don't use too many colours and avoid having too much information on each slide. Four lines of words, maybe three or four words to a line should be a maximum. If you need to convey more information, break that information into two slides.

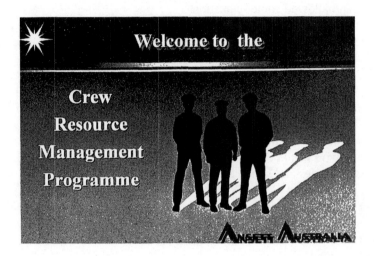

Colour schemes are interesting and help convey the message. Your computer will have some standard schemes supplied. They may not be what you like, but they are prepared by professional graphic artists. Be careful if you create your own. Have a few friends view them and give their impressions before sending them to the photographers. Add a logo or course name to each slide so they look like they are all from the same set and remember you will probably be more critical than your customers, so don't worry if they're not perfect. As we use them we often see ways in which they could be improved and we incorporate those ideas in the next set we produce.

Videos

Of all the communication media, we have found video to be the most powerful. Creating your own videos is a most effective method of delivering a CRM message, but you need the equipment and skills as well as the courage to say "Let's try it!"

Our first attempt was a simple interview with a company doctor and was a very low budget video clip. The technical flaws were overlooked by the aircrews who were pleased to see something from within their own airline rather

211

than from material produced externally, sometimes with professional actors. It's great to have biased customers! The clip showed a pilot interviewing the doctor by asking questions relevant to the stress component of our CRM program. There was a little bit of humour included which helped make the video more watchable and allowed some relaxation.

That first success led to another full length video which involved more people and scenes and as such was much more complicated. Now that we have the confidence and the budget, we will probably continue to use this medium each year.

However, there appear to be a few essentials to making a successful video. These are listed below. (Each is elaborated upon in the next section of the chapter.)

*Define your aim or message.
*Plan how you would like to achieve that aim.
*Write the scenes and script.
*Communicate with all involved.
*Shoot the scenes.
*Shoot extra footage.
*Log each bit of footage.
*Edit the movie.
*Polish and package it.
*Have a cut-off date or deadline so you don't keep trying to improve it.

Define your aim or message

This sounds simple, but it can take quite a bit of work because you need a clear vision of your aim at all times. If you're going to illustrate a CRM concept, there may be many ways to do it, but you will constantly need to ask "Does this achieve my aim, or illustrate my concept?". When making a CRM video about an incident, I found myself constantly reminding the other crew involved that even though the video depicted an inflight incident, the aim of the video was to illustrate the use of CRM principles. So define your aim, tell everyone involved what you're aiming for and keep focussed yourself.

Plan how you would like to achieve that aim

Lay out a plan of all the actions required, including gathering your information, studying it and from that write your sequence of scenes. You can change the plan as you go along, but other people on your team will need to know exactly what you plan to do. Include a time sequence in your plan and allow for all your other personal time requirements which could disrupt your sequence. List all the tasks in sequence and see if some can be done at the same time by other members of your team. One person may be researching the incident while another may be finding what film equipment is available. Make use of people who volunteer, but don't chase anyone that doesn't get around to doing their part. A small team working hard will be more successful than a big team of sluggish people.

Write the scenes and script

When writing the scenes, give a heading of the subject or purpose of that scene. Nominate all the people involved as well as location, time of day or other requirements. Below that write out the script, but allow the people some freedom in the way they say it. If you ask them to say it word for word you'll induce errors and the results won't look natural. Sometimes the spoken word must be exact if you're recreating a cockpit scene and you have a transcript of the cockpit voice recorder. The use of exact wording in this context allows for easier identification of the particular human factors failures under consideration.

Communicate with all involved

Now that you have done all that work, print a copy for everyone involved and expect some comments. You need to listen and then make changes as required. Remember that if they all don't like your favourite sequence, or miss the important point, your audience will probably react the same way.

Shoot the scenes

Now for the big day. If you've done the proper preparation, it should all go according to plan. Expect to reshoot scenes several times because something minor will inevitably go wrong. Don't despair because each of those pieces can be used later during editing. To get your subjects or actors to relax a little, tell them that this is only a practice and do it several times. Tell your camera operators beforehand that they should film these practices, if possible, because we have found that often the first few attempts can be the best because the subjects are more relaxed at that stage.

Shoot extra footage

Shoot from several angles and grab some "fill shots" as well. Scenes of engine instruments or aircraft taxiing, for example, can be spliced into the final movie as separators between scenes, or to cover over the visual errors while the sound track is still playing correctly.

If you only have one camera for an interview, try filming only the person asking the question and then only the person answering. This will involve shifting the camera and lights so film the whole interview first and then go back and get the interviewer just asking the questions. They might feel a bit silly at first but if you explain why you need it we find that they understand and will probably look quite natural. Do the same for the responses and that way you can splice the different visual angles together to produce a professional looking result.

Log each bit of footage

Logging is a tedious, critical job, but by the time you've completed this step you will be very familiar with the raw footage. Make a log of the start time of each piece of footage, the content, the length and any comments that will be helpful later. By knowing the start time you will be able to find it easily with your video recorder. You may have to view several scenes repeatedly to pick out the best one. Note that the audio from one section can be edited onto the video of another section, so if necessary record the location of good sound footage as well.

Edit the movie

You have a time frame from your movie plan, now select the best footage to fit into that plan. By logging the raw footage you build an introduction, for example, with ten seconds of company logo followed by ten seconds of the company flagship taking off and then the interviewer doing the introduction speech.

A little tip here, don't use too many small parts but don't underestimate the effect of short video segments. Advertisers on TV can convey very effective messages in segments of 20 seconds. We have found that you would rarely want to exceed 30 minutes duration for a video. Viewers will switch off after that time unless you have a very interesting subject.

Polish and package it

A professional-looking video should have some music at the beginning and a title page. This can be achieved on the computer or at the video shop, but if you don't have the resources for that, at least film some blank blue paper or blue wall. You can then splice this at the start and end of the movie and your customers won't be subjected to that video hash and noise. It is only a small point but it has a large effect if you don't do it. Remember that every extra little step you take will help to make your message seem more professional and important.

Have a cut-off date or deadline so you don't keep trying to improve it

Once you've finished the job you'll be relieved that its over. However, you'll see a lot of little errors that should be removed with a little more time and effort. Don't keep trying to improve the final result, you are probably much more critical than your customers. So have a cut-off date or deadline and leave the final version alone after that time. If you've enjoyed the experience you'll already be planning the next video that will be even better.

Concluding comment

It is important that the production of CRM programs be of the highest quality, even given the resource constraints that we see in training budgets. Well produced manuals, slides and videos have the potential to impart the human factors knowledge, skills and attitudes that are critical to safety in the aircraft. The experiences I have outlined in this chapter might prove useful to you and your organization as we move into a period of regulatory mandated CRM training. As I said earlier, you need a spirit of "Let's try it". Have fun.

18 Initial captain training - a systems approach

Graham Beaumont

Defining the problem

The past thirty years has seen enormous changes in the aviation industry. These changes encompass both hardware and liveware areas of the industry. The net effect is a dramatic shift in the way that aircrew are expected to go about their business. Arguably they do have more advanced equipment with which to complete their tasks and therefore can be asked to operate to far more exacting tolerances with a greater degree of safety.

Growth in the industry has brought with it ever expanding requirements for trained aircrew of all categories. Time to command has generally shortened and the average experience levels of airline captains has predicably decreased. Airline expansion has meant more personnel and this in turn has lead to a less familiar pilot corps. This lack of intimacy has placed greater emphasis on assessment systems which are not necessarily adequate substitutes. The ability of airlines to train captains 'just in time' with confidence has waned. Existing training approaches seem less capable of supporting the commercial imperative to turn out captains on time and on budget.

Why is this so? An examination of the changes should reveal the answer and supply direction for improving both training systems and the bottom line.

History revisited

The airline captain of yesteryear was by default a fairly rugged individual doing battle on one of the last frontiers. Interpersonal skills were not a consideration since the hierarchical system in which he worked expected leaders to lead without question. Selection systems were crude at best and pilots self selected to a large extent. Theirs was the right to challenge and challenge they did. A daunting prospect by any standard for subordinate crewmembers.

On the up side however, if one could survive the ordeal, it seems that a lot was learned in a very short time by subordinates. Vocational development was both rapid and thorough. Reporting for duty with a well prepared plan for the flight became a necessary aid to survival. This batch of subordinate crewmembers became well equipped to both attain command and cope with the redefinition of this office. This new-age Captain was required to be more than just Pilot in Command. The brief had been extended past the legal/safety barrier to include passenger comfort, schedule and economy. Market forces were beginning to drive role definition. Emphasis on communication and teamwork promoted behavioural if not attitudinal change. Challenge became coaching. The survival need for detailed preparation and planning by copilots faded away.

While this scenario may not accurately reflect the position in all cases, many airline captains of today will be able to identify with aspects of the described process.

Expectation and objectives

It is futile to commence any training program without first identifying the objectives and the expectations of the training. At this point in the debate the objectives shall refer only to the qualities of the end product and the expectations shall include those of all interested parties.

The role of the airline captain has changed. No person in the industry could deny this. Strangely enough, some airline captains themselves express disappointment at and lack of understanding of the changes which have overtaken them. Put bluntly, the airline captain has progressed from being an integral part of the management structure and is now more likely to be regarded as a major income earning asset. This ability to earn income depends not only on traditional and extended piloting skills but also upon customer interface abilities and skills. Regrettably, need for these skills was probably not foreseen at the recruitment stage years before. The commercial reality is that these skills in the airline captain give the organization a competitive edge and every edge counts.

Major changes in piloting skills have occurred. No longer has the airline captain to simply fly the aeroplane within tolerances. He must now possess a whole range of other skills, both overt and covert, which attract scrutiny during training. It is reasonable to ascribe meaning to the term overt which includes actions and behaviours. In the case of covert, attitudes and internalised processes are covered. Table 18.1 gives some examples of skills/practices/attitudes/ behaviours.

Table 18.1
Covert and overt skills of command

Overt	Covert
Manipulative ability	Practical Common Sense
Delegation practices	Ability to prioritise
Communication Skill	Assessment of self
Concern for others	Preparation and Planning
Knowledge	Situational Awareness
Personability	Motivation
Personal Standard	Receptiveness
Application of S.O.P's	Command of Respect
Motivational ability	Logic
Encouragement of feedback	Decision Making Processing

While clearly a discussion could be entered into as to what classification some of these attributes should be given, the purpose of the exercise has been to demonstrate where the thrust of the training effort should lie and where selection processes may not be delivering the necessary raw material. Table 18.1 also defines some of the expectations of airline captains and it is now reasonable to explore the differing sources of expectation.

The organization will expect any product of captain training to be commercially aware and faithful. It will expect service over and beyond when required to maintain the economic health of the organization.

Prudent and commercially astute decisions will be expected and use of initiative to further the organizational interests goes with the territory. In summary, the organization expects captains to use their best endeavours to maximise net income in areas under their direct control.

The Regulators are much less interested in the economic health of organizations except in so far as they realise that economically healthy organizations are less likely to have trouble meeting the intent of regulations. As far as the airline captain goes however, they expect that individuals so qualified will have a good working knowledge of the regulations and apply them as required in the operation of aircraft under their command. Where delegation of authority has occurred, organizations are expected to police the regulations on behalf of the appropriate authority. There is no escaping the fact that the airline captain is the final arbiter in the field as far as the Regulators are concerned.

When we begin to examine the expectations of Flight Operations departments, it is here that attributes listed in Table 18.1 are scrutinised. Even within such departments there can be differing emphasis depending on whether the primary focus is line or training oriented. Quite often the airline captain finds that he/she is trying to serve two masters. The less the integration between line and training managements, the more that this becomes a problem. Line Management within Flight Operations will expect that captains follow company laid down policy and at the same time uphold the values which are deemed necessary in the role of Captain.

Training management has two levels of expectation as far as Captains are concerned. Firstly, they will expect a candidate for Captain Training to have received on-the-job training during his career so far and that transition to the left hand seat will be just that to a large extent. Secondly, this arm of the organization will expect candidates to pass command training with enough margin to allow new Captains to settle into the less intensive recurrent training program without their standard falling below the minimum.

Captain training candidates on the other hand expect to be trained. Even if they have done little to help themselves during their period as co-pilots, they have expectations that the system will identify their short comings and apply remediation as required. Command training/captain upgrade training or some such can give the candidate a false sense of security that the system will meet individual needs. The tendency for candidates to equate command and captain as representing the same office also leads to confusion. Quite often the difference between pilot in command qualifications as defined by the regulators and captaincy as defined by the airline are two very different entities. The former generally can relate solely to the manipulative skills and the interpretion and application of rules while the latter embodies all of that together with the organization expectation overlay as previous described. Successfully combining the two is in essence the difference between copilots and captains within a company.

The onerous task for Training Departments within airlines is to closely examine the role of captain as described by regulation and organizational decree, determine the attributes required in the output and decide where and when to provide the necessary training. If expectations of all interested parties cannot be aligned, then facets of these expectations must be redefined. Clearly, any program which is not meeting the expectations of all concerned is failing.

Organizational alternatives

When deciding the format of captain training programs, the needs of the trainees as well as the system will require attention. The system may well rely on 'just in time' training. This can only be achieved if all of the prerequisite needs of the trainee have been addressed. In order to explore the alternatives which are available, it is of value to try to reduce the career of an airline pilot to major areas of activity during that career.

Table 18.2
Airline pilot career path

Activity	Average Time (in years)
Abinitio Commercial Pilot Training	2-5
Pre airline Experience	2-10
Induction and Initial airline Training	.5
Co-pilot Experience	5-20
Captain Training	.3-5
Airline captain	20-25
Recurrent Training	.5(total)

By examination of Table 18.2, it is clear that the time spent in formal training programs during a career in aviation is but a very small part of overall experience. In training terms, such an approach leads to a very plateaued skill/knowledge acquisition profile which requires of the system and the trainee short periods of intense concentration. By implication, if either the system or the trainee is neither prepared or flexible then the chances of success are reduced.

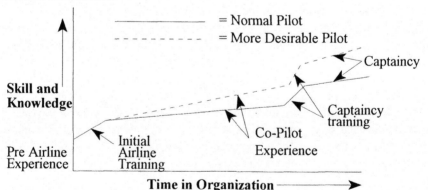

Figure 18.1 Desirable captaincy development

The unfortunate reality is that just-in-time training severely reduces flexibility. Just as real is the need to take advantage of the long period spent as a co-pilot to try to reduce the plateaued nature of training. By attempting to do this, a much smoother skill and knowledge acquisition gradient will result.

This does not mean that formal didactic training sessions are required or indeed desirable during this period as co pilot. What it does mean is that within the crew environment, learning through experience and from experience should be facilitated by the system and other crew members. No teachable moment should be lost. This sounds very simplistic but we are talking of making every line captain a trainer. We are talking of a support system which will provide back up for both copilots and captains. We are talking of replacing the fear/need based system of yesteryear with a meaningful coaching and feedback system capable of providing ongoing training. We are also talking of the devolution of responsibility for much of what could be considered to be captain training to line crews. We would also be responding to the needs of the copilots by providing structure to their knowledge/skill acquisition. How to implement such a plan remains the question.

Established models

There are many variations on the theme and to try to establish an existing generic model is quite difficult. What can be done however is to give an example of an existing model knowing that there will be other organizations which use a model very close to that suggested.

The management of most Flight Operations Departments is certainly not integrated. By that it is meant that many managers of segments of the department answer directly to the Director of flight Operations (see Figure18.2)

Such a model is purely licrachical with no lateral responsibility or accountability built in. Such a model promotes the notion that line captains simply fly the line with no other raison d'etre. Such a model stifles the cross flow of information and promotes vertical one way communication only. Indeed, such a model contributes to the development of separate cultures within fleets and the training department. Use of this model almost certainly guarantees that the resource of the line captain as an integral part of the overall training effort will go untapped or at least underutilised.

That is the macro picture. The organization of each crew and the way that this macro structure might impede training has also to be examined. More and more the basic crewing unit has become the two-man crew. Similarly the basic aircraft unit is becoming extended if not long range for added flexibility. Quite often the two do not go together and the two-man crew has to be augmented. There are two ways of doing this. Firstly, just add co-pilots until the regulations can be met or add a combination of captains and co-pilots. In the first instance

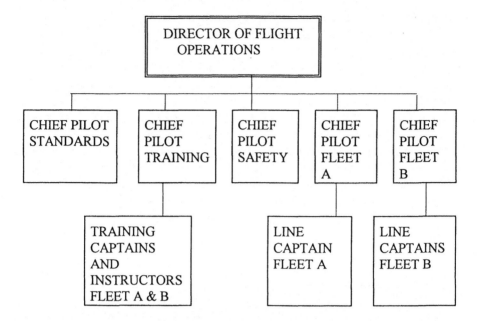

Figure 18.2 Flight operation organization chart

the exposure of each co-pilot to the experience of the captain will be reduced. Indeed if one of the co-pilots is licenced to provide cruise inflight relief for the Captain, then that co-pilot may not ever actually be on duty with the captain in low workload/training periods. In the second instance, the co-pilot is not deprived in this way but there are other factors at play which are peculiar to the two man crew.

CRM has generally been embraced as a good thing and the impact of this sort of training is beginning to be realised at the coal face. CRM is having a favourable impact on safety and that after all is the main reason it was introduced. There may however be a negative impact of CRM training which is only just emerging.

CRM is about teamwork, what helps and what gets in the way. Exponents of CRM principles are faced with a dilemma in day to day operations. Captains find that having to challenge a co-pilot to facilitate learning may actually get the co-pilot off side and downgrade the level of teamwork. Rather than do that, the challenge is left to one side and the team continues to meet its objectives in harmony and in the case of the co-pilot, ignorance.

When captains allow co-pilots to fly legs, the amount of learning achieved varies considerably. The rogue concept here is that of functional leadership.

This concept implies that the team member with the most knowledge about a problem assumes leadership of the team while the team deals with the problem. Captains generally have more knowledge about most operating problems than co-pilots. However if captains never allow co-pilots to take charge of the decision making process because of this, then the learning process has been downgraded.

In short, the way that airlines organise manpower at both the macro and micro level will impact on the value of any training opportunity for co-pilots.

The training culture

Not every airline will subscribe the need to develop a training culture within the organization. On the other hand most airlines will subscribe to the need to develop a safety culture. The reality is that the two are inextricably linked and to consider them separately is not advisable.

It is the attitudes and behaviours handed down through the training system which contribute to a large extent to the maintenance of the safety culture. Attitudes and behaviours have been mentioned just now. The level of support which a system demonstrates to a trainee will in turn be reflected in the support which a trainee gives the organization. If the established training system is not capable of supporting trainees in their vocational development, then win, lose or draw, captain trainees will be less include to support others once they check out. Fairly soon a 'no care no responsibility' system will have developed and any chance of developing a desirable training culture will have evaporated. Even aviators operate on role models, quite often in the negative sense. If the role model provided by the system is one of little support, then captains will operate the same way. Co-pilots generally expect some support in their vocational development. The simple fact is that if this is not forthcoming then their preparedness for captain training will be very much reduced.

The benefits and efficiencies which a well established training culture can bring to an organization are enormous both in human and material terms. It is therefore essential that some time, effort and money be applied to developing such a culture. In simplistic terms, what needs to be done is to train captains not to over look or bypass learning opportunities for co-pilots. Co-pilots in turn must be receptive to such input.

Overlaying an established system must start at captain training and be encouraged to spread from there. The system must lead by example and not just tell captains what to do but rather show them how to conduct this on-the-job training in the most effective manner. The establishment of this training culture is an important integral part of any captain training program.

A new training captain program can reduce attrition

Potential assessment

Accepted methodologies in this area of captain training have over the decades varied from a straight assessment of stick and rudder skills to a nod and a wink in the personalised atmosphere of a small organization. The truth is that neither of these methods or anything in between properly indicate chances of success in a captain training program.

Traditionally, there has been great reliance on some record of stick and rudder skills coupled with a subjective assessment of flight management skills. Stick and rudder skills are important but in the airline environment of today cannot be overweighted when trying to assess potential.

Overt indicators such as successful flight management are however only half of the rest of the story and some attempt should be made to examine the supporting processes to this area.

The old adage about right decisions being made for wrong reasons can hold true in aviation. Therefore, it is this examination of process which should occupy the minds of those charged with assessing potential to successfully complete captain training. Before being able to assess potential, the attributes of a good captain have to be agreed. There will be cultural differences between organizations and some of these attributes may be culturally based. Some attributes are however universal. Stick and rudder skills (particularly

224

asymmetric) is such a case. The evidence is in that one other such case is situational awareness (Orasanu 1995).

Situational awareness is something of a generic term which needs to be defined to make sense of it in this context. There is reasonable evidence to suggest that best performing crew operate sectors around a highly developed plan or blue print which includes worst case scenarios. This plan enables crew to free up metal capacity to cope with the unforeseen and unforeseeable. The accuracy of their mental model of the sector determines the amount of spare capacity available to attend to other tasks and to take an board modifiers to their mental model and adjust the plan accordingly.

It is therefore reasonable to expect a co-pilot arriving at captain training with a highly durable planning and preparation model to have a good chance of success. Of course there are other factors such as assertive ability, level of egocentricity, ability to receive constructive criticism, coaching ability and team attributes. While important, these factors must be given less weight in light of the evidence suggesting that captains must be good planners.

In order to achieve the best results, many factors need to be reviewed when trying to assess potential or indeed tailor training. An example of a starting point questionnaire designed to assess other than stick and rudder potential is given in Appendix 1 of this chapter. This questionnaire is designed to record the results of an interview with the candidate following a simulated or actual line sector. The areas which the questionnaire explores have been validated by either research or widely canvassed training captain feedback.

An integrated model

The argument so far has raised some of the problem and desirable outcomes associated with maintaining an effective initial Captain Training Program. It is timely therefore to explore a model which may cater for many of the needs identified during this discussion.

The truly integrated model for Initial Captain Training will start with the policy makers within the Flight Operations Branch applying some research to the necessary attributes of the airline captain of the future, no matter when this might be. This is where input from manufacturers and aviation think tanks is required to try to establish a profile for the captains of the future.

This profile can then be given to the psychologists to develop a series of selection tools which target the identified attributes. It would be in the national/international interest if some consistency in these tools could be achieved. That is not to say that national and organizational culture should be ignored but rather superimposed on a core instrument. It could also be adjudged of value to apply such testing to any pilot wishing to proceed past private pilot training so that the effects of self selection which the cyclical nature of aviation produces can be minimised as far as candidates for Initial Captain Training are concerned.

Notwithstanding, having inducted a pilot into an organization the task of training this pilot to be a captain has to be addressed. It would be fair to everyone concerned if there was a clear statement of the goals available to which reference could be made. Generally, there are statements to cover the overt requirements of captains within an organization but less often do we find documentation covering the covert requirements and how to meet them. The industry has been very good at telling their team members that they must win but the rules are often fuzzy and the equipment inadequate. For example, it is generally accepted that situational awareness is a necessary part of a captain's tool kit but what statement is made about the process of achieving this and what training is given to develop this skill?

The advantages of starting co-pilots into captain training as soon as possible after check out have already been explored. How to do this effectively and efficiently is the problem which now needs to be addressed. Historically, co-pilots were educated on the job by diverse drivers such as fear, chance and need. How one developed depended on with whom one flew, how often one flew and personal motivation. In a lot of cases that worked but at best it was a haphazard affair. Further, the system took little interest in this development until Captain Training loomed large on the horizon. Would it not be better to have a system which provided a continuously monitored development program? Clearly the answer is yes and such a program should commence the day the new pilot enters the organization. While training to be a co-pilot, the training system in providing such a program, but what then?

The answer could be in an age old process which fell from favour as formal education programs were developed. Reference is made here to mentoring. If does provide a workable alternative to fill the gaps discovered in many training programs.

Mentoring can be described as the process whereby an experienced person helps to shape and guide a newcomer. In the aviation, context, that would translate into the process by which an experienced captain helps to shape and guide a new co-pilot . It could be argued that already happens when people fly together. It has been suggested that two-man crews and CRM may work actively against this happening. Therefore it is not unreasonable to institute a formal system to fill the gap.

Clearly participants will need guidance to get started but the goals are clear. To establish a confidential relationship between a captain and a co-pilot where open two way communication can take place to allow the transfer of skills, philosophies and practices. Where strengths and weaknesses can be identified in a no threat environment and learning through challenge can take place. The captain mentor should become an adviser and advocate within the system at the same time maintaining awareness of the success of the process. Forced pairing should be avoided to ensure system integrity. Management will need to support the concept as a long term strategy and recognise the benefits in establishing the training culture. Recorded benefits include less plateauing in professional development, increased motivation on the part of the mentoree and raised levels of self confidence, satisfaction and displayed leadership. In all, desirable outcomes as far a Initial Captain Training is concerned.

Introduction of a mentoring system provides the perfect opportunity to integrate line captains formally into the training of co-pilots to be captains. Such a process has the potential to tap a hitherto underused resource and to provide human and economic benefits and efficiencies as well as impact favourably on organizational health. Getting such a program off the ground is the next challenge.

Authors on the topic are agreed about the fact that the effects of forced pairing can be quite negative consequently a voluntary system must be established. Clear guidelines as to how to go about the process have to be issued to participating captains and the goals of the process and indeed captain training have to be unambiguously stated. The organization must support the system by providing a focal point and a system of feedback for both mentor and mentoree. Participating captains must be able to assess success at a pairing and not be afraid to suggest to the mentoree that another mentor be found. If agreed by all parties involved, mentor input to readiness assessment may be important as part of the advocate role.

The final part of a more integrated model of Initial Captain Training involves the formal part to the process. The goal must surely be to integrate as much training as possible into the crew concept and indeed the organization at large. To come to grips with this aspect, let us examine the implications of crewing line training details with a training captain in the right hand seat throughout Initial Captain training. Apart from this representing a fairly artificial situation in so far as the trainee will still tend to defer to the training captain even though input may not be forthcoming, the opportunity to develop a personal style of crew management is severely hampered. Where possible it would be much better to have a regular line co-pilot in the right hand seat and for the training captain to do just that (ie train) from the jump seat. It does not mean that the training captain should not challenge the trainee as deemed necessary but if does mean that the trainee has normal resources with which to work and that management of these resources can be seen to work and develop normally.

Such an arrangement also limits the impact of functional leadership on the part of the training captain.

As far as the organization at large is concerned, it is important that some effort be made during initial captain training to foster role understanding on the part of the trainee of other departments and operations within the organization. By doing this, barriers to communication are overcome and the team led by the captain becomes a more integral part of the overall effort. While workshops are by far the best way of doing this other methods such as one on one sessions can be useful. Either way, if an understanding of the problems facing each area and how the aircrew team features in the overall scheme of things is achieved then, a degree of integration will result. At least, a building block will have been put in place.

Modifiers and barriers

The final shape of any program of this nature will be a result of the desirable modified by reality, even barriers. Management will always be faced with the problem of just where to spend what funds are available to be applied to achieve the result. With training, quite often there is a need to spend money to save money. The trouble is that having achieved the result, the need to have spent the money will always be a question mark. One fact remains that if a program can be found wanting, then a new approach, or at least fine tuning, will be necessary even if it does cost.

If an integrated approach to Initial Captain Training is the goal, there will be many things which define the degree of integration possible. The most influential of these will be the organizational culture. If that culture does not support change or does not have an established change orientation model, the going will be tough. Change threatens our perception of our model and most humans will resist excursions from their comfort zone. Consultation and education before proposing change can overcome this hurdle. Change for change sake is not the objective but rather change deemed necessary because of organizational introspection, egocentric attitudes and outdated values. Often it is very difficult to define these problems from within. The need to have an outsider look at the problem is a realisation which can be the first step to success. If a basic definition of culture is 'the way we do the things we do' the 'we' have enormous ownership of the process and 'we' will protect our vested interests.

That point leads us to explore the maturity of the system in which this training will take place. Immature systems will rely more heavily on 'canned' course, borrowed methods and industry standards than will a system which has great experience in the field. Such a system will already have tailored programs consistent with culture and needs. Such a system will be more able to shift the emphasis of training as required to meet the needs of all involved.

If the culture will allow, the ability to be innovative and responsive will be greater within a mature organization. It follows then that at least on the surface, a mature organization has more capability to implement an integrated Initial Captain training program. That is not to say that such a program cannot be initiated in any organization with the motivation.

System workload will greatly affect the ability to initiate new programs of any description. Manpower is always necessary to develop and implement training. The lead time required and the lack of available validation through instant results will always generate decision making dilemmas. This consideration coupled with short term economic imperatives make forward thinking decision taking very difficult. At some stage though, the pros and cons of the argument must be considered, and a course of action decided. System longevity is dependent upon foresight and commitment not expedience and decision taking must be viewed in this light.

The format of such a package will also depend on some of the more tangible assets which any system possess. Consideration of simulation sophistication and the development of meaningful LOFT within the organization will directly affect the micro format of the training. In the big picture, their influence will impact on program continuity. An integrated program cannot hope to be successful if it is interrupted continually by aircraft availability to complete training which could be simulator based. Removing as much of the training as is possible from the influences of the commercial imperative and environmental requirements will enhance flexibility and responsive capability. Tailored training becomes more a reality in this environment. Meeting the needs of the customer must surely be of major importance. Trying to assess such needs before commencement of training must give the individual and the system a better chance of success.

The calibration of check and training airmen is of vital importance to any system. Historically, aviators were considered to be craftsmen and women. The procedures and practices they employed grew out of home spun folklore and trial and error. The supervision of the craft was placed in the hands of the best craftsman. While each of these individuals was successful in their own right, each brought a slightly different emphasis to the job. Attempts to standardise overt requirements such as procedure, practices and technique have largely been successful. On the other hand, attempts to standardise the way that check airmen perceive and training airmen train these overt attributes have met with less success. A simple survey of these personnel asking for prioritised list of covert requirements may have interesting results. If it is found that the degree of calibration in these area is low, the validity of any assessment system using input from these personnel would have to be called into question.

This immediately throws up the problem faced by trainees. An inconsistent approach to training and checking can only produce a confused product.

If a trainee proceeds through his training only to be failed in check for something which was never picked up during training it is a system failure not a candidate failure. Calibration of all personnel involved is of vital importance and cannot be allowed to happen by chance.

PROCESS/EVENT	PRESENT IN SYSTEM	ABSENT FROM SYSTEM
VALIDATED SELECTION PROCESS		
INDEPENDENT SELECTION PROCESS FREE FROM COMMERCIAL OR OTHER PRESSURES		
BALANCED INDUCTION TRAINING		
GOALS (AND PROCESSES) OF INITIAL CAPTAIN TRAINING CLEARLY STATED		
MENTORING SYSTEM FOR CO-PILOTS		
CALIBRATED ASSESSMENT SYSTEM		
MEANINGFUL POTENTIAL ASSESSMENT		
CAPTAIN TRAINING CREW AS WELL AS INDIVIDUALLY FOCUSES		
FEEDBACK FROM/TO ALL STAGES USED TO FINE TUNE PROCESS		

Note: Absence of any component will increase the chances of failure.

Figure 18.3 Captain training checklist

Failure

It is doubtful whether a program can be put in place which will not have to face the reality of failure from time to time. In fact as far as individual failure goes it has been said that such occurrences validate the system. However, we should be very careful to identify the real cause of failure and be prepared to accept that the system is as capable of letting the trainee down as trainees are of letting themselves down. There should however be far less failure on all sides if the sequence of events described in Figure 18.3 is successfully implemented.

Figure 18.3 concentrated on system components rather than individual attributes. It is acknowledged that even if the selection process is sound and the attributes of all inductees are as required to achieve success in captain training, motivation in particular can vary. Proper mentoring and potential assessment systems should be capable of identifying such short comings in time to take remedial action. By the time co-pilots reach Initial Captain Training it is probably too late for remediation in process areas. When individual failure does occur or a system failure disadvantages the individual, it is very necessary that a support system be in place to reinvigorate self-esteem and return the individual to productivity. Once again, the mentoring system can be very useful.

Normally, there will be a captain within the system with whom the trainee has a close professional relationship. Possibly, this captain will have been involved as an advocate for the trainee in events leading up to the determination of failure. In any event, the mentor should be supported by the system to help the trainee overcome the grief and professional shame so often attached to failure. This support may take the form of access to professional counsellors, availability of leave, devising of a long term remediation program or other structural or scheduling procedures that may be seen as appropriate. A blinding reality of such failure is that the human cost can far outweigh the material cost and must be addressed properly.

Conclusion

It is fair to review what is hoped to be achieved by this systems approach to Initial Captain Training. Bearing in mind that it has not been an objective to discuss details of how to teach the various components of the syllabus, the aims and objectives will also be limited to philosophical and structural area.

As a general statement, it can be said that this approach aims to increase the success rate of Initial Captain Training by establishing a trainee centred system which is responsive to differing needs of the trainee. Additionally the trainee will be challenged, coached and guided from co-pilot checkout and potential to succeed will be carefully monitored. The proposed system will also reinforce the concept of a training culture.

Conversely, this systems approach is designed to minimise the waste, both human and material which can result from failure. As a result, organizations will be able to resort to " just in time" Initial Captain Training and meet crewing and budgetary targets.

The system aims to tap all available resources by bridging the gap between training department and line department. The proposal has the potential to draw all line captains into the training loop and infest all operations with a training overlay. In so doing , ownership of the outcomes of Initial Captain Training can be resident in all captains and the accountability which this produces can only positively affect the quality of the product. The saying "I taught him everything he knows" is a truism when voiced in the light of this proposed system. When pilots are heard to say these words, it is usually with some degree of pride in the fact that their ability to pass on knowledge has greatly assisted a fellow aviator.

This approach is not proposed as the perfect system but is offered as a skeleton upon which to hang the particular requirements of organizational and national culture. It has been devised knowing that there will be barriers to its implementation which can only be overcome at the local level. The complexity of the politics of embracing such an approach are not lost on the author. However, should it be see to have merit in total or in part then if the focus of debate can be maintained on the big picture, the corporate goals, then possibly the battles will not be so furious.

Further, this approach is designed to turn out quality products. Normally one would say that means more expense. In the light of being able to avert a percentage of potential failures, opponents way be forced to concede that cost offsets are achievable.

Only a systems approach to this major challenge for training departments can possibly hope to render a confident, aware and skilled product from Initial Captain Training Program.

APPENDIX 1

A	B	C	D	E
DISAGREE STRONGLY	DISAGREE SLIGHTLY	NEUTRAL	AGREE SLIGHTLY	AGREE STRONGLY

1 _____ This candidate displays a durable preparation/planning model.

2 _____ This candidate is able to formulate an accurate mental model of proposed exercises.

3 _____ The candidate accurately transfers his mental model to the aircraft/simulator.

4 _____ This candidate is aware that using all available resources achieves the best results.

5 _____ This candidate demonstrates the ability to input even under adverse circumstances.

6 _____ This candidate presents with a sufficient amount of commonsense and good manners.

7 _____ This candidate does not have a debilitating, egocentric attitude.

8 _____ This candidate displays a good balance between material and aesthetic employment drives.

9 _____ This candidate is conscious of the importance of our customers.

10 _____ This candidate believes in the value of and conducts good briefings.

11 _____ This candidate believes in establishing and maintaining good working relationships with cabin crew.

12 _____ This candidate believes that standard operating procedures are only for those who cannot think up their own procedures.

13 _____ This candidate believes that the required rate of knowledge

acquisition has reduced considerably.

14 _____ This candidate believes that crew agreement is necessary before committing to a course of action.

15 _____ This candidate demonstrates an acceptable ability to prioritise.

16 _____ This candidate regards making mistakes/being wrong as an integral part of a good learning model.

17 _____ This candidate recognises that not all possible circumstances can be covered by written procedures.

18 _____ This candidate is aware that safe and efficient flight is as much dependant on good communication and teamwork as technical proficiency.

19 _____ This candidate exhibits good situational awareness.

20 _____ This candidate expects participatory management styles to prevail in aircraft operation.

21 _____ This candidate responds well to constructive criticism.

22 _____ This candidate has the ability to coach co-workers

23 _____ This candidate demonstrates an ability to recover after an adverse performance.

References

Appelbaum, S.H., Ritchie, S., Shapiro, B.T. (1994) Mentoring Revisited: An Organizational Behaviour Construct, *Journal of Management Development*, 13, 4.

Argyris, C. Putnam, R. & Mclain - Smith, D. (1985) *Action Science.* Jossey-Bass, London.

Biddle, B.J., and Thomas, E.J. (Eds) (1966) *Role Theory: Concepts and Research.* John Wiley, Chichester.

Boyle, S.K. and Geiger - Dumond, A.H. (1995) 'Mentoring: A Practitioners' Guide. *Training and Development*, March.

Checkland, P. (1954) *Systems Thinking, Systems Practice.* John Wiley, Chichester.

Galbrith, M.W. (Ed) (1991) *Adult Learning Methods,* Kreiger Publishing Company, Malabar.

Morton - Cooper, A & Palmer, A. (1993) *Mentoring and Preceptorship.* Blackwell Scientific Publications, Oxford.

Wilson, B. (1984) *Systems: Concepts, Methodologies and Applications.* John Wiley & Sons, Chichester.

19 A checklist for improving training manuals

Phillip J Moore, Ross A Telfer and Jill J Scevak

Introduction

Despite the increasing use of Computer Based Training (CBT) and the expert production of CBT programs (e.g. Hickey, 1995), the manual still maintains its significance in initial, endorsement and cyclical training for pilots, and in initial and subsequent training of technical, maintenance and cabin crew. The source of such manuals varies from off-the-shelf providers such as aircraft and engine manufacturers, to in-house publications produced within an organization to satisfy its own unique needs. It is important to recognise the range of differing expertise needed to produce a successful manual. Off-the-shelf manuals tend to be constructed by experts in the knowledge domain working closely with writers/instructional design experts. In-house manuals are written by line and management pilots who may have little knowledge of the ways in which texts and graphics can be utilised to positively influence learning. This chapter aims to provide some practical guidance for in-house publication so that training manuals may be used more effectively by the wide range of learners in the aviation industry.

Many training manuals provide the prescribed knowledge and are essential tools and references for trainees. More than any other type of text, manuals are rarely read from start to finish, rather they are used in sections and also for quick reference on specific topics. Because of the nature of the information, and the ways in which individuals study the material, many manuals contain self-test sections so that learners can readily assess their level of knowledge competence against items that are similar to those likely to be in the final test. However, on many occasions the learners are isolated: from other learners and other materials, a combination that places great stress upon the quality of the manual itself. In such a context the use of a poorly-written, poorly-organised, conceptually-difficult training manual will not produce the desired outcomes, at least without a great deal of mental effort on the part of the learner. That effort is more efficiently expended elsewhere. Why divert it wastefully?

Mental effort can be reduced also by presenting information in both verbal and visual forms so that multiple codings of information can be formed. Multiple codings lead to more complete and complex mental models. Such models can be called upon reliably during operations. These are key points: a well designed manual can enable a trainee to concentrate effort on "real" learning, not learning in spite of the manual. Too many manuals rely on the expertise, experience and motivation the reader has developed independently.

Writing the manual

Evidence from research in The Netherlands indicates that the ideal mix for writing the manual is a teaming of subject matter expertise and instructional design expertise (Nijsen, Bustraan & de Haas, 1995). The combination of these perspectives ensures both content and format are given critical scrutiny. Another important recommendation is that organizations such as airlines use a checklist to review draft manuals. This chapter (see tables 19.1 and 19.2) provides such a checklist.

It has been claimed that "...there is no such thing as an ideal instructional text for everyone, in every situation. The syllabus, the reader, the expected learning outcomes, and the place of the manual in the training program are all determinants of manual design." (Nijsen, Bustraan & de Haas, 1995, p3). It follows that each of these criteria has to be considered and defined with precision. In broad terms they recommend a manual checklist covering the following:
* educational/instructional design;
* language and style;
* subject matter/content;
* lay-out/format.

As shown in Table 19.1, the specific checks are:
* content;
* format;
* readability;
* structure;
* graphics/illustrations;
* pilot involvement and activity.

Table 19.1
A checklist for aviation training manuals

FOCUS	CRITERIA
Content	Accuracy; sequence; clarity; completeness; new information flagged; acronyms explained; relevance; glossary.
Format	Lists; chunks; illustrations; fonts; levels of headings; boxes; legibility.
Readability	Sentence length; technical terms; result of readability formula; clarity; simplicity.
Structure	Key words in headings and sub-headings; topic sentences; italics; underlining; bold; cues and signals; contents indicated; index; links; overviews and summaries; guiding objectives; tabs; colour coding.
Graphics and illustrations	Relevance to text; location; quality; caption; labels and arrows; appropriate use of colour; sequence; uncluttered tables.
Reader involvement	Rhetorical questions; adjunct questions; tests; scenarios; case studies; further reading.

How are training manuals perceived by learners in aviation? Several examples will show that all is not rosy. From our own work (Moore, Farquharson & Telfer, in press; Telfer, Moore & Farquharson, 1995) with experienced pilots undergoing conversion training, we find negative comments about manuals such as "poorly organised publications", "unclear...poorly-written...manuals with information scattered in several places", "outdated manuals", "no introduction to the resources and sources of information" and "lack of guidelines". Walley's (1995) work with 665 pilots in Britain reflects these views with some 11 percent of supplementary comments related to manuals. Comments about manuals ranked 5 out of 15, indicating that they were seen as a problem area for training.

The process advocated in this chapter reflects that provided in CRM: use the expertise that is available to improve the quality of the result. The drafts of manuals can be distributed for critical review to a small sample of those who will have to use them, and to those who have the expertise to ensure the highest standard of content and presentation. This may require going outside the organization for input.

The characteristics of "good" manuals

Studies of reading, learning and text design (e.g Balan, 1989; Britton, van Dussen, Gulgoz & Glynn, 1989; Hartley, 1991; Hemmings & Battersby, 1989) have produced the following set of characteristics which can provide markers for "good" manuals. That is, manuals which show "considerateness" (Armbruster, 1985) and are "user-friendly". These terms refer to the ease in which information can be learned from the manual. We begin with perhaps the most obvious, the *content* of the manual.

Content

* The information is correct. While this is obvious, unfortunately this is not always the case (Telfer, Moore & Farquharson, 1995).
* The information is sequenced correctly to allow the development of ideas to flow.
* Important information is signalled (See Structural below).
* "New" information is explained when it is introduced. The reader is not left wondering about the new idea.
* Acronyms (e.g. TAT/EPRL) are explained when first introduced in the text.
* A glossary is used, preferably as a running glossary in margins.
* Interesting, unimportant (seductive) details are not included in the text. These may be fascinating but irrelevant.

Format

Text format refers to the ways in which written information is presented. Typically, the first focus of the reader is the layout of the page. Important aspects to keep in mind are:
* List-like materials are more easily perceived and learned if cued spatially (like this list).
* Group the text the way the information is "chunked".

* Split the text where the information divides.
* If there are sections, they should not be too long (and indigestible).
* Illustrations should be close to their textual references.
* Use **boldface** to emphasise important ideas or new terms.
* Have levels of heading (PRIMARY HEADINGS, **Secondary headings,** and *Tertiary headings*).
* Locate headings at side, centre and indented to show superordinate-subordinate relationships in ideas.
* Use boxes for supporting information such as anecdotes and examples.
* Use a text font that is large enough to read easily (not 10 point or less).
* Consider a loose-leaf format for initial versions of the manual (even the final version if the content is subject to updates or replacement sections) to encourage ongoing improvement. Do not lock the company in to a manual which may be incomplete, inaccurate or obsolescent.

Readability

Readability refers to how easy or difficult a manual is to read. Readability is one of the earliest efforts to provide revision guidelines for manuals. In order to determine the readability of material, a formula is applied to the material to gauge the reading level of the material. The result is usually shown as a grade level (e.g. suitable for grade 9, suitable for university, etc.). Typically, factors such as word length and sentence length are used to calculate the readability (see Anderson, 1983) and consequently material with long sentences and long words is seen as less readable than material with short sentences and shorter words. Of course, in technical material you cannot easily get away from long words so by any readability definition, the manual will not be easily readable.
So:
* Be mindful of the length of sentences, the longer the sentence the more likely it will be difficult for the learner to grasp the ideas.
* Be mindful of the number of long technical terms in a sentence, ensuring that each new term introduced is defined.
* For a "rough" idea of the difficulty of the material, run one of the easily applied readability formulae (such as Anderson's 1983 LIX) to gauge readability.
* Keep it clear and simple.

Structure

If the material in the manual is well structured so that the reader can quickly see how it all fits together, and what is important, then it is likely that learning will be more effective (e.g. Britton, van Dusen, Gulgoz & Glynn, 1989; Spyridakis, 1989). There are a number of ways in which the manual can highlight important information, including the following:

*   Using headings and sub-headings which include key words.
*   Placing the main idea of a paragraph at the beginning of the paragraph (using the so-called "topic sentence") and making it explicit.
*   Using italics, underlining, bolding etc (as described in *Format* above).
*   Using "cue" or "signal" words to highlight importance (e.g. "First, second, third..."; "It is critical that...."; " The problem here is...").
*   Having a "Contents" page for sections.
*   Having an index so readers can make quick reference to material they wish to check.
*   If there is more than one chapter or section, make explicit links between the sections so the reader can see how one "fits" with the other (e.g. " Here we have been talking about the benefits of INS, the next section considers how the accelerometers work.").
*   Using overviews and summaries of sections. An overview allows the reader to grasp quickly what the section is about before reading it (e.g. In this chapter we look at the APU (Auxiliary Power Unit) and how it operates. We also look at the APU's...."). In a similar way, a summary at the end of a section allows for a look at what was in the section (e.g. "To recap, ..."; "In summary, ..."; Overall then,...").
*   With the overviews, having a set of objectives that guide the reader. (e.g. "After reading this section you should be able to identify the conditions under which an airconditioning pack will trip automatically.")
*   Incorporate an overview (maybe in graphic form) of the whole manual after the *Contents* page. Here the reader can see the spatial relationships among the chapters or sections.
*   Pages, or tabs on pages, can be colour coded to simplify access.

Graphics/illustrations

Most manuals contain graphs, charts, maps, pictures, photographs, illustrations, and the like, to facilitate understanding. Such representations are usually quite powerful in the ways in which they carry the message. Remember the old saying, "A picture is worth a thousand words". However, it is not as simple as this as a number of factors come into play to make the graphic useful for learning. Here are the major factors involved.

*   The graphic is relevant to the text. Do not add photographs and illustrations to lighten up the presentation. Their reference to the text should be obvious, either through direct cueing (e.g. "Figure 3 shows how load busses are joined

together by bus ties." or "Below you can see how load busses are joined by bus ties.") or proximity to relevant text segment.

* This follows from the above. Graphics should be placed near their relevant text segment. We know that proximity is very important for effective use of the aid (Moore, 1994). If the reader has to turn the page to find the illustration, they may not do so.
* The quality of the graphic is critical. Simply stated, if they cannot be read due to poor reproduction or inappropriate size, then they may not be used.
* If captions are used, they should be clear.
* Graphics should not be too dense. You may not be able to see the woods for trees!
* Use labels and arrows etc to direct attention to important information in the graphic.
* If colour is used, the graphic should represent reality, or the colour should be used consistently throughout the manual. For example all hydraulic lines will be the same colour.
* The sequencing of graphics is appropriate to show some form of development (e.g. changes in triple mix positions in situations of different INS stations).
* For tabular material, space has to be used effectively to group and separate elements. A cluttered table will not invite processing.

Reader involvement and activity

There are many ways in which manual producers can get the reader to actually do something with the material they are reading. Basically, the argument is that interacting with the material will increase the level of processing of the material and hence the individual will have a better memory for the material as well as being more likely to transfer that knowledge for use in other contexts (Biggs & Moore, 1993). At the simplest level, a set of questions can be asked at the end of the section so that self-testing can be conducted. At a deeper level, scenarios can be developed that require the learner to integrate the information in order to solve the problem. What types of activities can be used to actively involve the reader?

* Rhetorical questions in the text itself. Such questions request the reader to ponder some issue as they read and the flow of reading is not usually interrupted. For example, which of these activities do you prefer as a means of active involvement when reading a training manual?
* Adjunct questions (questions seeking a response) in the text at specific and important points. Adjunct questions typically seek answers related to important information and can be placed before a section, or after it. Leaving

space for the learner to write their answers to the question at the point of asking may help.

* Test-type questions, usually multiple choice, at the conclusion of a section. It is relatively easy to write simple, detail oriented questions but they may be a poor measure of the learner's understanding. Attempt to have a range of questions, some detail oriented, others, targeting more important information. You will need to consider, too, how you will convey the correct answers. Not on the same page!

* Scenarios and problems at the end of each section of manual. Usually scenarios and problems require the reader to use their *understanding* of the material to generate alternatives and best-fit solutions. Instructionally, such scenarios can be used for group discussions and plenary type presentations. If they are boxed, they help with both interest and format.

* Suggestions for further reading. Here the motivated reader can pursue in greater depth issues they find of particular interest. (It might prove helpful if such materials were held at the training centre.)

* Provide spaces or pages for personal notes, examples, explanations and summaries.

The final product

Before the final product is readied for printing, it is useful to have others read the material and make comment. Table 19.2 provides a sample check-list and review summary based on the criteria listed in Table 19.1. Often, as writers, we get engrossed in our own views and thoughts and may miss something important. Similarly, during the use of the manual in training, it is beneficial to get feedback (formally or informally) from those who are actually using it. With their feedback, the next version may be even better than the first. Ultimately, though, a manual reflects the organization's commitment to its training. Content should be correct and well developed using the pointers we have mentioned above. Printing, reproduction of graphics and binding should be of the highest quality. It should invite the reader to get started: and to keep going.

Table 19.2
A checklist for reviewing training manuals

CRITERION	RATING* 1 2 3 4	CHANGES SUGGESTED
CONTENT		
FORMAT		
READABILITY		
STRUCTURE		
ILLUSTRATIONS		
READER ACTIVITY		
* *Rating Code*: 1 - Excellent (No changes needed) 2 - Satisfactory (Minor changes suggested) 3 - Unsatisfactory (Major changes required) 4 - Unacceptable (rewrite needed)		

Acknowledgement

This chapter is a revision of the paper entitled "Improving training manuals: Some practical pointers" presented by the same authors at the *Third Conference of the Australian Aviation Psychology Association*, Manly, Australia (November, 1995).

References

Anderson, J. (1983). Lix and Rix: Variations on a little-known readability index. *Journal of Reading*, 26, 490-496.

Balan, P. (1989). Improving instructional print materials through text design. *Performance and Instruction*, 13-18.

Biggs, J.B., & Moore, P.J.(1993). *The process of learning*. Sydney: Prentice-Hall Australia.

Britton, B.K., van Dusen, L., Gulgoz, S., & Glynn, S.M.(1989). Instructional texts rewritten by five expert teams: Revisions and retention improvements. *Journal of Educational Psychology,* 81, 226-239.

Hartley, J. (1991). Tabling information. *American Psychologist,* 46, 655-656.

Hemmings, B. & Battersby, D. (1989). Textbook selection: Evaluation criteria. *Higher Education Research and Development,* 8, 69-78.

Hickey, A. (1995). AIDA:Automated instructional design. In N.Johnston, R.Fuller & N.McDonald (Eds.). *Aviation psychology:Training and selection* pp240-245. Ashgate: Aldershot.

Moore, P.J. (1994). Metacognitive processing of diagrams, maps and graphs. *Learning and Instruction,* 3, 215-226.

Moore,P.J., Farquharson,T., & Telfer, R.A. (in press). Automation and human performance in airline pilot training. In M.Mouloua (Ed.)., *Human-automation interaction: Research and practice.* Erlbaum: Hillsdale.

Nijsen, E., Bustraan, J., & de Haas (1995). Involving subject matter experts and instructional design experts in the process of instructional design. Paper presented at the European Association for Research in Learning and Instruction Conference, Nijmegan, August.

Spyridakis, J.H. (1989). Signalling effects: A review of the research. *Journal of Technical Writing and Communication,* 19, 227-240.

Telfer, R.A., Moore, P.J. & Farquharson, T. (1995) Pilot learning and conversion training. Paper presented at the Third Australian Aviation Psychology Association Conference, Sydney, November.

Walley, S. (1995). Conversion training for commercial pilots. In N.Johnston, R.Fuller & N.McDonald (Eds.). *Aviation psychology: Training and selection* pp 324-329. Ashgate: Aldershot.

Part 3
Organization

20 Introduction to Part 3 - Organization

Ross A Telfer

The organization impinges upon the nature of aviation training in many ways. At the most obvious, it makes funds, facilities and personnel available. If one thinks of training in terms of a system, the organization controls not only vital inputs, but aspects of the process as well. It thus controls the output of the training system in both quantitative and qualitative terms.

There is a danger, if not naivete, in seeing the organization in its micro form as simply the airline, flying school or aviation college. The organization has to be seen in the macro or plural form and is much bigger...and much, much more powerful than that. It includes not only employers in the aviation industry, but governments and their bureaucracies, especially those administering aviation. Amongst other activities, the organization (as considered in its macro form):

• *decides laws, rules and regulations which govern standards;*
• *determines licensing requirements;*
• *prescribes examination content and format;*
• *funds air safety investigation and reporting; and*
• *provides safety seminars, publications and other communications with industry.*

The chapters in this section provide insight into the operation of organizations in both the micro and macro perspective. Initially, Sasso narrows the focus to organizational factors involved in CRM training. He shows how to start with a survey to establish the all-important base-line data (without which there is no criterion to trace change in the organization). Then comes the detail of instructor training, based on his experience with the 600 flight training staff at North West Airlines. Experiential methods, based on videotaped scenarios to provide simulated LOFT debriefs, are linked with a syllabus divided into four clusters: one being taught annually. This keeps the course, with its close attention to assessment techniques, up to date.

For readers in the southern hemisphere, the use of interns in LOFT instruction is an administrative aspect they would almost certainly not have considered. This relationship between the aviation industry and higher education in that continent serves as a model of reciprocal benefits. It is to be hoped that this innovation proliferates. If it does so, it will be because it has overcome a historical separation of roles.

Sasso introduces the notion of corporate culture and its potential to influence training. His frank discussion of the Red Book versus Green Book conflict will undoubtedly prove interesting (and, probably familiar) to readers who have been involved in company mergers. Similarly , there will be some deja vu in his identification of the difficulties involved in the transition to appropriate methods of Human Factors training. The excerpts from the LOFT Briefing Guide are valuable aids to understanding this process and to providing a guide for the analysis of CRM videotapes.

The second chapter in this part is the contribution from Cathay Pacific's Bent and Fry. They report on their unique experience as their undertook common type-rating training for a new, high-technology fleet, for its pilots. They show the problems which result from the use of traditional and obsolete training programs to prepare pilots for new technology. They describe a new efficiency resulting from emphasis on the initial stages of the conversion, and justify the costs involved.

Bent and Fry were commissioned by Cathay to investigate the crew training and operational aspects of converting to the A330/340. They detail what they found, and how the training design evolved. The chapter is a valuable guide for other companies which face a similar change, and includes examples of training notes. Especially interesting is their description of the division of duties between Pilot Flying and Pilot Non-Flying. From their experience, they conclude with a meaningful note which should be of interest to any airline's management:

> *... resource investment in training, before the delivery of the aircraft, is one of the a critical factors in ensuring the success of any airline training.*

In the following chapter, Farquharson reports on his study of airline management. It has a special value derived from the comparatively rare blend of the insight resulting from extensive experience, coupled with the application of theoretical models of occupational socialization. He argues that aircrew are characteristically distinct in the general population, and in ways which make them differ significantly from airline executives. He supports this argument with an analysis of how aircrew develop their behavioural norms and attitudes, showing the potential conflict with other groups in airline organizations.

He is able to identify the career indicators which show how and when management aircrew attain their status, developing the theme that such pilots are professionally motivated but rigidly moulded. As a solution, Farquharson provides five suggestions for the design of the aviation organization, emphasizing the development of both the person (manager) and the organization (management). Selection and training are the keys to good management.

Continuing the theme of the adapting aviation organization, MacLeod looks at the management of a perennial challenge for aviation organizations: *change.* And he makes the point that, in general, the industry does not handle it well. This argument is substantiated by using examples most readers will find persuasive...especially the rather unusual perspective on CRM. Causes of change are identified and discussed in terms of their implications for training.

The accretional model of change is contrasted with the trauma-induced trigger or the whim-based variety. Stakeholders and other barriers to change are discussed, together with the mechanics of resistance. In all, six aspects of change management are presented by MacLeod, who concludes with a method he advocates for handling future change. This is supported by a practical check list for this process.

Given the contemporary growing awareness of the CRM implications of culture for cockpit dynamics (see, for example, Merritt, 1995 and Johnston, 1993), Lie provides a timely analysis of the cultural and organizational challenges for Human Factors training. She describes her study of an Italian airline, with a focus on two of the dimensions identified initially in Hofstede's (1980) seminal work in the area of cultural influences. These two dimensions: Power Distance and Masculinity prove to have implications for training, especially in terms of how status affects communication. Masculinity may affect the accuracy of feedback and filter standards. Another challenge for the training process are the diverse subcultures which Lie describes.

She identifies, too, pathogens in the hierarchy: informational flow, motivation and care. Her recommendation is that airlines undertake an in-house survey, such as she conducted, before they commence Human Factors training. Policies, which may potential problems in the all-important processes involved, need to be identified.

A question many pilots must have asked is: "Why doesn't management use the CRM principles and techniques they are requiring us to implement?" This is the aspect of the organization addressed by Karlins and his colleagues where they trace the extremities of the CRM envelope at Singapore Airlines where the OASIS program has been established. This program brings pilots, cabin crew supervisors, ground engineers, station managers and traffic personnel together for a three-day residential seminar. The aims of this program, its process and materials, are detailed. For the many airlines seeking to attain such a goal, this chapter provides a helpful guide to the next generation of CRM. As Lie advocated in the previous chapter, Karlins et al also utilised an initial survey and used its results in the design of their OASIS program. They recommend this methodology.

Another successful OASIS method involved the use of an integrative case study which provided in full detail in this chapter. A third medium of training is the Qantas video of the *Dryden Accident,* emphasising the importance of ground staff and cabin crew. This is supported by another videotape from the ABC News: *What the Pilot Didn't Know.* OASIS thus provides a series of structured training activities which are designed to result in enhanced interpersonal awareness and an increased orientation to teamwork.

Two other organizational responses to operational problems are provided by Hayward. He continues the emphasis on the need for a company to extend the application of CRM beyond aircrew so that it is all-encompassing. He sees the need for the removal of the so-called "glass door" between the aircraft cabin and its cockpit, and supports this argument by referring to several classic instances in which all available resources were not utilized. The chronology of the inclusion of cabin crew in CRM is traced, indicating the extent to which the innovators moved ahead of the regulators.

A case study analysis shows how an Australian airline reacted to a pilot dispute which led to a major change in the composition of its aircrews. The Team Building Workshop is described in detail, providing a valuable model for the development of positive attitudes and cohesion. Hayward's concluding evaluation of the effect of the pilot dispute, however, is quite sobering.

The second case is that of the merger of two Australian airlines. A CRM program was designed to unify the resultant new pilot workforce, integrate cabin and cockpit crew, and to utilise the existing Emergency Procedures course structure. As other authors in this group of chapters have emphasized, Hayward points to the need for management support of such programs. A strong case is made for custom-built as opposed to off-the-shelf imported Human Factors programs which are usually forced-fits.

From an airline training and compliance manager's perspective, Miller describes an instructional cycle which starts with philosophies, then moves to regulatory and corporate training requirements. The next stages of the cycle to be detailed are assessment, hardware, software, constraints and testing. Miller emphasises in-house development so that the training cycle reflects corporate ethos and values. The self-development also ensures that the training meets parochial needs. Though localised in application, the typical training requirements he describes are generic, giving the chapter an informative value beyond a one-off application.

If training is to be effective, and more effective, the dynamics of the organization have to be considered. The control of resources, priorities, personnel, syllabus, standards, licensing and testing gives organization critical power over the training cycle. Common goals and philosophies are essential between all participants in the aviation training domain.

References

Hofstede, G. (1980) *Culture's consequences: International difference in work-related values. California: Sage.*

Johnston, N. (1993) CRM - Cross cultural perspectives. In E. Weiner, B. Kanki and R Helmreich (Eds.), *Cockpit resource management.* San Diego: Academic Press.

Merritt, A. (1995) Creating and sustaining a safety culture: Some practical strategies. Paper presented at the *Third Australian Aviation Psychology Synmposium,* Manly, November.

21 Organizational issues in human factor training

Anthony C Sasso

In aviation, there are several matters which must be taken into account before embarking on a training program. In addition to concentrating on the mind of the learners and the skill of the instructors, one must take a serious look at the numerous organizational factors. To properly address the organizational factors involved in the entire realm of aviation training from ab initio to recurrent to refresher would take an entire book in itself. This chapter describes those organizational factors involved in just one aspect of aviation training: Crew Resource Management (CRM).

There is no doubt among aviation professionals worldwide that the study of human factors is a key piece of the entire training puzzle in any flying organization. Despite the fact that the annual worldwide commercial jet aircraft fleet accident rate is steadily declining, from an average of 43 accidents per million departures in 1960 to under 5 accidents per million departures in 1994 the amount of these accidents attributed to human factors continues to average over 60 percent (BCAG, 1995). The most disturbing fact about this statistic is that one half of these accidents occurred in the approach and landing phases of flight. These phases of flight make up only 4 percent of the total flight time in a typical airline flight (BCAG, 1995). The causes of these accidents were not engine, hydraulics, electrical or other mechanical system failures; they were *human* system failures. Recognizing the critical role of human factors in determining the effectiveness of technically proficient flight crews in both normal and emergency situations, the aviation community has embraced the concept of CRM training (Helmreich & Foushee, 1993). However, despite the desire and need, implementing a CRM training program is a difficult task. There are numerous organizational factors which play a major role in the development and implementation of an effective CRM training program. This chapter will describe some of these organizational obstacles, and show how one major airline in the United States is attempting to overcome them.

The first steps on the road to CRM

The first thing that any aviation organization should do when developing a CRM program is to obtain an accurate representation of the attitudes and feelings of its work force. There should be an efficient way to survey the potential work group to determine what specific type of training program would work best. The Flight Management Attitudes Questionnaire is an extremely effective tool which has been used by numerous United States and international airlines (FMAQ, 1993). The FMAQ contains 82 questions designed to measure attitudes toward leadership and command, crew interaction and communications, stress, work values, team behaviors, and attitudes towards cockpit automation. In addition to these CRM related issues, the questionnaire also contains items which describe the organizational climate of the organization (Merritt, 1995). An immediate organizational problem emerges; one must get a quantitative sample of responses from the surveyed group in order for the survey to be valid and significant. In an airline with a small number of pilots, this shouldn't pose much of a problem. In an airline with several thousand pilots, as is the case in many major air carriers, the challenge is to get a legitimate number of responses that is representative of the survey group, to make the survey valid. It is equally important to help the potential survey group see that it is in their best interest to respond to the survey. Whether this information comes from mass quantity mailings, newsletters, articles, company publications, video releases, or even telephone calls, the bottom line is to reach a majority of the work force for survey effectiveness.

Instructor training

The check airmen corps clearly determines the extent to which CRM concepts taught in the classroom are translated into behavior on the line. This should be the first group trained in any organization implementing a CRM program; specific training for this group should focus on how to assess, coach, and reinforce crew performance on the line or in the flight simulator (Chidester, 1993). Acknowledging the importance of instructor training leads to such issues as "How do you train the instructors?" and "How long should they be trained?". Most major air carriers have established instructor training programs for CRM instruction and Line Oriented Flight Training (LOFT) administration, and each company's program is as different as the livery of their aircraft. For example, DELTA Airlines has a one-day training session each year between October and December for all CRM/LOFT facilitators. At Federal Express, Captain Mark Klair has designed a unique two-day training course for all CRM/LOFT facilitators. British Airways has a four day course for CRM/LOFT facilitators, with ample opportunity for each student to practice facilitation and debriefing. While the design and implementation of each of the aforementioned programs differs, the end result of all three, as well as any aviation organization, is to expertly train the instructors. For a more in-depth look at one specific program and the organizational issues involved in training, let's look at the CRM/LOFT instructor training program at Northwest Airlines (NWA).

Discussing work load management

Weakness in numbers

NWA currently has approximately 600 flight instructors. Each of these instructors is expected to administer CRM training, and specifically, administer LOFT scenarios in flight simulators. As each instructor approaches LOFT facilitation in a different manner, there inevitably arises a great amount of variability in teaching techniques and styles, leading to a paucity of standardization among the instructor work force. The simple solution would be to train all of the instructors at the same time in the same manner to ensure standardization of CRM training. However, this proves to be one of the major organizational issues at NWA.

It is impractical and undesirable to assemble all 600 instructors for a combined training session, primarily because of the difficulty of training such a large group at one time. Secondly, even with an available facility, the quality of the training would be less than ideal. In a two-day CRM/LOFT Instructor Qualification Course (IQC), NWA emphasizes the differences between technical-type instruction and LOFT facilitation. Using adult education methods, a large part of our facilitation training involves one-on-one, instructor-to-student interaction and practice in actual facilitation of debriefings. To accomplish this practice training, the learners view video tapes of actual LOFT scenarios. They then "role-play" the parts of the crew from the video, while another learner facilitates a CRM debrief. By actually practicing this facilitation, the learners internalize much more than by watching an instructor lecture on facilitation. This is also known as "experiential learning". With a group of 600 instructor pilots to train for CRM/LOFT events, it would be impossible to achieve the desired one-to-one relationship for each of them. Not only would there be an insufficient amount of video tapes to view, but the entire process would take an inordinate amount of time.

Instructor dual responsibilities

Another organizational issue at NWA is the off-line versus line-flying dual relationship of the flight instructors. Every instructor pilot is required to spend six months out of each year flying as a line pilot and the other six months performing instructor duties. These six month periods do not have to be consecutive; this is where an organizational problem exists. Any instructor, by virtue of the schedule, can alternate back and forth at random, from line flying to instructing, on a month to month basis. Imagine this worst case scenario: an instructor receives CRM/LOFT facilitation training in January, but then does not perform instructor duties until June. Even the most effective instructor training program loses some of its value if the skills taught in that program are not utilized until many months later.

Recurrent training: A necessity

For a CRM program to be effective, the curriculum must be revitalized and revamped each year. At NWA, the CRM model is divided into four main headings called "Clusters." These Clusters are Communication, Team Building, Workload Management, and Technical Proficiency (See Figure 21.1).

In order to make CRM training intriguing and original, NWA concentrates on only one of the Clusters each year. For example, in 1995, the annual focus was Workload Management. In 1996, the Cluster being emphasized was Communication. As one might expect, the instructor training must also be continuously updated and improved to match the annual Cluster emphasis. There must be continuous recurrent training for instructors, just as there is continuous recurrent training for pilots.

The success of any CRM training program will ultimately depend on the skills of the personnel responsible for administering the training and observing/measuring its effects. Thus it is important that CRM instructors (course developers), check pilots (operational reinforcers), and course designers (developers), be highly skilled in all areas related to the assessment and practice of CRM (FAA, 1995). The Human Factors Practices section at NWA conducts recurrent training sessions for instructors several times throughout the year. These training sessions come in the form of instructor newsletters, presentations at instructor standardization meetings, articles in the flight operations monthly magazine, and, in the near future, via electronic mail on CompuServe.

LOFT administration

An additional problem with availability of instructors has a direct impact on the actual administration of the LOFT events themselves. A LOFT event is planned to be administered in real time, as if it were an actual line flight. It is the responsibility of the instructor to make the LOFT as realistic as possible by making all the necessary radio calls, responding to all crew inputs, playing the role of the flight attendants, if applicable, and operating the flight simulator. The instructor should not intervene at any time during the LOFT, letting the flight continue uninterrupted. For NWA's two-person crews (DC-9, B-757, B-747-400, MD-80, and A320), only one instructor is scheduled for each crew. This instructor must perform all the required duties mentioned above, and at the same time, perform the primary duty of *observing the crew's CRM performance*. As one can imagine, this is an extremely difficult workload management task. More often than not, the instructor is so busy performing all the required duties necessary to make the LOFT realistic that there is little time to observe and document crew performance, the instructor's most important role.

NORTHWEST AIRLINES			
CREW RESOURCE MANAGEMENT			

Communication	Team Building	Workload Management	Technical Proficiency
I. Briefs crew thoroughly. II. Clearly communicates decisions about operation of the flight. III. Explicitly encourages participation. IV. Seeks information and direction from others when necessary. V. Asserts with appropriate level of persistence to maintain a safe operation. VI. Critiques self and other appropriate.	I. Exercises secure authority. II. Involves entire crew in decision making process. III. Uses appropriate techniques to manage interpersonal and operational conflict. IV. Adapts to crew interpersonal differences. V. Crew members cope effectively with operational stress.	I. Distributes tasks to maximize efficiency. II. Prioritizes tasks for effective accomplishment. III. Manages time for accomplishing tasks. IV. Monitors and analyzes all relevant operational factors to remain situationally aware.	I. Adheres to SOPA, SMAC and FARs. II. Demonstrates technical skills. III. Demonstrates knowledge of aircraft systems and normal, abnormal and emergency procedures.

Figure 21.1 Northwest Airlines CRM model

The simple solution would be to have two instructors in the LOFT so that they can share the workload and therefore have a better chance of documenting crew performance. At NWA, due to pilot instructor availability, pay issues, and scheduling constraints, this is not a possibility. NWA is using a creative program to rectify this situation by training college interns to assist the LOFT instructors. These interns are aviation majors, instrument rated pilots, and knowledgeable of the airline aviation industry. The intern is assigned to the Human Factors Practices section, specially trained to be intimately familiar with the LOFT scenario, and is used primarily to assist the LOFT instructor with the administration tasks. The intern operates the simulator and performs the necessary roles of ATC, Flight Dispatch, Maintenance, Flight Attendants, etc., making the LOFT more realistic.

As a result, the workload of the LOFT instructors is significantly reduced, and they are therefore able to spend more time performing the primary duty of observing crew CRM behavior. The intern program is in its initial stages at the time of this writing. NWA has only one intern devoted to this test program, and only in its Boeing 757 fleet. However, the early results are extremely favorable. Each of the LOFT instructors who were assisted by the intern expressed great satisfaction in the assistance received, saying the reduction on workload resulted in more observance of the crew's behavior, and ultimately a more constructive LOFT debrief.

In NWA's three-person crews (DC-10, B747-200, B-727), two instructors (Captain, Second Officer) are assigned to administer LOFT events. One would think that the observance of crew behavior would benefit, as there are two instructors to share the workload of the required LOFT duties. However, since NWA has twice as many Captains as Second Officers, the Second Officer instructor sometimes has to "fill in" and be the "crew" Second Officer during the LOFT. When this happens, the quality of the LOFT training is repressed. For example, when the Second Officers must talk directly to the flight attendant, and are "filling in" and acting as the Second Officer *crew member*, they would have to talk to themselves. This type of situation is highly discouraged for effective LOFT training; however, it is a better alternative to cancelling the LOFT completely.

747 LOFT mission

Culture: Benefit or problem?

Another organizational problem that may exist is the very culture of the aviation organization itself. As we become a global village and begin to see further integration of crews from differing cultures, we need to be sensitive to those issues and to develop training strategies that are sensitive to cultural differences (Helmreich, 1993). Most people think of culture as only a problem in multinational or international airlines. However, the problem of corporate culture can also affect the training program. At NWA, there isn't a problem with nationality culture, but there is a unique corporate culture. On November 19, 1986, Northwest Orient merged with Republic Airlines to form Northwest Airlines, as it is known today. For a period of several years, the airline dealt with "Red Book" (Northwest Orient) versus "Green Book" (Republic) issues. There were two sets of aircraft operating procedures, a reorganized seniority order, and personal differences within the pilot work force. With an emphasis on cooperation and collaboration in the cockpit as a focus in CRM training, one can imagine the interpersonal barriers that had to be overcome with a "Red Book" pilot and a "Green Book" pilot in the same aircraft. When Northwest began its CRM training, significant progress was made with "Red/Green" issues through an increased sensitivity in "Red/Green" problem areas for both line pilots and instructor pilots. However, despite the fact that the Northwest Orient-Republic merger occurred over ten years ago, NWA was still dealing with occasional "Red/Green" issues in 1996.

Training facilities

Another organizational factor that directly impacts aviation training is the actual training facility itself and the types of equipment available. Air carrier training and certification of the future will utilize Line Operational Simulations (LOS) as the primary training vehicle for airman certification and pilot recurrent training (LOFT Design Focus Group, 1994). It is imperative that airlines make use of full motion simulators to conduct CRM/LOFT training. The simulators must be maintained to the highest levels, so that the optimum amount of realism can be maintained. Depending on an aviation organization's operating budget, it can either maintain its own set of flight simulators or send its pilots to a remote training facility. There are obvious additional costs associated with owning flight simulators or renting simulator time from an outside facility. Consequently, even though the industry recognizes that LOS will be the primary vehicle for pilot training, there will always be aviation organizations that will not be able to "drive" this vehicle.

A difficult transition

In 1993, when the CRM LOFT was first introduced at NWA, the instructors were required to learn a completely new set of responsibilities. No longer could they resort to lecture-type technical training. They were now tasked to facilitate a LOFT event utilizing the "reverse briefing" method, which calls for the learners to do most of the talking. This new type of training proved to be very difficult for some instructors, as it was very new to them. NWA instructors were tasked to commence the LOFT training by asking their learners to describe their own CRM experiences from the line. Most of the time, the instructors didn't get much response from their learners, and it was a very uncomfortable situation for both groups. Learners were accustomed to listening to an instructor lecture, so it was very awkward for them to suddenly have to do most of the talking. This problem endured for the majority of the CRM/LOFT training in NWA's first year of conducting LOFT, and the instructors looked to the Human Factors Practices section for assistance. The relief came in the form of a pre-LOFT video tape to be used as a tool during the briefing period prior to the CRM/LOFT.

Pre-LOFT video tape

For 1995, the annual CRM emphasis for NWA was to concentrate on the concepts of Workload Management. These concepts included distributing tasks to maximize efficiency, prioritization of tasks for effective accomplishment, managing time for accomplishing tasks, and monitoring and analyzing all relevant operational factors to remain situationally aware (Northwest CRM, 1989). For 1995, the pre-LOFT video tape was designed to address these concepts, and at the same time, make it very easy for an instructor to facilitate a CRM discussion on workload management. The video consisted of three short segments depicting different crew behaviors. The instructor showed the learners the video segments, one at a time, pausing between each segment to ask a series of questions. The pre-LOFT briefing guide that accompanied the video contained questions the instructor was expected to ask after each segment, as well as typical answers the learners might give.

The video depicted an A-320 Airbus crew handling an engine fire procedure in three different ways. The first segment showed poor workload management and team building skills, the second segment showed improved CRM skills, and the third segment showed the optimum use of CRM skills. Questions such as "How well did the Captain distribute the tasks?", "How well did the crew prioritize their duties?", and "How well did the First Officer manage his available time?" were included in the briefing guide. A page from the 1996 Pre-LOFT Briefing Guide is shown below as an example of the types of information contained for instructor guidance.

Instructor Note: Play the first video segment of Western Airlines 2605. You can refer to the Western 2605 TAB for some additional information. When the segment is over, stop the tape at the blank screen and ask the following questions:

"Let's examine some of the communication issues present in this accident by considering the crew's performance in terms of the Communication Crew Performance Indicators."

1. *"What were the barriers to communication in this situation?"*

The first officer had a grudge against the captain for writing a discrepancy report on him. This was probably the reason why he was so vague in telling the captain which runway was in use. Also, since the first and second officer had both landed on the closed runway AFTER it had been NOTAMED closed, they may not have realized the danger of landing on the closed runway once again.

2. *"Was this an example of clear communication between the crew members? Between ATC and the aircraft?"*

No. The first officer was very vague in relating to the captain which runway was being used. Although the FO knew that the approach was to the RIGHT (versus LEFT) runway, he never made it clear to the rest of the crew. Even when the Captain said "We're cleared on the right?", the FO's responses were ambiguous. He said "the other runway". Also, when ATC cleared the crew to the 23 RIGHT approach, the first officer answered back with only "twenty three", not "twenty three right."

3. *"If you were the first officer in this incident, how would you have handled it?"*

You will obviously get different responses when you ask this question. Try to solicit a response from each student.

---

4. *"Did the FO assert himself with the appropriate level of persistence to maintain a safe operation?"*

No. He let his emotions get in the way of logic and his lack of communication was a direct factor in the cause of the crash. He played the "nonreactive" role, and he didn't assert himself or speak up despite the fact that the aircraft was entering an obviously dangerous situation.

Figure 21.2 Example from pre-LOFT Briefing Guide

For 1996, NWA used a different variation of a three segment video tape, but the annual emphasis changed to the concepts under the Communication Cluster. These concepts include briefing crews thoroughly, clearly communicating decisions, explicitly encouraging participation, seeking information and direction from others when necessary, asserting with the appropriate level of persistence to maintain a safe operation, and critiques of self and others when appropriate (Northwest CRM, 1989). Rather than have the learners analyze the performance of the same crew in three different situations, the 1996 pre-LOFT video contains cockpit voice recorder (CVR) reconstructions of three different actual aircraft accidents. The three accidents portrayed in the video are: Western Airlines 2605, a DC-10 that crashed in Mexico City in 1979; US Air 5050, a Boeing 737 that ran off the end of the runway at LaGuardia airport in Flushing, New York in 1989; and United Airlines 232, the DC-10 that crashed in Sioux City, Iowa in 1989. Communication, or the lack thereof, played a major part in the outcome of these accidents. Similar to the 1995 Briefing Guide, the 1996 Briefing Guide contained all the questions and appropriate responses written directly into it.

Even if the instructors were uncomfortable facilitating a CRM discussion, they could still conduct an effective pre-LOFT briefing simply by following the guidelines in the pre-LOFT briefing guide. After observing several of NWA's LOFT scenarios, Captain Roy Butler, a leader in the field, made this comment about NWA's pre-LOFT briefings: "NWA's use of a pre-LOFT briefing video and associated briefing guide is an extremely effective way for the instructors to conduct a thorough pre-LOFT briefing. The concepts of CRM are clearly spelled out for the instructors to discuss, and the students' learning potential is greatly increased. In fact, if the instructors simply used the briefing guide as written, it would be difficult to conduct a poor pre-LOFT briefing" (Helmreich, Wilhelm, Bell, Butler, & Connelly, 1995).

In addition to the questions and answers for the CRM discussion, the pre-LOFT briefing guide contained several pages of information designed to assist the instructor during the LOFT event. The guide contained background information on NWA's CRM program, some historical information on the accident and incident rates industry-wide, and helpful hints for conducting effective LOFT debriefs. The next challenge for NWA's Human Factors Practices department was to train the instructors how to use the video and briefing guide. This challenge was addressed by the production of the NWA Instructor Refresher Video.

Instructor refresher video

The Instructor Refresher video was designed with the NWA instructor in mind. It was produced by NWA's Flight Training Development section, and it was intended to solve the organizational problems of recurrent training, CRM/LOFT standardization, and facilitation training. The video ran 30 minutes in length, and contained all the necessary information on how to conduct a CRM/LOFT event at Northwest Airlines. The video was divided into three sections.

The first section contained information on how to conduct the CRM/LOFT briefing. It included directions on the conduct of the CRM/LOFT briefing, a step by step guide for using the pre-LOFT video tape and briefing guide, and several items for instructors to remember about the major differences between facilitation and instruction. The second section of the refresher video contained information on how to use the simulator video recording equipment. This section also demonstrated the operation of the Video Cassette Recorders and cameras in the flight simulators, as well as how to mark the video tape in order to highlight specific video segments for later use in the LOFT debrief. The third and final section of the refresher video detailed techniques for an effective CRM LOFT debrief. These techniques came from NWA's own LOFT experiences, as well as from the direct results of research conducted by NASA/Ames, California scientists and researchers from NASA/University of Texas. In addition, the video contained a list of do's and don'ts for CRM LOFT facilitation and debriefing.

Every CRM LOFT instructor was required to view the Instructor Refresher video prior to administering a CRM LOFT. The video actually served two purposes. First, for any instructors who hadn't administered a CRM/LOFT in the current year, the video gave them sufficient information and instruction on how to conduct the CRM/LOFT effectively. Second, for any instructors who experienced a substantial delay between instruction and coming "off-line" to administer CRM/LOFT events, the video fulfilled its title. It "refreshed" the instructors on the conduct and administration of the CRM/LOFT. This video was the first of its kind at NWA, and it has been something that the instructors desired for a long time. It is hoped that this and future refresher videos will help to diminish the problem of instructor training and standardization, if not solve the problem entirely.

As with any training program, the study of Human Factors is a continuous on-going process, not just a one time lesson. The entire aviation community must embrace the concepts of Human Factors training. Despite the numerous organizational barriers mentioned above, we must strive to overcome these barriers and continue to develop newer and more productive methods of learning. It is our responsibility to disseminate the message that the pay-offs from investments in this area will be great in terms of safety and effectiveness of the aviation system (Helmreich, 1993). Let none of us be like the Chief Executive Officer of one major airline who experienced a serious accident, and then was heard to comment "I can't believe this happened to us. We *did* CRM training over 3 years ago."

References

ATA, AQP Focus Group (1994) *Line Operational Simulations: LOFT Scenario Design, Conduct and Validation.* LOFT Design Focus Group, ATA, AQP Subcommittee, November 2, 1994.

BCAG.(1995) *All Accidents.* In Statistical Summary of Commercial Jet Aircraft Accidents, Worldwide Operations 1959-1994.(p.5-14) Boeing Commercial Aircraft Group. Seattle, Washington.

Chidester, T. (1993) *Critical Issues for CRM Training and Research.* In E. Wiener, B. Kanki, & R.Helmreich (Eds), *Cockpit Resource Management* (p.320). San Diego, California: Academic Press.

FAA (1995) Advisory Circular No. 120-51B, Crew Resource Management Training, Federal Aviation Administration, p. 14.

FMAQ, (1993) Helmreich, Merritt, Sherman, Gregorich, & Weiner. NASA/University of Texas, Austin, Texas.

Helmreich, R. (1993). *Future Directions in Crew Resource Management Training.* ICAO Journal, Volume 48 No. 7, September 1993, p. 9.

Helmreich, R., & Foushee, H.C. (1993). *Why Crew Resource Management? Empirical and Theoretical Bases of Human Factors Training in Aviation.*

In E.Wiener, B. Kanki, & R. Helmreich (Eds), *Cockpit Resource Management* (p. 40). San Diego, California: Academic Press.

Helmreich, R., Wilhelm, J., Bell, J., Butler, R. and Connelly, E. (1995) *Observations of the Northwest Airlines LOFT Program*. Proprietary Report, Appendix B. (p. 3) NASA/UT/FAA, August 18, 1995.

Merritt, A. (1995) *Cross-Cultural Issues in CRM/LOFT Training*. NASA/University of Texas/FAA Aerospace Research Project, Presented at the IATA Human Factors in Aviation Seminar, Bahrain, March 1995.

NWA CRM Model (1989) *Northwest Airlines CRM Reference Manual*. Northwest Airlines Flight Training Development department (pp.5-14).

22 Airline training for new technology

John Bent and Rick Fry

Comments from a number of publications show that cockpit automation increases, decreases, and redistributes workload. It enhances situational awareness, takes pilots out of the loop, increases head-down time, frees the pilot to scan more often; reduces or increases training requirements; makes a pilot's job easier, increases fatigue, changes or fails to change the role of the pilot, makes things less or more expensive; is highly reliable or highly unreliable, minimises human error, leads to error, changes the nature of human error, tunes out small errors, raises likelihood of gross error; is desired by pilots, is not trusted, leads to boredom, frees pilot from the mundane, and finally increases or has an adverse affect on safety.
(Adapted from comments by J.Lauber)

Introduction

Efficiency is the designers' goal, and advances with new technology. For new transport aircraft, improvements in efficiency demand that pilots understand the changes, and find new ways to operate. It is the intention of this chapter to take these issues and show how Cathay Pacific Airways handled the challenge of relatively rapid introduction of fly-by-wire aircraft into its operations. We use a number of examples from our training programs to highlight the procedures we used. Before we do that, however, some general background to the problem.

Change in aviation technology development has largely been driven by designers and engineers, with only scant consideration of the man-machine interface. Pilots have been expected to adapt. More recently, considerable efforts have been made to design aircraft for the operators, but pilots still find unfriendly engineering solutions on the modern flight deck. Once pilots were eventually included in the design evaluation process, the assumption seems to have been made by manufacturers that senior airline pilot managers would be able to identify the ergonomic solutions most expertly. Pilots, however, are usually conservative by nature. Like most people, experienced pilots see the familiar and comfortable as safer than the unknown. If only senior pilots are involved at the design stage, the resulting airliner flight deck may meet *traditional* pilot expectations, rather than those of optimal efficiency.

With contemporary computer power, there is already the capability to design control systems to provide pilots with traditional aircraft feel and handling qualities. This has been partially achieved on the B777 fly-by-wire aircraft. However, in order to do this, there is a need to provide feedback loops which increase complexity over simpler systems, incurring weight, cost, and maintenance penalties. Weight, however small, carried in the air over the twenty to thirty-year life of a modern airliner, is a crucial factor in airline operating costs. So, in the battle for efficiency, designers are forced to constrain aircrew operating space and interface.

Practical improvements will probably lead to more standardised handling qualities, almost independent of aircraft size and mission. However, the dramatic advances of computer power behind these advances are also likely to lead to yet more change for pilots. The safe development of new man-machine interfaces will require increasingly close cooperation between designers, engineers, trainers, and pilots.

Immediately following almost all historical leaps in aviation technology, there were traumatic periods of adjustment in the industry. During the "changeover periods", accident rates rose, and the cynics prevailed for a while. Surprisingly, with almost every change, pilots were exposed to *traditional* training programs which were ill-suited to the new technology. Military accident rates rose dramatically during peace-time periods of adjustment, particularly post- war when jets were introduced, and later with the introduction of early military fly-by-wire fighters. Too little emphasis was placed on operational differences, or on research of how the man-machine interface had changed. Appropriate pilot training for new technology always eventuated, but often some time after the new aircraft had entered service.

Subscribing to the inevitability of future leaps in technology, we must find coping mechanisms before the introduction of any significantly new aircraft. We must recognise the needs of humans in training pilots for changing flight decks. Training courses must include consideration of the need for trainee pilots to replace old concepts with new ones. Just as the aircraft themselves have become more efficient, their operators want more efficient training programs. Changed technology applies to instructional design, too. Improved, more powerful training programs can also appeal to airline accountants. With more appropriate training of a higher quality, course lengths can be reduced, providing long term payback for the higher initial investment in course design and equipment.

With hindsight, it is easy to be critical. The solution remains relatively simple, however. While aircraft design is one of mankind's most successful team efforts, pilots are still not appropriately recognised as members of the team. The training of pilots for new technology must be given more resources and emphasis at the earliest stage. Operational differences must be identified, risk analysis of the new man-machine interfaces made, and appropriate training courses devised.

Prior to the aviation recession of the early nineties, resources were in reasonable supply to provide for research into improved flight crew training. Since the deepest point of the recession, the huge airline deficits of the world have resulted in a slash and burn mentality, with resources re-allocated to survival. Advanced CRM and LOFT training concepts, just launched in many airlines, became still-born or were often aborted. It was a testing time for airline management to show real commitment to funding improved training.

A330/A340 flying training in Cathay Pacific Training School

Cathay's new approach to introducing high technology aircraft

For many years, Cathay Pacific Airways has been operating high technology jet transports of the day. The Convair 880, was followed by the B707, the Tristar L1011, B747, and Cathay then became an early operator of the B747-400, flying more than twenty of the type on ultra long haul routes. More recently, Cathay introduced twelve new fly-by-wire Airbus Aircraft (four A340s and eight A330s) followed by the B777-200, and in 1998, the B777-300 stretch.

As a largely self-contained operator, having its own simulators and training programs, Cathay commissioned, over a two year period, both authors of this chapter to research the flight crew training and operational aspects of the A340/A330. Part of this research involved an A340 familiarisation in the Miami simulator; then flying a number of test aircraft; and, finally, line captain experience with Dragonair as line captains over a six month period, operating the A320 mainly into China. Under management of the authors, Cathay became the first airline in the world where pilots fly both twin (A330) and quad (A340) aircraft.

Pilots were trained at an average rate of sixteen pilots per month, requiring a new style of preparation. The pace and complexity of the launch of over fourteen aircraft, at the rate of one aircraft per month, had no company precedents. In the late eighties, Cathay Pacific Airways ordered the first Airbus aircraft for the airline, the A330. As an all US-equipped carrier, the introduction of the A330 was a change in direction for the company. This was the first Airbus with Rolls Royce engines, and continued the Cathay tradition of an all Rolls airline. Firm orders were made for ten aircraft due for deliveries commencing in early 1995.

However, following detailed aircraft analysis, the decision was made in early 1994, to add six A340-300 aircraft to the existing ten A330 order. These aircraft would be preceded by four leased A340-200s. The deliveries commenced with only nine months' lead time. The combined acquisition rate thus escalated to an average of one aircraft per month, of different variants, for the first eleven months of introduction. Subsequently, Cathay purchased two Airbus A330 test aircraft for delivery in late 1996. Beyond the seventeen firm aircraft orders there were options on a further sixteen A330/A340 aircraft, reaching a potential fleet size of 33 aircraft.

While the introduction of the A330 had been well resourced, the addition of the A340 at an introduction date earlier than the A330, generated some very significant challenges. For Cathay, without significant previous Airbus experience, the combination of the two variants, at a rate of introduction unprecedented in the company, became a major challenge. At the same time, the underlying organizational structures of Cathay were being modified in response to recessionary and competitive pressures, inflation in Hong Kong, and a need to be proactive about a challenging future.

For the first six months of 1994 the two authors completed an A320 conversion in Toulouse, and flew with Dragonair, an associated airline in Hong Kong, as Line Captains on the A320. This involved 100 sectors each, flying into China - representing some invaluable exposure to fly-by-wire technology. This experience was most important in the launch process in terms of both experience gained and credits achieved towards training at introduction due to family commonality.

The CAE simulator, previously ordered for the A330, was fitted with a quick changeover kit to allow both A330 and A340 training. A Level 5 flight training device was also ordered and modified in the same way. For annual recurrent training, Cathay applies a minimum of eight, four- hour sessions per pilot. This training is considered to be a high priority in the maintenance of standards. Video-facilitated LOFT is also a significant element of training. A second A330/A340 convertible simulator was planned to be in service in mid-1977.

- ESTABLISH THE DIFFERENCES

- ASSESS THE OPERATIONAL IMPACT

- ESTABLISH *APPROPRIATE* PROCEDURES

- PREPARE TRAINEES

- DESIGN AN *APPROPRIATE* TRANSITION TRAINING PACKAGE

- DESIGN AN *APPROPRIATE* RECURRENT TRAINING PACKAGE

- MONITOR THE PROCESS

- THE WORD IS "*APPROPRIATE*"

Figure 22.1 Checklist for hi-tech introduction

Seamless Training

The two authors surveyed accident data and training issues with other airlines and safety organizations, and presented internal forums for Cathay Management and Flight Crew in order to de-mystify the technology, and to try to correct any extreme and inaccurate perceptions. From this we learned that certain important steps must be taken to prepare pilots for new technology (See also Figure 22.1).
  1. Analyse the differences between the new technology and what currently exists;

2. Assess the operational impact;
3. Find ways to explain the differences to pilots as early and as simply as possible;
4. Establish appropriate procedures;
5. Provide pre-training and advance information to trainees;
6. Monitor the process and provide feedback for modification and improvement.

It is not enough to just apply traditional training programs to significantly new technology. The operational impact of new technology is in human terms. These are thus the focus for the new training design. Attitudes, values and expectations have to be addressed.

This can be achieved through such forums, or by means of pre-course reading to prepare pilots for the mainstream transition program. Some samples of the information disseminated in Cathay are shown in Figure 22.2. As indicated earlier in this chapter, anxiety and suspicion have to be expected when experience pilots face the unknown. A trainee commencing training without confidence and enthusiasm, is a trainee already partially lost.

Traditional pilot training methods assumed the need for pilots to learn through various phases of training, from ground school (technical) through simulator, to flight training. However, this process misses a fundamental point. Pilots will not be operating the aircraft in such a phased manner, moving slowly from theory to practice, and from the parts to the whole. They will be using all skills simultaneously. Their perspective at work on the flight deck is unrelentingly operational. They need to know at the start of their training how to operate the aircraft in its practical requirements. The traditional separation of the necessary skills in training is a compartmentalisation of memory into the multiple processes of the flight deck. The different instructors involved in each phase inevitably bring differing emphasis to the trainee, and sometimes inappropriate information, requiring unlearning and re-learning later in the operational environment. Confusion sown during early training can become an accident factor later.

In order to overcome the limitations of conventional flight training for new technology aircraft, Cathay and Lufthansa have independently developed transition courses designed by flight crew aimed at more operational and seamless learning. Each day, a combination of training aids produces an immediate transfer from theory to practice. Computer Based Training (CBT), using checklists and procedures in use, combined with same-day simulator sessions, completes the circle of operational integration. CRM and LOFT is integrated and emphasised.

Cathay developed the Lufthansa integrated training (as applied to the LH A340) into seamless training, using a regular mix of CBT/tutorials/flight training device/full flight simulator. The objective targeted from the start of training is operational learning. Traditional barriers between technical and simulator training are removed. Technical and Simulator Instructors have became part of a single team, and are given regular route familiarisation flights. Additional LOFT inputs to the course from Flight Instructors are fed back, as the check and training team grows in experience and numbers.

Basic FMGS trainer, A340/A330

An advanced CBT training program was ordered from TRO. For over one year, this CBT program was customised to align the content directly and operationally with aircraft procedures and checklists. For almost every instructional day, the trainee pilot applies the CBT learning of part of the day to the full flight simulator in the second part of the day. The program is intended to provide shorter, more enjoyable and effective training programs which are more directly aligned to the task of the modern pilot.

SIDESTICK:

PIO (Pilot Inducted Oscillation) is the most significant trainee handling challenge to overcome with sidestick operation. It must be understood from the outset that the sidestick changes the aircraft vector, which the computers WILL THEN MAINTAIN. The experience of **releasing the sidestick** in rough air will demonstrate this fact effectively and permanently. Due to the lack of **sidestick feedback**, trainers should think of making inputs only in TWO stages:

1.Verbal

2.Take Control

Remember that ADDING a control input achieves nothing from a training perspective.

FMA

From the start of training the trainee must call FMA as pilot flying.

TAXYING (Taxy by wire):

Taxying: ALL inputs to a taxiing trainee MUST BE VERBAL. "Adding" a steering input could be disastrous, especially in a turn.

Turns must be well overhung, to avoid the mains cutting the corner. The C/L should be felt "over the shoulder" before tracking around a turn. For pilots ex-L1011, the turning position is very similar to that aircraft. Use diff. thrust as necessary. <7 kts you get bogged down, especially if a 90 degree turn. Best entry speed 10-13 kts.

Max speed on straight taxiway (clear of A/C): 30 kts (but beware of higher brake temps). Decelerate with SINGLE brake applications to <10kts, rather than "riding the brakes".

Exactly on C/L: RT/LFT knee over C/L for Capt/FO respectively.

Note that sudden steering inputs can place a significant side force on the nosewheel and tyre assembly which, if seen, can leave a lasting impression!

Figure 22.2 Examples of Cathay training notes for new technology

Some of the main lessons stemming from the Cathay A340/A330 introduction follow.
1. The new technology training cake should include the ingredients shown below:
   *   An operational perspective.
   *   Time to absorb the training.
   *   The questioning of the validity of old concepts.
   *   The abandonment of comfortable well-trodden attitudes, if inappropriate to the new technology.
   *   The learning of new habits, and the conscious disposal of the old.
   *   Clear explanations, with reasons (objective education).
   *   Understanding the increasing importance of effective task sharing/communication in two-pilot hi-tech operations (CRM).

* Identification of "man-machine" design objectives, and operational "traps" for the pilot.
* Regular re-enforcement.

2. The process must include emphasis on critical man-machine interface areas such as:
   * the hazard of reversion to old habits under stress;
   * the place for automation as a tool;
   * who is in control: pilot or aircraft?
   * airmanship (experienced common sense) must still dominate;
   * the avoidance of over-reliance on automation;
   * how to revert to the simple fix.

3. Early operational experience must be fed back into training as rapidly as possible, especially for practical problems, such as interpretation and workload. Much of the modern airliner is software driven. Here the manufacturer can play a critically helpful part by making designers freely available for the airline to communicate with, as difficulties of software or interpretation occur. For example, Cathay had an Airbus test pilot available for consultation when required.

4. Rapid communication is vital between the airline and manufacturer. It is equally important within the airline. The Cathay A340/A330 team of 27 launch flight trainers, seven simulator instructors, and five technical training instructors were linked by E-Mail through which information was available on-line day or night, at home or at work. Co-ordination of all aspects of the launch could be effected world-wide via E-mail.

5. The lessons learnt at Cathay fell mainly into the realm of *Human Factors*. We have known about the issues raised for a long time, and the practical verification serves to remind us of the broadening team attitude necessary to produce safer air transport. Appropriate training for new technology is the key to a safer operation. To get this, manufacturers and airlines must invest, *in advance of delivery* of new technology aircraft, in the most effective training tools and, most importantly, in the training of effective trainers.

Glass cockpits / FMS equipped flights decks are powerful tools for efficient flight, but can also become powerful traps if they are given priority over common sense and airmanship. A NASA analysis of commercial aviation incidents which occurred over one year in US terminal areas revealed that over 90% involved FMS/Glass cockpit aircraft. To a great extent, the responsibility for appropriate training for such new technology must lie with the manufacturer.

On the A340 and A330 pilots can navigate laterally at 3000' in the climb out with 5-10 easy "head-down" keystrokes, when 0-2 moves would achieve the same result with heads-up. Pilots must be taught how to fly sophisticated aircraft by the shortest, most straightforward methods, especially in terminal areas where weather and other traffic should dominate their interest. They should be trained to revert to the simple fix. Obsession with peripheral system details is a symptom of a carry-over of concepts applicable to previous aircraft.

There is a need for a further elevation of the need for enhanced CRM skills in the two-pilot, hi-tech cockpit, especially in terms of communication and task sharing. To promote these aspects, in Cathay we changed procedures for the A330/A340 fleet to "hot mike" communications below FL 150. Also, all pilot duties (except a rejected take off) have been split fifty/fifty PF/PNF, including starting and taxying the aircraft. This is to maintain the simplest and clearest separation of tasks and duties, as well as preparing First Officers for command.

Mixed fleet flying

How realistic is mixed fleet flying? The experience of other airlines with A320 and A340 operations is one of steady progress, frustrated by industrial or organizational factors external to the arguments. Cathay committed commercially to fly mixed-fleet, and is now fully converting all pilots to mixed fleet flying. In developing the mixed fleet flying procedures, Cathay adopted a similar process to that employed by the AQP Development Team in the USA. This involved working together with the Hong Kong Civil Aviation Department towards practical rules designed to protect the highest levels of safety, via a phased and evaluated process. In practice, most of the challenges were nothing to do with the technology, but more to do with adaptation of existing regulations to fit the new situation.

It must be remembered that the A340 and A330 are designed for commonality of both components and operation. These aircraft are operationally extremely close, by any measure. Existing rules do not permit common ratings for the pair as they have differing numbers of engines. However, in reality, fly by wire and computer architecture (wings level signalling, and interactive identification feedback) remove the traditional effects of these differences. Cathay, therefore applied to operate the two variants on two endorsements.

It is interesting to note how many years the B757 and B767 have been operated safely on common type ratings. Yet these aircraft have differences of a greater practical relevance to pilots than the A330 and A340 having a common management of aircraft systems and procedures in every sense. We join the response from cross-qualified Airbus training captains: what's all the fuss about?

Mixed fleet flying: What's all the fuss about?

The piloting perspective

An entirely long-haul pilot roster reduces handling skills to a minimum level. There is obviously a safety-related benefit to exposing pilots to both short and long haul operations on the same roster. The personal and professional satisfaction stems from piloting two aircraft with identical handling on routes ranging from the shortest to the longest in the world, on a balanced roster. The slight differences between variants do not threaten flight safety, because pilot response to emergencies is ECAM led and system-interactive. ECAM management protocol is the same for both aircraft. In fact, the slight differences generate an optimum balance of interest, motivation, and arousal levels, enhancing pilot professionalism. The possibility of remaining on Airbus fly-by-wire aircraft throughout a career is, as a result of the varied nature of the operation, attractive to pilots. For their employers, it goes a long way towards the elimination of the cross-fleet training costs which come with traditional operations.

INTRODUCTION
As pilots we tend to be rather conservative in our outlook; a healthy quality in aviation. Because Airbus fly-by-wire technology represents a significant new step in design philosophy, we have sometimes taken a cynical view of the new concepts involved, especially when all the facts are not available to us. The adjustments which were necessary with the

advent of jet and swept wing transports are a matter of record, and the Airbus fly-by-wire family represents another leap forward, requiring similar changes of outlook.

PURPOSE OF THESE NOTES

It is appropriate, before commencing training, to look at the Airbus issues which are perceived to be significant, as outlined in these notes. They are provided in order to try to explain some of the issues which may cause uncertainty. It is recommended that they are read in conjunction with the CPA customised Standard Operation Procedure Section, issued before the course. The sources for these notes are broad, and include current operators of A320s, A330s, and A340s. Our own A320 conversion and 100 sectors/230 hours each of line flying in China and the region, followed by cross crew qualification to the A340, provide a further practical basis for the information provided...

EXPERIENCE

Fly-by-wire A320s have been flying for many years. The experience gained in the process of conversion to this technology has been well analysed. Research undertaken to review Airbus conversions has shown that trainees with reservations about the integrity of Airbus technology prior to starting the conversion, have had greatest difficulty with the training program. It has also been found that although age plays a part in terms of the "rate" of learning, more experienced pilots are more able to retain a sense of awareness that the aircraft still requires knowledge, good judgment, and airmanship to operate safely...

ACCIDENTS & INCIDENTS

There have been some "high profile"A320 accidents, which have received a considerable amount of media publicity. Until recently, there has been the perception that Airbus have not actively provided responsive public defences against media inaccuracies. By the time official enquiries are complete, the accidents reported are no longer prime news, and negative opinions have already been formed. Because of this, and the impact of the first news reports, these opinions are not substantially reversed once the findings are available...

As with previous aircraft introductions, design and procedural weaknesses have been found, which have been corrected by modifications to equipment or procedures.

A balanced examination of accident investigation reports and flight safety sources reveals that almost all recent Airbus accidents contained significant human factors, such as training, the dissemination of information, inter-crew communications, crew task sharing, and CRM.

Examples of A320 stories include the "*stuck-in-the-hold*", and "*unable to descend*" "incidents". We have carried out extensive research with BA, LH, Ansett, Canadian, and other A320 operators which reveals no recorded evidence that these "incidents" ever occurred. Indeed, from a technical point of view, it is impossible to understand how either incident could have occurred because the "basic modes"of fly-by-wire, "Heading and V/S", are always available. Nevertheless, these unsubstantiated stories continue to circulate freely. [Lufthansa has even seen fit to establish a folder entitled "Specially Heard Insider Talk", the initials of which summarise the content to some extent!]...

THE COMPUTERS

As is well known, transport aircraft preceding fly-by-wire A320/330/340 aircraft used computers to drive FMS, EFIS, manage navigation, and enable automatic approaches to be flown safely. Such technology was to some extent "add-on", rather than "built in", as the rest of the aircraft usually functioned conventionally.

The designers of Airbus fly-by-wire aircraft have taken the use of computers a step further by building the **entire** aircraft around computer control. Deliberately different manufacturers and software formats have been employed in order to eliminate the potential for "common faults". When studying the A340 or A330, it will become apparent that every major system has some sort of interaction with other systems or flight situations (e.g. changes to the condition of the hydraulic and electrical systems directly effect flight control laws)...

FLIGHT "PHASES"

Performance, and vertical and lateral navigation obviously depend on the phase of flight. The Flight Management & Guidance System (FMGS) computers respond to changes of flight phase automatically, altering *performance/speed* targets to fit with the phase of flight. ECAM information is presented in a pre-set sequence from start up to shut down, as a function of each flight phase. Awareness of what flight phase the computers "think they are in" is important...

SIDESTICK CONTROL - FLY-BY-WIRE

The sidestick is the pilot's input to the computers. The "Envelope" part of the Fly-by-wire computers is pre-programmed to limit aircraft attitudes (in Normal Law) to 67 degrees of bank (2.5G in level flight) and usually +30 to- 15 degrees of pitch, regardless of pilot sidestick input...

There is **no direct mechanical connection** between the sidestick and the control surface. The means of transmission from *sidestick to computers to control surfaces* is via shielded low impedance electric cables. As part of the A320 European and US certification process, the system was bombarded by radiation from military radars and the aircraft was deliberately flown into multiple lightning strikes. There have been no recorded cases in airline service where electro-magnetic interference has affected the A319, A320, A321, A330 or A340 fly-by-wire system. In fact, it is understood that the electro-magnetic protection standards for fly-by-wire transports have now been reduced.

The sidestick provides **no direct feedback** through the grip. Feedback is **indirect** via the RESULTS of the application. The sidestick is moved against spring pressure. The designers wanted to avoid complex back-driven feedback systems, sidestick linking, jam or feedback monitoring devices, and control-splitting systems, all of which increase weight, complexity and cost.

If an **incapacitated pilot** freezes his sidestick into full deflection, the other pilot simply presses his instinctive button on his sidestick and immediately takes control. After holding the button depressed for 30 seconds, he can lock out the other sidestick completely. However, the **last** pilot to press and hold this button **always** takes control.

If **both pilots make a sidestick input** together, the result is the algebraic sum of BOTH inputs. It is therefore important in the training environment to give priority to the other cues which measure trainee inputs, such as the visual cues used in the past. It is important for pilots to pre-warn each other of the need for a clear allocation of control, and for a trainee to be advised that the instructor may take control completely at times.

Control in Pitch:

Control is **via the computers**. Throughout flight, the elevators move under the control of the Flight Computers **with no pilot input.**

In NORMAL or ALTERNATE LAW, the sidestick **does NOT select a control deflection** or ATTITUDE directly, as would be the case with a conventional aircraft, and the elevator deflection is NOT proportional to sidestick movement. A "fore or aft" sidestick application **selects "G".** If a pitch input is made and held, the aircraft will pitch at a constant G until the flight envelope limits are met.

Moving the sidestick back creates a demand greater than 1.0G, and forward creates a demand less than 1.0G. When the sidestick is released (**STICK FREE**), the DEMAND fed to the computers is to **maintain flight at 1.0G** (relative to the earth). You can therefore consider your selected input as a SELECTED VECTOR THROUGH SPACE, which the computers will MAINTAIN, even through turbulence. There is no need to ride the sidestick as you would conventional controls.

In NORMAL LAW there is **no requirement to trim**. Without autotrim, the A340 would be no different from a conventional aircraft in that as it slows down it would try to maintain its in-trim speed, and as a result would pitch nose down, losing altitude. However, in Normal Law, the flight control computers now detect a pitch-down tendency as a G less than 1.0G and so cause the elevators to move up, returning the aircraft to flight at 1.0G. As a result the A340 or A330 will decelerate in level flight with no pilot input, maintaining 1.0G to the earth and continuously adjusting the trim as it does.

Control in Roll:

In NORMAL LAW in roll the sidestick **demands ROLL RATE**. If the sidestick input in roll is held, the aircraft will roll until the flight envelope limits are met. This is apparent during a Cross wind Take Off, if a normal control input is made into wind and held after rotation. While on the runway, the sidestick applies aileron directly, and then as the Flight Control Laws blend in, the aircraft will roll into the crosswind at a RATE proportional to the sidestick deflection. Up to 33 degrees of bank, the aircraft is automatically trimmed to generate 1.0G relative to the earth (no trimming required in a turn).

In ALTERNATE LAW(2) in roll the sidestick demands **DIRECT TO CONTROL SURFACE,** which is virtually the same as a conventional aircraft. It may be found that Alternate Law roll is rather more sensitive than Normal Law.

Summary:

In NORMAL LAW, in both PITCH and ROLL, when a movement of the sidestick is made, the resulting attitude or bank angle will be maintained with the sidestick returned to neutral. Therefore, as a general principle, whenever the desired flight path has been established, pressure on the sidestick should be removed.

The Sidestick - practical:

It takes most pilots *10 minutes to get used to it.*

It makes flying the aircraft a *more precise skill,* and easier to master.

The lack of "through-stick" feedback is a much more minor issue in practice than might be expected. *Alternative feedback cues are abundant,* and are quickly substituted for the traditional feel.

The *automatic trim function* is a delight once experienced, and further improves precision flying.

Enjoy the course. The A330 and A340 are the product of large commitments of research, development, and testing by some of the best aeronautical designers and engineers from four countries. Airbus fly-by-wire types have now accumulated significant amounts of in-service experience. They are of course quality products, as we have seen on factory visits. There is widespread appreciation of the quality of engineering and finish on these aircraft. We believe that you will find that you are embarking on a most enjoyable and professionally rewarding part of your aviation career.

Figure 22.3 Some selections from the Cathay pre-course information for Airbus trainees

Conclusion

When this chapter was written, we had converted over two hundred pilots from non-Airbus to A330/A340 aircraft, in under eighteen months. Airline training for new technology necessitates a newer, more integrated approach to training. In this chapter we have attempted to show how Cathay proceeded in its introduction of a fleet of fly-by-wire aircraft using a variety of theory-into-practice strategies such as seamless training. Our personal experiences, and those of our colleagues, played important roles in guiding the process, the pilot perspective cannot be underestimated. For us, however, resource investment in training, before the delivery of the aircraft, is one of the critical factors in ensuring the success of any airline training.

23 Training and developing the aircrew manager

Terry L Farquharson

Introduction

At the professional level, the aviation industry can be commended for its response, to challenges offered by issues such as increasing and rapidly changing technology, the efficient and safe management of new generation cockpits and their resources, and today's more complex and legalistic operational environment.

However, there is a small group of aircrew which, by virtue of its supervisory role, functions in both the professional and the management arenas. History suggests that management is not a comfortable role for aircrew and lore and literature are littered with accounts of both personal and organizational tragedies.

This chapter firstly examines reasons why aircrew have difficulty with the transition to the management role. Next, there is discussion on the role the organization plays in this process. Finally, there are proposals for a system of selection, training and development which will benefit both the individual aircrew manager and the organization.

Differences

There are three principal areas where aircrew show themselves to be different from both the general population and, importantly, executives.
- personality
- decision making
- role and occupational socialization

Personality

In 1980 the American Psychiatric Association defined personality as follows:

> *The characteristic way in which a person thinks, feels and behaves;*
> *the ingrained pattern of behaviour that each person evolves, both*
> *consciously and unconsciously, as the style of life or way of being in*
> *adapting to the environment.*

This definition can be broadened to include groups such as aircrew or other professions. Dolgin and Gibbs (Jensen, 1989) reviewed the results of several personality assessment inventories used to predict success in pilot training and concluded that aircrew showed statistically significant personality differences from the general populations on which the studies were based. However, one test, the Cattell 16 Personality Factors Test, allows a direct comparison between results for aircrew and executives. Table 23.1 summarizes the areas where aircrew and executives differ.

Recognition of these differences can be used to advantage in establishing the selection, training and development processes for prospective aircrew managers.

Table 23.1
Areas of difference between aircrew and executives

- Pilots are more self assured than executives.
- Pilots are more controlled and precise than executives.
- Pilots are very much more relaxed than executives.
- Pilots are much less prone to anxiety than executives.
- Pilots have much tougher poise than executives. They tend to be bold, hard and decisive. Pilots make decisions quickly but may take action without sufficient thought or consideration.
- Pilots are generally less outgoing than executives.
- Pilots tend to be more emotionally stable than executives.
- Pilots are likely to be more spontaneous, enthusiastic and cheerful than executives.
- Pilots are more conscientious, conforming and moralistic than executives.
- Pilots are more tough minded, self-reliant, realistic and cynical than executives.
- Pilots are more trusting, more accepting of conditions and easier to get along with than executives.
- Pilots are more practical and less imaginative than executives.

(adapted from Farquharson, 1993)

Decision making

A Director of Flight Operations for a major airline once commented to the writer about aircrew managers and their decision making:

> *It is never difficult for a pilot to make a decision, whether it's the correct one, only hindsight will tell. They are decision makers....(but) we had the problem of quick decision making, short-sightedness and not looking at all the issues as these should have been over-viewed before the decision was made.*
>
> (from Farquharson, 1993)

Some understanding of the aircrew decision making process can be gained by examining their professional "management" environment. One set of problems lasts only as long as a flight. The time available in which to make critical decisions is determined by the high velocity and three dimensional movement of the "office". The decision making environment is highly structured and regulated. Principal interactions are with groups with similarly disciplined outlooks. Lastly, professional training is centred about achieving almost total conformity with standard procedures. But, clearly, this mode of decision making is ideally suited to the operational environment.

In contrast the executive's decision making scenario is framed much more about a "nonprogrammed" environment. Decisions which deal with unusual or unique problems requiring more lengthy deliberation before formulating policy or strategic responses to achieve a successful outcome. Feedback is used to constantly alter system responses but the process takes place over a much longer time frame than for the pilot and is likely to involve inputs from many people.

These results support the conclusions contained in Table 23.1 and strongly suggest that this could be an area in which training would be required for the prospective aircrew manager.

Role and occupational socialization

In common with other professional groups, aircrew are socialized into their role. Many factors combine to create an individual or group's observed behaviour. The important outcome of this process is not only that people/groups hold expectations about how they should behave in certain circumstances but they also hold expectations about how other people/groups should behave.

Figure 23.1 shows a four dimensional model of aircrew behaviour developed by Telfer (1988) which is particularly useful in explaining the inter-relationship of the factors affecting behaviour. The two most important factors for understanding aircrew occupational socialization, and therefore behaviour, are the weak organizational influence, resulting from aircrew being a largely absentee work force, and the strong group, or social psychological dimension, governed by the aircrew's professional peers. In this situation there is a high probability of conflict with other groups such as management.

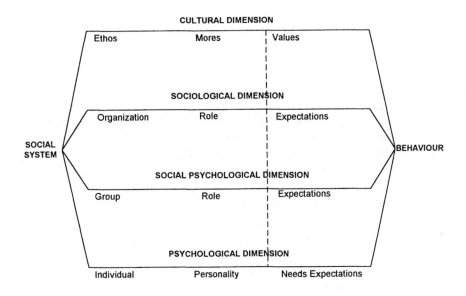

Figure 23.1 A four dimensional model of flight crew behavourial analysis (Telfer, 1988)

A reasonable conclusion would, therefore, be that aircrew are likely to come to a management position with a strong socialization into their professional role, but that set of individual and group values and expectations is likely to be either partly or wholly at odds with those required to successfully perform in a management environment. Resocialization is likely be a necessary development strategy.

The organization's influence

In the same way as peer groups, organizations have considerable influence in determining how individuals or groups within that body behave. Organizations also set their standards for legitimate and correct behaviour. Ouchi (1981) has observed that:

> *Tradition and climate makes up a company's culture. More than that, culture implies a company's values....Managers instill that pattern in their employees by their example and pass it on to succeeding generations of workers"*

Telfer and Moore (1995) further underscore the pervasive influence organizations exert in creating not only the climate (i.e. the set of internal characteristics that differentiate one organization from another and which also influences the behaviour of its members) but also the internal learning environment.

However, surveys and interviews conducted by Farquharson (1993) indicated that senior management in Flight Operations Departments generally had a low level of awareness about the influences they exerted in these areas and, hence, the messages being transmitted. More often than not the means of providing guidance to aircrew managers relied on processes more akin to osmosis than to any set of clearly articulated principles and goals. Several other interesting observations can be made about today's system of bringing aircrew into management positions:

- On average aircrew spend approximately twenty years in professional aviation before entering management. This phenomenon can largely be explained by the rigid seniority and social system that ensures it takes about twenty years to achieve a position of professional credibility; usually that position is associated with rank.
- On average aircrew in major airlines take up their first management appointment at age forty.
- In the organizations surveyed, the level of aircrew management experience was low. For example, in the fifty to fifty five age group, at which time some aircrew occupied relatively senior management positions, professional experience often exceeded thirty years but management experience averaged between five and ten years.
- Training has remained focused around professional areas with only twenty percent of training being associated with non-professional areas. There is a general perception that management training and development can be achieved purely by sending people on courses.
- The check and training stream is by far the preferred area from which to recruit management aircrew. In the organizations surveyed eighty nine percent of aircrew managers had their origins in training. The expressed reason for this preference was that these individuals were the company's best professional aircrew; however, this begs the question as to whether their

      background naturally equips these individuals as the best choice for management positions or whether there is merely the assumption that training skills equate and directly transpose to management skills?
- The recruitment process for aircrew managers is often socially based and few organizations adopt any formal assessment processes to judge a candidate's suitability against any predetermined standard.
- However, once in management positions aircrew are generally positively disposed toward their task and appear to be motivated more by professional than personal issues such as remuneration and recognition.

That this situation has developed is most curious given the professional aircrew's almost pathological predilection for rigid standards and accurate socialization into a role. Clearly, there does not seem to be the same sense of urgency involved in ensuring newcomers have a quick, efficient and guided transition into the management arena. The position is all the more remarkable when today's commercial environment and consequent pressures are considered. In an industry where profit margins are shrinking, or in many cases negative, it seems incongruous that aircrew managers are not positively selected, trained and developed to achieve the standards demanded of other managers in the aviation industry.

The nature of flight operations management

Before making prescriptions for a new approach it is essential to have some understanding of the nature of the flight operations management task. As with any operations management scenario, flight operations faces the task of balancing the commercial desirability constraint with the operational feasibility constraint. The commercial constraint can be conceived as the business opportunities identified by the commercial areas of an airline, while the feasibility constraint is set by aircraft and crew capabilities and the vast amounts of laws and regulations governing airline and aircraft operations.

      Aircrew managers are initially recruited for their specialist knowledge in the operational areas and often see these functions as separate from the commercial enterprise. However, the clear picture emerges that, while flight operations can be viewed as one area of the business, it is not isolated; rather, it is heavily influenced by other business functions and policies. Therefore, aircrew managers must be conversant not only with their professional skills but also with the general management skills applied in other areas of the business. The level of general management skill required will depend on the individual's positions in the management hierarchy.

Characteristics of a new approach to training and developing aircrew managers

If aircrew are to function efficiently and effectively as managers and the costly personal and organizational failures seen in the past are to be minimized, then it is suggested that the organization and the training and development system should have the following characteristics.

- The organization's charter should be clearly stated and made known to all. Periodic revision of these goals will be necessary to ensure the operating system (i.e. the departmental structure and function) is in harmony with the department's actual role and function.
- Jobs should be fully defined in relation to the stated objectives. This definition must also include a person specification which annunciates the skills and experience required of the incumbent.
- Only the minimum number of aircrew should be recruited for management training. History suggests that many positions occupied by aircrew have been essentially clerical in nature and, given the high salary differential paid to aircrew in their professional role, this misapplication of resources cannot be economically justified. Provided the two preceding steps have been accomplished the number of aircrew required to perform management functions will be minimized.
- The system should recognize that general management skills and flying/training skills are different and, therefore, recruitment should not focus exclusively on people with high level professional skills. The aim must be to select those with the best prospect of becoming competent managers. However, one caveat should be applied here; due to the reduced opportunities to fly when in a management role and the need to maintain professional credibility, potential managers should have not only high management potential but also high professional competence.
- The system should understand the nature of the aircrew personality and accept that the time available to develop the required skills is short, therefore, any training and development process must be structured, guided and actively managed.

Management and manager development

Examination of these suggested characteristics reveals two areas of focus, the organization and the individual. Drucker (1977) proposed that development takes place through not one but two related tasks that impact each other.

- *Management Development* - where the concentration is on the management environment and considers age structure, skill base, organizational structure and job content and design; and
- *Manager Development* - where the goal is to enable individuals to develop their abilities to the fullest extent. Fundamental to manager development are:
  - Self motivation.
  - Active participation, encouragement and guidance from superiors and the organization.
  - A performance appraisal system that looks at what individuals do well, what they can do better and what shortcomings in their skills need to be overcome in order to improve their performance capability.

Management development

Why should management development be considered important and necessary? Firstly inappropriate structure may lead to dysfunction and inefficiencies and, secondly, with the passage of time and change of environmental forces, re-organization may be necessary to align departmental structure and tasks with current needs.

Within this framework it is now possible to present a model for management development in a flight operations department. The model, shown at Figure 23.2, is a six step sequential process and is linked to a complimentary model for manager development. The management development model requires positive action in the following areas:

- *Structure.* The structure must be matched to the task. Most flight operations departments use a functional structure.
- *Job Specification.* Jobs should be specified in detail with the result that position holders are clear as to what the job entails and how it relates to the goals set for the department.
- *Person Specification.* The person specification is the natural compliment to the job specification and should take into account the personal attributes needed for the task, the skills and skill levels required and the experience level needed.
- *Selection.* Selection should be aimed at recruiting those with the highest management potential. Here the use of a development centre is recommended as it will result in analysis and identification of an individual's strengths and weaknesses against the specification and in general terms. Two

clearly identifiable benefits are gained; the individual gains personal insight; and, the organization identifies the specific areas on which to concentrate training resources with the consequent reduction in time and cost combined with a greater probability of success.

- *Performance Assessment.* If organizational performance is to be validly assessed some form of feedback is necessary and a personal performance assessment system is an integral part of this process.
- *Organizational Feedback.* Adoption of an individual performance assessment system allows feedback in two directions; feedback into the organization to allow a determination on the job itself and the assessment system, leading to continued management development; and, individual feedback leading to manager development.

Another benefit gained through the use of this process is the establishment of positively defined formal relationships. Responsibility, authority and accountability associated with each position are known and ambiguity is removed. For the aircrew manager the world becomes more certain. For senior management the benefits are the surety that personnel are properly matched to tasks which in turn are aligned with the organizations goals.

Manager development

Manager development flows from and is the natural complement to management development. The process of manager development can be viewed through three related models.

- *The Relationship Between Specialist Knowledge and General Management Skills.* Each level of management in which aircrew might be employed requires a different balance between specialist knowledge and general management skills. At the junior levels the focus is on specialist knowledge, however, with increasing seniority more emphasis must be placed on developing general management skills.
- *The Concept of Development Over Time.* The aircrew manager, like any other manager, cannot be expected to acquire the necessary skills and management experience overnight. Just as flying skills grow with time and experience, so do management abilities. However, what makes the aircrew situation unique is the generally late start in the formal management arena. The clear message, therefore, is that the process of acquisition of knowledge and experience must be compressed as well as actively guided and managed. Figure 23.3 gives an indication of the types of skills and knowledge that might be suited to each level in the management hierarchy.

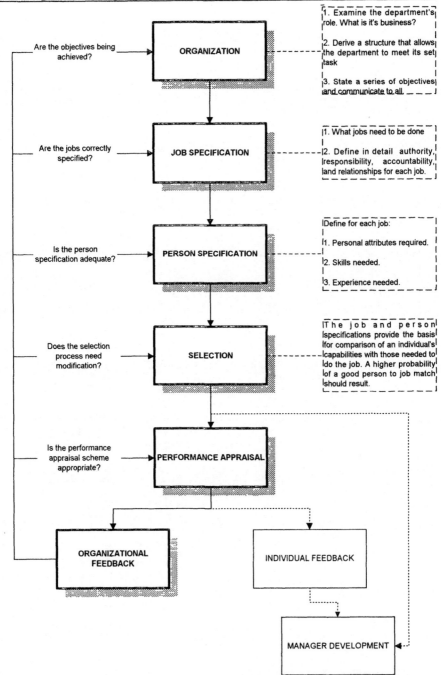

Figure 23.2 Model of a process of management development

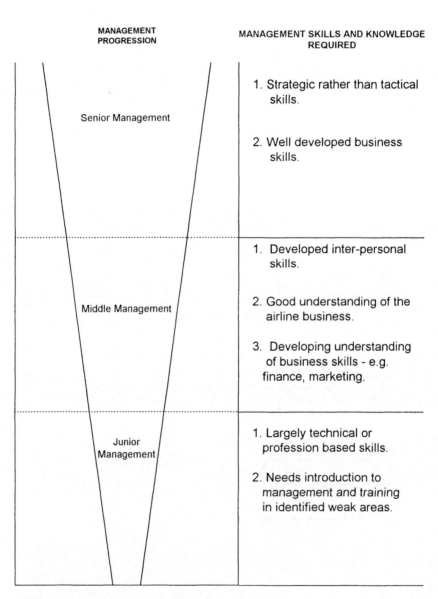

Figure 23.3 The concept of development over time

- *The Extension of Manager Development From Management Development.* Figure 23.4 shows how manager development links to management development. This process allows four areas of training needs to be identified, the focus of which shifts according to the position needs, the individual's strengths and weaknesses, and the needs identified through periodic perfomance assessments.

For the following reasons the four areas of training and development outlined in Figure 23.4 provided a rational guide to solving the vexing problem of equipping aircrew managers with the necessary skills and knowledge.

- *Selection Based Training Needs.* If individual strengths and weaknesses can be identified in the selection process, appropriate training can be given to boost the weak areas. This assumes a standard has been established against which to assess individuals. The clear benefit is that scarce resources are properly directed and the process of resocialization is set off on the correct path.
- *Core Training Needs.* Each organization should be able to identify core areas for training, examples of which might be departmental administrative functions, budgeting processes or relationships with the local regulatory authority. For the new recruit this training will set the scene and further solidify the resocialization process, while for those progressing through the system it will provide the proper foundation for advancement.
- *Performance Assessment Based Needs.* A fundamental element of the feedback system is a periodic assessment of performance. At the individual level this not only gives direction but also leads to the identification of any supplemental training needs.
- *Development Through Exposure and Periodic Job Rotation.* While some formal training is necessary, it is essential that the aircrew manager be given broad exposure to all aspects of the airline business in the shortest possible time. Some avenues available to facilitate this process are interdepartmental projects and committees and selective job rotation.

Active career management

There is the temptation to say that, because of the cost involved in taking aircrew away from their professional task, they should be excluded from management; however, the parallels with other professional groups strongly support the need for aircrew to function in management positions. But, clearly, economic factors will limit the number of practitioners. Therefore, given that aircrew normally start a management career much later than other aviation industry managers, it is essential that the process is actively monitored and controlled. The responsibility for this task falls directly to senior flight operations management staff.

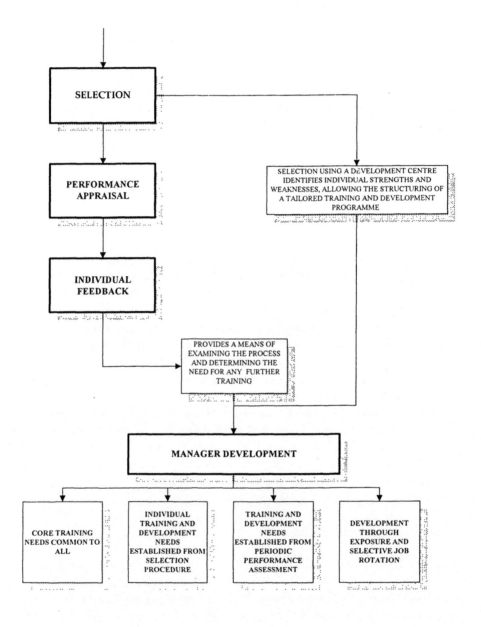

Figure 23.4 Model of a process of manager development

Conclusion

Despite what history and folk lore suggest, aircrew can become good managers. Certainly there is nothing faulty about the basic raw material; one airline that conducted some basic IQ assessments of its potential aircrew found that, judged on this scale, these individuals rated in the top thirty percent of United Kingdom university graduates (Farquharson, 1993). However what must be recognized is that, as with other highly trained professional groups, aircrew have developed the skills and outlook that ensure success and survival in their chosen field. In common with other professionals, the assumption is often incorrectly made that the ability to perform at a high standard within the profession is a guarantee that individuals can also perform well as a manager. History clearly contradicts this view.

By recognizing and understanding the problems and processes involved in bringing aircrew into management positions, many of the expensive personal and organizational tragedies that have occurred can be avoided or at least minimized, with the result that both the organization and the individual benefit.

References

Drucker, P.F. (1977), *Management*, Pan Books, New York.

Farquharson, T.L. (1993), Issues in Developing General Management Skills In Specialist Aircrew Managers", MBA Dissertation, Brunel University.

Jensen, R.S.(ed) (1989), *Aviation Psychology*, Gower, London.

Ouchi, W. (1981) *Theory Z: How American Business Can Meet the Japanese Challenge*, Avon, New York.

Telfer, R.A. (1988), From Pilot Judgement Training to Cockpit Resource Management, Paper presented to the Forty First IASS Flight Safety Foundation, Sydney.

Telfer, R.A. and Moore, P.J.(1995), Learning, Instruction and Organization in Aviation, Paper presented at the Eighth International Symposium on Aviation Psychology, Columbus, April.

24 The management of change in aviation training

Norman MacLeod

Introduction

We talk about change as though it is the exception rather than the rule. We talk of change management as if it is an activity which is outside the normal course of events. Yet, change is with us every day; what is remarkable is how badly we tend to deal with it. It is true that most people do not like change. It is unsettling. It prevents the establishment of habits and routines which reduce the turbulence in life. Instructional systems are especially prone to slipping into grooves, given the sometimes repetitive nature of the material being delivered.

This chapter will examine change in aviation training, from a personal perspective. First, we will look at what we mean by change and what events can give rise to it. Then we will discuss the modes in which change can be implemented as well of some of the barriers which will be encountered. The mechanics of resistance will be examined next before, finally, we outline a change management strategy.

What is change?

In an organizational setting we tend to consider change as being some form of departure from a steady state. Quite often, it is an event which requires planning, communication and, ultimately, some project management in order to arrive at a desired end-state. Change is a step shift in the normal mode of peration such that the new mode is quantitatively different. For example, replacing a fleet of basic training aircraft will require changes in operating procedures and the associated ground instruction. The scope of change may vary. We could simply replace old with new. We may take the opportunity to replace fixed-pitch props with variable-pitch. We may even decide to replace piston with turboprop. The ultimate decision is most likely to be made on economic grounds but each case has implications for the training system. Unfortunately, the full scope of the required modifications to existing practices may not always be readily apparent.

Take the simplest case, for example, of exchanging new for old. Systems and sub-systems may be substantially different in what is, superficially, the same model of aircraft as manufacturers refine and update products or find new suppliers. This will require alterations to operating procedures which will cascade down to training. However, the apparent similarity between old and new can mask the scope of change required. Consider the experience the crew of the Shuttle 'Endeavour' in 1992. Having failed to deploy the 'Intelsat' satellite using either the primary or backup circuits, the checklists used aboard the orbiter were compared with those in use at Mission Control and with those issued to the other three Shuttles in service. All were found to be the same; what had been overlooked was the fact that the wiring in 'Endeavour' was different and the change was not reflected in the checklists. Change, then, can be insidious as well as overt and planned: It can also be a mess. Consider this view of a recent training initiative (Figure 24.1).

Crew Resource Management (CRM) training is a direct result of the recognition that human failings in social situations are a significant contributor to aircraft accidents. Having been spawned in the US, the approach has spread outwards until most airlines now have some identifiable CRM activities in place. But what exactly is the problem and is CRM training the solution? I was talking to a young female European pilot on a 747 captain's course. When asked about flightdeck management, she said that the real difficulty for her was the attitude of female cabin attendants, many of whom were older than her and, she felt, resented her success. It seems that the overt change, CRM training, has been designed to remedy a situation which reflected a particular set of circumstances which existed on American flightdecks twenty years ago. The insidious change is the current set of social relationships found in the team which do not necessarily reflect the training assumptions. CRM as a planned change activity is a good example of the messiness inherent in the process. It demonstrates the importance of clearly identifying the problem before taking action.

Figure 24.1 A training initiative

The causes of change

So, what can be considered as specific causes of change? Perhaps the most obvious are developments in the technology and organization of operations. The arrival of new aircraft on the fleet and the retrofitting of new systems such as TCAS all require additions to initial and recurrent training syllabuses. The move to two-man cockpits clearly emphasises different pilot skills but the merger of two airlines might similarly generate a training requirement in order to harmonise procedures. Although changes in technology will have an immediate impact on line training, it will have a more delayed effect on ab-initio systems as ground training syllabuses are modified and changes are reflected in classroom instruction.

Pilot schools also have to contend with variations in input standards. Changes in state education and in the social development of children will affect the nature of candidates presenting themselves for selection and training. The globalisation of aviation training market means that a course tailored for one ethnic group does not meet the needs of students from a different group. An example of this is the use of the traditional UK classroom instructional method to teach foreign students. The UK system puts a responsibility on students to ask questions of the instructor to clarify any areas of uncertainty. However, some Asian students tend not to ask questions on the grounds that to do so would be an imposition on classmates who are forced to wait on an individual. What is needed is a mechanism to clear up misunderstandings out of class and yet instructors can resent the fact that students failed to take the opportunity when it was offered; in their eyes, the fault is the students' not the system's.

Whereas changes in technology of operations and procedural activity fall into the category of identifiable step change, the type of event traditionally classified as change, the mismatch between the design of the course and the students arriving for training does not. Instead, it typifies insidious change. Lying someway between the two is the case of educational technology. The mechanics of the delivery of instruction have changed enormously. We have seen chalk and a blackboard replaced by video projectors linked to dynamic simulation models capable of presenting aircraft instrumentation behaving in real-time. The decision to invest in a particular level of technology can be seen as a step-type change event and yet, in reality, it is remarkable how often the decision is made only after competitors have upgraded and suddenly your school is looking old and tired.

This section has attempted to identify some of the more significant causes of change in training systems. However, the outcome of the change process is not simply a response to an initial cause. The mode of change can be seen as an intervening variable, and this is what will be considered next.

Triggering change

Change may be characterised not just by the cause but also by the way in which the reaction to the cause has been initiated. At one extreme we have the accretional model of change initiation. Something happens and we alter our systems accordingly. This model is particularly appropriate to describe the development of training syllabuses. As new technology enters service, training requirements are added to the ground instructional syllabus. Unfortunately, material is often added at a faster rate than it is removed. The result is a net growth in ground training content and the requirement to teach material because it is tested in the exam and not because it has any relevance to the real world. For example, in a review of a seven month practical phase of a electronic engineers course, 43% of the instruction was found to relate to equipment no longer in service with the company.

At the other extreme, we see change that can be trauma-induced. Examples abound of an accident or some shift in public perception being sufficient to bring about change. The very first amendment to the UK pilot training syllabus was the direct result of two aircraft colliding over France in 1919. A similar event over the Grand Canyon in 1956 did much to promote the formation of the US Federal Aviation Administration. Again, TCAS technology has been available for many years but only became a requirement after an accident. Finally, we saw earlier that the increasing implication of group behaviour in aircraft accidents has given rise to the requirement for CRM training.

Both the accretional model and the trauma model are predicated on the concept of there being a relationship between the real world and the training system. In the accretional model, the system attempts to track reality by continually updating requirements. However, it fails to recognise the gap which develops when too many obsolete practices accumulate. The trauma model, on the other-hand, fails to keep track of developments and is suddenly brought into line. However, a third 'whim-based' model can be identified which makes no attempt to establish any links with the real world.

Change which derives purely and simply from some, usually senior, manager's bright idea is not uncommon. Quite often, investment in classroom technology is based on a whim. It may be rationalised after the event but, nonetheless, is still no more than a spontaneous action. For example, consider the description in Figure 24.2 of a school's introduction to CBT.

It would be wrong to underestimate the importance of whim-based change but, for our purposes, it serves as an introduction to the non-rational aspects of change which are the subject of the next section.

The CBT vendor approached the school with a view to a collaborative project. The vendor was keen to get a product into service which would hopefully revive the prospects of its bespoke authoring system. The school had not considered CBT as it was deemed too costly and, in any case, was not sanctioned by the regulator as an acceptable means of instruction. Initially, the intention was to apply CBT to maintenance training. Then, the focus was shifted to the commercial pilot course. A notional block of time was identified and subjects found to fill the allocation. The managing director had decided that the adoption of CBT would differentiate the school from the competition, despite that fact that the system could only be used outside of normal teaching as a means of revision. Courseware production was fraught with difficulty and, when the lessons were delivered, they caused considerable dissatisfaction among instructors. Apart from being demonstrated to visiting airline executives, the CBT was never integrated into the school curriculum.

Figure 24.2 Introduction of CBT

Barriers to change

Change is usually considered in terms of an alteration of state or notional location. So, we consider our present condition and decide what needs to be altered in order to better fit the prevailing circumstances. We talk of where we are now and where we want to be. In so doing we set up a logic of motion. Anything that then blocks or deflects that motion is deemed to be an obstacle, a barrier. Obstacles imply resistance and to resist logic is illogical, to defy rational change is to be irrational. However, the truth of the situation is that change does not affect all involved in an equal manner; it is not equally rational in the eyes of all those affected. Fund-holders who will have to foot the bill may need to enter into painful negotiations with some other part of the organization in order to keep budgets under control. Working practices may change. Effort will need to be expended by someone to bring about the change. Power relationships may be affected. It is interesting to note that the US FAA Advanced Qualification Program (AQP) has been kept under centralised control, some may say in order to avoid subversion by regional inspectors. The regional organization of the FAA has resulted in District Offices having considerable power. The initial resistance to AQP from within the FAA was quite strong and it was felt that the initiative could not work as intended if left to the regional network to implement. However, this action on the part of Washington may have offended some regional staff who see their traditional roles being usurped.

Everyone has a stake in the organization and change needs to recognise the differing views of stakeholders. First, let us list whom we mean by stakeholders. In an ab-initio commercial pilot school we can readily identify ground and air instructors, students and school management as immediate interested parties. Equity holders in the school are also concerned to get a return on their investment as are sponsors of students. The Regulatory authority has a remit to guarantee the quality of the product and the general public has an interest in the safe outcome of the training process. We can extend the list further to include administrative staff, canteen workers, airfield operator and so on, all of whom might, to some degree, be affected by a change in the training process. What is clear is that few, if any of these groups, have views that directly overlap and so change will require a trade-off of interests.

Change does not affect all involved in an equal manner

Stakeholders, then, have different perspectives on the organization and, as such, are qualified to comment on change to varying degrees. The implication is that all stakeholders can contribute to planned change and should be ignored at peril. Resistance to change occurs primarily when stakeholders' views are out of synchronisation. We need to differentiate between resistance to change and the failure of change. The one can lead to the other although the accomplishment of change can subsequently be deemed a failure. We also need to differentiate between the politics of change, which is effectively what a stakeholder analysis illuminates, and the project management of the activity.

305

Perceived resistance can often be the result of inadequate project management. We will try to make clear this difference by looking at the mechanics of resistance.

The mechanics of resistance

The ways in which change can be resisted are many, various and quite legitimate. Perhaps one of the most effective is sheer inertia. If we accept the concept of change as movement in a direction, then change requires inertia to be overcome for movement to start. However, quite often, the change process is not factored into the daily routine and so normal work output must be maintained. This leaves little time for change. Time is just one of the resources which project managers underestimate when putting plans together. Sometimes the case for change is poorly made. Therefore, those affected by the process do not see the need and the inertia to be overcome increases proportionately.

Organizational change can sometimes founder because of an incomplete view of the problem or because inadequate steps are taken to deal with ambiguity. This next case study brings together many aspects of change and will serve as the raw material for the final part of this chapter which deals with change management. The example, in Figure 24.3, considers a school's plan to introduce classroom monitoring of instructors.

For some time the head of the school had been considering introducing some form of instructor monitoring. Student failure rates in some subjects were high and, having been newly appointed, the head was of the opinion that classroom methods were in need of updating. Furthermore, some airline representatives and a few graduating students had made adverse comments about instructors. A discussion paper was produced by an outside consultant which outlined the implications of instructor monitoring in terms of what could be measured and what the school could do with the output. It was stressed that the instructors needed to be made aware of the purpose of the scheme and what the outcomes would be in terms of updating classroom activity. It was also stressed that suitable measurement instruments would need to be tested before the system could be made to work. Without any real discussion of any of the issues, it was decided to trial a simple post-lesson questionnaire with a newly-arrived class. The students were given the form and told that it was a trial document. They were asked to identify a specific lesson for which they would all complete the form. They were told that the purpose of the trial was to comment on the suitability of the questionnaire. Their experiences would then be used to devise the final format which would be used at some yet-to-be-decided time in the future. Before the nominated lesson arrived, the project was scrapped. The instructors did not believe that students were in a position to comment on instructional standards. The students were uncertain about participating in an activity which could jeopardise their relationship with instructors who were in a position to influence their futures. No further attempts at instructor monitoring were attempted.

Figure 24.3   Monitoring of instructors

Change management

We have seen that change can be a messy business. To some degree it can be anticipated and planned for. It is also a creeping disease which only becomes apparent when an event shows up the gap between what you think you are doing and what you should be doing. Change cannot be considered as a rational move towards a clear goal; we all see things in a different light. However, there is still a need to exercise control. Insidious change should be covered by normal management techniques. The enthusiastic adoption of Total Quality Management (TQM) by industry probably says more about the failure of management to keep track of the fundamentals than it does about the merits of the approach. Planned change needs additional effort. It could be argued that change management is a sub-set of project management. In reality, though, the impact of change usually affects more of the organization than the specific project being managed.

There are six aspects of change management which we need to consider; clearing the way, breaking down barriers, keeping control, taking decisions, implementing change and planning for the future. Specific actions are detailed in the Change Management Checklist at the end of the chapter. It would be worth applying the checklist to the instructor monitoring exercise at this point to see how things could have been handled differently.

Conclusion - Future change

We have seen that change management involves keeping track of evolutionary developments as well as controlling planned alterations to working practice. It is a political event and rarely do all interested parties - stakeholders - share the same view about the relative merits of the planned change. But we cannot avoid change and it therefore it is to everyones' advantage if it can be managed effectively. Change management requires a negotiated progress towards a goal. It requires a broader vision of the organization and its activities than is probably held on a day-to-day basis by team members - whatever their management grade. It also requires change initiators to recognise that their planned solution might not be the best.

But what about the future? What can we start planning for now? Without a doubt we are going to see greater use of PC-based technology to provide simulation capabilities. The ability to develop aircraft-related skills whilst studying theory in a classroom will have an impact both on the organization of ground instruction and on the conduct of flight training. Environmental pressures might force training out of aircraft and into ground-based devices and the concept of a zero flight-time, ab-initio student arriving on the line is not that far-fetched. Changes in our understanding of the nature of learning may influence the design of instruction. Current procedural approaches to teaching flight deck automation seem to be flawed, partly because we have an incomplete knowledge of the way conceptual modelling of the inter-relationships between systems is developed. Perhaps we need a new approach which capitalises on computer graphics and virtual reality techniques to visualise data.

Changes in employment patterns may affect the way pilots are recruited to the industry and the time they remain within it. In Europe, barriers to free movement of labour are being broken down and the harmonised flight crew licensing proposals reflect that trend. But in addition to moving to find work, we are increasingly led to believe that the "careers" and a "job for life" are things of the past. If we imagine aviation as a job which someone does when they are young, and just for a couple of years, then there will be a greater need for training to maintain the workforce. However, this training bill may need to be offset by shorter, cheaper courses. And if you accept that CRM may be a response to yesterday's social problem, then what are we doing today which will put the next generation of pilots, and their aircraft, at risk?

Clearing The Way

- Do you have a clear idea of what you are trying to do?
- WHO will be doing WHAT differently?
- How will things look different?
- How will you tell if the change has been successful?
- Have you worked out what needs to be done and how are you telling people?
- Are all the issues involved clear?

Breaking Down Barriers

- Who feels uncomfortable with the change and what is their objection?
- What might these objections tell us about our plan?
- Is management enthusiastic about change and how do they show it?
- Who is involved in planning the change?
- Why are these people involved and no-one else?
- What rewards are there for being involved?
- Are you listening to the rumours and what are they saying about the change?
- Do you express support for decisions made which do not match your plan?

Keeping Control

- Is it clear who is in control?
- Do you carry out face-to-face checks with individuals?
- Do you have necessary facts and figures to hand?
- Do you set targets after consultation?
- Have you clarified the end product so that everyone is working to the same plan?
- Have you delegated major areas of work?
- Do you walk the floor and gather views of stakeholders?
- Do you say how often you will visit or consult?

Taking Decisions

- Are you taking decisions by consensus?
- Do you identify time-scales and gather information?
- Do you consult with those affected?
- After deciding, do you inform EVERYBODY?
- Do you check that decisions are carried out?

Implementing Change

- Are you field-testing on a small scale?

- Are you field-testing with a unit supportive of change?
- Are the objectives clear to the pilot group?
- Do you have a clear picture of the results desired?
- Does the pilot group know that it is acceptable to make mistakes?
- Is the time right for change?
- Do you know how the change will impact on other parts of the organization?
- Do you have supporters in the organization with the clout to keep the change on track?
- Is the change manager and the project manager the same person? If it is then WHY?

Learning for the Future

- Do you review, at regular intervals, the lessons from implementation?
- Do you seek negative as well as positive feedback?
- How do you gather information about the change?
- What is the information telling you?
- Are you prepared to alter plans?
- Do you explain why plans are changing?
- Do you write down good practice?

Figure 24.4 Change management checklist

25 Cultural and organizational challenges for human factors training

Anne Marit Lie

Why culture?

Why connect culture and human factors training? Are there any practical lessons to be learnt and taken into consideration through "measuring the temperature" of the organization before "treating" its pilots? What do actually we mean by culture? Culture has a kind of "taken for granted" existence, you may not notice it until you are faced with a world outside of you usual cultural environment. It is a social construction, created and maintained by a group of human beings, emotionally charged and visible through attitudes and behavior. "The way things are done" and the "rights and wrongs" are compellingly obvious within the culture.

Human Factors training touches these social constructions or cultural frameworks as it, to a large extent, deals with interpersonal relationship between crew members. We used to presume that all human factors issues were valid everywhere, that, for example, teaching all co-pilots assertiveness would cure most communication problems between them and the captain. We have now reached a training philosophy where there is agreement on common human factors problems, but we have moved away from the standpoint of there being only one way of solving these problems; the methods of solving cooperation problems in Japan is likely to differ from the solution employed in USA. For training to reach its audience or participants, it is important that the training values and methods nest within the culture maintained by the group.

These cultural reflections inspired an in-house study of an Italian airline (Lie, 1994). The study was going to serve as a guide to the development of a Crew Resource Management course for this airline company. Interviews and questionnaire data were evaluated to establish particular issues to be handled during the training course. Let us have a look at the theory on which we based our study, and the cultural facets that challenged us during the training development.

311

**It is important that the training values and methods
nest within the culture**

Vérité en-deçà des Pyrénées, erreur au-delà
(There are truths on this side of the Pyrenees which are falsehoods on the other
[Pascal])

Our basic understanding of what appears right and wrong, and the education
which makes our own social rules and regulation appears reasonable, are first
absorbed through our family, and later friends and teachers. We learn to accept
our society's or culture's codes and disciplines as legitimate. Hofstede (1984)
made a study of work-goal and attitudes in an international corporation, and
through his analysis he managed to pinpoint several cultural dimensions. To be
able to focus our study of the Italian airline better, we concentrated our research
on the effect of two of these cultural dimensions, Power Distance and
Masculinity, both of which had been claimed to have a distinct effect on Latin
culture.

All animals are equal, but some are more equal than others
(Orwell, G, "Animal Farm")

The power distance dimension considers the habitual exercise of power within a culture. It refers to the extent to which superiors and subordinates accept, and expect, the unequal distribution and exercise of power, and to the level at which social inequality is accepted as proper and legitimate. Inequality exists within any culture, but the degree to which it is tolerated varies between one culture and another. In a high power distance culture, social inequality is readily accepted and leaders are expected to be autonomous and decisive, while their subordinates are expected to know their place and implement their leader's directives. In a low power distance culture, superiors and subordinates view and treat each other as colleagues; here information tends to be much more freely offered by subordinates who are, in any case, more likely to be consulted spontaneously by their managers. It should be mentioned that in a low power environment, the problem of unresponsiveness to legitimate authority could arise.

High power distance seems likely to provide a potent source of CRM problems, since it is closely associated with social stratification and perceptions of social status. In high power distance countries, junior crew members are more likely to fear the consequences of disagreeing with leaders, possibly with good reason (Johnston, 1993). Leaders are themselves likely to feel comfortable with paternalistic behaviour, and leaders, rather than followers, tend to initiate communication. It is important to remember that leadership does not exist in a social vacuum - it is directly related to the social perception and acceptance of "followership" or "subordinateship".

The in-house study, sited within a country strongly influenced by high power distance, consequently influencing the cockpit atmosphere, revealed potential danger areas. More than half of the co-pilots stated that the captain sometimes ignored their suggestions. During interviews one of the co-pilots expressed "The old captains... they think they are God" a feeling which was echoes by many other co-pilots. The co-pilots at times also felt being treated "like dogs". It captures a potentially dangerous effect high power distance can cause in the cockpit; the captain may adhere so strongly to his self-perceived status, that his autocracy overrules the assistance of the co-pilot. The co-pilot reinforces the effect by feeling discouraged or by not finding it his right to express his opinion. The results showed that more than half of the first officers agreed or partly agreed to a question stating that their duty was to fulfil the order of the captain in all situations. It supports the theory that high power distance is sustained by the way subordinates perceive their duties. The hazardous aspect is: submissiveness at the expense of constructive criticism and corrections related to safety.

The established atmosphere of communication in the cockpit is important. An Italian first officer put it like this during an interview: "The problem if you talk too much in the cockpit is that the other think you are not reliable or trustworthy.

At the same time you should speak up if something is wrong; it is like walking on a thin line."

The reply on one questionnaire statement from the study (Figure 25.1), indicates a difficulty in communicating with seniors, putting the exchange of information at risk:

I find it hard to communicate with superiors

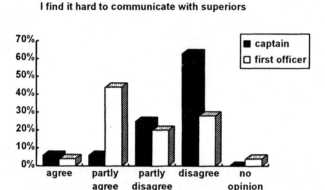

Figure 25.1 Responses on questionnaire displaying differences in attitudes towards communication with superiors

Considering the cultural restrictions, one might understand that revealing upsetting or correcting information in the cockpit is not as easy as it is important.

The fact that the airline company was small and translucent, that is, relationships between employees were obvious, magnified the communication problems. More than a third of the co-pilots stated that they would hesitate to criticise the captain as they would have to fly with him later.

In a routine situation the effect of restricted communication is only irritation or uneasiness, but the effect in an emergency situation may be more salient, and put a strain on the information exchange and co-operation necessary to solve the dilemma, the consequences being disastrous and putting people's lives in danger.

And the Lord God said, It is not good that the man should be alone: I will make him a help meet for him. (*Genesis*. 2:18)

The dimension of masculinity considers the extent to which a culture uses the biological existence of two genders to define very different social roles for men and women. More masculine cultures (e. g., Japan, Austria, Venezuela, Italy) expect men to be socially dominant, assertive, ambitious and competitive, and to strive for money and material success. They expect women to serve and to care for the non material quality of life, for children and for the weak. In more feminine cultures (e.g., Sweden, Norway, Netherlands, Denmark), where the social roles of the sexes are relatively overlapping, neither men nor women need to be ambitious nor competitive (Hofstede, 1991). Both sexes may go for a different quality of life than material successes.

Masculine societies tend to have a belief in the "independent decision-maker," and leaders value their decision-making autonomy. Decisiveness, interpersonal directness, and machismo are common in masculine cultures. Typical masculine traits are competitiveness and the race for materialistic and monetary values with the effect that young men are expected to make a career; those who do not see themselves as failures (Hofstede, 1984). One can imagine the consequence of masculinity in the milieu of pilots, where high and impeccable performance is constantly asked and sought for. Admitting mistakes and accepting correction with an open mind is difficult enough in everyday life; in an environment where a little mistake may have big consequences, where professionality is alpha and omega and where competition to be promoted is high, it is hard treating correction and criticism as valuable information. Masculinity in the light of pride may rise as a wall between the pilots shutting out critical (in both senses of the word) communication. High power distance have the potential to amplify the consequence of 'macho' captains not acknowledging corrections: "Sometimes the F/O waits and lets the captain go through with the mistake without telling him. This is extremely stupid, but when you have this kind of relationship with these people, if they do something wrong we let them do it, as long as they are not cracking the plane."

The competitiveness and the difficulty with which a person accepts his own weaknesses and faults are not difficult to picture having a serious impact on cockpit co-operation. The feminine cultures might have an advantage in that imperfectness is more readily accepted. It was discovered, that being a female researcher in a masculine environment had positive consequences. In front of the 'weak' gender it was no longer necessary for the male pilot to keep up the competitive guard and it paved the road to an understanding of the consequences of masculinity in the pilot milieu.

How to make sense of how people in organizations that do not make sense try to make sense of what they do.
(Czarniawska-Joerges, 1992)

The sense-making mechanism, the organizational culture, is like a galaxy within a cultural universe. It is vast but has comprehensible boundaries. It has a gravity force keeping the organization together, and it reduces confusion, insecurities and fears which are existent within the company.

This culture is not unilateral in the sense that everybody shares the same values, attitudes and basic assumptions. Personal characteristics, shared experience, and differential interaction lead different sets of people to developing different understandings of their worlds. These subgroups or subcultures of the organization can be constituted by different professions, departments, age groups, genders, etc. Social cohesion reinforces cognitive and emotional bonds between subgroup members and tends to raise barriers between them and others, who are seen as outsiders or different (Trice & Beyer, 1993).

Applying the consequences of subcultures to aviation, it can be argued that different goals and priorities may evolve in flight and ground operations departments, promoting different degrees of focus on safety issues amongst flight and ground personnel. A comment taken from the in-house requirement study revealed these two typical subgroups: "There are two big parts in the company; the operational and 'the others'. The operational people, the ones who 'live' near the aircraft, pilots, C/A, technicians, operating room, and then you have the ground personnel. The relationship is not very good..."

For companies operating long-haul flights the problem is exacerbated, as the working life and priorities of the pilots compared to the ground staff is widely different. The pilots spend a minimum of time at home base doing a job that is a far cry from a regular nine-to-five job. In the eyes of the ground personnel the aviators spend most of their time "on vacation"; collecting a huge salary for it. The opinion of the pilots is quite contrary. They view their responsibilities as far more important than "an office job anyone can fulfil".

Professional sub-cultures, such as pilot and cabin attendant cultures, are often existent within airline companies. They stay within the boundaries of the same aircraft, but may have different values and priorities and often lack an understanding of each other's tasks and goals. We only considered the pilots in our study as they were our target group for the training. Our basis of evaluating the presence and relation between these professional subcultures in the company is therefore weak.

The study identified diverse subcultures in the company. It contains a challenge for training, to bring people from different sub-cultures together during training in order to enhance safety through mutual understanding of each others goals and priorities. Another great challenge seems to be to persuade the management of the importance of such integrated training.

Management philosophy - pathogens in the hierarchy

During the period of performing interviews and analysing questionnaire data, several organizational problems became apparent that a human factors course would not solve. The study touched on issues or failures that cannot be "treated" simply by giving a human factors training course to the pilots. It revealed that the training may cure the symptoms of an "illness", but probably not the "illness" itself.

Reason (1990) has indicated that the higher an individual's position within an organization, the greater is his or her opportunity for generating so-called pathogens or latent failures: the result of a decision or an action made well before an accident. These failures usually originate at the level of the decision-maker, regulator or line-management, that is, with people far removed in time and space from the event. The consequences of these failures may lie dormant for a long time.

Information flow

One possible pathogen related to management priorities is related to information flow. Information flow and feedback have through several studies been benchmarked as important in the development and maintenance of a healthy safety culture. Continuous information flow and quick feedback are established as indicators of companies with low accident rates (Cohen, 1977, Flight Safety Foundation, 1990, Turner et al., 1989).

Companies within a high power distance culture may have a drawback as managers may have a different view on the benefit of information flow and feedback in general. Communication is generated at the top and is passed down as far as superiors find it necessary. Feedback is not regarded as significantly important, as opinions from subordinates do not have a high value. The study revealed a clear difference in opinion between first officers and captains regarding communication flow (Figure 25.2) which can possibly be traced to the consequences of information flow in a high power distance society. Information reaches the co-pilot with difficulty possibly because management does not find it a priority to inform the people at the bottom of the ladder.

Power distance is likely to influence the information flow and communication pattern outside the boundaries of the cockpit, particularly where there is a lack of formal information channels. The status gap caused by high power distance leads the first officers to be reluctant at an informal pursuit of information, as it means the action of asking a superior. The difficulty in communicating with superiors indicated in Figure 25.1, enlarges the obstacle for co-pilots to keep updated on reliable information. One pilot expressed: "A step in the right direction could be that top management realise how important it is that the information flow exists."

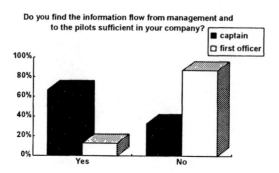

Figure 25.2   Pilot evaluation of the information flow between management and pilots

Motivation and care

Another pathogen may be an identified lack of care and concerns from the management. In the small Italian airline, embedded in masculine and competitive surroundings, we found eager pilots doing more than their required duty. The management had drained a lot of energy from their young and ambitious pilots, but was failing to motivate them and showing them appreciation. One pilot put it this way: "In the beginning pilots were asked a lot, much more than they were supposed to do just to keep the company going. The response has always been positive, because motivated people were employed. What is happening now is that this positive attitude has been taken for granted by the management. They expect people to always be like this, but we are starting to see another attitude, because if you do not gratify people, they do some extra once, twice maybe three times and then they think, well, why should I do it, I never even get a thank you for it. I can see now that people are becoming less positive". The lack of care and concern from the top was exhausting the previous enthusiasm and dedication.

The learning experience of a near miss, and the positive effect of the transfer of experience are known and acknowledged facts; hence to solve the problem of publicly admitting mistakes, anonymous reporting has been applied. Professional errors are hard to admit in a masculine society, where competitiveness is a strong trait. The questionnaire exposed a factor that does not promote admitting mistakes (Figure 25.3):

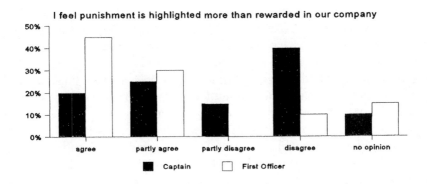

Figure 25.3 Pilot responses in respect to how they feel management evaluates rewards contra punishment

How would anonymous reporting work in a small airline where everybody knows everybody, and how easy is it to criticise people you encounter regularly on a professional basis? An excerpt from a safety manager interview in the airline explained: "No, we don't receive many anonymous reports, because the F/Os are afraid that, since we're a small company, the captain will find out. He then thinks, well I'm flying with this guy again, and I do not want trouble." In a small and translucent company, bringing a pilot's mistake into light, and at the same time cover their identity, is not easily done, even though it serves all pilots and has the potential to improve flight safety.

The process is as important as the goal

We first believed that our main product was a tailor-made human factors training course for a high power distance and masculine culture. We focused our human factors course around limits and possibilities of the human, disussing effects of masculine attitudes and high power distance in the cockpit environment. Through case studies we invited elaboration of the meaning of teamwork and leadership, and how communication can be influenced by cultural factors. In the course-surroundings everybody was equal, the facilitators were both captains and first officers, and problems associated with the relationship between captain and first officer were discussed freely. Realizing relationship problems may be the problems half solved.

During the study-process of the in-house requirements, we discovered possible organizational barriers to the effect of the training, worrying a bit whether the course was going to be apprehended as "yet another management ploy". We also started asking ourselves about the comparative value of the study-process, was it equally valid to the human factors training itself? The regular encounters between the pilots and the members of the development team resulted in discussions and reflections around the issue and purpose of human factors, before the course was developed. Even though the course was setting a scene for discussing interpersonal-related issues, the initiated debates and the awareness phase caused by the pre-study seemed equally important.

It is therefore recommended, and this is particularly feasible in small airlines, that an in-house study is done before developing and implementing a Human Factors training course. It is one way of addressing the issue of Human Factors at an early stage (it may not be that apparent to all pilots what it entails), and for the airline to get an impression of the pilot attitudes. It may be helpful to involve an external person, to have someone, who may see the airline with different eyes, to bounce ideas and findings back and forth with. We carried out the in-house study using a student which kept the costs low.

What are our most important and valuable experiences? We used the knowledge and opinions of the pilots to highlight problem issues, and we feel we have succeeded using the study in practice. One may say we invented a treatment to cure failure symptoms, but we are concerned that some of the causal factors are still lying dormant. We never questioned the positive effect of Human Factors training, but it became clear to us that it isn't enough to improve the Human Factors related skills and abilities of the pilot if the status quo of the organization remains. If an airline company truly wants to reduce the probability of accidents, then management must also look at its policies and "the way things are done" to make sure it supports a firm base for a healthy and safety-building culture.

We discovered that the process appears to be as important as the goal. In the not too distant future, when Human Factors training, it is hoped, will include the whole corporation, accomplishments will issue from the process. The aim will be not so much to arrive, as to travel productively.

Acknowledgements

I would like to thank Johan Kjær-Hansen for his constant motivation and belief in my work, and Monica Bacchi for her support and analytic insight which has always impressed me. Simon Grant gave me through his proof reading an invaluable possibility to clarify my thoughts, and last but not least I am grateful to the Socio-Technical Systems Safety Sector at the Joint Research Centre in Ispra, Italy, for giving me the possibility to collect the experiences which laid the basis for this chapter.

References

Cohen, A. (1977). Factors in successful occupational safety programs. *Journal of Safety Research.* 9(4), pp. 168-178.

Czarniawska-Joerges, B. (1992). *Exploring Complex Organizations.* USA: Sage.

Flight Safety Foundation, (FSF), (1990). *Lessons Learned from Safety Audits.* Flight Safety Digest. August.

Hofstede, G. (1984). *Culture's consequences: international differences in work-related values.* Newbury Park, CA: Sage.

Hofstede, G. (1991). *Cultures and organizations: software of the mind.* London: McGraw-Hill.

Johnston, A. N. (1993). CRM: Crosscultural perspectives, in E. Wiener, B. Kanki and R. Helmreich (eds), *Cockpit Resource Management.* San Diego: Academic Press.

Lie, Anne Marit (1994), *Safety Culture in an Airline Company; and its impact on Crew Resource Management*, Diploma Thesis at the Norwegian Institute of Technology, Trondheim.

Reason, J. (1990). The contribution of latent human failures to the breakdown of complex systems. In D.E. Broadbent, D.E. Baddeley, and J.T. Reason (Eds.). *Human factors in hazardous situations.* Oxford: Clarendon Press.

Trice, H. M. & Beyer, J. M. (1993). *The cultures of work organizations.*

Englewood Cliffs, N. J.: Prentice Hall.

Turner, B.A., Pidgeon, N., Blockley, D., & Toft, B. (1989). Safety culture: Its importance in future risk management. Paper presented at the Second world Bank Workshop on Safety Control and Risk Management. Karlstrad, Sweden, November.

26 Expanding teamwork beyond the cockpit door:

An Integrative Program ("OASIS") for Pilots, Cabin Crew, Station Managers/Traffic and Ground Engineers

Marvin Karlins, Freddie Koh, Len McCully and C T Chan

Although the format and content of various Cockpit Resource Management programs may vary from airline to airline, most emphasize and encourage *teamwork* as "the way to fly" when it comes to optimizing safe and efficient performance in the cockpit. Such a focus is both appropriate and worthwhile, as the dramatic experiments of Ruffell Smith and other aviation-science pioneers have clearly demonstrated. It is through teamwork that the individual skills, experiences and perspectives of each crew member are "drawn out" and utilized in maximizing flight deck performance.

But what about teamwork *beyond* the cockpit door? In the early 1980s, developers of the Singapore Airlines CRM program began to suspect that the teamwork concept could and should be expanded to encompass not only technical crew but cabin crew as well. This suspicion was fueled by the very positive outcomes observed when a small number of cabin crew supervisors were invited to attend the CRM program. It became readily apparent that this opportunity for tech crew-cabin crew interaction provided the impetus for discovering, discussing and defusing some of the cockpit-cabin problems that, left untreated, could compromise the overall effectiveness of aircrew performance during flight.

The result? By 1985 it appeared both reasonable and practical to expand the concept of CRM teamwork to include not only the interaction between pilots, but also the interaction between pilots and cabin crew: an approach that recognized the need to strive for a *total aircraft team effort* where cabin crew and tech crew worked together in the pursuit of better performance and personal satisfaction on the job.

And why stop there? Having discovered merit in stretching the boundaries of teamwork to encompass both cockpit and cabin crew, it seemed appropriate to extend the frontiers of territorial teamwork further still to include other personnel impacting directly on flight operations. Such a step was taken in 1988 when Singapore Airlines developed the OASIS (Operational Areas Seminar In

Synergy) program. This program, first introduced in 1989, brings pilots, cabin crew supervisors, ground engineers and station managers/traffic personnel together for a three-day residential seminar devoted to the enhancement of intergroup effectiveness through the spirit and practice of teamwork.

The OASIS Program

Even though it "makes sense" for different groups in an organization to work together as a team...it is not always easy to do so. Why should this be so? An insightful answer is provided by Neuhauser in her book *Tribal Warfare in Organizations* "Any organization with specialized functions and departments is made up of groups--which I call 'tribes'--that look at their work and at the organization in very different ways. Anthropologically, these groups in organizations are very much like 'real' tribes; they have their own dialects, values, histories, ways of thinking, and rules for appropriate behavior. What if we took some Apaches, Cherokees, and Pygmies, added a few Japanese and Germans--plus a Texan or two--and then said to this group, 'Now go work together and get the job done!' No one would be surprised if tribal warfare broke out in this group. And yet in many ways, this is exactly what happens in most organizations today."

Placed in an airline context, pilots, cabin crew supervisors, ground engineers and station managers/traffic personnel can be seen as four different "tribes"...each group having its own rules of conduct, values, ways of thinking and beliefs concerning what is important in their jobs. When the beliefs or behaviors of one group are not congruent with the thoughts or actions of a different group...intergroup hostility, rather than teamwork, is usually the outcome.

The OASIS program was designed to reduce intergroup conflict and enhance intergroup cooperation and effectiveness--*teamwork*--between the airline's four operational areas. In attempting to achieve this objective, the program's participants were encouraged to accept two recommendations in their own worklife:

(1) Even though the four operational groups might vary in some of their beliefs and needs, it should never be forgotten that these differences pale in comparison to the similarity that comes with sharing the same superordinate goal: the safe and efficient operation of the aircraft at all times. When pilots, cabin crew, ground engineers and station managers/traffic personnel work together as a team, they will be better able to achieve their common goal while enhancing individual and interpersonal job satisfaction at the same time.

324

(2)   To reach the highest levels of intergroup teamwork, each operational group member (pilot, cabin crew supervisor, ground engineer and station manager) needs to: (a) *understand* that each workgroup has, in fact, its own set of problems and hassles to contend with; (b) *learn* what these problems/hassles are and (c) *use* this information to avoid doing those things that increase these problems and hassles for your colleagues and, on a more positive note, undertake those behaviors which can facilitate a co-workers performance and job satisfaction.

There is a major problem encountered, of course, when one attempts to follow the two recommendations: namely, *knowing* what the problems and hassles are for members of the various operational workgroups. This was clearly demonstrated by OASIS seminar participants when they were asked--during the initial portion of the seminar--to make lists of the various workplace problems they faced. Although most participants were fully aware of problems occurring *inside* their various operational areas (e.g., a cabin crew supervisor might speak of dealing with difficult passengers; a ground engineer might be concerned with finding the right part for rectifying a defect; a pilot might mention difficulties with ATC and a station manager might be uneasy about an on-time departure); very few participants listed problems or hassles occurring *outside* their own operational areas. Also noticeably absent from the list were problems occurring

Teamwork needs to go beyond the cockpit door

between groups in the operational areas.

One of the major objectives of the OASIS program was to remedy this knowledge gap by providing participants with the information they needed to: (a) be more aware of the unique challenges faced by members of the other operational workgroups (not just their own); (b) discover what they did that helped and/or hindered the performance of their colleagues in the other operational groups and (c) how to use this new-found information to work more effectively as a team.

Providing seminar participants with an *awareness* of how they could help their colleagues from the various operational areas was accomplished in three ways: (a) The OASIS questionnaire ("survey results") exercise; (b) an integrative case study; (c) a video re-creation of an airline tragedy.

The OASIS questionnaire

One of the best ways to learn how to work more effectively across and between operational groups is by going directly to the source and asking the various operational group members what they think should be done to enhance intergroup teamwork. In 1988, a year before the first OASIS seminars were conducted, a questionnaire was developed. These questionnaires were then mailed to a random sample of employees in all four operational areas, soliciting their anonymous responses to a set of inquiries designed to identify those behaviors undertaken by members of the various operational groups which helped and/or hindered them in their performance of their duties. Members of each operational work group answered survey questions about members of the other three work groups to which they did not belong. Thus, for example, ground engineers were asked to assess their interactions with pilots, cabin crew supervisors and station managers based on three questions:

(1) Consider all the work encounters (experiences) you have had with pilots. Also, think about what your colleagues have had to say about *their* interactions with pilots. Based on what you've experienced and what you've heard, *make a list of some things pilots do that make your job more **difficult** (reduce productivity and/or job satisfaction).*

(2) Based on what you've experienced and what you've heard *make a list of some things pilots do--or could do--to help you perform your job more **effectively.***

(3) To help pilots and my group work most effectively together, I would make the following recommendations:

The answers of these staff (which generated 100+ pages of single-spaced typewritten material) were recorded, arranged into categories based on content and frequency of response, and presented in summary form to all seminar participants as part of "The Survey Results Exercise."

The Survey Results Exercise

The Survey Results Exercise was divided into an individual and group phase. During the individual phase seminar participants were given time (45 minutes) to read through and consider the 24 pages of summarized survey results on their own. During the group phase seminar participants had the opportunity to discuss the survey results in small groups, each group containing at least one representative from each of the four operational areas (thus, there was at least one pilot, one cabin crew supervisor, one ground engineer and one station manager/traffic person in each of the five person groups). The importance of the Survey Results Exercise was emphasized by the seminar presenter who said: "I believe this Exercise is the single most important activity in your OASIS seminar. It is your best chance to gain an understanding of what you and your colleagues can do to help (or conversely, not hinder) each other in the performance of your duties." Instructions for the two parts of the Exercise were as follows:

Individual phase of the Survey Results Exercise "This designated period of time will allow each of you sufficient time to read through the summary of the questionnaire responses. Of special interest, of course, will be the comments of the other three operational areas towards your operational group (e.g., station managers/traffic personnel will want to see what pilots, cabin crew supervisors and ground engineers have to say about them). However, there should be adequate time to allow you to read through the comments made about all groups. During this phase of the Exercise you might want to make some notes concerning what you have read...to be used during your group discussion later on. If so, feel free to make use of the paper we have given you for that purpose."

Group phase of the Survey Results Exercise "This designated period of time will give representatives of the various groups the opportunity to question, challenge, answer, elaborate upon and generally discuss the various points brought up in the Surveys. Some groups choose to go item by item through the listed comments...others use the comments as a kind of 'starting point' for discussions. Whichever way your group decides to use the comments is fine with your presenter. Here is the important thing to keep in mind: *this might be the only chance you ever get to have a discussion with members of **all four** operational groups together in one place in an off-line, relaxed atmosphere. Take advantage of this unique opportunity to better understand what the*

327

various intergroup problems are...and what can be done to reduce or overcome them."

Once the individual and group phase of the Survey Results Exercise was completed, the seminar presenter led a general discussion of the activity and highlighted some findings for participants to consider.

Impact of the Survey Results Exercise:

The Survey Results Exercise allowed Singapore Airlines personnel from the four operational areas the opportunity to identify, confront and attempt to solve those problems they had personally specified as impediments to effective teamwork in the workplace. As such, the Exercise was not a "canned" activity for use with any airline but, rather, meaningful and relevant to the specific audience for which it was intended. Although many of the problems mentioned were, in fact, generic to many (if not all) airlines; nevertheless, it is the authors' belief that the effectiveness of the Exercise was enhanced because seminar participants were aware that the comments they were reading came from their own colleagues rather than some "aviation consultant" with a "dog and pony" list. *For that reason, the authors recommend that any airline wishing to run an OASIS-type seminar poll their own employees in compiling a relevant list of problems for individual and group consideration.*

Based on the feedback from OASIS participants (supplied when they filled out a seminar evaluation form at the end of the program) the Exercise achieved its objectives. Some excerpts:

This exercise made me aware of what I could do to help others from different operational areas work more effectively. Now that I have this information I can be a better colleague.

Gave me new insights on how to work better with others.

Expanded my horizons when it came to including others in a teamwork effort.

This activity made me realize I was doing things to cause problems for other staff I wasn't even aware of. Now that I know what these things are I can avoid doing them in the future.

This seminar, particularly the Survey Exercise, helps us learn what we can do to make worklife better for everyone. Talking with members of the other workgroups about the survey results really helped me appreciate their point of view and why they act the way they do.

This exercise made me aware of a lot of things I never realized before...what I did that hassled others; and what I can do to make things better all around.

Taught me the need for communication and cooperation between flight ops, cabin crew and ground staff.

Underscored the importance of treating others with tact and professionalism if you want things accomplished right.

Helped me see the bigger picture. We're all in this together and need to work as a team.

The integrative case study

The OASIS questionnaire was one approach used by the authors to make seminar participants more aware of what they could do to enhance teamwork among and between aviators, cabin crew and ground staff. The second approach involved use of a case study, *"The Zurich Incident"*, which was created specifically to highlight some common problems that can arise between operational groups during line operations. It was the task of the participants, working in groups, to identify what those problems were and what they could do to help their colleagues within and between operational areas solve the problems most effectively. In tackling the task assignment, seminar participants came to understand the importance of *teamwork* in getting their jobs done safely and efficiently while enhancing interpersonal relationships and job satisfaction at the same time.

Why use a case study to emphasize a teamwork approach to problem-solving?

The case study approach, used so successfully at leading universities and business seminars has several advantages: (1) It adds a sense of "realism" to the topic under discussion (2) it involves "active learning" on the part of seminar participants--an approach which enhances participant motivation to both learn and put that learning into practice. (3) Working together in a group context can often lead to useful insights that would be impossible to achieve by an individual working alone. (4) Because all four operational areas were represented in each case study group, so were their unique perspectives and viewpoints. This gave participants the opportunity to see things "from the other person's point of view" while learning to work together as a team in developing effective problem solving strategies.

Case study instructions

Seminar participants were given the following instructions before undertaking their assignment:

*This case study is divided into two parts. In **Part One**, the Individual Phase, you will be given ten minutes, working alone, to read through the Case and give it some initial thought. In **Part Two,** the Group Phase, you will join your team in its assigned breakout room. Your team will then have one hour, working together, to discuss and arrive at a consensus answer to the two questions below. Please select a member of your team to report out your findings at a later session. This individual will have up **to eight minutes** to present your teams' answers to all seminar participants.*

Here, then, are the two questions for your consideration:

Question #1: *Based on your reading of the case, what were the constraints on: (a) the ground engineer; (b) station manager; (c) in-flight supervisor; (d) captain.*

Question #2: *Based on your reading of the case, how could each party have done better? (a) the ground engineer; (b) the station manager; (c) the inflight supervisor; (d) the captain.*

"The Zurich Incident" Case Study:

Prologue

The inbound flight was late. It had been scheduled to come in at 1235 and depart at 1345 hours. It is now 1330 and the aircraft has just landed. The flight has already been rescheduled to depart at 1430 hours.

It is snowing heavily and this has been one of the worst winters in European history. Ground Engineer has made arrangements for de-icing the aircraft.

The flight is 3/4 full and several of the nearby airports are already closed by weather. This has increased the congestion at your station.

******

-60 from revised STD
Aircraft arrived at gate.
Transit passengers kept on board.
Station manager is advising passengers of the delay at check-in. IFS (inflight supervisor) and crew at gate.
Captain at flight dispatch.
Ground engineer doing his walk around check.

-55 from revised STD
Captain arrives at aircraft.
IFS and Crew do handover and normal checks.

-50 from revised STD
Captain informs the Engineer de-icing is required and begins Cockpit checks.
Engineer says de-icing is arranged.
Cabin crew starts pre-flight duties.

IFS requests passengers to remain seated over the PA. Station manager in the process of finalizing flight closure. IFS requests Ground engineer to repair unserviceable toilet flush motor. He was told at the last station that it would be fixed in Zurich. Zurich Ground engineer said he did not have time to do it.

-35 from revised STD
Station manager requests clearance from IFS to board passengers. IFS denies clearance.

-30 from revised STD
Station manager commences boarding in accordance with established schedule for boarding. IFS is visibly annoyed as cleaners are just leaving the aircraft.

-10 from revised STD
Catering completed. Cabin crew discovers that they are short of 10 economy class meals.
IFS informs Station manager.

-7 from revised STD
Captain reminds first officer of his 5 minutes before start up call to ATC to ensure slot time is not lost.

-5 from revised STD
F/O makes call to ATC and receives clearance. SM informs IFS that meals

cannot be catered.

IFS agrees to take aircraft in spite of the shortage.

SM asks for headcount as it appears that there is a passenger who has not boarded.

SM advised total on board should be 327 but stub count was only 326.

-02 from revised STD

Captain calls IFS and asks why aircraft doors still not closed. IFS informs him of the situation. Captain asks why he was not told about this earlier.

Captain calls ATC to inform them that the flight will be delayed by 15 min.

-01 from revised STD

Captain informed by ATC that the next slot available will be in 50 mins time.

Captain informs GE that second de-icing is required.

+1 from revised STD

IFS reports headcount of 327. SM requests second count.

+3 from revised STD

GE informs Captain that de-icing will only be available at +35 and completion is expected at +45. GE warns Captain that he cannot get another de-icing slot.

Captain announces 50 mins delay over PA. Reason given is ATC slot time.

+5 from revised STD

IFS insists on uplift of missing meals as flight now delayed for more than 30 mins.

SM says additional uplift might not arrive in time but he will try. IFS looks for GE to fix toilet flush motor. GE not around.

+8 from revised STD

Second headcount by cabin crew confirmed 327 on board. At the same time, ground staff confirmed boarding stub count in order. (Lost stub found.)

+12 from revised STD

IFS reports to Captain all doors closed. Captain tells IFS off about how badly co-ordinated the whole transit had been.

+30 from revised STD

Engineer tells Captain that de-icing equipment is expected at any time but has not arrived yet.

+35 from revised STD

De-icing truck arrives.

GE tells Captain that de-icing completion time is expected to be +50 to +55.

End of case

Presenter debriefing after group interaction and seminar presentations:

After listening to the group presentations, the seminar leader made some specific observations relating to what was said by each group. Then he made some general comments that were repeated throughout all the seminars. These included: (a) the importance of seeing things from the other person's perspective or point of view; (b) the value of using information gained from other members of the operational team; (c) the value of teamwork in getting the job done more productively and with greater personal satisfaction and (d) the need to practice the "3-C's" in line operations: Communication, Coordination and Collegiality. Finally, the presenter answered any questions posed by seminar participants.

Video presentation: "The Dryden Accident"

In the 1995-96 OASIS seminars, participants were provided with a third learning tool (in addition to the Survey Results Exercise and integrative case study) to raise their awareness of the need to interact effectively across the operational areas to achieve the teamwork necessary for safe, efficient operation of the aircraft.

The Dryden Accident

During Cockpit Resource Management seminars conducted by the authors in the 1980s it became apparent that video presentations could be used as effective learning tools with aviators, so long as the films were factually accurate, current, aesthetically superior and presenting material worthwhile to learn. *The Dryden Accident is* such a film, a video which poignantly demonstrates the importance of teamwork for the safe operation of the aircraft. The 18 minute film, owned and available from Qantas Airways, details the factors leading up to the crash of Air Ontario Flight 363 on March 10, 1989. Of particular interest to aviators in general, and OASIS seminar participants in particular, is the role played by ground staff and cabin crew in the unfolding tragedy.

To make the impact and message of the Dryden film even more salient, the authors screen a second video produced and available from ABC News. This film, from the program *20-20*, is entitled "What the Pilot Didn't Know" (ABC News, Oct. 30, 1992), and describes the final moments of USAir flight 405 which crashed on take-off from Laguardia Airport on March 22, 1992. One factor that makes the USAir crash particularly disturbing is its striking similarity to the Dryden tragedy...right down to the type of aircraft flown, the cause of the crash and the kind of interaction between cabin staff and cockpit crew before the accident. After viewing *The Dryden Accident* and *What the Pilot Didn't Know* the viewer cannot help but be reminded of two critical aviation axioms: (1) good crew coordination and teamwork is vital in maximizing flight safety; and (2) those who do not learn from the lessons of history are bound to repeat them.

Conclusion

Pilots don't operate in a vacuum (Karlins, Koh & McCully, 1989). To maximize safety *and* efficiency in flight operations requires teamwork within the cockpit *and* beyond, where technical crews must interact effectively with other operational staff in the conduct of their duties. The OASIS seminar was created to bring employees from the different operational areas together in a cordial, relaxed learning environment (away from the pressures of line operation) where they were given the opportunity to learn more about each other and what could be done to enhance safety, efficiency and personal satisfaction through greater interpersonal effectiveness and teamwork on the job.

Through a series of structured activities (the Survey Results Exercise, an integrative case study and a discussion of an airline tragedy depicted in a video presentation), seminar participants were encouraged to achieve the basic seminar objectives:

(1)　Interpersonal awareness:　　To be aware of (a) the kinds of pressures/challenges/problems encountered by employees in all four operational areas and (b) how members of each workgroup can help and/or hinder members of other workgroups in the performance of their duties; so that when pilots, cabin crew and ground staff interact they can do so with the sensitivity that develops from understanding each other's problems and points of view.

(2)　*A teamwork orientation*: To recognize the symbiotic interdependence of the four operational areas and realize that it is only through teamwork that pilots, cabin crew, ground engineers and station mangers/traffic personnel can transform the workplace into a WORTHplace: a place where maximum personal satisfaction and organizational success (safe, efficient flight) are mutually achievable.

Based on seminar participant evaluations, the OASIS experience has been successful in furthering interpersonal awareness and teamwork among operational staff at Singapore Airlines while reducing misunderstandings (conflicts) that can arise between different groups in the workplace. For that reason the authors recommend that other airlines establish similar-type programs in an effort to enhance job satisfaction and safety throughout the aviation industry.

Acknowledgements

The authors would like to thank the following individuals for their assistance and efforts in developing the OASIS seminars for Singapore Airlines. Captain Albert Koh, Mr. Cyril Teo, Mr. Edward Seow, Mr. Tan Soon Hock, Mr. Francis Lee, Mr. Hui Keen Ming, Mrs. Aileen Kong, Mr. Tan Siow Phing, Mr. Fong Weng Pow, Mrs. Lam Seet Mui and Ms. Sim Sai Ting.

References

ABC News. (October 30, 1992). "What the pilot didn't know." Film & Tape Practices, ABC News, 47 West 66th Street, New York, NY 10023-6290.

Karlins, M., Koh, F., & McCully, L. (1989). "The spousal factor in pilot stress." *Aviat. Space Environ. Med.* 60(11), 1112-1115.

Neuhauser, P. (1988). *Tribal Warfare in Organizations.* Cambridge, Mass: Ballinger Publishing Co.

Qantas Airways Limited. (1996). "The Dryden Accident." Qantas Airlines Limited, Flight Operations Support, Qantas Centre, 203 Coward Street, Mascot NSW. 2020, Australia.

27 Human factors: Training for organizational change

Brent Hayward

Introduction

The Australian commercial aviation industry enjoys an enviable safety record. This is at least partially due to the highly regulated environment that the industry has operated within for most of its history. This environment fostered high standards of selection, training, licensing, and aircraft maintenance and inspection, modern fleet equipment, technological advancement, and a generally healthy attitude towards individual and corporate safety. Australia's good safety record has also been assisted by the existence of a relatively benign operational flying environment, including light traffic and comparatively stable weather patterns, and by an indeterminate amount of good fortune.

From a human performance perspective, the major Australian airlines have also been in a position to fund the development and implementation of quality human factors training initiatives for flight crew. While the explicit motivation for the introduction of such courses invariably centres on flight safety, some have also been precipitated by the need to address specific operational and/or cultural problems or deficiencies. This chapter will review developments in Crew Resource Management (CRM) training, and move on to focus on two programs that are testament to the potential for organizations to detect and respond to such problems, and to affect changes in organizational culture through the introduction of human factors training principles.

Crew Resource Management training

The widely respected Aircrew Team Management (ATM) program developed by Australian Airlines (formerly TAA), and the CRM courses implemented by Qantas Airways and Ansett Australia are solid examples of the genre. These programs all complemented pre-existing regimens of what is now known as Line

Oriented Flight Training (LOFT) for cockpit crews. They also set out to address the issues identified as the major causes of flight crew involved accidents in the 1970s and early 1980s: poor communication, poor teamwork, poor leadership, poor followership, and poor judgement. In summary: poor management of available resources.

These and most other CRM programs embraced the maxim best articulated by John Lauber in his definition of Cockpit Resource Management as "the effective utilisation of all available resources - information, equipment and people - to achieve safe and efficient flight operations" (Lauber, 1984). The shortfall of such courses, and of the *application* of this definition is apparent with the benefit of some years of hindsight: they only addressed part of the problem, that which related solely to crew members working within the cockpit. In doing so they ignored the valuable contribution to safety and efficiency to be made by the inclusion of other personnel, particularly cabin crew, as an integral part of a flight's operating crew. The exclusion of cabin crew from the core operational team is still widely practised today. While most airlines have now altered the nomenclature of their courses to reflect the fashionable transition to *crew* rather than cockpit resource management, for many companies only the name has changed.   CRM remains as a form of cockpit crew, rather than total crew, training.

The glass door

In many cases the exclusion of cabin crew from the core operational team is not overt. It is implied rather than stated, and functions as a form of "glass door" between the cabin and the cockpit. Degani and Wiener's (1994) thoughts on the "Fourth P" of flight deck operations - *practices* - can be extrapolated here, with reference to intra-crew performance. In many airlines, it is understood through accepted workplace practices, if not formalised through company philosophy, policies, or procedures, that there are areas of operation and responsibility which are strictly the domain of cockpit crew, and others which fall just as solely on the shoulders of cabin crew. While delineation of some duties is entirely appropriate, there are many areas of operations where a total crew or team approach to duties can pay large dividends in safety, operations, and service. Many airlines continue to ignore these areas, probably at their peril. The double irony of such practices is that not only do these companies lose out on the valuable contribution that cabin crew can make to flight safety and operational efficiency, but they also ignore the fundamental value that cockpit crew can add to, say, customer service.

The case for including cabin crew as an integral component of a flight's operating crew is now well established (Hayward, 1995a). The British Midland

B737 accident at Kegworth (UK Air Accidents Investigation Branch, 1990) and the now infamous Air Ontario F-28 accident on take-off at Dryden, Canada (Moshansky, 1992; Maurino, Reason, Johnston & Lee, 1995) are classic case studies of the perils of ineffective use of all available resources, and have been used to justify the integration of crew Emergency Procedures (EP) training at some carriers (Hayward, 1993). The salient feature of each of these accidents is that the operating crew were acting as two crews - one running the cockpit and the other the cabin - rather than one. The paradox is that this is the way these crew members were *trained* to operate, so their actions were supported by company philosophy, policy and procedures, in addition to accepted practices. The sobering concern is that this continues to be the case within many major airlines today.

Integrated crew training

As the 1980's drew to a close, several airlines began to include cabin crew in CRM-style training. America West Airlines were amongst the first to include cabin crew in a fully integrated CRM program (Vandermark, 1991), while others, including Australian Airlines (Baker & Frost, 1993) and American Airlines (Chidester & Vaughn, 1994), devised strategies for the infusion of some CRM principles for cabin crew by including them in integrated EP or CRM refresher training. At Australian Airlines, following the success of ATM training for cockpit crew, it was felt that there were significant benefits to be gained by including cabin crew in the program. However, when it became apparent that the airline was unable to commit the resources required to put all cabin crew through the full ATM course, a strategy was devised to achieve a workable compromise. In 1991 the company's EP training course was expanded from one to two days, the syllabus and all procedural manuals were fully revised to cater for total crew training, and the crews were placed into joint training sessions. These included the primary components of the annual ATM recurrent training modules, in addition to fulfilling all requirements for EP revalidation training. This new approach proved highly successful, and served to increase mutual understanding and respect for the professionalism, role and responsibilities of each crew group.

What of the regulators?

As with most developments in aviation safety, in CRM training the leaders amongst the operational community have also led the regulators. The 1993 revision of the US Federal Aviation Administration's Crew Resource Management Advisory Circular (Federal Aviation Administration, 1993) formally redefined a flight's operating crew to include "...not only the cockpit crew but also all other groups that routinely work with that crew and are involved in decisions required to operate a flight safely". Dispatchers, maintenance personnel and air traffic controllers were included with cabin crew as part of the extended operating crew. Since 1993 several other State regulators have followed or have plans to follow suit.

While neither CRM nor more generic human factors training is as yet mandatory for Australian operators, in July 1995 the Australian Bureau of Air Safety Investigation (BASI) issued an Air Safety Interim Recommendation (Bureau of Air Safety Investigation, 1995) recommending that the Civil Aviation Safety Authority (CASA) "...require operators involved in multi-crew air transport operations to ensure that pilots have received effective training in crew resource management (CRM) principles". BASI further recommended that CASA establish a timetable for the phased introduction of CRM training, in order to ensure that:

i. CRM principles are made an integral part of the operator's recurrent check and training program and where practicable, such training should be integrated with simulator LOFT;
ii. CASA provides operators and/or CRM course providers with an approved course syllabus based on international best practice;
iii. such training integrates cabin crew into appropriate aspects of the program; and
iv. the effectiveness of each course is assessed to the satisfaction of CASA.

Adding to global acceptance of human factors training, in 1995 the International Civil Aviation Organization (ICAO; Maurino, 1995) amended Annex 6 (Operation of Aircraft) to the Chicago Convention to require mandatory human factors training for flight crew. The amendment introduces standards and recommended practices for human factors training for cockpit crews, calling for training programs to include "training in knowledge and skills related to human performance and limitations", and requiring that the training be given on a recurrent basis, and include an examination to determine competence.

Developments downunder

Australian team building

In August, 1989, the Australian aviation industry was rocked by the resignation of all but a handful of the nation's domestic airline pilots. For a country with a land mass roughly the size of the continental United States, this was no everyday industrial dispute. The conflict which followed was to become the most bitter and damaging industrial dispute in Australia's history, throwing the transport and tourism industries, along with the rest of the nation's business community, into chaos (for further detail on the dispute, see Norington, 1990). Over the next few weeks and months, as talks between the domestic pilot's union and the airlines continued to falter, and the dispute dragged on, the military and many foreign carriers were called in to get the country moving again, and the domestic airlines set about rebuilding their pilot workforces. When it became apparent that only a trickle of pilots were breaking from union ranks and returning to their old jobs, the airlines intensified their recruiting efforts, both at home and abroad.

When an official end to the dispute was finally called in March, 1990 the pilot group at Australian Airlines included the handful of pilots who had not resigned, a substantial number of ex-employees who had returned at various stages throughout the dispute, new pilots recruited from the military and general aviation, expatriates who had returned from flying abroad, and a minority (about 16%) of foreign nationals, recruited primarily from North America and Britain.

Given the diverse origins of the new pilot group, and the range of experiences and opinions which they were likely to possess regarding the dispute, it was decided at Australian Airlines to develop and run a series of "Team Building" workshops for pilots and their partners (see Hayward & Alston, 1991). The workshops were designed as an extension to the company's ATM program, with the primary objectives of integrating and bonding together the new pilot workforce, and acting as a cathartic release for the jumble of emotions and experiences resulting from the dispute. The workshops also served to review touchstone principles of flight safety and ATM, and attempted to ensure that dispute-related baggage would not interfere with the safe and efficient performance of flight crew duties. Partners were included as it was recognised that the dispute had potentially been just as stressful and difficult an experience for them as it was for the pilots.

Evaluations of the Team Building Workshops were very positive. Most participants took the opportunity to work through their experiences and feelings about the dispute and to put it behind them and look to the future. Some interesting data, both quantitative and qualitative were collected. Rankings of factors characterising the dispute for participants were quite revealing in terms of stressors encountered, particularly for those who chose to return. Not only had the family's economic welfare been severely threatened, workshop participants reported that they commonly experienced loss of important friendships, harassment after returning to work/taking up the job, severe domestic disruption, and feelings of confusion, despondency, anger, hostility, humiliation, embarrassment, and uncertainty over the future. Harassment of partners and even children was not uncommon following a decision to return to work.

However, the other side of this tragic industrial dispute has never been told. Six years down track, while Australia's domestic airlines have moved on, it is estimated that more than half of their pre-dispute pilot workforce are still pursuing flying careers overseas. Airlines too numerous to name, based from Stockholm to Jakarta, Frankfurt to Hong Kong, and Vienna to Dubai are all benefiting from the experience and training of Australia's domestic pilot dispute refugees.

Qantas and Australian Airlines: The merger

The mid-1992 announcement of the merger of Qantas and Australian Airlines was a surprise reversal of Australian Government policy. After recovery from the initial shock of the announcement, a team was formed within Flight Operations to begin working towards the integration of two culturally distinctive approaches to human factors training. While employees of the new entity were all "Aussies" of some description, the corporate cultures of the two companies - until the merger both fully government owned - were radically different. Those who have been touched by organizational mergers will recognise the difficulty to be faced in attempting to meld similar corporate cultures together, let alone to merge two organizations which may have flirted with each other at some levels from time to time, but have different ways of doing business, are at different stages of maturity, and are then suddenly thrust down the aisle by their parents to forge a "shotgun wedding" alliance. Organizational mergers are complex, highly stressful, and life changing events. The evidence is that most mergers are poorly planned and managed, and do not deliver gains promised. It can be argued that some workers never fully recover from such an event. For further discussion of the human impact of mergers, see Hayward (1995b).

While both Qantas and Australian had been involved in Human Factors training for cockpit crew for some years, the culture of their cockpits and cabins, and their approaches to CRM training differed considerably. Also, while Australian Airlines had been conducting fully integrated joint EP training (including annual ATM refresher training) for all crew members for several years, Qantas had not conducted joint crew training sessions since the 1970's, and no Qantas cabin crew had been exposed to any form of CRM awareness training. Given the differing orientations of the two companies, including the different nature of their operations, it was not surprising that the early proposals of the CRM working group, which included the introduction of joint *Crew Resource Management* training across the airline, encountered considerable resistance.

In the 20 years since Qantas Airways had last conducted joint crew training, many factors contributed to an erosion of the working relationship between their cockpit and cabin crews, and to the development of two crews, rather than one. Different industrial awards, industrial disagreements, logistical problems, separate transport and accommodation arrangements, and separate management of cockpit and cabin crew within the airline, all contributed to a physical and psychological distancing of the two groups. Additional physical and psychological separation of the crews was effected on board through the sheer size of today's wide-bodied jet liners and their correspondingly large crew complements (for some years Qantas operated the world's largest all B747 fleet). Most of these factors still operate today, where it is possible for a cabin crew member on a B747-400 to complete a 10 day trip overseas without setting eyes on some members of the cockpit crew. At most airlines such factors can create the potential for a break down in the understanding of the roles and responsibilities of crew members, both in routine operations and most critically during emergencies, and Qantas is no exception.   In fact at most airlines today cabin crew belong to the *marketing* department rather than to the operational side of the company. This situation was rectified at Qantas in 1994 when technical and cabin crew were brought together under the one management.

New CRM?

In consideration of the above, it was decided at Qantas to develop a new CRM program which would address several primary issues for the company. First, it would be a course which would aid in the unification of the four broad groups of air crew now employed by Qantas: international (ex-Qantas) and domestic (ex-Australian) technical and cabin crew. These crew groupings represented some unique training problems. They encompassed four distinct levels of CRM experience to be catered for when developing the new course: from the domestic pilots, many of whom had been exposed to ATM principles at Australian since 1985, the international pilots, who had completed CRM at Qantas in the early 1990s, the domestic cabin crew, who had been provided with two or three years of basic CRM awareness training, through to the company's international cabin crew, the vast majority of whom had never heard of CRM.

Second, the new course would be a true total crew resource management course, integrating the cockpit and cabin crews via joint training sessions, and using practical, experiential training exercises. When it came to the structure and content of the syllabus, it was considered important to ensure that crew members had ownership of the new course. In this respect, Qantas returned to the guiding principles used in development of the original Australian Airlines ATM syllabus (Margerison, McCann & Davies, 1987), and since adopted by several other companies, including America West and Delta Air Lines (Byrnes & Black, 1993). As had Delta and many other airlines, Qantas also relied significantly on the expertise and guidance provided by the work of Professor Bob Helmreich and his colleagues from the NASA/FAA-sponsored Aerospace Crew Research

Project at The University of Texas at Austin.

To guide course development, a CRM Steering Committee was established with representation from all crew sub-groups, management, unions, the company aviation psychologist, and advisers from external agencies such as BASI. Having decided not to totally reinvent the wheel, the Steering Committee revisited the existing CRM syllabus material developed by Qantas and Australian. While some of this material was repackaged for use in the new course, much of it was omitted due to developments within the industry and a desire to avoid direct repetition of earlier training for some staff.

To minimise the commitment of additional training resources and expenditure, it was decided to adapt another training concept developed by Australian Airlines: the EP course shell would be used as a vehicle for conducting CRM training, while still fulfilling all mandatory EP revalidation requirements. Course time was expanded from one to two days for international crew members, while domestic crews already had a two day course, so would require no additional training time. The total EP syllabus was then dismantled and reconstructed, ensuring that all new exercises were developed with an appropriate CRM flavour. The remaining training time was then allocated to additional CRM activities. A good example of the joint purposes to be served by the new EP exercises is the revised raft exercise or "wet drill". In its new format the exercise involves participant role plays, and is briefed and de-briefed on aspects of CRM-style behaviour (team work, communication, leadership, etc.) in addition to the more traditional EP requirements. Participant reaction to the raft exercise has been excellent, with a typical comment being: "I've been doing these raft drills for 15 years, but have never learnt so much about what might happen, and in particular how I and other people might react in a real ditching".

Selling the training to management

As detailed by Bob Helmreich (1993) in his treatise on "the CRM wars", the history and evolution of CRM training can be viewed as a series of battles, and the battle most frequently fought is for resources. A major obstacle to any plans for introduction of a new training course is the task of enlisting management support. At Qantas, the concept of the new CRM course involved the commitment of significant additional resources, not the least of which was an additional training day for all international technical and cabin crew, totalling in excess of 7,000 additional work days per annum. And hadn't cockpit crews already "done" CRM training? While senior management appreciated the commercial and moral value of keeping the Qantas safety record intact, as with most safety-related initiatives it is difficult to demonstrate the value of CRM training *a priori*.

So, the Steering Committee re-thought the benefits of CRM training. It was reasoned that while the stated objectives of CRM training may be wide and varied, the bottom line value is invariably to improve the safety and efficiency of operations. This would be achieved on the Qantas CRM course by enhancing team performance through better communication, cooperation, and understanding of each others' roles and responsibilities. Would it not then follow that this enhanced team performance would also lead to better customer service, and through better customer service to repeat business, and then on to the real bottom line, which is of course increased profitability? Given the turmoil kindled by the merger, a further objective could be to use the CRM training vehicle to improve relationships between members of the merged entities.

These arguments formed the basis of the sales pitch to management and were felt to be a major factor in securing approval and funding to proceed with development and implementation of the new Qantas CRM course. This was granted and course delivery commenced to all Qantas Air Crew in April 1995. Efficacy will rely heavily on the extent to which management continues to support the program, in addition to the quality of the training design and delivery.

The future

The examples described above represent a fraction of the range of developments in human factors training in recent years. The proliferation of new courses, global and regional training seminars and conferences, papers, articles and texts promoting the virtues of human factors in aviation would seem to indicate that it is here to stay. This notion is supported by the spread of human factors training and principles from flight operations to other components of the aviation system (Hayward, 1995a), including the aircraft cabin, aircraft maintenance (eg., Hobbs, 1995), air traffic control (Ruitenberg, in press) aviation safety and accident investigation (Maurino, Reason, Johnston & Lee, 1995), and aircraft systems design (eg., Graeber, in press).

However, is this a notion entrenched in reality? A problem currently faced is that with aviation psychology and human factors now becoming so very fashionable, some organizations launch themselves into human factors programs without really thinking through their true needs or objectives, or the long-term consequences of introducing a program that may not work as promised. In some cases this can be a knee-jerk reaction to the glare from the publicity of an incident or accident, and in others it may just be simply "filling the square" to ensure that management have a program to point to if questions are asked. In some organizations CRM has been the victim of such motivations, with predictable consequences. There is a danger that this practice may in fact be increased in the future with the mandating of certain types of training.

Human factors training initiatives can act as powerful agents for organizational and cultural change. However, they must be well designed and marketed, operationally relevant, skill-based and solution oriented. They must also be responsive to organizational needs, and be developed with due deference to the intricacies of the professional, organizational and national cultures within which they will operate. Merritt and Helmreich's (in press) architectural metaphor for CRM training prescribes the need for varied design requirements to suit different locations and environments. The human factors community has learnt from experience that one architectural style does not fit all purposes, and that if a program is to be successful in meeting its objectives it must be custom built. This chapter has described two specific programs which were tailored to meet perceived organizational needs. The Australian Airlines Team Building workshops extended the principles of CRM to make a valuable contribution to group cohesion, and in all likelihood, to flight safety. The new Qantas CRM program shares similar objectives and carries the potential to achieve organizational change. The extent of its success, as with all such programs, will rely on a durable commitment to appropriate ideals by management.

That is so because any human factors training initiative must be sincerely and strongly supported by management - not just by what management says, but also by what management does. Research indicates that if CRM training does not have true management support it will wither, never realising its full potential (Helmreich, 1993). The same is true of all flavours of human factors training. If the guiding principles described above are followed, if the lessons learnt and in particular the imperative of commitment can be communicated to management, and if human factors training delivers on the organizational outcomes it promises, then its future in aviation and its contribution to flight safety will be assured indeed.

References

Baker, R.L.A., & Frost, K. (1993). Australian Airlines' integrated crew training. In B.J. Hayward & A.R. Lowe (Eds.), *Towards 2000: Proceedings of the 1992 Australian Aviation Psychology Symposium*. Melbourne: The Australian Aviation Psychology Association.

Bureau of Air Safety Investigation (1995). *Air Safety Interim Recommendation No: IR950101*. July, 1995. Canberra.

Byrnes, R.E., & Black, R. (1993). Developing and implementing CRM programs: The Delta experience. In E.W. Wiener, B.G. Kanki, & R.L. Helmreich (Eds.), *Cockpit Resource Management*. San Diego: Academic Press, Inc.

Chidester, T., & Vaughn, L. (1994). Pilot/flight attendant coordination. *The CRM Advocate, 94*(1), 8-10.

Degani, A., & Wiener, E.L. (1994). *On the design of flight-deck procedures* (NASA Contractor Report 177642). Moffett Field, CA: NASA Ames Research Center.

Federal Aviation Administration (1993). *Advisory Circular 120-51A: Crew resource management*. Washington, DC: Author.

Graeber, R.C. (in press). Integrating human factors and safety into airplane design and operations. In B.J. Hayward & A.R. Lowe (Eds.), *Applied aviation psychology: Achievement, change and challenge*. Aldershot, UK: Avebury Aviation.

Hayward, B.J. (1993). The Dryden accident: A crew resource training video. In R.S. Jensen & D. Neumeister, (Eds.), *Proceedings of the Seventh International Symposium on Aviation Psychology*. Columbus, OH: Ohio State University.

Hayward, B.J. (1995a). Extending crew resource management: an overview. In N. McDonald, N. Johnston, & R. Fuller (Eds.), *Applications of psychology to the aviation system*. Aldershot, UK: Avebury Aviation.

Hayward, B.J. (1995b). Organizational change: the human factor. In N. McDonald, N. Johnston, & R. Fuller (Eds.), *Applications of psychology to the aviation system*. Aldershot, UK: Avebury Aviation.

Hayward, B.J., & Alston, N.G. (1991). Team building following a pilot labour dispute: Extending the CRM envelope. In R.S. Jensen (Ed.), *Proceedings of the Sixth International Symposium on Aviation Psychology*. Columbus, OH: The Ohio State University.

Helmreich, R.L. (1993). Fifteen years of the CRM wars: A report from the trenches. In B.J. Hayward & A.R. Lowe (Eds.), *Towards 2000: Proceedings of the 1992 Australian Aviation Psychology Symposium*. Melbourne: The Australian Aviation Psychology Association.

Hobbs, A. (1995). Human factors in airline maintenance. *Asia-Pacific Air Safety*, March 1995.

Lauber, J.K. (1984). Resource management in the cockpit. *Air Line Pilot, 53,* 20-23.

Margerison, C., McCann, D., & Davies, R. (1987). Aircrew team management program. In H.W. Orlady and H.C. Foushee (Eds.), *Cockpit Resource Management training: Proceedings of a NASA/MAC workshop* (NASA CP 2455). Moffett Field, CA: NASA Ames Research Center.

Maurino, D.E. (1995). ICAO annex amendment introduces mandatory human factors training for airline flight crews. *ICAO Journal, 50*(7), September.

Maurino, D.E, Reason, J., Johnston, N., & Lee, R.B. (1995). *Beyond aviation human factors.* Aldershot, UK: Avebury Aviation.

Merritt, A., & Helmreich, R.L. (in press). CRM in 1995: Where to from here? In B.J. Hayward & A.R. Lowe (Eds.), *Applied aviation psychology: Achievement, change and challenge.* Aldershot, UK: Avebury Aviation.

Moshansky, V.P. (1992). *Commission of inquiry into the Air Ontario crash at Dryden, Ontario: Final report.* Ottawa: Canadian Ministry of Supply and Services.

Norington, B. (1990). *Sky pirates: The pilots' strike that grounded Australia.* Sydney: ABC Books.

Ruitenberg, B. (in press). Human factors aspects in CNS/ATM systems. In B.J. Hayward & A.R. Lowe (Eds.), *Applied aviation psychology: Achievement, change and challenge.* Aldershot, UK: Avebury Aviation.

UK Air Accidents Investigation Branch (1990). *Report on the Accident of Boeing 737-400 G-OBME, near Kegworth, Leicestershire on 8 January, 1989* (AAIB Aircraft Accident Report 4/90). London: HMSO.

Vandermark, M.J. (1991). Should flight attendants be included in CRM training? A discussion of a major carrier's approach to total crew training. *International Journal of Aviation Psychology, 1* (1), 87-94.

28 The training cycle: An organizational perspective

Roger Miller

What are the organizational considerations in aviation training, and the training cycle in particular? They include:
- training philosophies;
- training requirements (both regulatory and corporate);
- training value (measurement methods);
- training hardware and software;
- training constraints (budgets and scheduling);
- testing mechanisms.

It is not difficult to see why aviation training continues to present many challenges to those involved in its administration. Significant among the many training demands are the operation of different generation fleets, with old and new technology; the total integration of CRM and Human Factors training; the design of efficient, effective, and readily-measurable training programs within the multitude of training demands. In an industry fast becoming self-regulating, it is the last which is gathering increasing importance, as exemplified by the FAA Advanced Qualification Program.

Actual change, however, is relatively recent with many organizations relying on traditional methods. Change is also being driven by the need for increasing efficiencies in the modern business environment in which aviation is a particularly expensive enterprise. Modern aircraft with glass cockpits, complex computer management and flight systems require training derived from contemporary educational design and development.

Training philosophy

The principal intention of training is to provide pilots with high quality skills and knowledge to accomplish their tasks while meeting both safety and commercial goals of the airline. Such training must also reflect and reinforce the culture of the airline.

What is this culture? It is difficult to define but often readily observable as a projection of individuals' behaviour. The culture incorporates the values and attitudes of the organization, and can be exemplified by communication styles (both formal and informal); dress, uniform styles and personal presentation; societal norms; decision making philosophies at all levels; the service ethic; and safety emphases. An airline culture will include an operating discipline and a motivation derived from business goals.

A Flight Operations Department may orient new pilots to the company culture by means of a comprehensive induction program. It is important to illustrate the culture at work through examples drawn from the functioning of other departments, then emphasising the *link* with Flight Operations and the interdependence of the network of departments for the effective functioning of the whole organization. The company's culture can also be reflected in all its training programs. This can be facilitated if the company uses its own resources in the design and conduct of training workshops and associated materials. Its usual to find valuable resources and talent in individual staff members. Too often, off-the-shelf training programs are purchased to meet training requirements. These packages have been developed in a way that reflects another culture: sometimes national as well as corporate. Design expertise can be imported, but is best utilised in conjunction with a development group representing the expertise available within the airline. Trainees are quick to react to inappropriate content or presentation when it conflicts with their own organizational culture or operational discipline.

The training cycle

There is an ongoing training cycle, shown in Figure 28.1 which provides five opportunities for a representation of the organizational philosophy and its attitude to operational training.

Most organizations will create the objectives, design a syllabus, prepare instruction, and prepare evaluation methods and materials (which tend to vary significantly in effectiveness), but seldom promulgate continuous monitoring systems to provide ongoing feedback for refinement of the objectives, methods and materials of instruction. Each of the five elements of the training cycle requires sustained review and development.

In order to initiate and maintain the training cycle, it has to be funded. This is where the evaluation component of the cycle can play an important role.

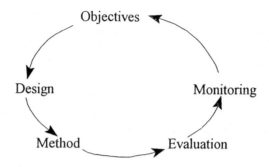

Figure 28.1 The training cycle

Training needs at times can be ill-conceived when management sees the need for a short-term fix for a problem which is more effectively approached over the longer term. The training may well be necessary, but can be integrated with other areas of the company's activities in order to get better results. For example, the training could be built into Induction or Recurrent Training programs in more than one department (such as Pilots and Cabin Crew).

Typical training requirements

The typical training requirements of an organization will vary according to the operation conducted : regional, commuter, international, etc. In broad terms, however, the training requirements are dictated by two sources: Regulatory and Company.

The *regulatory requirements* can include:
• Aircraft Type Ratings;
• Multi-engine Instrument Rating;
• Recurrent Licence Renewal;
• Instructor and Check Airmen Training;
• CRM/Human Factors Training.

The *company* training needs include:
• Induction of a new intake of pilots;
• Line Training Captain/First Officer Training;
• Check Airmen if not regulated;
• CRM facilitator training;
• Command Training programs (both preparatory and graduation);
• Second Officer to First Officer upgrade;

- ETOPS courses;
- Customer service programs for pilots.

Most organizations will be required to administer such programs, and probably others, which involve syllabus design; instructor/facilitator/presenter training; development of a reliable and valid means of evaluation, monitoring and feedback; and maintenance of the full training cycle.

Training hardware, software and liveware

Training hardware and software consists of such tools needed for training as the equipment and the programs or materials needed to support them. The all-important liveware includes the instructors and the recipients of training. The actual range of hardware and software used in training has become quite extensive.

For example, typical airline training requirements include computer programs and linked audio-visual displays, simulators (both fixed-base and full-flight), part-task trainers, individualised study carrels, manuals and other reference materials, notes and hand-outs, textbooks, instructional aids, and a range of resources varying from aviation periodicals to journals, bulletins and the proceedings of relevant symposia and conferences.

Consider the training involved in an Aircraft Type rating. Aircraft systems and operating practice may be based on individual computer-based training (CBT) modules. These are interactive and usually supported by classroom involvement with an instructor to provide clarification, explanation, application and testing. Next will be some time on a fixed base simulator, which may be integrated with the CBT rather than end-on in design. Then comes the full-flight simulator (FFS) phase to consolidate and extend knowledge and operating techniques, and to provide the final test schedules. Non-revenue aircraft operation is involved where the FFS accreditation does not meet the requirements of the Zero Flight Time Regulation. To attain trainee confidence in the real world of aviation, some operators provide actual aircraft time as a non-revenue flight. This is especially useful when take-offs and landings are infrequent in revenue operations. Usually a trainee's first landing will be in normal revenue operations.

In training for a Type Rating, it is difficult for instruction with the primary tools to produce conditions which replicate those found on the line. A quality training design is needed to produce a confident, safe and capable pilot. Such programs are often based on those produced by Aircraft manufacturers. Optimally, these need to be linked with the airline's culture, training philosophies, and standard operating procedures. Two frequently-used methods of doing so are training support documentation (such as Reference and

Operating Manuals) and the use of video.

Manuals need to be clearly indexed, giving both a quick-search capability and indicating the key areas for revision. Layout can promote readability by the use of boxed overviews, purposeful variations in font or type face, and subheadings or summaries to help the reader. For the trainee who seeks additional information, links and references to other documentation is handy. Manuals give an opportunity for the training department to show a practical example of applied Human Factors in aviation. Simple, clear language promotes comprehension and minimises (or, hopefully, removes) ambiguity.

A small working group can take responsibility for proof reading draft manuals, both to correct any errors and to test the readability and appropriate level of text. A loose-leafed format will facilitate ongoing refinement and make revision easier. The inclusion of white space or blank pages for personal note taking is usually appreciated by trainees.

To promote feedback, an evaluation form can be incorporated in training documents. This evaluation is based upon the program's objectives, and normally taps reactions to content, scheduling, materials, presentation, and facilities. An open-ended component for suggestions will complement a tick-the-box rating scale for the other dimensions.

Video is a powerful training medium, but in my view is best used as a support to the main instructional thrust. As such, it can provide examples and emphases. It has a major role as a stimulus to promote discussion: a major source of learning for adults. Duration is also important. Around fifteen minutes seems to be quite sufficient. More than this and the attention span may be exceeded and the training value lost. Another solution is to divide the longer video into segments separated by opportunities for discussion.

There is a lot to be said for in-house production of training videotapes. They then convey the organizational culture, with company examples, characters and procedures. By involving company crews in the concept from the outset, then in the production and evaluation, there will be both commitment to, and ownership of, the product. The participation of the Flight Operations management also enables them to be personal, visible and communicable to line pilots. The appearance of authority also lends endorsement to the training program.

Video can be usefully applied to CRM programs (as in the re-enactment of a company incident); Check Airman training (re-enacting a check situation and using it as an aid to de-briefing); Recurrent programs (in which a short presentation from a Flight Department manager can be used to introduce a topic or provide a context). The techniques for developing such a training videotape are provided in the chapter by Holling in part 2 of this book.

Pre-Course Reading distributed before the actual training occurs can stimulate relevant thought, and prepare the trainee for the instruction and activities to follow. Questions in the Pre-Course Reading establish a mental set and provide personal input which can be called upon by presenters as contributions to discussion. They are also a valuable means of establishing what the candidate already knows. In a recurrent training process the questions can provide an ongoing stimulus for learning. When linked with the major training document, such as the Course Manual, the Pre-Reading can combine to form a permanent source of reference. Again, if it can be provided in a loose-leaf folder (appropriately presented with the company logo and glossy cover to reflect the importance given the training), with note-taking blank spaces or pages, it will form a valued working document.

The trainers, instructors, presenters or facilitators (according to the style of training provided) need special preparation, too. Whether the training expertise is coming from within the company or from an external source, total reliance on an individual is not wise. The preferred option is to use a company development working team, steered by a Training project Manager. The company's organizational culture is thus transmitted, and company ownership and control is assured. Most importantly, the product will be one with which the trainees will relate.

A valuable by-product is that individuals within the company are being developed as a residential and expanding base of training expertise.

In summary, then, there is no simple recipe for successful training, which consists of interlinked aspects of development, materials, and methods. As an example, consider the *Training Captain Workshop* developed by *Ansett Australia* in consultation with Professor Ross Telfer (*Instructional Research and Development*).

Design of a Training Captain Workshop

This workshop was intended as training for both new or existing Training Captains. The design consisted of:
• Pre-Course Reading
• Reference Notes
• A Course Manual
• Evaluation Form

The *Pre-Course Reading* was distributed to participants about a week before the workshop. It included a formal welcome from the Flight Training Manager, details of the objectives of the training, and further explanation of the rationale of the course and what participants could expect. The timetable for the two days of training was given, as well as the evaluation form so that participants would be aware of the dimensions upon which they could provide feedback. There were several questions requiring participants to write their personal views, ideas or examples. An opportunity to provide these responses was built into the design of the workshop, and has proved to be a valuable discussion period in which Training Captains have the opportunity to compare their views and solutions with those of their peers, as well as contemporary instructional theory and research evidence.

The *Reference Notes* form the major component of the *Course Manual*. The information provided in the Pre-Reading is presented in full detail, with a topic by topic treatment outlined the initial index. The design hinges in the involvement of participants, and on a process which reflects the content provided in the Manual. Thus the early topic on adult learning is characterised by discussion and activity. The psychology of learning is reflected in the schedule which has longer periods early in the day, gradually reducing in span. More abstract and demanding topics are presented early in the day, with greater use if activities and videos later in the day. Immediately prior to coffee breaks or lunch are topics or exercises designed to promote discussion which will continue into and over the recess.

Table 28.1
Examples of evaluation items

Workshop Content

How satisfied were you with the content of the workshop, that is, what was introduced, discussed or practised?

V. Dissatisfied   Dissatisfied   Satisfied   V. Satisfied

Comment/Suggestion:
....
....
....

Workshop Presentation
Was the presentation of the workshop (the ways sessions were introduced and conducted) appropriate?

No   Sometimes   Yes

Comment/Suggestion:
....
....
....

Surveying pilots for input

In the design phase, the training syllabus can usually be improved by considering the line pilots' perspective. To ascertain this, a survey to help identify course components can be undertaken. One of the perennial problems with such a survey is the attrition rate: the number of replies received considering the number of forms distributed. Additionally, up to date information is going stale while late responses are pursued. A simple, confidential and efficient form of return is vital. The format shown in Table 2 has achieved an 80% return rate. Return mail boxes were located in all areas where pilots reported for duty at each base. The boxes were cleared regularly so contents could be returned via the company mailing system.

Table 28.2
Response format for pilot survey

> **INITIAL INTAKE INDUCTION COURSE**
> **SURVEY**
>
>
> **THANK YOU**
>
>
>
> Please fold this form along the dotted line, then staple
> and place in company mail. Return by Friday, 22nd
> November, 1996.
>
> ---
>
>
> *Captain Joseph Bloggs*
> *Manager Flight Training*
> *Flight Airlines*
> *Room 63, Level 2*
> *Airport Building*
> *Ecksville*

As an attachment to the survey questionnaire, a letter of introduction can also help the response rate. This letter should indicate the purpose of the survey, how the results will be used in the design of the training course, and how the line pilots can be involved. This can help gaining acceptance of the program and recognition of the value given the line pilots' viewpoint.

Training constraints

The schedule and budget are the two major constraints, and they are linked. Both can be driven, at least in part, by regulatory and company requirements. At one extreme, a company can choose to meet the minimum requirements. Most organizations, however, will want to pursue a superior product. This is where the constraints begin to become more apparent. Management may be prepared to fund the extensions to the minimum training program: but they are going to need convincing. The justifying argument is the key.

Can the additional content of the training program be justified in terms of measurable gain? The cost of the course development is one factor, but a more significant one is the additional cost of loss of productivity. Person days, staff numbers, and cumulative training needs are the sorts of terms on which the accountants will focus. For management, pilots are a very expensive commodity. Time is the key variable: expressed in terms of the duration and frequency of training. The basic justification, apart from regulatory requirements, is improved safety and minimized risk. The safety image of an airline is essential for its commercial survival. Passengers make decisions based on their perception of an airline's safety record. How does a training manager convince management that these benefits accrue from additional training?

Training effectiveness in an airline is measurable. Performance data can be collected in several ways:
• Incident Reporting Programs;
• Confidential Reporting Systems;
• Real-time QAR Programs; and,
• The Check System.

Despite this evidence, there remains the problem of communicating benefits to accountants when the actual value will not be apparent for some time. Further, the value may have effect in the absence of incidents rather than through their quantification.

Checking

The checking system is designed to measure crew performance ensuring compliance with regulatory and company requirements. As indicated above, it also provides an opportunity to gather data about training effectiveness. These data refer not only to technical, but to non-technical or human factors training. There is emphasis here on the performance of the crew as well as that of the individual.

This emphasis extends, through LOFT, into simulator checking as well as line operations observations. Assessment generally involves technical, manipulative, and human factors performance. Assessment criteria and grading system design is an important element of then system, if it is to be effective in providing feedback within the cycle.

Assessment items would usually involve, for example:

Pre-Flight/Post Flight	Team work
Take Off, Climb	Briefings
Cruise, decent	Situational awareness
Approach, Landing	Communications,Flight & Cabin Crew
Systems knowledge	Workload management/Decisions
Instrument Flying	Leadership (c)
Flight Management	Support, (F/O) approp.assertive
Assymetric Flight	Automation management

Grading systems vary but usually involve the following in their design:

Below standard
Minimum standard - minimum acceptable, safe. A repeat of exercise necessary. Consistent performance required to be above this level.
Satisfactory standard- some margin over required standard
Very good - desirable Company standard. A comfortable margin of performance
High standard-

Whatever designs are used, it is essential that they are incorporated into a database which can acccurately track trends, identify consistently weak areas which feed back to the training system. A Quality Control system measuring consistency amongst the Check and Training personnel is also an important component. An evaluation system for the human factors area could utilise the NASA/UT Effectiveness Marker system.

CRM principles and practice need to be reflected throughout the various operational and training manuals. CRM course design should include a comprehensive initial/induction program which would cover the theory, awareness and skills components. The latter either experiential based involving use of simulator LOFT , or role playing exercises which directly relate to the practical environment. Ideally both are utilised.

A quality control system is an important component of training

The initial course is recommended to reinforced with an annual Recurrent Training programmme, which links or extends from the initial. Such a program would again contain theory and awareness elements but the primary emphasis should be skill development. A ive year recurrent cycle migh be considered, designed to cover the CRM principles over the period. This concept would permit application to greater depth than covered initially, and incorporate any updated concepts.

Check pilot training

A key factor in the quality of airline checking is the selection of check airmen. The availability of committed, highly-experienced staff who are able to evaluate skills, knowledge and attitudes is vital. With such a group, initial training can include extensive classroom instruction, then technical preparation for the operation of the simulator. There needs to be a focus on interpersonal skills as well as objective assessment. This requires interactive training and accurate feedback to promote self-awareness and empathy. Role play and the use of videos based on scenarios of simulator check sessions, used for briefings and debriefngs, are valuable tools in the training process.

A check pilot training program needs to be quite comprehensive and include development of competency in effective communication and human factors performance. The latter could involve specific training in the use of the NASA/UT crew effectiveness marker system. Check training program outcomes additionally could address:

* developing the essential knowledge, skills and atttiudes to enable effective interpersonal communication to be an integral part of the checking process;
* developing an awareness of the essential competencies involved in interpersonal communication;
* gaining practice and performance appraisal in the implementation of competencies;
* developing and action plan for transfer and implementation of competencies to the checking process.

A three or four day program could include topics such as:

Communication difficulties in checking
Concerns and goals of problem check situations
Barriers to effective communication
Major components of a debrief
Listening/Responding skills
Personality and self-concept
Assertion styles/techniques/practise
(Extensive use of video and role playing incorporating these topics.)

Evaluation methods, consistency of approach, reliability and validity aspects require consideration.

The cycle completed

The performance data gathered through the range of evaluations brings the training loop back to its starting point. From the evaluative data, modified or new training objectives are devised and innovative or adapted courses begin. The training cycle is now complete.

Author index

Subject index